**OT 29**
**Operator Theory: Advances and Applications**
**Vol. 29**

**Editor:**
**I. Gohberg**
Tel Aviv University
Ramat Aviv, Israel

Editorial Office:
School of Mathematical Sciences
Tel Aviv University
Ramat Aviv, Israel




Birkhäuser Verlag
Basel · Boston · Berlin

# Topics in Operator Theory and Interpolation

**Essays dedicated to M. S. Livsic on the occasion of his 70th birthday**

**Edited by**

**I. Gohberg**

**1988**

**Birkhäuser Verlag**
**Basel · Boston · Berlin**

Volume Editorial Office:

School of Mathematical Sciences
Tel Aviv University
Tel Aviv, Israel

**CIP-Titelaufnahme der Deutschen Bibliothek**

**Topics in operator theory and interpolation** : essays dedicated to M. S. Livsic on the occasion of his 70th birthday / ed. by I. Gohberg. – Basel ; Boston ; Berlin : Birkhäuser, 1988
(Operator theory ; Vol. 29)
ISBN 3-7643-1960-7 (Basel ...) Pb.
ISBN 0-8176-1960-7 (Boston) Pb.
NE: Gochberg, Izrail' [Hrsg.]; Livsic, M. S.: Festschrift; GT


Printed in Germany
ISBN 3-7643-1960-7
ISBN 0-8176-1960-7

CB-SHK
SCIMON

CONTENTS

*M. S. LIVSIC*

# BIOGRAPHY OF M.S. LIVSIC

Moshe Livsic (Mikhail Samuilovich Livsic) was born on the 4th of July, 1917 in the small town of Pokotilova near Uman, a province of Kiev, in the Ukraine (according to the 1897 census, Pokotilova numbered 3030 citizens, including 1670 Jews). When he was four years old, his family moved to Odessa where his father held the position of associate professor of mathematics in an academic institute. His father's influence on Moshe, an only child, was very great, and until today he has fond memories of the Yiddish songs and Jewish prayers sung by his father, who before his mathematical career, was a cantor at the synagogue.

Moshe Livsic's father often spoke about the great mathematicians who were active at that time in Odessa: N.G. Chebataryov, an outstanding algebraist; V.F. Kagan, an outstanding expert in geometry, especially non-Euclidean; Yu. I. Timchenko, an expert in mechanics; M.G. Krein, who was at that time a young post-graduate student; and S.O. Shatunovsky. They were all close friends of Moshe's father.

S. O. Shatunovsky was an especially intimate friend of the elder Livsic. Shatunovsky was an excellent lecturer and an extraordinary person, well known to many of the townsfolk. Even today the older generation still recall the professor whose fascinating lectures in mathematics were attended by hundreds of students from all the faculties of the university.

In the West relatively little is known about the work of S.O. Shatunovsky (1859-1929). He was one of the first representatives of constructive mathematics, and a pioneer in intuitionist logic and modern algebra. He devoted much time to the law of the excluded third, and in 1901 he was the first to indicate that the formal transfer of this law to infinite sets is not obvious. In his dissertation, completed in 1917, S.O. Shatunovsky constructed a foundation of algebra and in particular of Galois theory as a theory of congruences with respect to the functional moduli introduced by Cauchy, without invoking the law of the excluded third to infinite sets. S.O. Shatunovsky found an original generalization of the limit notion. Without using limits, he defined the volume of a polyhedron as a certain invariant. Independently of Hilbert, and approximately at the same time (1897-1898) he laid the axiomatic foundation of the theory of areas. In 1910, together with V.F. Kagan, S.O. Shatunovsky founded a mathematical publishing house in Odessa. This publishhing house, "Matesis", played a significant role in mathematical education and the popularization of mathematics in Russia. "Matesis" published translations of European classics in mathematics and a number of textbooks, including the well-known book of Dedekind on the theory of irrational numbers. In 1923 "Matesis" published S.O. Shatunovsky's book "Introduction to Analysis" which contained his lectures on the subject. "Matesis" continued operating until some time after the October revolution.

In 1931 Moshe graduated from school, which at that time comprised seven grades. At school he became friendly with Israel M. Glazman, and their friendship continued intermittently until the tragic death of this outstanding mathematician on May 30th, 1968. At the age of sixteen, the two friends worked out a plan for their future education which culminated in a deep study of philosophy (Kant, Hegel, and the works of a number of English and French philosophers). It was clear to them that the study of philosophy in the 20th century had no value without a fundamental knowledge of the natural sciences and so they planned to study physics and chemistry first. However, since a study of the natural sciences was impossible without a fundamental knowledge of mathematics, the two friends reached the logically inevitable conclusion that they should begin by studying mathematics. Many years later M.S. Livsic light heartedly summed up the youngsters' program: "I succeeded in thoroughly studying some fields in mathematics. I succeeded less in studying some fields in physics. There was no time for philosophy." Nevertheless a tendency to a philosophical understanding of scientific results remained.

As a youth Moshe Livsic was attracted to the new technology of radio, and he dreamed of becoming a radio technician. After graduating from school he entered the radio class at the Technical College for Communication in Odessa. However, in 1933, he interrupted these studies to enroll in the newly created Department of Physics and Mathematics at the Odessa State University.

During the first years at the university mathematics was taught by M.G. Krein, F.R. Gantmakher (who shortly thereafter left for Moscow), and M. A. Naimark, who was a graduate student, assistant and, subsequently, a colleague of M.G. Krein. Later, when Moshe Livsic was already a third year student, B. Ya. Levin, a prominent specialist in the theory of analytic functions, joined the faculty.

Those who influenced Moshe Livsic most during his university years were M. G. Krein and B. Ya. Levin. He especially remembers B. Ya. Levin's course on theory of functions of a complex variable, and M. G. Krein's courses on integral equations and on the differential equations of mathematical physics, both from the viewpoint of functional analysis. These courses were on the frontiers of research of that time.

Among his fellow students and friends, Moshe Livsic remembers especially his schoolfriend I.M. Glazman. He also remembers V. Smushkovich, a very talented mathematician and a handsome young man (lost in the Second World War), and A.P. Artyomenko, the most talented student of M.G. Krein (and much older than the others). Artyomenko obtained important results in the theory of Hermitian positive-definite functions. He and M.S. Livsic had a warm relationship. After World War II, A.P. Artyomenko disappeared and all attempts to find him were of no avail. A younger student who entered the university a year after Moshe Livsic was V.P. Potapov, who later also became an eminent mathematician. The two, having common scientific interests, became close friends.

Among the older students whom Moshe Livsic remembers were V. L. Shmulyan, D. P. Milman, and M. A. Rutman, all of whom became graduate students of M.G. Krein and later outstanding mathematicians. Along with Moshe Livsic they were active participants in the seminar on functional analysis. This seminar and its participants became famous in the mathematical world where they were known as the Odessa School of functional analysis, with M.G. Krein as its undisputed leader. This school had a great impact on the development of functional analysis both in the USSR and abroad. V.L.Shmulyan perished at the front in the Second World War. His achievements were highly appreciated and were later continued by other mathematicians. From the front Shmulyan wrote letters with mathematical results, and M.S. Livsic corresponded with him until his death.

M.G. Krein devoted much of his time to his students. He could often be seen taking a stroll on Deribassovskaya Street (the main street of Odessa), in the company of his students, deep in discussions of a mathematical, philosophical and ethical nature. M.S. Livsic and I.M. Glazman admired and loved M.G.Krein. They often visited him at his home where discussions would continue long into the night. These were fruitful and pleasurable hours, which made life more vital and interesting. The students were preoccupied with the role of abstract and classical analysis and M.G. Krein impressed them with his balanced attitude towards both of these streams. This attitude was reflected in his work and served as a source of inspiration.

From B. Ya. Levin Moshe Livsic learned a love of the theory of analytic functions. He used the ideas, techniques and methods of analytic functions theory throughout all of his research. B. Ya. Levin made friends easily with his students, and they regularly visited him at his home. He was a batchelor, and in his small room, thick with tobacco smoke, lively discussions on literature, philosophy, mathematics, and politics took place.

M.S. Livsic's first research paper, published in "Mathematicheskii Sbornik", was a joint paper with B. Ya. Levin.

M.S. Livsic began his research work at the end of his student period. His initial scientific interests were formed under the influence of his teachers, M.G. Krein and B. Ya. Levin. After graduating in 1938 from the Odessa University he continued his studies in the same university as a Ph.D. student under the supervision of M.G. Krein.

During those years M.G. Krein was involved in research related to the moment problem, and B. Ya. Levin was occupied with the theory of quasianalytic functions. M.S. Livsic's masters thesis and his research works published during the following three years were all devoted to these topics. However, soon afterwards he abandoned them both. He became interested in operator theory to which he came directly from the moment problem He often recalls the following episode which had some influence on him. It was a remark made by M.G. Krein during the defense of a Ph.D. thesis (one of the first in the Odessa University) to the effect that the person who could construct a spectral theory of nonselfadjont operators had not yet been born. Moshe had read the famous book of M.H. Stone on operator theory, and the papers of J. von Neumann in which the theory of unbounded operators was exposed for the first time. The lecture series of N.I. Akhiezer "Infinite Jacobi matrices and the moment problem" also sparked this interest. In this lecture series the connection between Jacobi matrices, the moment problem and general operator theory was traced out in a clear and lucid way. The first edition of these lectures appeared in Kharkov in mimeograph form; later they were published in Uspekhi Mat. Nauk, V. 9, 1941. In the same issue of this journal also appeared, for the first time in the USSR, a review paper on operator theory by A. Y. Plessner. The work of N.I. Akhiezer and A.Y. Plessner also had a great influence on M.S. Livsic.

During World War II, M.S. Livsic was evacuated, together with the University from Odessa, first to Maikop and then in

1942, when the Nazis approached the town, to Bairam-Ali in Turkmenia. Because of his bad eyesight he was not conscripted. In Maikop, in 1942, M.S. Livsic defended his Ph.D. thesis which was devoted to applications of Hermitian operator theory to the generalized moment problem. His opponents were M.G. Krein and F.R. Gantmakher.

In 1945, whilst in Bairam-Ali, Moshe Livsic completed the dissertation for his second doctoral degree. It comprised two parts. The first part was a continuation of his previous research and showed the connection between the extension problem for symmetric commuting operators and the extension problem for Hermitian positive-definite functions. These results were never published. In the second part he generalized the extension theory of J. von Neumann. He introduced a certain matrix valued analytic function which characterized the nonselfadjoint extensions of a symmetric operator with finite coefficiency indices, and named it the characteristic function of a nonselfadjoint operator. This function has a number of remarkable properties. In particular the nonselfadjoint operator may be recovered from it up to unitary equivalence. Later the notion of characteristic function was introduced also for bounded operators.

In May 1945 at the age of 28, just three years after his first Ph.D. degree, he successfully defended his second dissertation in the Steklov Mathematical Institute of the USSR Academy of Sciences in Moscow. His opponents were S. Banach, I.M. Gelfand, M.A. Naimark and A.Y. Plessner.

During the postwar period the situation in Odessa changed considerably. The first indications were felt by Moshe when his name was dropped by the administration from the list of faculty members returning to Odessa to work in the University because, in the words of the vice-rector, "he was not suited to represent the Ukranian culture." Instead he was sent to work at a relatively minor institution in Kirovograd, also in the Ukraine. In 1944 M.G. Krein was dismissed from Odessa University and his students also had to leave. Thus, the famous school of functional analysis which had existed at this university for many years, came to an end. Shortly after B. Ya. Levin left for Kharkov. In 1945 Moshe Livsic returned to Odessa to head the Mathematics Department of the Odessa Hydrometerological Institute (a second rate academic institute with no mathematics majors), where he remained until 1957. He found his part time work in the Odessa Pedagogical Institute more interesting. Here he collaborated with M.S. Brodskii and P. Potapov, who at that time proved an important theorem which generalized Blaschke product decompositions to the case of analytic matrix valued functions. This theorem arose from the problem of factoring the characteristic function into elementary factors. M.S. Livsic used Potapov's theorem to construct triangular models for nonselfadjoint operators. M.S. Brodskii developed the theory of nonselfadjoint operators, the theory of characteristic functions and triangular models, using geometric methods.

During the period 1955-57 Moshe Livsic became interested in physical interpretations of his theory. He published a number of papers in which it was shown that, under certain conditions the characteristic matrix function coincides with the Heisenberg scattering matrix. M.S. Livsic's students at that time included L.A. Sakhnovich, A.V. Kuzhel and B.R. Mukminov. Their research was also related to the theory of nonselfadjoint operators and was an extension of the M.S. Livsic theory and his philosophy. The M.S. Livsic theory was already recognized at this time as a major contribution to functional analysis. It was utilized by many researchers and had great impact. The monographs of I. Gohberg with M.G. Krein, and B.Sz.-Nagy with C. Foias, may serve as examples.

In 1957 Livsic moved with his family to Kharkov, where until 1962 he was head of the mathematics department of the Kharkov Mining Institute. He then joined the department of mathematical physics in the Kharkov State University, where N.I. Akhiezer was chairman of the department. Here he continued working on the physical interpretation of the theory of nonselfadjoint operators and developed his theory of "open systems" which are physical systems which interact with the environment. These investigations are described in two monographs: "Operators, oscillations, waves. Open systems" and "Theory of operator colligations in Hilbert spaces" (the latter jointly with A.A. Yantzevich), both of which are published in English translation. E. R. Tsekanovski, L. L. Waksman, A.G. Rutkas, A.A.Yantzevich, and V.K. Dubovoi were among the students of M.S. Livsic in Kharkov.

In 1975 M.S. Livsic moved with his family to Tbilisi, where he worked for three years in the Institute of Agricultural Machines. The reason behind this move was his desire to immigrate to Israel and he knew that for various reasons it would be impossible for him to do so whilst in Kharkov. It was at that time that Livsic first became interested in extending the theory of one nonselfadjoint operator to the case of two or more commuting nonselfadjoint operators. During this period he obtained his first results in this direction, which included in particular a generalization of the Cayley-Hamilton theorem to the case of two commuting operators with finite dimensional non-Hermitian components.

In 1978 M.S. Livsic arrived with his family in Israel. He settled in Beersheva and began working at the Ben Gurion University of the Negev. It was the third time in his life that he actively engaged in building up a new school. There he started working with N. Kravitsky on developing a theory of several commuting operators. It turned out that the theory of pairs of commuting operators is closely connected with a problem of algebraic geometry of obtaining a determinantal representation of algebraic curves. Certain elementary transformations which allow one to find all the possible non-equivalent determinantal representations of a given algebraic curve if one such representation is given were recently found by V. Vinnikov, Moshe's most recent student. In all of the investigations of this period an active part was taken by N. Kravitsky. H. Gauchman, another colleague at the Ben Gurion University, recently generalized a number of these results to the case of Hilbert bundles.

From his early days at Beersheva, Moshe organized and succesfully ran an active seminar on operator theory and systems. Since 1985 Moshe holds the David and Helena Zlotowski Chair in Operator Theory and Systems.

Moshe has always been very active and dedicated to his work. His recent breakthroughs in the theory of characteristic functions for several commuting operators indicate that in spite of his seventy years, mathematically Moshe is still a young man. He is loved by his friends, colleagues and students for his wonderful qualities of integrity, honour and benevolence, and respected as a great mathematician.

Harry Dym Israel Gohberg Naftaly Kravitsky

# LIST OF PUBLICATIONS OF M.S. LIVSIC

PAPERS


1. On some questions concerning Hamburger's moment problem, Math. Sbornik 6, 1939, 293-306

2. Quasi-analytic classes of functions represented by Fourier series, Math. Sbornik 9, 1941, 693-712 (with B. Ya. Levin)

3. On some special classes of quasi-analytic functions, Trans. of Odessa University 3, 1941, 23-24

4. An application of the theory of Hermitian operators to the generalized moment problem, Doklady 44, 1944, 3-7

5. A class of linear operators in the Hilbert space, Math. Sbornik 19, 1946, 239-262

6. A contribution to the theory of isometric operators with equal defect numbers, Doklady 58, 1947, 13-15

7. A contribution to the theory of elementary divisors of Hermitian operators, Doklady 60, 1948, 17-20

8. A linear function of operators which is invariant with respect to a group of translations, Doklady 68, 1948, 213-216 (with M.S. Brodskii)

9. A theorem on multiplication of characteristic matrix functions, Doklady 72, 1950, 625-628 (with V.P. Potapov)

10. A contribution to the theory of selfadjoint systems of differential equations, Doklady 72, 1950, 1013-1016

11. Isometric operators with equal defect numbers, quasiunitary operators, Math. Sbornik 26, 1950, 247-264

12. On reduction of non-selfadjoint operators to the triangle form, Uspekhi 7:3, 1952, 110-111

13. On reduction of linear non-Hermitian operators to a "triangle" form, Doklady 84, 1952, 873-876

14. On the resolvent of a linear asymmetric operator, Doklady 84, 1952, 1131-1134

15. Spectral expansion of linear nonselfadjoint operators, Math. Sbornik 34, 1954, 399-402

16. An inverse problem of the theory of operators, I.; Doklady 94, 1954, 399-402

17. An inverse problem of the theory of operators, II.; Doklady 97, 1954, 589-592

18. The theory of nonselfadjoint operators and its application Trans. of the 3rd Soviet Math. Congress, Volume 2, 1956, Moscow 40-41

19. On the dispersion matrix of an intermediate system. Doklady 111:1, 1956

20. On an intermediate system arising from dispersion of elementary particles, Doklady 111:4, 1956

21. An application of nonselfadjoint operators in the dispersion theory, Journal of Experimental and Theoretical Physics 31:1, 1956

22. The method of nonselfadjoint operators in the dispersion theory, Uspekhi 12:1, 1957, 212-218

23. Spectral analysis of nonselfadjoint operators and intermediate systems, Uspekhi, 13:1, 1958, 1-85 (with M.S. Brodskii)

24. The theory of nonselfadjoint operators and its applications, Proceedings (Trudy) of the 3rd Soviet Mathematical Congress, Volume 3, 1958, 269-276

25. On a mathematical problem concerning the theory of lengthwise polarized particles, Doklady, 131:4, 1960, 797-800

26. Decomposition of a reactive quadripole into a chain of primitive quadripoles, Doklady, 135:3, 1960, 542-544 (with M.S. Flexer)

27. Chebyshev matrix and Hamiltonian of a free particle, in the book "Functional Analysis and its Applications", Baku, 1961, 157

28. Design of a transmitting line by given frequency characteristic, Translactions of Kharkov University 28, 1961, 149-162 (with M.S. Flexer)

29. Method of nonselfadjoint operators in the theory of wave guides, Radio Engineering and Electronics, 7, 1962, 291-297, Moscow

30. Open systems as linear automata, Izvestia AN (Mathematics) 27:6, 1963, 1215-1228

31. Some problems in the theory of linear open systems, 3rd Soviet symposium on Wave Diffraction, Moscow, 1964, 41-42

32. On noı. unitary representations of groups, Functional Analysis and its applications, 3:1, 1969, 62-70

33. Open geometry and operator colligations, Trans. of Kharkov University, 1973, 16-35 (with L.L. Waksman)

34. Discrete linear systems and their connection with M.M. Dzharbashan's theory of factorization of meromorphic functions, Soviet Math. Doklady 15, 1974, 1657-1662

35. Commuting nonselfadjoint operators, Bulletin of Georgian Academy of Sciences, USSR, 1978

36. Operator waves in Hilbert space and related partial differential, Integral Equations and Operator Theory, Vol. 2/1, 1979, 26-47

37. The inverse problem for the characteristic functions of several commuting operators, Integral Equations and Operator Theory, Vol. 2/2, 1979, 264-286

38. A method for constructing triangular canonical models of commuting operators based on connections with algebraic curves, Integral Equations and Operator Theory, Vol. 3/4, 1980, 489-507

39. An introduction to the theory of open systems: Signal Processing Theory and Application, North-Holland Publish. Co., 1980, 105-109

40. On scattering and transfer matrices. 1981 European Conference on Circuit Theory and Design, North Holland Pub. Co., 1981, 1022-1029

41. Commuting operators and fields of systems, distribution in Euclidean space, Operator Theory: Advances and Appl., 4 1982, Birkhauser Verlag, Basel, 377-413, Toeplitz Centennial

42. Cayley-Hamilton theorem, vector bundles and divisors of commuting operators, Integral Equations and Operator Theory Vol. 6, 1983, 250-273

43. System theory and wave dispersion, Lecture Notes in Control and Informations Sc., No. 58, Springer-Verlag 1984, 663-575

44. Collective motions of spatio-temporal systems, Journal of Mathematical Analysis and Applications, Vol. 116 £ 1, May 15, 1986

45. On commuting nonselfadjoint operators, Integral Equations and Operator Theory, Vol. 9, 1986

46. Characteristic functions of commuting nonselfadjoint operators and mapping of vector bundles on algebraic curves, Operator Theory: Advances and Applications, Vol. 19, 1986

47. Commutative nonselfadjoint operators and collective motions of systems, Lecture Notes in Mathematics, Springer-Verlag, 1272, 1987, 1-39

BOOKS

1. Operators, Oscillations, Waves. Open Systems. "Nauka" Moscow, 1966, 1-298 (Transl. Math. Monographs, Vol. 34, Amer. Math. Soc. 1973)

2. Theory of Operator Colligations in Hilbert Spaces (Monograph), Kharkov, 1971, 1-160. Translated into English by Scripta Trans. Comp., 1978, Washington, U.S.A. (with A.A. Yantsevich)

Operator Theory:
Advances and Applications, Vol. 29




# ON SKEW TOEPLITZ OPERATORS, I

Hari Bercovici  Ciprian Foias  Allen Tannenbaum

Dedicated to Professor Moshe Livsic, a great mathematician and a man of the highest integrity, on the occasion of his seventieth birthday.

This paper is concerned with the study of the invertibility properties of a certain class of operators which we call "skew Toeplitz". Besides being of mathematical interest, these operators appear quite frequently in engineering applications. Our results will also be seen to be closely related to the classical theory of Hankel and Toeplitz operators. We wish to acknowledge the pioneering influence of Professor Livsic in the uses of operator theory in systems which was an inspiration for the present work.

## 1. INTRODUCTION

In the past ten years, the (engineering) field of systems and control theory has motivated a number of interesting problems in operator theory and functional analysis. (See for example the monograph [8].) The subject area being studied in the present work has precisely such an origin.

Indeed if one considers the problems of model reduction, robust stabilization, and sensitivity minimization one is naturally led to study the invertibility of a certain kind of operator which we call "skew Toeplitz". (See Section 2.) In the present mathematical work we shall only briefly discuss the physical origins of this problem and simply take it as an interesting question in operator theory. The connections with control engineering will be considered in great detail in a forthcoming applied paper. We will only note here however, that the techniques elucidated in the present paper should prove useful in the determination of the singular values for the block Hankel operators that typically arise in systems theory.

We shall give a precise definition of the class of operators which we shall study in the next section. However in order to give the reader a flavor of the subject, we would like to discuss a special case here. Set $H := H^2(\mathbf{C}^N) \ominus \Theta H^2(\mathbf{C}^N)$ where $\Theta$ is a nonconstant inner $N \times N$ matrix-valued function. Let $\hat{C}$ denote the compression of $C$ a constant $N \times N$ self-adjoint matrix (considered as a linear operator on $H^2(\mathbf{C}^N)$) to $H$. As a corollary of our techniques we shall give necessary and sufficient conditions for the invertibility of $\hat{C}$ (as an operator on $H$). Note that for $N = 1$ this is of course trivial. ($\hat{C}$ is invertible just in case $C \neq 0$.) For $N > 1$ the question is considerably more subtle and will be covered as an interesting example of the general invertibility problem of skew Toeplitz operators. (See Section 5.)

We should also note that the work considered here relies on some of the ideas already contained in [4-7]. However the problem which we shall study below is considerably more difficult and hence demands some different methods. In fact we feel that the techniques exhibited here are an interesting blend of the factorization ideas of Gohberg and Krein (and their numerous co-workers; see the recent book [3] and the references therein), and the dilation theory and work on contractions of class $C_0$ of Sz.-Nagy and Foias (see [13] and the references therein).

We now briefly summarize the contents of this paper. In Section 2 we define the notion of "skew Toeplitz" operator and briefly discuss some connections with control theory. In Sections 3 and 4, we formulate and prove our key results about the essential invertibility of skew Toeplitz operators. Here we make contact with the classical theory of matrix Hankel and Toeplitz operators, and the matrix version of the Nehari theorem. In Section 5, we specialize our results to the case of the compression of constant matrices (as mentioned above), and in Sections 6 and 7 we give a determinantal criterion for the invertibility of skew Toeplitz operators. In Section 8 we discuss the important case of scalar skew Toeplitz operators and relate these results to our previous work on these problems in the numerical case ([4], [6], [7]). Finally in Section 9 we consider some future research directions on this topic.

As is obvious from our title, we regard this paper only as a first in a series on an interesting research topic which we plan to explore both from the theoretical and applied points of view.

This research was supported in part by grants from the Research Fund of Indiana University, NSF (DMS-8521683, ECS-8704047), and the AFOSR.

## 2. NOTATION AND PRELIMINARY REMARKS

In this section we would like to define the precise class of operators which we will be studying as well as prove some preliminary results and make an important technical assumption.

We follow the standard notation from the book [13]. In particular for $\Lambda$ an $r \times s$ matrix-valued inner function, we set

$$H(\Lambda) := H^2(\mathbf{C}^r) \ominus \Lambda H^2(\mathbf{C}^s).$$

Moreover for $P_{H(\Lambda)} : H^2(\mathbf{C}^r) \to H(\Lambda)$ orthogonal projection, we let $S(\Lambda) := P_{H(\Lambda)} U_+ | H(\Lambda)$ where $U_+$ is the canonical shift on $H^2(\mathbf{C}^r)$.

Next let $\Theta$ denote a fixed $N \times N$ matrix-valued non-constant inner function. Then we set $H := H(\Theta)$, $T := S(\Theta)$, and let $U_+$ be the isometric dilation of $T$ on $H^2(\mathbf{C}^N)$ (i.e. $U_+$ is the canonical shift on $H^2(\mathbf{C}^N)$). Note that $T \in C_0(N_1)$, i.e. the defect operators $D_T$, $D_{T^*}$ have rank $N_1 \leq N$, and $T^k h \to 0$, $T^{*k} h \to 0$ for all $h \in H$ as $k \to \infty$. (See [13] for details.) In particular $I - T T^*$ and $I - T^* T$ are compact, and hence $T$ and $T^*$ are Fredholm (i.e. essentially invertible). We will also let $U$ denote the unitary dilation of $T$ defined on $L^2(\mathbf{C}^N)$. Note that $U$ is the bilateral shift on $L^2(\mathbf{C}^N)$, and $U_+ = U | H^2(\mathbf{C}^N)$.

Now for $Q \in L(\mathbf{C}^N)$ (the space of linear endomorphisms on $\mathbf{C}^N$), we set $\hat{Q} := P_H Q | H$, where $Q$ is regarded as a multiplication operator on $H^2(\mathbf{C}^N)$. We are now at long last ready to define the object of study of this paper. Set

$$A := \sum_{j,k=0}^{n} T^j \hat{C}_{jk} T^{*k}$$

where $C_{jk} \in L(\mathbf{C}^N)$ and $C_{jk}^* = C_{kj}$. (Thus $A = A^*$.) Notice that

$$A = P_H\left(\sum_{j,k=0}^{n} C_{jk} U_+^j U_+^{*k}\right) | H,$$

where $P_H : H^2(\mathbf{C}^N) \to H$ denotes orthogonal projection. For obvious reasons we will call such an operator $A$ *skew Toeplitz*. The matrix Laurent polynomial

$$a(z) := \sum_{j,k=0}^{n} C_{jk} z^{j-k}$$

may be regarded as the symbol of the skew Toeplitz operator $A$. Note however, that the correspondence between operator and symbol is not in general 1-1 in either direction.

The problem treated in this paper is that of determining the invertibility and essential invertibility of a skew Toeplitz operator. Before doing this in the next two sections, we would like to briefly discuss a physical problem from control engineering in which the invertibility of a skew Toeplitz operator arises, and which motivated much of the present work. In what follows we will of course only sketch the relevant engineering material in a special case, and so for a more complete picture we refer the interested reader to [8].

The $H^\infty$ optimal sensitivity problem [8] may be formulated as follows. Let $W$ be in $H^\infty(L(\mathbf{C}^N))$. This represents a "weight" or a "filter" in a given control problem. Let $\Theta \in H^\infty(L(\mathbf{C}^N))$ be inner. $\Theta$ is the "plant" or the fixed part of a control system. Then the optimal sensitivity problem (in this circumstance) reduces to the following. Compute

$$\mu := \inf \{\|W - \Theta Q\|_\infty : Q \in H^\infty(L(\mathbf{C}^N))\}.$$

Physically, $\mu$ represents the minimal sensitivity over all possible stabilizing compensators for the plant $\Theta$ relative to a class of energy-bounded disturbances filtered by $W$. (See [8] for details.)

Let $M_W : H^2(\mathbf{C}^N) \to H^2(\mathbf{C}^N)$ denote the multiplication operator induced by $W$ on $H^2(\mathbf{C}^N)$, and let $P_H : H^2(\mathbf{C}^N) \to H^2(\mathbf{C}^N) \ominus \Theta H^2(\mathbf{C}^N) =: H$ denote orthogonal projection. Then by the results of [13], we have that

$$\mu = \|P_H M_W\|.$$

More generally in many control problems, one wants to compute the singular values of the operator $P_H M_W$ (for example in problems involving Hankel norm approximation theory.) If one now invokes the fact that $W$ is a rational ($N \times N$ matrix-valued) function, using an argument based on [4], [5], and [7], one gets that the problem of the determination of the singular values of this operator (and in particular the optimal sensitivity) reduces to a question on the invertibility of a skew Toeplitz operator. See also example (8.1) below.

**REMARKS (2.1).** We close this section with a few general remarks. We have just indicated that the question of the invertibility of a skew Toeplitz operators arises quite naturally. There is of course a large related literature on the invertibility of ordinary Toeplitz operators, e.g. see the book of Clancey and Gohberg [3] and the references therein. We were of course influenced by this literature, and indeed the techniques which we use here can be regarded as a combination of the work on contractions as presented in [13] and some of the factorization ideas as discussed in [3]. Of course as in the standard Toeplitz case, we will see that the theory of skew Toeplitz operators is also closely related to the classical spectral theory of the Hankel operator and the matrix Nehari problem.

## 3. INVERTIBILITY OF COMPRESSED OPERATORS

Since by definition skew Toeplitz operators are compressions of certain operators on $H^2(\mathbf{C}^N)$, in this section we would like to make some observations about the invertibility of compressions. Throughout this section, $K$ will denote a Hilbert space, $H$ a closed subspace of $K$, $X : K \to K$ a bounded linear operator, and $Y := P_H X \mid H$. Set $H_1 := (XH)^-$, and define operators $Z : H \to H_1$ and $W : H_1 \to H$, by $Z := X \mid H$ and $W := P_H \mid H_1$. Clearly we have that $Y = WZ$.

We would like to state now two elementary results whose proofs we leave to the interested reader. However, we will see that these will be essential in determining the invertibility of skew

Toeplitz operators in the next section. The first result is:

**LEMMA (3.1).** *The operator $Y$ is invertible (resp., left-invertible, Fredholm, essentially left-invertible) if and only if both $Z$ and $W$ have the corresponding property.*

We now conclude this section with the following simple observation:

**LEMMA (3.2).** *Let $H$ and $H_1$ be closed subspaces of $K$. Then the operator $P_H \mid H_1$ is invertible (resp., left-invertible, right-invertible, Fredholm, essentially left-invertible, essentially right-invertible) if and only if $P_{K \ominus H_1} \mid K \ominus H$ has the corresponding property.*

**REMARKS (3.3).** We should note that concerning the proof of (3.3), it suffices to prove only the one-sided assertions (either from the left or the right), since the other direction then follows immediately by taking adjoints. Moreover, regarding the essential left-invertibility, one can also show that

$$\dim \ker P_H \mid H_1 = \dim \ker P_{K \ominus H_1} \mid K \ominus H.$$

In particular, this implies that if these operators are Fredholm, then their indices are equal.

## 4. ESSENTIAL INVERTIBILITY OF SKEW TOEPLITZ OPERATORS

In this section we prove one of our key results about the essential invertibility of the skew Toeplitz operator $A$. This will be seen to be closely related to the essential norm of a certain associated Hankel operator. We use the notation of the Section 2. In particular, we have

$$A = \sum_{j,k=0}^{n} T^j \hat{C}_{jk} T^{*k} = P_H \sum_{j,k=0}^{n} C_{jk} U_+^j U_+^{*k} \mid H.$$

Since the operator

$$\sum_{j,k=0}^{n} C_{jk} U_+^j U_+^{*k}$$

does not have good commutation properties with either $U_+$ or $U_+^*$, we will study at first the essential invertibility of an operator closely related to $A$. Before doing this we need to set up the following notation.

Let

$$B_+ := \sum_{j,k=0}^{n} C_{jk} U_+^{n+j-k},$$

$$B := \sum_{j,k=0}^{n} C_{jk} U^{n+j-k},$$

and

$$C(z) := \sum_{j,k=0}^{n} C_{jk} z^{n+j-k}.$$

Moreover we put $d(z) := \det C(z)$, and let $C^A(z)$ denote the algebraic adjoint of $C(z)$ so that

$$C^A(z)C(z) = C(z)C^A(z) = d(z)I.$$

We can now state the following lemma:

**LEMMA (4.1).** *The following conditions are equivalent:*

(i) *$A$ is essentially left-invertible;*

(ii) *$AT^{*n}$ is essentially left-invertible;*

(iii) *$P_H B_+^* | H$ is essentially left-invertible.*

**PROOF.** The equivalence of (i) and (ii) follows from the fact, noted in Section 2, that $T^*$ is essentially invertible. For the equivalence of (ii) and (iii) we note that

$$P_H B_+^* | H - AT^{*n} = P_H B_+^* | H - P_H \sum_{j,k=0}^{n} C_{jk} U_+^j U_+^{*n+k} | H$$

$$= P_H B_+^* | H - P_H \sum_{j,k=0}^{n} C_{jk} U^{*n+k-j} | H + F = P_H B_+^* | H - P_H B_+^* | H + F = F$$

where $F$ is a finite rank operator. (Note $(I - U_+ U_+^*)$ has rank $N$.) □

**REMARK (4.2).** The advantage of considering the operator of (4.1) (iii) in studying the essential invertibility of $A$ is that $B_+^*$ commutes with $U_+^*$, and hence the space

$$H_1 := (B_+^* H)^-$$

is invariant under $U_+^*$. Consequently from the Beurling-Lax theorem, we infer the existence of an inner function $\Theta_1 \in H^\infty(L(\mathbf{C}^M, \mathbf{C}^N))$ $(M \leq N)$ such that

$$H_1 := H(\Theta_1) = H^2(\mathbf{C}^N) \ominus \Theta_1 H^2(\mathbf{C}^M).$$

The function $\Theta_1$ will be crucial in the determination of the essential invertibility of $A$.

Set $T_1 := S(\Theta_1)$. Note that $T = S(\Theta)$. Moreover we set $Z := B_+^* | H : H \to H_1$. Then we have the following result:

**LEMMA (4.3).**

(i) $T_1^* Z = Z T^*$.

(ii) $T_1$ *is an operator of class* $C_0$.

(iii) $M = N$.

**PROOF.** (iii) is an immediate consequence of (ii) since an operator of class $C_0$ is of class $C_{00}$ (see [13]). (i) follows from the fact that $B_+^*$ commutes with $U_+^*$. Finally, to prove (ii), let $m$ denote the minimal function of $T$. By (i), we get

$$m(T_1)^* Z = Z m(T)^* = 0,$$

and hence $m(T_1)^* = 0$ since $Z$ has dense range. □

Following the elementary observations that we made in Section 3 (note that $B_+^*$ corresponds to $X$ there), we now consider the essential invertibility of the operator $W := P_H | H_1$. In order to do this we will now make contact with the classical Toeplitz and Hankel operators. More precisely, let $\tau : H^2(\mathbf{C}^N) \to H^2(\mathbf{C}^N)$ be the Toeplitz operator defined by

$$\tau h := P_{H^2(\mathbf{C}^N)}(\Theta_1^* \Theta h)$$

for $h \in H^2(\mathbf{C}^N)$. Further define the Hankel operator $\chi : H^2(\mathbf{C}^N) \to L^2(\mathbf{C}^N) \ominus H^2(\mathbf{C}^N)$ by

$$\chi h := P_{L^2(\mathbf{C}^N) \ominus H^2(\mathbf{C}^N)} \Theta_1^* \Theta h$$

for $h \in H^2(\mathbf{C}^N)$. Then we have the following:

**PROPOSITION (4.4).** *Notation as above. (In particular $H = H(\Theta)$, $H_1 = H(\Theta_1)$.) The following conditions are equivalent:*

(i) $W = P_H | H_1$ *is essentially left-invertible;*

(ii) $P_{\Theta_1 H^2(\mathbf{C}^N)} | \Theta H^2(\mathbf{C}^N)$ *is essentially left-invertible;*

(iii) $\tau$ *is essentially left-invertible;*

(iv) *the essential norm of* $\chi$ *is less than one;*

(v) *distance* $(\Theta_1^* \Theta, H^\infty(L(\mathbf{C}^N)) + C(L(\mathbf{C}^N))) < 1$.

*(Note that* $C(L(\mathbf{C}^N))$ *denotes the space of continuous* $L(\mathbf{C}^N)$ *valued functions defined on the unit circle.)*

**PROOF.** First of all the equivalence of (i) and (ii) follows from (3.2). We now demonstrate the equivalence of (ii) and (iii). In order to do this, we note that if $M_{\Theta_1^*} : L^2(\mathbf{C}^N) \to L^2(\mathbf{C}^N)$ denotes multiplication by $\Theta_1^*$, then $M_{\Theta_1^*}$ is unitary. Hence $P_{\Theta_1 H^2(\mathbf{C}^N)} | \Theta H^2(\mathbf{C}^N)$ is essentially left-invertible if and only if

$$M_{\Theta_1^*}[P_{\Theta_1 H^2(\mathbf{C}^N)} | \Theta H^2(\mathbf{C}^N)] M_{\Theta_1} = P_{H^2(\mathbf{C}^N)} | \Theta_1^* \Theta H^2(\mathbf{C}^N)$$

is essentially left-invertible. Further, we have

$$\tau = (P_{H^2(\mathbf{C}^N)} | \Theta_1^* \Theta H^2(\mathbf{C}^N))(M_{\Theta_1^* \Theta} | H^2(\mathbf{C}^N)),$$

and $M_{\Theta_1^* \Theta} | H^2(\mathbf{C}^N)$ is unitary from $H^2(\mathbf{C}^N)$ to $\Theta_1^* \Theta H^2(\mathbf{C}^N)$. The required equivalence now follows immediately.

Next the equivalence of (iii) and (iv) may be derived from the equality

$$\begin{aligned} \|u\|^2 &= \|\Theta_1^* \Theta u\|^2 \\ &= \|\tau u\|^2 + \|\chi u\|^2 \end{aligned}$$

for $u \in H^2(\mathbf{C}^N)$. Finally, the equivalence of (iv) and (v) is a consequence of the fact that the essential norm of $\chi$ is the distance of $\Theta_1^* \Theta$ to $H^\infty(L(\mathbf{C}^N)) + C(L(\mathbf{C}^N))$. (See [11].) □

**REMARK (4.5).** We should note here that an analogous result to (4.4) holds for left-invertibility. Moreover if one replaces $\Theta_1^*\Theta$ by $\Theta^*\Theta_1$ one gets an analogous result for essential right-invertibility, and of course right-invertibility.

We now consider the essential invertibility of the operator $Z$. We can only give a set of sufficient conditions for invertibility here. We use the notation that we set up at the beginning of this section as well as that of Section 2. Note that $B_+$ is an analytic Toeplitz operator with symbol $C(z)$. We can now state:

**PROPOSITION (4.6).**

(i) *If*

$$\{z : d(z) = 0\} \cap \sigma(T) = \emptyset, \tag{1}$$

*then $Z$ is invertible.*

(ii) *If*

$$\{z : d(z) = 0\} \cap \sigma_e(T) = \emptyset, \tag{2}$$

*then $Z$ is Fredholm (i.e. essentially invertible).*

*(Note that $\sigma_e(T) = \sigma(T) \cap \partial D$ where $\partial D$ denotes the unit circle.)*

**PROOF.** Let $B'$ be the Toeplitz operator with symbol $C^A(z)$ (notation as above), so that

$$B_+B' = B'B_+ = d(U_+).$$

We have then

$$B'^* B_+^* = d(U_+)^*,$$

and hence

$$B'^* B_+^* \mid H = d(T)^*.$$

Now if (1) is satisfied, then $d(T)$ is invertible, and hence $B_+^*$ is bounded from below on $H$, from which we get (i). Next if (2) is satisfied, then $d(T)$ is Fredholm, and so $B_+^*$ is essentially bounded from below on $H$, from we deduce (ii). □

We are now ready to formulate and prove the main result of this section:

**THEOREM (4.7).** *With the above notation, assume that condition (2) holds. Then $A$ is Fredholm if and only if*

$$\text{distance}\,(\Theta_1^*\Theta\,,\,H^\infty(L(\mathbf{C}^N)) + C(L(\mathbf{C}^N))) < 1.$$

**PROOF.** First of all since $A$ is self-adjoint, it is Fredholm if and only if it is essentially left-invertible. But by (4.1) we have therefore that $A$ is Fredholm if and only if $Y := P_H B_+^* \mid H$ is essentially left-invertible. Now by (4.6), we have that $Z$ is Fredholm (we have assumed condition (2)), and hence by (3.1) $A$ is Fredholm if and only if $W = P_H \mid H_1$ is essentially left-invertible, from which we get the desired conclusion from (4.4). □

**REMARKS (4.8).** (i) A similar argument shows that under the hypothesis (2), $A$ is essentially right invertible (and hence Fredholm since $A = A^*$) if and only if

$$\text{distance}\,(\Theta^*\Theta_1\,,\,H^\infty(L(\mathbf{C}^N) + C(L(\mathbf{C}^N))) < 1.$$

Moreover clearly this last condition is equivalent to the existence of a rational $R \in L^\infty(L(\mathbf{C}^N))$ such that

$$\text{distance}\,(\Theta^*\Theta_1 + R\,,\,H^\infty(L(\mathbf{C}^N))) < 1. \tag{3}$$

In certain cases it is condition (3) that we will find most convenient to work with in considering the essential invertibility of $A$.

(ii) We finally note that if $A$ is Fredholm, then

$$\text{distance}\,(\Theta_1^*\Theta\,,\,H^\infty(L(\mathbf{C}^N)) + C(L(\mathbf{C}^N))) < 1$$

regardless of condition (2).

## 5. COMPRESSIONS OF CONSTANT MATRICES

A neat corollary of the above theory is that it is possible to give a necessary and sufficient condition for the invertibility of the compression of a constant $N \times N$ matrix. Once again following the notation of Section 2 for $\Theta$ a fixed nonconstant $N \times N$ matrix-valued inner function, and $C \in L(\mathbf{C}^N)$, $C = C^*$, we set $\hat{C} := P_H C \mid H$ (where $H = H(\Theta)$). For $N = 1$, we have of course that $\hat{C}$ is invertible iff $C \neq 0$. The case of $N > 1$ is more interesting!

In order that condition (2) of Section 4 be satisfied, we assume that $C$ is invertible. Indeed using the notation of Sections 2 and 4, notice that we are studying the case in which $A = \hat{C}$, i.e. $n = 0$. Then obviously $C(z) \equiv C$, $\Theta_1$ is precisely the inner factor of $C^{-1}\Theta$, and $d(z) = \det C$ is a nonzero constant. We can now state the following:

**THEOREM (5.1).** $0 \notin \sigma(\hat{C})$ *(i.e.* $\hat{C}$ *is invertible) if and only if*

$$\text{distance}\,(\Theta^* \Theta_1, H^\infty(L(\mathbf{C}^N))) < 1.$$

**PROOF.** Basically the theorem follows if we simply note that the argument given in Section 4 applied to $\sigma_e(A)$ works for $\sigma(A)$ when $A = \hat{C}$. More specifically, if we consider (4.1) (and its proof), we have that since $n = 0$, $F = 0$. Consequently, if we now follow the reasoning up to (4.8), we see that we may remove the word "essential" in the formulation of the various results, and hence we get that for $A = \hat{C}$, $0 \notin \sigma(A)$ if and only if (3) is satisfied with $R = 0$ which is precisely the required statement. □

We would like to illustrate (5.1) now with an example which we feel shows the great difference in complexity between numerical and matrix skew Toeplitz operators.

**EXAMPLE (5.2).** Set for $m_1, m_2 \in H^\infty$ inner functions

$$\Theta = \begin{bmatrix} m_1 & 0 \\ 0 & m_2 \end{bmatrix}$$

$$C = \begin{bmatrix} 0 & 1 \\ 1 & 0 \end{bmatrix}.$$

Since $\Theta_1$ is the inner part of $C^{-1}\Theta$, we get that

$$\Theta_1 = \begin{bmatrix} 0 & m_2 \\ m_1 & 0 \end{bmatrix}$$

and hence

$$\Theta^* \Theta_1 = \begin{bmatrix} 0 & \overline{m}_1 m_2 \\ \overline{m}_2 m_1 & 0 \end{bmatrix}.$$

But this means by (5.1) that $0 \in \sigma(\hat{C})$ iff

$$\max \{\text{distance}(\overline{m}_1 m_2, H^\infty), \text{distance}(\overline{m}_2 m_1, H^\infty)\} = 1.$$

Moreover by (4.8) we have that $0 \in \sigma_e(\hat{C})$ iff given any rational functions $\phi_1, \phi_2 \in L^\infty$ we have

$$\max \{\text{distance}(\overline{m}_1 m_2 + \phi_1, H^\infty), \text{distance}(\overline{m}_2 m_1 + \phi_2, H^\infty)\} \geq 1.$$

Let us take more specific $m_1$ and $m_2$ and complete our analysis. First suppose that $\deg m_1 \neq \deg m_2$. Then by the above argument and the results of [1], we have that $0 \in \sigma(\hat{C})$, i.e. $\hat{C}$ is not invertible. Next suppose $m_1 = m$, $m_2 = m^2$. Then

$$\text{distance } (\overline{m}_2 m_1, H^\infty) = \text{distance } (\overline{m}, H^\infty) = 1$$

and so once more $\hat{C}$ is not invertible. Further, $\|\chi h\| = \|h\|$ (see (4.4)) iff $h \in H(m)$, and hence $0 \in \sigma_e(\hat{C})$ iff $\dim H(m) = \infty$.

## 6. FACTORIZATION CONSTRUCTION

In this section we will make a certain construction based on factorization theory which will be essential to us in finding a determinantal formula for the invertibility of $A$. We will assume that condition (1) from Section 4 holds throughout this section.

Then first we note that from (4.6) we have that $H_1 := B_+^* H$ is closed, and

$$H_1 = H^2(\mathbf{C}^N) \ominus \Theta_1 H^2(\mathbf{C}^N)$$

where $\Theta_1 \in H^\infty(L(\mathbf{C}^N))$ is inner (see Section 4).

Next if $P_{H^2(\mathbf{C}^N)} : L^2(\mathbf{C}^N) \to H^2(\mathbf{C}^N)$ denotes orthogonal projection, we see that

$$H = P_{H^2(\mathbf{C}^N)}\Theta(L^2(\mathbf{C}^N)\ominus H^2(\mathbf{C}^N))$$

and so we get that $\Theta_1^* B_+^* \, P_{H^2(\mathbf{C}^N)}\Theta(L^2(\mathbf{C}^N)\ominus H^2(\mathbf{C}^N))$ is orthogonal to $H^2(\mathbf{C}^N)$. But since $P_{H^2(\mathbf{C}^N)}B^* \mid H^2(\mathbf{C}^N) = B_+^*$ we have that

$$\Theta_1^* B^* \Theta(L^2(\mathbf{C}^N)\ominus H^2(\mathbf{C}^N)) \subset L^2(\mathbf{C}^N)\ominus H^2(\mathbf{C}^N)$$

and so

$$\Theta_1^* C^* \Theta = \Omega^*$$

where $\Omega \in H^\infty(L(\mathbf{C}^N))$. But from this (using the fact that $\Theta$ is inner) we obtain

$$C\Theta_1 = \Theta\Omega. \tag{4}$$

Now from (4.6), we have that $B_+^* \mid H$ is an isomorphism of $H$ to $H_1$. Hence $(B_+^* \mid H)^*$ is an isomorphism of $H_1$ to $H$. Set $T_1 := S(\Theta_1)$. (Notation as in Sections 2 and 4.) Then since $(B_+^* \mid H)^* = P_H C \mid H_1$ intertwines $T$ and $T_1$, we see by virtue of the commutant lifting theorem that there exists $C^{(-1)} \in H^\infty(L(\mathbf{C}^N))$ such that

$$C^{(-1)}C = I + \Theta_1 E, \; C^{(-1)}\Theta = \Theta_1 E_1 \tag{5}$$

$$CC^{(-1)} = I + \Theta F$$

where $E_1$, $E$, $F \in H^\infty(L(\mathbf{C}^N))$. Equations (5) will be crucial in writing down a certain determinantal formula for the invertibility of $A$ in Section 7.

We conclude this rather technical section with an important identification which we will need later on in our analysis. More precisely, we want to give a very simple characterization of $\Theta_1$ using factorization theory.

First note that since $T_1$ and $T$ are similar we have that (see [12]) det $\Theta =$ det $\Theta_1$, and so from equation (4)

$$d(z) = \det C(z) = \det \Omega(z)$$

and

$$C^A \Theta = \Theta_1 \Omega^A \tag{6}$$

where $\Omega^A$ denotes the algebraic adjoint of $\Omega$. (Note that $\Omega\Omega^A = \Omega^A \Omega = d(z)I$).

Let

$$\Omega^A = \Omega_i^A \Omega_o^A$$

be the inner-outer factorization of $\Omega^A$. From (6) it follows that $\Theta_1 \Omega_i^A$ is the inner factor of $C^A \Theta$. Moreover it is clear that we have that det $\Omega_i^A$ is the factor of $d(z)$, say $\hat{d}(z)$, which corresponds to the zeros of $d(z)$ in the open unit disc $D$.

We therefore see that $\Omega_i^A$ is the right inner factor of $\Theta_1 \Omega_i^A$ corresponding to these zeros. More precisely define

$$\Gamma := \{v \in H(\Theta_1 \Omega_i^A) \mid \hat{d}(S(\Theta_1 \Omega_i^A))^k v = 0 \text{ for } k \text{ sufficiently large}\}.$$

Then

$$H(\Theta_1) = H(\Theta_1 \Omega_i^A) \ominus \Gamma. \tag{7}$$

(7) defines $\Theta_1$ uniquely up to a constant unitary right factor. Hence we have a precise characterization of $\Theta_1$ from elementary factorization theory.

## 7. DETERMINANTAL FORMULA

In this section we would like to derive a determinantal formula for the invertibility of a skew Toeplitz operator $A$ as we did in [4] and [7] in the numerical case. We assume throughout this section that (1) holds and moreover that

$$\text{distance } (\Theta^* \Theta_1, H^\infty(L(\mathbf{C}^N))) < 1. \tag{8}$$

Then we have

**LEMMA (7.1).** $0 \in \sigma(A)$ *if and only if* $0 \in \sigma_d(A)$ *(where* $\sigma_d$ *denotes the discrete spectrum.)*

**PROOF.** Immediate from (8) and (4.8). □

**REMARK (7.2).** Notice that (7.1) means that $0 \in \sigma(A)$ if and only if there exists a nonzero $f \in H(\Theta) = H$ such that $Af = 0$. But this last condition is equivalent to the existence of $f \in H$, $g \in H^2(\mathbf{C}^N)$ such that $f \neq 0$ and

$$\sum_{j,k=0}^{n} C_{jk} U_+^j U_+^{*k} f = \Theta g. \tag{9}$$

Now define the Toeplitz operator $\mathfrak{t}$ on $H^2(\mathbf{C}^N)$ by

$$\mathfrak{t}h := P_{H^2(\mathbf{C}^N)}(\Theta^* \Theta_1 h)$$

for $h \in H^2(\mathbf{C}^N)$. We will now need the following technical result:

**LEMMA (7.3).** *With assumptions* (1) *and* (8), *the Toeplitz operator* $\mathfrak{t}$ *is invertible.*

**PROOF.** First of all from (4.8), we see that $0 \notin \sigma_e(A)$, and hence $A$ is Fredholm and index $(A) = 0$ (since $A = A^*$). Moreover (8) insures that $\mathfrak{t}$ has a left inverse. Thus $\mathfrak{t}$ is semi-Fredholm, and

$$-\infty \leq \text{index } (\mathfrak{t}) \leq 0.$$

Further from the proof of (4.4) (see also (4.5)), we can now deduce that $P_{\Theta H^2(\mathbf{C}^N)} | \Theta_1 H^2(\mathbf{C}^N)$ is semi-Fredholm, and

$$\text{index } (P_{\Theta H^2(\mathbf{C}^N)} | \Theta_1 H^2(\mathbf{C}^N)) = \text{index } (\mathfrak{t}). \tag{10}$$

Now from (3.3), we see that

$$\text{index } (P_{\Theta H^2(\mathbf{C}^N)} | \Theta_1 H^2(\mathbf{C}^N)) = \text{index } (P_{H_1} | H), \tag{11}$$

and since $Z = B_+^* | H : H \to H_1$ is an isomorphism (see (4.6)), we have

$$\text{index } (P_{H_1} | H) = - \text{ index } (P_H B_+^* | H). \tag{12}$$

Finally from the proof of (4.1) and our above argument, we get

$$\text{index}\,(P_H B_+^* \mid H) = \text{index}\,(A) = 0\,,$$

which implies via the above string of equalities that index ($\mathfrak{t}$) = 0. From this of course, we immediately infer that $\mathfrak{t}$ is invertible as required. □

This allows us to make the following:

**DEFINITION (7.4).** Let $F \in H^\infty(L(\mathbf{C}^N))$, $x \in \mathbf{C}^N$. Then we set

$$\Gamma(F)x := \mathfrak{t}^{-1} P_{H^2(\mathbf{C}^N)} \Theta^* Fx. \tag{13}$$

Note that if we endow the space $L(\mathbf{C}^N)$ with the standard Hilbert-Schmidt structure, we get that (13) defines a matrix-valued function satisfying

$$\Gamma(F) \in H^2(L(\mathbf{C}^N)).$$

We moreover set

$$C_l(z) := \sum_{0 \le j \le n,\, l < k \le n} C_{jk} z^{n+j-k+l}$$

and

$$\Gamma_l(z) := \Gamma(C^{(-1)} C_l)(z) \tag{14}$$

for $0 \le l \le n-1$.

With this notation from (9) we get that $0 \in \sigma(A)$ iff there exist $f$, $g$ as above such that

$$C(z) f(z) - \sum_{l=0}^{n-1} C_l(z) f_l = z^n \Theta(z) g(z) \tag{15}$$

where $f(z) = f_0 + z f_1 + \cdots$ is the Taylor expansion of $f(z)$. We now apply the matrix function $C^{(-1)}$ to (15) and using equations (5) we get that

$$f(z) - \sum_{l=0}^{n-1} C^{(-1)}(z) C_l(z) f_l = \Theta_1(z)\, (z^n E_1(z) g(z) - E(z) f(z)) =: \Theta_1(z) h(z). \tag{16}$$

If we apply the operator $P_{H^2(\mathbf{C}^N)} \Theta^*$ to (16), and use (13) and (14) we see

$$h(z) = -\sum_{l=0}^{n-1} \Gamma_l(z) f_l .$$

Hence

$$f(z) = \sum_{l=0}^{n-1} (C^{(-1)}(z) C_l(z) - \Theta_1(z)\Gamma_l(z)) f_l . \tag{17}$$

If we now plug (17) into (15) and use equations (4) and (5), we have

$$\begin{aligned} z^n \Theta g &= Cf - \sum_{l=0}^{n-1} C_l f_l \qquad (18) \\ &= \sum_{l=0}^{n-1} C_l f_l + \Theta F \sum_{l=0}^{n-1} C_l f_l - \Theta\Omega \sum_{l=0}^{n-1} \Gamma_l f_l - \sum_{l=0}^{n-1} C_l f_l \\ &= \Theta \sum_{l=0}^{n-1} (FC_l - \Omega\Gamma_l) f_l . \end{aligned}$$

Now since $\Theta(z)$ is unitary for almost all $z \in \partial D$ (the unit circle), we get that (18) holds iff

$$\sum_{l=0}^{n-1} (FC_l - \Omega\Gamma_l)(z) f_l \equiv z^n g(z). \tag{19}$$

But this brings us to the key point. Indeed since $g \in H^2(\mathbf{C}^N)$, the Taylor series of $z^n g(z)$ has its first $n$ coefficients equal to 0. Thus (19) is valid iff for the Taylor expansions $(0 \le l \le n-1)$

$$(FC_l - \Omega\Gamma_l)(z) = X_{l0} + zX_{l1} + \cdots \tag{20}$$

we have

$$\sum_{l=0}^{n-1} X_{li} f_l = 0 \tag{21}$$

for $0 \le i \le n-1$. Moreover by (17), $f \ne 0$ iff the vector $(f_0, \cdots, f_{n-1}) \ne 0$.

Our above argument proves the following:

**THEOREM (7.5).** $0 \in \sigma(A)$ *if and only if*

$$\det \begin{bmatrix} X_{00} & X_{10} & \cdots & X_{n-1,0} \\ X_{01} & X_{11} & \cdots & X_{n-1,1} \\ \cdot & \cdot & \cdots & \cdot \\ X_{0,n-1} & X_{1,n-1} & \cdots & X_{n-1,n-1} \end{bmatrix} = 0. \tag{22}$$

**PROOF.** Immediate from the above discussion. □

**REMARKS (7.6).** Notice that we can determine the invertibility of $A$ (modulo the above assumptions) via the determinant of an $n \times n$ block matrix. (Each of the $X_{ij}$ is $N \times N$.) When $N = 1$, we actually have an $n \times n$ matrix. Previously (see [4], [6], [7]) our determinantal formulae for such a problem involved $2n \times 2n$ matrices. Hence it seems that the present theory gives us a improvement in the scalar (numerical) case. We will discuss this further in the next section.

## 8. THE SCALAR CASE

In this section, we would like to make a few remarks about the case in which $T \in C_0(1)$ in the definition of $A$ in Section 2, i.e. the scalar case when $N = 1$. Once more we assume that (1) holds. Then we first note (using the notation of Section 6; see in particular equations (5)) that we have here

$$\Theta_1 = \Theta,\ E = F,\ \Omega = C = E_1,$$

and all of the above functions are scalar-valued and contained in $H^\infty$. Moreover, (11) is always satisfied since $\Theta^* \Theta_1 = 1$ (and so the corresponding distance is zero).

Next following the program of the previous section, given $C$, $\Theta \in H^\infty$ coprime (in the strong Corona sense; see (1)) with $C$ a polynomial such that

$$C(z) = \sum_{0 \le j,k \le n} C_{jk} z^{n+j-k}$$

$$C_{jk} = \overline{C}_{jk},$$

we are required to find $C^{(-1)}$, $F \in H^\infty$ such that

$$1 = CC^{(-1)} - \Theta F. \tag{23}$$

We would like to give here a method for constructing $C^{(-1)}$ and $F$. More precisely, let $z_1, \cdots, z_k$ $(k \le 2n)$ denote the roots of $C$. It is easy to see that if some nonzero root $z_i \in D$ (the open unit disc), then $1/\overline{z_i}$ will also be a root of $C(z)$. Note that by (1), $\Theta$ is analytic in a neighborhood of each $z_i$. Then we set

$$C^{(-1)}(z) := \frac{1 - x(z)\Theta(z)}{C(z)} \tag{24}$$

$$F(z) := -x(z) \tag{25}$$

where $x(z)$ is a polynomial obeying the interpolation conditions

$$1 - x(z_i)\Theta(z_i) = 0 \tag{26}$$

for $i = 1, \cdots, k$. Clearly since $\Theta$ and $C$ are coprime and $\Theta$ is inner, this interpolation problem can always be solved. (Indeed for $z_i \in D$, $\Theta(z_i) \ne 0$. Moreover if $z_i \ne 0$, then $\Theta(1/\overline{z_i}) = 1/\overline{\Theta(z_i)}$.) It is then trivial to check that $C^{(-1)}$ and $F$ as defined in (24) and (25) solve the Corona equation (23). (See also [9].)

Given this, we note in this case that

$$X_l := FC_l - \Omega\Gamma_l = FC_l - CP_{H^2}\Theta^* C^{(-1)}C_l \tag{27}$$

for $0 \le l \le n-1$. From this one derives the $n \times n$ matrix of (22) from the first $n$ coefficients of the (scalar) Taylor expansions of the $X_l$.

We would like to illustrate these ideas with a simple example:

**EXAMPLE (8.1).** Let $w \in H^\infty$ be rational, $\Theta \in H^\infty$ nonconstant inner, and set $H := H(\Theta)$, $T := S(\Theta)$. We would like to consider here the problem of computing the singular values of $w(T)$. Note that if express $w = p/q$ as a ratio of two relatively prime polynomials, it is easy to see that this problem amounts to determining if $0 \in \sigma_d(P_\rho)$ where

$$P_\rho := q(T)q(T)^* - (1/\rho^2)p(T)p(T)^*$$

for $\rho$ a positive real number. (Note that $P_\rho$ corresponds to $A$ above.) This question has been considered in great detail in [4-7] and has motivated much of the research considered in the present paper.

Let us now take

$$w(z) = \frac{1-z}{2}, \quad \Theta = \exp\left(\frac{z+1}{z-1}\right)$$

(our favorite example and test case), and apply the procedure discussed above. Then one may compute that here

$$C(z) = \frac{1}{\rho^2}z^2 + \left(4 - \frac{2}{\rho^2}\right)z + \frac{1}{\rho^2}$$

and

$$C_0(z) = -\left[\frac{1}{\rho^2}\right] + \frac{1}{\rho^2}z.$$

(Note that $n = 1$ in this case.)

Moreover, the roots of $C(z)$ are given by

$$z_1 = (1 - 2\rho^2) + 2i\rho^2\sqrt{(1/\rho^2) - 1},$$

and $z_2 = \overline{z}_1$. (Since $\|w\|_\infty = 1$, we may clearly take $\rho \in (0,1)$.) Hence we get that

$$\Theta(z_1) = \exp\left(-i\sqrt{(1/\rho^2) - 1}\right),$$

and $\Theta(z_2) = \overline{\Theta(z_1)}$. With this data, we may then compute an interpolating function (as in (26))

$$x(z) := \frac{z - z_2}{2}\left[\frac{\sin\sqrt{(1/\rho^2) - 1}}{\rho^2\sqrt{(1/\rho^2) - 1}}\right] + \exp\left(-i\sqrt{(1/\rho^2) - 1}\right).$$

Finally using (26) (note that since $n = 1$, we need only calculate the constant term of $X_0$), we derive that the singular values of $w(T)$ are precisely the roots of

$$\tan\sqrt{(1/\rho^2) - 1} + \sqrt{(1/\rho^2) - 1} = 0$$

contained in the interval (0,1), which agrees with the answer we obtained in [6] using a completely different method.

## 9. CONCLUSIONS

The results above are the beginning of a study of an interesting class of operators that appear in numerous physical applications. There are of course several important and nontrivial problems which must be resolved first before one can claim to have a satisfactory theory.

First of all from the purely mathematical perspective we like to have a better understanding about the invertibility of skew Toeplitz operators and not just the essential invertibility. Next there remains the question of how to (more explicitly) solve the Nehari problem for $\Theta^* \Theta_1$ as defined above. (See equation (11).) This matrix-valued operator does have a special form (both $\Theta$ and $\Theta_1$ are inner), and results in the scalar case from [1] (on nondeformable "minifunctions") give us some reason to expect that similar results may be obtained here (perhaps in terms of the factorization indices of the operators [3]). Moreover it may be illuminating to understand the relationship of (22) to previous determinantal formulae derived in [4-7].

Of course, the ultimate aim is to develop algorithms suitable for the computation of the singular values of the block Hankel matrices for the kinds of infinite dimensional systems which appear in control engineering. We hope that the present paper raises a whole series of research issues that will be worth considering in the near future.

## REFERENCES

[1] V.M. ADAMJAN, D. Z. AROV, and M. G. KREIN, Analytic properties of Schmidt pairs for a Hankel operator and the generalized Schur-Takagi problem, *Math. USSR Sbornik* **15** (1971), 31-73.

[2] V.M. ADAMJAN, D. Z. AROV, and M. G. KREIN, Infinite Hankel block matrices and related extension problems, *Amer. Math. Soc. Transl.* **111** (1978), 133-156.

[3] K. CLANCEY and I. GOHBERG, "Factorization of Matrix Functions and Singular Integral Operators", Birkhauser, Basel, Switzerland, 1981.

[4] C. FOIAS and A. TANNENBAUM, On the Nehari problem for a certain class of $L^\infty$ functions appearing in control theory, to appear in *J. Functional Analysis* .

[5] C. FOIAS and A. TANNENBAUM, On the Nehari problem for a certain class of $L^\infty$ functions appearing in control theory II, Technical Report, Department of Electrical Engineering, Univ. of Minnesota, October 1986. Submitted for publication.

[6] C. FOIAS, A. TANNENBAUM, and G. ZAMES, On the $H^\infty$-optimal sensitivity problem for systems with delays, *SIAM J. Control and Óptimization* **25** (1987), 686-706.

[7] C. FOIAS, A. TANNENBAUM, and G. ZAMES, Some explicit formulae for the singular values of certain Hankel operators with factorizable symbol, Technical Report, Department of Electrical Engineering, Univ. of Minnesota, March 1987. Submitted for publication.

[8] B.A. FRANCIS, "A Course in $H^\infty$ Control Theory," Lecture Notes in Control and Information Science, Springer, New York, 1987.

[9] E. W. KAMEN, P. KHARGONEKAR, and A. TANNENBAUM, New techniques for the control of linear infinite dimensional systems, in "Frequency Domain and State Space Methods for Linear Systems," edited by C. Byrnes and A. Lindquist, North-Holland, Amsterdam (1986), 355-367.

[10] N. K. NIKOLSKII, "Treatise on the Shift Operator," Springer, New York, 1986.

[11] L. B. PAGE, Bounded and compact vectorial Hankel operators, *Trans. Amer. Math. Soc.* **150** (1970), 529-539.

[12] B. SZ.-NAGY and C. FOIAS, Modèle de Jordan pour une classe d' opérateurs de l'espace de Hilbert, *Acta Sci. Math. (Szeged)* **31** (1970), 93-117.

[13] B. SZ.-NAGY and C. FOIAS, "Harmonic Analysis of Operators on Hilbert Space," North-Holland, Amsterdam, 1970.

Hari Bercovici and Ciprian Foias
Department of Mathematics
Indiana University
Bloomington, Indiana 47405

Allen Tannenbaum
Department of Electrical Engineering
University of Minnesota
123 Church Street SE
Minneapolis, Minnesota 55455
and
Department of Mathematics
Ben-Gurion University of the Negev

Submitted: September 7, 1987

Operator Theory:
Advances and Applications, Vol. 29
(c) 1988 Birkhäuser Verlag Basel



# ON LOCAL INDEX AND THE COCYCLE PROPERTY FOR LEFSCHETZ NUMBERS

R.W.Carey and J.D. Pincus

Dedicated to M.S. Livsic
on his seventieth birthday.

Let $T=(T_1,\dots,T_s)$ be a commuting $s$-tuple of elements in the algebra of bounded operators on a complex Banach space. When the $(2s-2)$-dimensional Hausdorff measure of $\sigma_{ess}(T)$ is zero we introduce certain Lefschetz number ratios which give the transition functions for a holomorphic line bundle $E_T$ on $\mathbb{C}^s \setminus \sigma_{ess}(T)$. The Lefschetz numbers themselves define a meromorphic section of $E_T$ whose divisor is a complex analytic cycle carried on the Taylor spectrum; its local degree at $z$ has a natural interpretation as a maximal ideal index for $(T-z)$. This index has jumps on the singular locus of the spectrum and sometimes determines the $K_1$-homology class of $T$. The correspondence $T \rightarrow E_T$ has the property that $E_{T \oplus T'} = E_T \otimes E_T{}'$, and if $s$ is even, $E_{T^t}=-E$, where $t$ denotes transpose. Furthermore, when $M$ is a Hilbert space, $\sigma_{ess}(T)$ is smooth and $K$ is compact, $E_{T+K}=E_T$. The present note details the construction of the map $T \rightarrow E_T$ and its relationship to the fundamental trace form of crypto-integral algebras.

## TABLE OF CONTENTS

## 1. INTRODUCTION

A natural and fundamental problem in the index theory of commutative Banach algebras is to determine how global index formulae for enveloping $C^*$ - algebras localize. The aim of this series of papers is to make some initial steps towards a realization of that goal. In so doing we shall explore the relationships between the complex geometry of the spectrum and its boundary, and between spanning currents and cyclic cocycles. The focus of the present paper is on Koszul complexes and the analytic functional calculus.

The simplest non-planar algebras involve a pair of commuting Fredholm operators. In order to motivate some of our ideas we shall begin by noting certain reciprocity results pertaining to their study.

### (i) The cocycle property

Suppose $A$ and $B$ are commuting operators on a complex Banach space $M$. If $w \notin \sigma_{ess}(A)$ and $z \notin \sigma_{ess}(B)$, the multiplicative Lefschetz number of $B-z$ relative to $A-w$ is the quotient of characteristic polynomials

$$\psi(B-z;\, A-w) \equiv \frac{det(B-z \mid ker(A-w))}{det(B-z \mid coker\,(A-w))}.$$

Using methods from algebraic $K$-theory, in particular the group $K_2$, the authors showed in [6] that the divisors in $\mathbb{C}^2$ defined by $\psi(B-z;\, A-w)$ and $\psi(A-w;\, B-z)$ are equal. Indeed, we proved that

$$\Psi(B-z;\, A-w) \equiv \frac{\psi(B-z;\, A-w)}{\psi(A-w;\, B-z)},$$

which is defined whenever $(w,z)$ is in the complement of the Taylor spectrum $Sp(M,A,B)$, has a non-vanishing holomorphic extension through $Sp(M,A,B)$. Consequently, when the essential spectrum $\sigma_{ess}(A,B)$ of the pair $(A,B)$ is not too large, i.e., if it's 2-dimensional Hausdorff measure is zero, it turns out that such quotients defined from linear combinations of $A$ and $B$ form transition functions for a holomorphic line bundle $E_{A,B}$ over $X \equiv \mathbb{C}^2 \setminus \sigma_{ess}(A,B)$ while the individual Lefschetz numbers define an element in the vector space of meromorphic cross sections of $E_{A,B}$. The divisor of this section is a complex analytic cycle in $X$ whose local degree at point $(z,w)$ can be interpreted as an index for the maximal ideal $(A-w,\, B-z)$ generated by $A-w$ and $B-z$ in the norm closure of the Taylor functional calculus [37]. A description of the local degrees has also been given in [7] in terms of a decomposition series for the module $M$.

The original motivation for this work was the desire to use local equations to define the (unique) complex analytic cycle in $X$ which represents the $K_1$-homology class of the extension $\xi(A,B)$ when these operators act on a Hilbert space and are almost normal [1], [22]. In that context the cycle represents an element in $H_2(X)$ (using Borel-Moore homology) while the bundle $E_{A,B}$ defines an element in the Picard group of $X$ which is Poincaré dual to $\xi(A,B)$. This correspondence of commuting tuples to line bundles has the property that the direct sum of two such tuples maps to the tensor product of their respective bundles, while the transpose tuple maps to the dual or inverse bundle.

Our plan in this paper is to develop the higher dimension hypersurface analogue for $s$-tuples of commuting operators. While the theorems established here carry over to higher codimensions, that framework involves some technical difficulties which we presently wish to avoid.

We should mention that recent studies of M.S. Livsic [26] also encounter line bundles associated to pairs of commuting operators. However, that work goes in another direction with different bundles, and utilizes quite different techniques since the operators considered there are finite rank perturbations of self-adjoint operators and therefore have a trivial index theory. On the other hand, the authors anticipate some interesting connections with their work when the Livsic results are thought of in the context of Riemann-Hilbert problems and determining functions.

The algebraic set up is as follows:

Let $R$ be a commutative ring and $M$ a left $R$-module. Suppose that $T=(T_1,\cdots,T_s)$ is a commuting $s$-tuple of endomorphisms on $M$. We will use the notation $E(M,T)=\{E_s^k(M),d_k\}_{k\in Z}$ to denote the Koszul complex associated with the action of the elements $T_i$ of $T$ on $M$. When $M$ is a Banach space $\sigma_{ess}(T)$ denotes $Sp(\mathfrak{a},T)$ where $\mathfrak{a}$ is the Calkin algebra $L(M)/$ (compact operators) and the elements $T_i$ act by left multiplication.

Thus, if $s=2$, we have

$$E(M,T):\ 0 \rightarrow M \xrightarrow{d_2} M\oplus M \xrightarrow{d_1} M \rightarrow 0$$

where $d_2m=-T_2m\oplus T_1m$, $d_1(m_1\oplus m_2)=T_1m_1+T_2m_2$ for $m_1$ and $m_2$ in $M$.

The homology modules $ker\, d_k\,/\,ran\, d_{k+1}$ of the complex $E(M;T)$ will be denoted $H_k(M;T)$ for $k=0,1,\cdots,s$.

If the complex $E(M,T)$ is exact and the homology of the subcomplex $E(M,\hat{T})$, where $\hat{T}=(T_1,\cdots,T_{s-1})$, is finitely generated and projective, then $T_s$ induces an automorphism on each $H_k(M;\hat{T})$ and the canonical homomorphism between $Aut\,[H_k(M;\hat{T})]$ and $K_1(R)$ gives an element

$$\prod_{k=0}^{s-1}[H_k(M;\hat{T}),T_s]^{(-1)^{k+1}}$$

in $K_1(R)$. The determinant map for finitely generated projective modules induces a homorphism $K_1(R)\rightarrow R^*$, the group of units in $R$. When $R$ is a field, $K_1(R)\simeq R^*$ and we have the multiplicative Lefschetz number

$$\psi(T_s;\hat{T})\equiv\prod_{k=0}^{s-1} det\,[H_k(M;\hat{T}),\ T_s]^{(-1)^{k+1}}$$

For the construction of the cycle in the hypersurface case the basic result is the following:

Suppose $T=(T_1,..,T_s)$ is an $s$ - tuple of commuting bounded linear operators on a complex Banach space $M$. Let $f=(f_1,\cdots,f_s)$ and $(g=g_1,\cdots,g_s)$ be bases for the dual space $(\mathbb{C}^s)^*$ such that

$$\hat{f}(T)=(f_1(T),\cdots,f_{s-1}(T)) \text{ and } \hat{g}(T)=(g_1(T),\cdots,g_{s-1}(T))$$

are Fredholm $(s-1)$ - tuples, i.e., the associated homology modules are finite dimensional vector spaces.

**COCYCLE THEOREM 1.1** *There is a non-vanishing holomorphic function* $\Sigma(z_1,\cdots,z_s)$ *defined in some neighborhood* $\Omega$ *of the origin in* $\mathbb{C}^s$ *so that for* $z\in\Omega\setminus Sp(M,T)$

$$\Sigma(z_1,\cdots,z_s)=\frac{\psi(f_s(T-z);\ \hat{f}(T-z))}{\psi(g_s(T-z);\ \hat{g}(T-z))}.$$

Thus, the value of $\Sigma$ even at $0 \in Sp(M,T)$ is defined although the Lefschetz numbers themselves are not defineable as such on the spectrum, i.e., at $z$ in $\mathbb{C}^s$ where $E(M,T-z)$ fails to be exact. This cocycle result generalizes Corollary 1.3 of [6] to arbitrary dimensions and provides a means for relating local and global aspects of index theory. For example, it enables us to identify the fundamental trace invariant from commutative local data (see Theorem 1.13 below). It also leads to higher dimensional analogues of the tame symbol formulae obtained in [6]. These applications will be addressed elsewhere.

It follows as we shall see from Theorem 1.1 that the Lefschetz numbers will give the Cousin data for a holomorphic line bundle with the $\Sigma$ as transition functions. The divisor of the Cousin data is a holomorphic chain supported on $Sp(M,T)$. This is a consequence of the fact that the homology of the complexes $E(M,f(T))$ and $E(M,\hat{f}(T))$ are connected through the long exact sequence of homology

$$\cdots \to H_{\mu+1}(M;f(T)) \to H_\mu(M;\hat{f}(T)) \to H_\mu(M;\hat{f}(T))$$
$$\to H_\mu(M;f(T)) \to \cdots$$

where the connecting homomorphism

$$\Delta\colon H_\mu(M;f_1(T),\cdots,f_{s-1}(T)) \to H_\mu(M;f_1(T),\cdots,f_{s-1}(T))$$

is multiplication by $(-1)^\mu f_s(T)$. (cf. [29] prop. 2, pg. 365).

We also observe the following two suggestive relationships which are proved in the appendix.

**PROPOSITION 1.2** *If $E(M,T)$ is exact, then*

$$\psi(T_s;\hat{T}) = \frac{\prod_{k=0}^{s-2} det[\,coker\ T_{s-1} | H_k(M;T_1,\cdots,T_{s-2}),T_s]^{(-1)^k}}{\prod_{k=0}^{s-2} det[ker\ T_{s-1} | H_k(M;T_1,\cdots,T_{s-2}),T_s]^{(-1)^k}}$$

**PROPOSITION 1.3** *With $\hat{T}' = (T_1,\cdots,T_{s-2},T_s)$, and $E(M,T)$ exact, we have*

$$\frac{\psi(T_s;\hat{T})}{\psi(T_{s-1};\hat{T}')}, = \prod_{k=0}^{s-2} [det_* \circ \partial_k[\{T_{s-1},T_s\} | H_k(M;T_1,\cdots,T_{s-2})]^{(-1)^k}$$

Here $det_* \circ \partial_k$ denotes the determinant homomorphism on the Milnor group $K_2(R_k)$ of the ring $R_k$ generated by $T_{s-1},T_s$ and their pseudo-inverses as operators on the homology module $H_k(M;T_1,\cdots,T_{s-2})$ and $\{T_{s-1},T_s\}$ denotes the Steinberg symbol of $T_{s-1}$ and $T_s$. This last result is an extension to the multi-operator context of Reciprocity Theorem 1.1 in [6].

**(ii) Local index**

If $\pi=(\pi_1,\cdots,\pi_{s-1})$ is an $(s-1)$ - tuple of independent linear functionals on $\mathbb{C}^s$ which do not vanish simultaneously on the joint essential spectrum $\sigma_{ess}(T)$ of $T$, the spectral mapping theorem [37] gives a neighborhood $\Omega$ of the origin in $\mathbb{C}^s$ disjoint from $\sigma_{ess}(T)$ so that the modules $H_k(M;\pi(T-x))$, $x \in \Omega$ corresponding to the Koszul complex $E(M,\pi(T-x))$ are finite dimensional vector spaces for $k=0,1,\cdots s-1$. Consequently, it makes sense to consider a relative index

$$ind(T-x,\pi)\equiv-\sum_{k=0}^{s-1}(-1)^k \, dim\ Root\ space\ [T-x \mid H_k(M;\pi(T)]$$

or more generally if $L$ is a Fredholm tuple in the commutant of $T$ let

$$ind\ (T,L)=-\sum_k(-1)^k\ dim\ Root\ space\ [T \mid H_k\ (M;L)]$$

where if $X_1,\ldots,X_q$ is a $q$ - tuple of commuting operators on a vector space $W$, the expression *Root space* $[X \mid W]$ denotes the set $\{w \in W \mid X_i^n\, w=0,\ i=1,2,\ldots,q$ for some positive integer $n\}$. In other words *Root space* $[T-x \mid H_k(M;\pi(T))]$ is the spectral subspace at the point $x$ of $T$ acting on $H_k(M;\pi(T))$.

A basic question is: how does this index depend on $x$ and $\pi$?

We shall give a precise answer in Theorem 1.5 below.

In order to explain this we first recall there are results of Markoe [27] which imply the germ of $Sp(M,T)$ at the origin, $Sp_0(M,T)$, is represented by an analytic set of dimension less than or equal to $s-1$. Thus, suppose $V=V_1\cup V_2\cup\ldots\cup V_t$ is the irreducible decomposition of the $(s-1)$ dimensional component $V$ of $Sp_0(M,T)$. If $W\subset\mathbb{C}^n$ is a local variety of dimension $r$ let $C_p(W)$ denote the tangent cone to $W$ at $p$. The $(n-r)$-plane $T^{n-r}$ through $p$ is said to be excellent for $W$ at $p$ if $T^{n-r}\cap C_p(W)=\{p\}$. There is a well known result which we now recall (cf.[43]).

**THEOREM 1.4** *Given $p\in W\subset\mathbb{C}^n$, dim $W=r<n$ the set, $E_p(W)$, of excellent planes for $W$ at $p$ is the complement in the Grassmanian of $(n-r)$ - planes in $\mathbb{C}^n$, $G^{n,n-r}$, of a proper subvariety $E'_p(W)$, and hence is open, arcwise connected and dense in $G^{n,n-r}$. Furthermore, $\mu(W,p,T^{n-r})=\mu(W,p)$ if $T^{n-r}$ is excellent but $\mu(W,p,T^{n-r})>\mu(W,p)$ if $T^{n-r}$ is not excellent.*

Here $\mu(W,p,T^{n-r})$ denotes the intersection multiplicity of the plane $T^{n-r}$ with $W$ at $p$, and $\mu(W,p)$ denotes the multiplicity of the local ring of $W$ at $p$.

With $W=V_1\cup\cdots\cup V_t$ this geometric theorem has an operator theoretic analogue which enables us to compute the maximal ideal index.

**STABILITY THEOREM 1.5.** *The map $\pi\longrightarrow ind\ (T,\pi)$ is constant on the set of those Fredholm $(s-1)$ - tuples $\pi(T)$ for which the line $\bigcap_{i=1}^{s-1} ker(\pi_i)$ in $\mathbb{C}^s$ is excellent for $V$ at $p$; furthermore, if dim $Sp_0(T,M)\le s-2$ then ind $(T,\pi)=0$ for any* *choices of the Fredholm tuple* $\pi(T)$.

Note that *ind* $(T,\pi)$ can change when $\bigcap_{i=1}^{s-1} ker(\pi_i)$ is not excellent while for excellent planes $\pi^{\perp}$ we may view *ind* $(T,\pi)$ as a maximal ideal index.

**iii) Global index , line bundles.**

When the $(2s-2)$ - dimensional Hausdorff measure of the joint essential spectrum $\sigma_{ess}(T)$ is zero the cocyle condition expressed in Theorem 1.1 leads to the construction of a line bundle $E_T \mapsto X$ on the complement of the essential spectrum and the Lefschetz numbers give a meromorphic section of $E_T$. Let $[V]$ denote the divisor of that section. We have noted above that the local degree of the cycle $[V]$ is a maximal ideal index. Our next result provides a generalization of that fact which globalizes to give an intersection formula for the total index of Koszul complexes. In section 8 we study algebras of singular integral operators of dimension $s-1$ and connect the intersection formula of the next theorem with cyclic cocycles acting on characteristic classes represented by Bochner - Martinelli forms.

**THEOREM 1.6** *Let* $U$ *be a neighborhood of* $Sp(M,T)$ *and suppose* $F=(F_1, \cdots ,F_{s-1})$ *is an* $(s-1)$ *- tuple of complex functions which are defined and holomorphic in* $U$. *Furthermore, suppose* $F$ *never vanishes on* $\sigma_{ess}(T)$. *Then*

$$ind\,((T-x),F(T))=(D_1\cap \cdots \cap D_{s-1}\cap[V])_{\{x\}}$$

*where* $D_i$ *is the divisor of* $F_i$. *That is, the index of* $T-x$ *relative to* $F(T)$ *is the local intersection number at* $x$ *of the divisors of* $F_i$ *and the cycle* $[V]$.

**COROLLARY 1.7** *Suppose* $F$ *satisfies the conditions of Theorem 1.6. Then*

$$ind\,F(T)\equiv-\sum_{k=0}^{s-1}(-1)^k\,dim\,H_k\,(M;F(T))=D_1\cap D_2\cdots\cap D_{s-1}\cap[V]$$

*where* $D_i$ *is the divisor of* $F_i$ *and the right hand side denotes the total intersection number.*

**COROLLARY 1.8** *Suppose* $h$ *is holomorphic in* $U$ *and* $h(x)\neq 0$. *Then*

$$\prod_{k=0}^{s-1}(det\,h(T)\,|\,Root\ space\ [T-x\,|\,H_k(M;F(T))])^{(-1)^{k+1}}$$
$$=h(x)^{(D_1\cap\cdots\cap D_{s-1}\cap[V])_{\{x\}})}$$

**COROLLARY 1.9** *Suppose that* $h$ *doesn't vanish on the common zeros of* $F_1, \cdots ,F_{s-1}$ *which lie in* $Sp(M,T)$. *Then*

$$\psi(h(T);F(T))=\prod_{x\in Sp(M,T)} h(x)^{(D_1\cap\cdots\cap D_{s-1}\cap[V])_{\{x\}}}.$$

If the joint essential spectrum has some additional smoothness properties then we can use a generalized Stokes' theorem so that Corollary 1.7 can be rephrased in terms of integration.

**THEOREM 1.10.** *Suppose that* $\sigma_{ess}(T) = Y \cup S$ *where* $Y$ *is an immersed, oriented* $(2s-3)$ *dimensional* $C^1$*-submanifold of* $\mathbb{C}^s$ *having finite volume and* $S$ *is a closed subset of* $\sigma_{ess}(T)$ *of Hausdorff* $(2s-3)$*-measure zero. Then there exists a unique extension* $[\tilde{V}]$ *of* $[V]$ *to a locally rectifiable current on a neighborhood* $U$ *of* $Sp(M,T)$ *and* $d[\tilde{V}] = \sum_j m_j [Y_j]$ *where* $m_j \in Z$ *and* $Y_j$ *is a connected component of* $Y$ *for each* $j$*. Furthermore,*

$$ind(F(T)) = \sum_j m_j [Y_j] \, f^*(k_0^{BM})$$

*where* $k_z^{BM}$ *denotes the Bochner-Martinelli* $(s-1, s-2)$ *- form in* $\mathbb{C}^{s-1} \setminus \{0\}$ *given by* $k_z^{BM} =$

$$\frac{(-1)^{(s-1)(s-2)/2}\,(s-2)!}{(2\pi i)^{s-1}\,\|\xi - z\|^{2(s-1)}} \sum_{j=1}^{s-1} (-1)^j (\bar{\xi}_j - \bar{z}_j) d\xi_1 \wedge \cdots \wedge d\xi_{s-1} \wedge d\bar{\xi}_1 \wedge \ldots \wedge \widehat{d\bar{\xi}_j} \wedge \ldots d\bar{\xi}_{s-1}.$$

The reason for allowing a scar set $S$ is to include the case where the singular locus of $V$ is not just discrete.

The notation $[Y_j]$ denotes the current of integration over $Y_j$ with the stated orientation. Since $d[\tilde{V}]$ is a real MC - cycle (see definition section 8) we deduce the fundamental geometric fact (see [17]) that those components $Y_j$ having $m_j \neq 0$ are maximally complex in the sense that

$$dim_{\mathbb{R}}(Tan_z\, Y_j \cap J(Tan_z\, Y_j)) = 2s - 4$$

where $J$ denotes the almost complex structure of multiplication by $\sqrt{-1}$.

A similar formulation holds in higher codimensions. In our study of more general complexes which have curvature work centers on Hirzebruch - Riemann - Roch type formulae involving the Todd class of the analytic cycle and an analogue of the Chern - Weil theory developed in the context of cyclic cocyles [8]. These aspects will be discussed elsewhere.

Although the number of functions in $F$ is smaller than the dimension of $\mathbb{C}^s$, the ambient space, Theorem 1.6 gives explicit numerical relations between the indices of $T$ and $F(T)$. This result may be contrasted to the remarks of M. Putinar [32; section 3] which question the feasibility of such relations when the Fredholm spectrum is not an open subset. (We also note that Theorem 3.1 of [32] follows immediately from Theorem 1.6 by taking $T_s$ as the zero operator in which case $Sp(M,T) \setminus \sigma_{ess}(T)$ is an open subset of the hyperplane $z_s = 0$).

Another basic question involves the stability of local indices under perturbations.

Suppose $T' = (T_1', T_2', \cdots, T_s')$ is an $s$-tuple of commuting operators so that $T_j - T_j'$ is a compact operator on $M$ for each $j = 1, 2, \cdots, s$. Let $E_{T'}$ and $[V]'$

denote the corresponding bundle and cycle, respectively. Is $E_{T'}=E_T$? or equivalently $[V]'=[V]$? When $M$ is a Hilbert space the answer is yes.

**THEOREM 1.11.** *If $T$ and $T'$ satisfy the conditions of Theorem 1.10 and $T-T'$ consists of compact operators then $[V]=[V]'$. In particular, $ind(T-x,\pi)=ind(T'-x,\pi)$, $x\notin\sigma_{ess}(T)$. That is, the local index is stable under compact deformations provided the essential spectrum is a manifold with scar set.*

**PROOF OF THEOREM 1.11.** Let $C=d([\tilde V]-[\tilde V]')$. By Theorem 1.10 and the invariance of index under compact perturbations on Hilbert space (see Curto [9] and Vasilescu [40] Thm. 3.8 and Cor. 3.9)] we have $F_*C(k_z^{BM})=C(F^*k_z^{BM})=0$ for all $z\notin F(\sigma_{ess}(T))$. Consequently, since $C$ is locally rectifiable it follows by the homotopy equation for the $\bar\partial$-operator, i.e., $\bar\partial\circ E+E\circ\bar\partial=id$ (cf. [17], [14]) (see also the proof of Theorem 1.13 below) that $F_*(C)=0$ for all holomorphic maps $F$. From the geometric Lemmas 3.4 and 3.5 of [18] we can recover $C$ from the collection $F_*(C)$ for sufficiently many $F$, and thus deduce that $C=0$. Consequently, $[\tilde V]=[\tilde V]'$ by the fundamental uniqueness theorem for holomorphic chains [17], [18]; that is, holomorphic chains with compact support and the same boundary are equal.

**(iv) Fundamental trace forms and boundaries of extended analytic cycles.**

Several authors have sought to clarify the link between index theory of $C^*$ - algebras and totally antisymmetric forms [30], [19], [3], [4], [31], [11], [5], [6], [7]. In section 8 we shall apply local index theory to study this question for $C^*$ - algebras generated by a commuting $s$-tuple $(T_1\cdots T_s)$ of operators on a Hilbert space $H$. In this case the fundamental trace form is a real MC-cycle in the sense of R. Harvey and B. Lawson [17].

**DEFINITION 1.12** A current $C$ on an open subset $U$ of $\mathbb{C}^n$ is called *locally flat* if every cut-off $\phi C$ by a function $\phi\in C_0^\infty(U)$ can be expressed in the form $\phi C=R+dS$ where $R$ and $S$ are currents having locally integrable functions as coefficients.

An alternate characterization of locally flat currents can be given in terms of the flat norm

$$F_K(C)=sup\,\{|C(\eta)|:\ \|\eta\|_K\le 1\ \text{and}\|d\eta\|_K\le 1\}$$

for each compact set $K$. A flat current is a limit in the norm $F_K$ of *locally normal currents* supported on $K$, where a current $S$ for which both $S$ and $dS$ have measure coefficients is called locally normal.

Note that if $C$ is flat so is $dC$. The importance of locally flat currents stems from Federer's *Support Theorem* ( [13] 4.1.15, 4.1.20).

Suppose $M$ is a locally flat current of dimension $r$ defined in an open subset of $\mathbb{C}^s$, and supported in a closed subset $Y$ of $U$. Let $\Lambda_r$ denote $r$-dimensional Hausdorff measure.

(a) If $\Lambda_r(Y)=0$ then $M\equiv 0$.

(b) If $Y$ is an $r$-dimensional oriented submanifold of $U$ then $M$ is of the form $M=f[Y]$ where $f$ is a locally integrable function on $Y$.

The following theorem generalizes Theorem 4.2 which was announced in [5], a circulated but unpublished preprint of 1982.

**STRUCTURE THEOREM 1.13**

*Let $A$ be a cryptointegral algebra of dimension $s-1$ whose essential spectrum satisfies the conditions of Theorem 1.10. Let $C$ be the $(2s-3)$ - dimensional current associated with the fundamental trace form*

$$(\sqrt{-1})^{s-1}\cdot Tr(\sum_{\sigma}\epsilon(\sigma)A_{\sigma(1)}A_{\sigma(2)}\cdots A_{\sigma(2s-2)}),\quad A_{\sigma(k)}\in A.$$

*Suppose $C$ is locally flat. Furthermore, suppose the operators $T_i$ corresponding to the coordinate functions $z_i$ commute. Then the analytic cycle $[V]$ has a unique extension to a locally rectifiable current $[\tilde{V}]$ in a neighborhood of $Sp(H,T)$ such that* $d[\tilde{V}]=-\dfrac{(2\pi)^{s-1}}{s-1}C$.

Thus, the fundamental trace invariant is the boundary (in the weak sense) of $[V]$ when extended to a current over $Sp(H,T)$. Since $C$ is closed it follows by the support theorem of Federer that $\dfrac{(2\pi)^{s-1}}{s-1}C=\Sigma c_j[Y_j]$ where $c_j\in Z$. Again if $c_j\neq 0$ then $Y_j$ is maximally complex. For planar algebras it can easily be checked that the property that $C$ be locally flat is equivalent to the existence of the principal function [4]. For the algebras of zero-order pseudo-differential operators on compact manifolds and Toeplitz operators on odd-spheres the work of W. Helton and R. Howe [19] can be used to identify $C$ explicitly as integration over the essential spectra.

Cryptointegral algebras were defined by [19] as generalizations of singular integral operators in arbitrary dimensions and include classical zero order pseudo - differential operators and Toeplitz operators. More general examples of pseudo - differential operators introduced by R. Beals were shown by J. Janas [21] to also generate cryptointegral algebras.

For the case of pseudo-differential operators on a manifold $W$ having real dimension $s-1$ one thinks of $Y$ as an embedding or immersion of the cosphere bundle of $W$ under the map given by the principal symbols of an $s$-tuple of commuting pseudo-differential operators on $W$.

**COROLLARY 1.14.** *Suppose* $f = (f_1, \cdots, f_{s-1})$ *are* $C^\infty$ *functions on* $Y$ *which have no common zeros. Then*

$$index\,(\rho(\hat{f})) = \Sigma\, c_j\, [Y_j](f^* k_0^{BM}),$$

*where* $\rho(\hat{f})$ *is the Bott operator defined by* $f$.

In the next two sections we gather results concerning Lefschetz numbers and local divisors which are needed to prove our theorems.

## 2. LEFSCHETZ NUMBERS AS RATIONAL FUNCTIONS

We recall certain results and definitions which play a role in our proofs.

A complex of Banach spaces is a sequence $(X,\alpha) = (X_p, \alpha_p)$, $p \in Z$ of Banach spaces $X_p$ and operators $\alpha_p \in L(X_{p+1}, X_p)$ such that $ran\,(\alpha_{p+1}) \subset ker(\alpha_p)$ for all $p \in Z$. An endomorphism $\theta$ of $(X,\alpha)$ is a sequence $(\theta_p)_{p \in Z}$ such that $\theta_p \in L(X_{p+1})$ and $\alpha_p \theta_p = \theta_{p-1} \alpha_p$ for all $p \in Z$. The set of all endomorphisms of $(X,\alpha)$ is denoted by $End\,(X,\alpha)$.

A complex $(X,\alpha)$ is said to be Fredholm if, with $H_p(X,\alpha) = ker\ \alpha_p / ran\ (\alpha_{p+1})$,

i) the function $p \longrightarrow dim\ H_p(X,\alpha)$ is finite and has finite support, and

ii) $\gamma(\alpha_p) = inf\,\{\gamma(\alpha_p) : p \in Z\} > 0$ where $\gamma(\alpha_p)$ is the reduced minimum modulus of $\alpha_p$.

If $X_p = 0$ for all but a finite number of indices, then (ii) is a consequence of (i).

The set of all Fredholm complexes on $X$ is denoted by $\Phi(X)$. We define the set $F(X) = \{(\alpha,\theta) : \alpha \in \Phi(X),\ \theta \in End(X,\alpha)\}$.

**DEFINITION 2.1.** *Let* $(\alpha,\theta) \in F(X)$. *The characteristic function of the pair* $(\alpha,\theta)$ *is the rational function*

$$\chi(\alpha,\theta)(z) = z^{ind\ \alpha} \prod_{k \in Z} \frac{det\,(z^{-1} - \theta_{2k}) H_{2k}(X,\alpha)}{det\,(z^{-1} - \theta_{2k+1}) H_{2k+1}(X,\alpha)}$$

This function is well defined for $z$ in a neighborhood of 0 in $\mathbb{C}$. If $dim\ H_p(x,\alpha) = 0$, the corresponding determinant is equal to one by definition.

M. Putinar and F.-H. Vasilescu prove in [34]:

**THEOREM 2.2.** *Let* $X = (X_p), p \geq 0$ *be a sequence of Banach spaces and let* $\Omega \subset \mathbb{C}^m$ *be open. Suppose that the map*

$$\Omega \ni \lambda \longrightarrow (\alpha(\lambda),\ \theta(\lambda)) \in F(X)$$

*is analytic. Then the map*

$$(z,\lambda) \longrightarrow \chi[\alpha(\lambda),\ \theta(\lambda)](z)$$

*is also analytic on its domain.*

Analyticity of the map $\lambda \to (\alpha(\lambda), \theta(\lambda))$ means that $\alpha_p(\lambda)$ and $\theta_p(\lambda)$ are analytic for each $p \in Z$.

We require a little more than this result and will indicate a proof, largely based on the argument in [34].

**THEOREM 2.3** *There are functions $p(z,\lambda)$ and $q(z,\lambda)$ which are monic polynomials in $z$ with coefficients varying analytically in $\lambda$, so that*

$$\chi[\alpha(\lambda), \theta(\lambda)](z) = \frac{p(z,\lambda)}{q(z,\lambda)}$$

*whenever $\chi[\alpha(\lambda), \theta(\lambda)](z)$ is defined.*

**PROOF.** Fix a point $\lambda_0$ and consider

$$n+1 = n(X,\alpha(\lambda_0)) = min\,\{m \geq 0 \,|\, H_p(X,\alpha(\lambda_0)) = 0,\ p \geq m\}.$$

Suppressing $\lambda_0$, take $M_n$ a complement of $ran\,(\alpha_n)$ in $ker\,(\alpha_{n-1})$, define $Y_{n+1} = X_{n+1} \oplus M_n$, and take $\beta_n$ as the extension of $\alpha_n$ to $Y_{n+1}$ so that $ran\,(\beta_n) = ker\,(\alpha_{n-1})$ and $ker\,(\beta_n) = ker(\alpha_n)$. Further take $\beta_p = \alpha_p$ and $Y_p = X_p$ for $p \neq n$.

It is shown in [34] that these constructions can be made so that $(\beta(\lambda), \theta(\lambda))$ depends analytically on $\lambda \in \Omega$ and that, for $\lambda_0 \in \Omega$

$$\frac{\chi[\alpha(\lambda), \theta(\lambda)](z)}{\chi[\alpha(\lambda_0), \theta(\lambda_0)](z)} = \frac{\chi[\beta(\lambda), \theta(\lambda)](z)}{\chi[\beta(\lambda_0), \theta(\lambda_0)](z)} \cdot \left(\frac{\phi(\theta_{n-1}(\lambda), z^{-1})}{\phi(\theta_{n-1}(\lambda_0), z^{-1})}\right)^{(-1)^n}$$

where

$$\phi(\theta_{n-1}(\lambda), z^{-1}) = det_{M_n}(z^{-1} - P_n\, \theta_{n-1}(\lambda) \,|\, M_n)$$

and $P_n$ is the canonical projection of $Y_{n+1}$ onto $M_n$.

Theorem 2.3 will follow by induction on $n(X,\alpha)$. The construction has been arranged so that if $n(X,\alpha) = n+1$ then $n(Y,\beta) = n$.

By the inductive hypothesis, $\chi[\beta(\lambda), \theta(\lambda)](z) = \dfrac{p_1(z,\lambda)}{q_1(z,\lambda)}$ in a neighborhood of $\lambda_0$ and the map $z^{m_n}\phi(\theta_n(\lambda), z^{-1})$ depends analytically on $\lambda$, since $\theta_n(\lambda)$ depends analytically on $\lambda$ in a neighborhood of $\lambda_0$ $(m_n = dim\, M_n)$.

Consequently, near $\lambda_0$

$$\chi[\alpha(\lambda), \theta(\lambda)](z) = \frac{p(z,\lambda)}{q(z,\lambda)}$$

where we can take $p(z,\lambda)$ and $q(z,\lambda)$ in lowest terms.

Now suppose $\lambda$ varies in a connected component of $\Omega$. Let $\{U_\gamma\}$ be a covering of $\Omega$ so that in each neighborhood $U_\gamma$ we have

$$\chi[\alpha(\lambda),\beta(\lambda)](z)=\frac{p_\gamma(z,\lambda)}{q_\gamma(z,\lambda)}.$$

For $\lambda \in U_r \cap U_\mu$ the unicity of the decomposition in lowest terms implies

$$p_\gamma(z,\lambda)=p_\mu(z,\lambda) \text{ and } q_\gamma(z,\lambda)=q_\mu(z,\lambda).$$

Consequently, there are monic polynomials $p(z,\lambda)$, $q(z,\lambda)$ defined in $\mathbb{C}\times\Omega$ so that

$$\chi[\alpha(\lambda),\ \theta(\lambda)](z)=\frac{p(z,\lambda)}{q(z,\lambda)}.$$

This will be true for all $(z,\lambda)$ such that

$$\prod_p det(z^{-1}-\theta_{2p+1}(\lambda)\mid H_{2p+1}(X,\alpha(\lambda))\neq 0.$$

Note that the zero set of $q(z,\lambda)$ is contained in the set where the characteristic function is not defined while the zero set of $p(z,\lambda)$ is a subset of

$$\{(z,\lambda)\mid det\,(z^{-1}-\theta_{2p}(\lambda)\mid H_{2p}(X,\alpha(\lambda)))=0\}$$

for some $p$.

We conclude this preparatory section with some familiar remarks about divisors. Suppose that $\chi$ is a meromorphic function on a complex manifold of dimension $n$. Since $\chi$ is locally of the form $g/h$, with $g$ and $h$ holomorphic, and any two representations of $g/h$ differ (multiplicatively) by a never vanishing holomorphic function, we may associate a zero set $Z$ and a pole set $P$ to $\chi$ which will both be hypersurfaces. Let $\{Z_i\}$ and $\{P_i\}$ denote the irreducible components of $Z$ and $P$, respectively. Now let $z$ be a manifold point of $Z$. There is a unique positive integer $m_1$ associated to each component $Z_i$, called the multiplicity of $\chi$ on $Z_i$. Similarly, $\chi$ has a multiplicity $n_i$ on the components $P_i$.

The holomorphic $(n-1)$ chain

$$D_\chi=\sum_i m_i[Z_i]-n_i[P_i]$$

is called the divisor of $\chi$.

Because $\chi$ locally has the form $g/h$, the function $log\,|\chi|$ is locally integrable. A fundamental result is the following Poincaré - Lelong formula (see [24]).

**THEOREM 2.4**

*If $\chi$ is a meromorphic function on a complex manifold, then*

$$(i/\pi)\partial\,\bar{\partial}\ log\,|\chi|=D_\chi.$$

## 3. SUPERFICIAL ELEMENTS AND SLICED HOMOLOGY

Our investigation of the various divisors corresponding to different choices of bases will depend on some concepts in local ring theory. The book of M. Nagata

[28] is recommended for a discussion of the details of that subject.

Let $a$ be an ideal of a ring $R$ and let $M$ be an $R$-module. Set $F_n = a^n/a^{n+1}$ and $G_n = a^n M/a^{n+1}M$, for $n = 0,1,2 \cdots$.

When $a \in F_m$, $b \in F_n$ define $ab$ as follows: let $a'$ and $b'$ be elements of $a^m$ and $a^n$ respectively such that $a = a'$ (modulo $a^{m+1}$), $b = b'$ (modulo $a^{n+1}$); define $ab = a'b'$ ( modulo $a^{m+n+1}$). This multiplication defines a graded ring structure for the direct sum $F$ of the $F_n$. Furthermore, since $F_n = a^n/a^{n+1}$, $F_n = (F_1)^n$ and so $F$ is a homogeneous ring. Similarly the direct sum $G$ of the $G_i$ becomes a graded module over $F$.

Now let $R = \Sigma R_n$ be a Noetherian homogeneous ring. An element $f$ of $R$ is called a superficial element if $f \in R_1$, and if there is an $m$ such that $(0{:}fR) \cap R_n = 0$ for any $n \geq m$. Our reason for introducing superficial elements is the fact that certain homology modules which occur naturally from an algebraic point of view fail to be topological spaces.

**THEOREM 3.1 ([28])** *Suppose that $R_0$ is a semilocal ring with maximal ideals $m_1, \cdots, m_s$ such that every $R/m_i$ contains infinitely many elements and that $R_1$ is a finite $R_0$ module. Let $n_1, \cdots, n_t$ be proper submodules of $R_1$. Then there is a superficial element $f$ of $R$ which is not in any of the $n_i$.*

It is further known (cf. [28]) that when $M$ is a graded module over $R$ and $R$ and $M$ are Noetherian and depth $a = 0$, there is a numerical polynomial $p(x)$, the Hilbert - Samuel polynomial, such that

$$length_{R_0} a^n M/a^{n+1}M = p(n)$$

for all $n$ sufficiently large.

Now suppose that $\pi = (\pi_1, \cdots, \pi_{s-2}, f)$ and $\pi' = (\pi_1, \ldots, \pi_{s-2}, g)$ are $(s-1)$ - tuples of independent linear functionals on $\mathbb{C}^s$, and that $\pi(T)$ and $\pi'(T)$ are Fredholm. Consider the unital ring $R(H_*)$ generated by the operators

$$\pi_1(T), \cdots, \pi_{s-2}(T), f(T), g(T)$$

acting on $H_* \equiv H_*(M; \pi_1(T), \cdots, \pi_{s-2}(T))$, $* = 0,1, \cdots, s-2$. Since $\pi_i(T)$, $1 \leq i \leq s-2$ annihilates these modules it suffices to consider the pair $f(T), g(T)$. Since these operators are algebraically Fredholm in the sense that they have finite kernel and cokernel in their action on these modules, we see that

$$dim_{\mathbb{C}} a^n H_*/a^{n+1}H_*$$

is a polynomial for large $n$ if $a$ is the ideal in $R(H_*)$ generated by $f(T)$ and $g(T)$. By considering dual spaces a similar result holds for $dim_{\mathbb{C}} ker_* a^{n+1}/ker_* a^n$, where $ker_*$ is taken relative to each of the spaces $H_*$.

Next consider the graded ring $\Sigma F_n$ with $F_n = a^n/a^{n+1}$. Since $F_0$ is the field of complex numbers, it follows by Theorem 3.1 that there is a superficial element $L$ belonging to $F_1$ and represented by $\mu f(T)+vg(T)$ for some choice of complex numbers $\mu$ and $v$. Further, since $dim_{\mathbb{C}} F_n$ is constant for large $n$, it is not difficult to check that $L$ induces isomorphisms

$$a^n H_*/a^{n+1}H_* \rightarrow a^{n+1}H_*/a^{n+2}H_*$$

and

$$ker_* a^{n+2}/ker_* a^{n+1} \rightarrow ker_* a^{n+1}/ker_* a^n .$$

Let $c$ be chosen so that for $n \geq c$, $L$ induces isomorphisms between all of these quotients, and for all the modules $H_* = H_0, \cdots, H_{s-2}$.

For each $n \geq c$ one can form the determinants:

$f_{*n}(z_1,z_2) \equiv det_n[z_1 f(T)+z_2 g(T)]$ where $z_1 f(T)+z_2 g(T)$ is the induced endomorphism $a^n H_*/a^{n+1}H_* \rightarrow a^{n+1}H_*/a^{n+2}/H_*$ where we take these determinants equal to one if $a^n H_* = a^{n+1}H_*$.

For each $n$, $f_{*n}(z_1,z_2)$ is not the zero polynomial in $(z_1,z_2)$, since for some choice of $z_1,z_2$ we have the isomorphism induced by $L$. Thus the zero set $Z_{*n}$ of $f_{*n}(z_1,z_2)$ is a proper complex subvariety of $\mathbb{C}^2$. Consequently, $\bigcup_{n \geq c} Z_{*n}$ is nowhere dense. Now we can consider all $H_*$ as well as all $ker_* a^{n+1}/ker_* a^n$. We still get only a nowhere dense set in $\mathbb{C}^2$ outside of which $z_1 f(T)+z_2 g(T)$ is an isomorphism.

Let $[L]$ denote the map induced by $L$ on the graded module. Since

$$[L]:\ a^n H_*/a^{n+1}H_* \rightarrow a^{n+1}H_*/a^{n+2}H_*$$

is an isomorphism it is an easy exercise to see that

$$dim\ a^n H_*/a^{n+1}H_* = dim\ Root\ space\ [a\,|coker\ L\ |\ a^n H_*]$$

provided $L$ is also chosen to be algebraically Fredholm on $H_*$.

Similarly, by virtue of the Hilbert-Samuel polynomial theorem, one has

$$dim\ ker_* a^{n+1}/ker_* a^n = dim\ Root\ space\ [a\,|\,ker\ L\ |\,ker\ a^n H_*].$$

Further, as it straightforward to check that

$$dim\ Root\ space\ [a\,|ker\ L\,|a^m H_*] - dim\ Root\ space\ [a\ |\,coker\ L\ |\,a^m H_*]$$

is independent of $m \geq 0$, we may conclude that for $(z_1,z_2)$ chosen from an everywhere dense subset of $\mathbb{C}^2$ the difference of root-space dimensions

$$dim\ Root\ space\ [a\,|ker[z_1 f(T)+z_2 g(T)|H_*]$$

$$- dim\ Root\ space\ [a\,|coker[z_1 f(T)+z_2 g(T)|H_*]$$

is constant in $(z_1,z_2)$ for each $* = 0,1,\cdots,s-2$.

## 4. PROOF OF THE COCYCLE THEOREM

After dispensing with the case where $Sp_0(M,T)$ has dimension $\leq s-2$, we proceed by induction on the size of the intersection $\{\pi_1, \cdots, \pi_{s-1}\} \cap \{\rho_1, \cdots, \rho_{s-1}\}$. We will show the existence of a functional $\tau$ so that $(\pi_1, \ldots \pi_{s-2}, \tau)$ and $(\rho_1, \cdots, \rho_{s-2}, \tau)$ both define Fredholm tuples. This enables us to reduce the proof to a comparison of $s$ - tuples $(\pi_1, \pi_2, \cdots, \pi_{s-1}, \pi_s)$ and $(\pi_1, \pi_2, \cdots, \rho_{s-1}, \rho_s)$, these in turn are handled by considering the action of $\pi_{s-1}(T)$ and $\rho_{s-1}(T)$ on each of the sliced homology modules $H_i(M; \pi_1(T), \cdots, \pi_{s-2}(T))$, $i = 0,1, \cdots, s-2$. These spaces are perhaps not Banach spaces so the results from [6] may not apply. The difficulty is overcome using superficial elements.

From Theorem 2.3 we have for $x$ near 0, and $x \notin Sp(M,T)$

$$\psi_\pi(x) = \frac{p_\pi(x)}{q_\pi(x)}$$

where $p_\pi(x)$ and $q_\pi(x)$ are monic polynomials in $\pi_s(x)$ having coefficients which are analytic in $(\pi_1(x), \cdots, \pi_{s-1}(x))$, and $q_\pi(x) \neq 0$ for $x \notin Sp(M,T)$. As noted above, results of Markoe [27] imply the germ of $Sp(M,T)$ at the origin is analytic of dimension at most $s-1$. If $Sp_0(M,T)$ has dimension less than $s-1$ then $q_\pi(x) \neq 0$ near $x = 0$, so that $\psi_\pi(x)$ has an analytic extension to a neighborhood of the origin. But the zero set of $p_\pi(x)$ is contained in $Sp(M,T)$, hence, again by dimensional reasoning, $p_\pi(x)$ is also non-vanishing and so $\psi_\pi(x)$ has a never vanishing extension. Since $\pi$ is arbitrary, the same conclusion applies to the ratio $\psi_\pi(x)/\psi_\rho(x)$. We therefore assume hence-forward that *dim* $Sp_0(M,T) = s-1$.

We continue the proof by considering the ratio $\psi_\pi(x)/\psi_\rho(x)$ where $\rho$ has the special form $\rho = (\pi_1, \pi_2, \cdots, \pi_{s-2}, \rho_{s-1}, \rho_s)$.

Near $x = 0$, consider

$$D_{\psi_\pi} = D_{p_\pi} - D_{q_\pi} = \sum_\alpha m_\alpha^\pi [V_\alpha]$$

where $\bigcup_\alpha V_\alpha \subseteq Sp_0(M,T)$ and the $V_i$ are germs of irreducible analytic subvarieties containing the origin.

Similarly

$$D_{\psi_\rho} = \sum_\alpha m_\alpha^\rho [V_\alpha]$$

We will prove that $m_\alpha^\pi = m_\alpha^\rho$ for each $\alpha$.

For this purpose it suffices to consider these divisors near manifold points of $\bigcup_\alpha V_\alpha$. For such a point, $y$, we can assume that $y$ is in only one of the varieties, say $V_1$. By translation $T \rightarrow T-y$ we can take $y = 0$. Moreover, since $V_1 \cap \pi_1^{-1}(0) \cap \cdots \cap \pi_{s-2}^{-1}(0) = W_1 \cup \cdots \cup W_v$ is a finite union of irreducible varieties containing zero, any divisor obtained by restriction to $\pi_1^{-1}(0)\cap \cdots \cap\pi_{s-2}^{-1}(0)$ has the form $\sum_j n_j[W_j]$ for some integers $\{n_j\}$. Thus, to show that the restricted divisors are equal, we consider what happens at manifold points of the variety sliced in the $\rho_{s-1},\rho_s$ direction.

Also by translation in this direction we can reduce to the case where the origin is regular for $V_1\cap\pi_1^{-1}(0)\cap \cdots \cap\pi_{s-1}^{-1}(0)$.

First suppose that

$$\pi_{s-1}=\mu\rho_{s-1}+\sum_{\alpha=1}^{s-2}\lambda_\alpha\pi_\alpha$$

where $\mu$ is necessarily not zero. From Proposition 1.2 we have (with obvious suppression of some notation)

$$\psi_\pi(x)=\prod_{p=0}^{s-2}\left(\frac{det[\pi_s(T-x)|coker\ \pi_{s-1}(T)|H_p(\pi_1(T),\cdots,\pi_{s-2}(T)]}{det[\pi_s(T-x)|ker\ \pi_{s-1}(T)|H_p(\pi_1(T),\cdots,\pi_{s-2}(T)]}\right)^{(-1)^p}$$

$$=\prod_{p=0}^{s-2}\left(\frac{det[\pi_s(T-x)|coker\ \rho_{s-1}(T)|H_p(\pi_1(T),\cdots,\pi_{s-2}(T)]}{det[\pi_s(T-x)|ker\ \rho_{s-1}(T)|H_p(\pi_1(T),\cdots,\pi_{s-2}(T)]}\right)^{(-1)^p}$$

$$=\psi_{(\pi_1,\cdots,\pi_{s-2},\rho_{s-1},\pi_s)}(x).$$

But $\pi_s=\sum_{\alpha=1}^{s-2}v_\alpha\pi_\alpha+\eta\rho_{s-1}+\lambda\rho_s$ and $\lambda\neq 0$, since $\pi_s$ is independent of $\pi_1,\cdots,\pi_{s-1}$. Hence, since $\pi_s(T-x)$ acts like $\lambda\rho_s(T-x)$ on the indicated spaces we have

$$\psi_\pi(x)=\lambda^{r(x)}\psi_\rho(x)$$

where

$$r(x)=ind(\pi_1(T-x),\cdots,\pi_{s-2}(T-x),\rho_{s-1}(T-x))$$

$$=\sum_{k=0}^{s-1}(-1)^k\ dim\ H_k(M;\pi_1(T-x),\ldots,\pi_{s-2}(T-x),\rho_{s-1}(T-x)).$$

Since $r(x)$ is constant for $x$ near the origin, $\psi_\pi(x)/\psi_\rho(x)$ does not vanish. We turn now to the case where $\pi_1,\pi_2,\cdots,\pi_{s-1},\rho_{s-1}$ is a base for $(\mathbb{C}^s)^*$.

For $\alpha=(\alpha_1,\alpha_2)\in\mathbb{C}^2$ form $s_\alpha=\alpha_1\pi_{s-1}+\alpha_2\rho_{s-1}$. Choose a dual basis $\{v_1,\cdots,v_s\}$ for $\{\pi_1,\cdots,\pi_{s-1},\rho_{s-1}\}$ and let $w_\alpha,\mu_\alpha$ be in the span of $\{\nu_{s-1},\nu_s\}$ with

$$s_\alpha(w_\alpha)=0,\quad s_\alpha(\mu_\alpha)=1.$$

Choose $r_\alpha\in(\mathbb{C}^s)^*$ so that

$$r_\alpha(w_\alpha)=1,\quad r_\alpha(\mu_\alpha)=r(v_i)=0$$

for $1\le i\le s-2$.

Next choose $\alpha$ so that

(i) $(\pi_1,\pi_2,\cdots,\pi_{s-2},s_\alpha)$ does not vanish on $\sigma_{ess}(T)$, i.e., $(\pi_1(T),\cdots,\pi_{s-2}(T),s_\alpha(T))$ is Fredholm.

(ii) $s_\alpha(T)$ is superficial relative to $\pi_1(T),\cdots,\pi_{s-2}(T)$, i.e., relative to $H_k(M;\pi_1(T),\cdots,\pi_{s-2}(T))$, $0\le k\le s-2$.

(iii) *ker* $w_\alpha$ corresponds to an excellent plane for the variety $W_1$ at the origin.

By the results of section 3 and Theorem 1.4 the collection $\Lambda$ of $\alpha\in\mathbb{C}^2$ for which (ii) and (iii) hold is everywhere dense.

Let $\pi^\alpha=(\pi_1,\cdots,\pi_{s-2},s_\alpha,r_\alpha)$. For $\alpha$ near $(1,0)$ the tuple $(\pi_1(T),\cdots,\pi_{s-2}(T),s_\alpha(T))$ is Fredholm and we can form the corresponding Lefschetz number $\psi_{\pi^\alpha}$.

According to Theorem 2.3 we can write

$$\psi_{\pi^\alpha}(x)=\frac{p(x,\alpha)}{q(x,\alpha)},$$

since the Koszul complex and endomorphism $r_\alpha(T-x)$ vary analytically in $(x,\alpha)$. Now

$$p(x,\alpha)=\Sigma_z^k a_k(x,\alpha)=\Sigma r_\alpha(x)^k\, b_k(x,\alpha)$$

where $b_k(x,\alpha)$ is analytic in $(x,\alpha)$. Similar considerations apply to $q(x,\alpha)$. Consequently,

$$\lim_{\alpha\to(1,0)} p(x,\alpha)=p(x,(1,0))$$

and

$$\lim_{\alpha\to(1,0)} q(x,\alpha)=q(x,(1,0))$$

Now, near $x=0$,

$$D_{p(\cdot,\alpha)}=m_\alpha[V_1]$$

$$D_{q(\cdot,\alpha)}=n_\alpha[V_1]$$

thus, for $\alpha$ near $(1,0)$ we have

$$m_\alpha=m,\quad n_\alpha=n$$

if $D_{p(\cdot,(1,0))}=m\,[V_1]$ and $D_{q\cdot,(1,0))}=n\,[V_1]$.

Accordingly, for such $\alpha$ we have that $\psi_\pi(x)/\psi_{\pi^\alpha}(x)$ extends to a never vanishing holomorphic function near zero.

In order to obtain the requisite conclusion for $\psi_\pi(x)/\psi_\rho(x)$ it suffices to consider $\psi_{\pi^\alpha}(x)/\psi_{\pi^\beta}(x)$ with $\alpha,\beta$ in $\Lambda$ and near $(1,0)$ and $(0,1)$ respectively.

Let $\psi_{\pi^\alpha}(x)=p(x,\alpha)/q(x,\alpha)$ with $p(x,\alpha)=\sum_k r_\alpha(x)^k\, a_k(x,\alpha)$, and

$q(x,\alpha)=\sum_k r_\alpha^k\ c_k(x,\alpha)$. For $x \in ker\ s_\alpha \cap \bigcap_{c=1}^{s-2} ker\ \pi_c$ and $|r_\alpha(x)|$ large, we have

$$\frac{p(x,\alpha)}{q(x,\alpha)} = \prod_k \left( \frac{det[r_\alpha(T-x)\,|\,H_{2k}(M;\ \pi_1(T),\cdots,\pi_{s-2}(T),s_\alpha(T))]}{det[r_\alpha(T-x)\,|\,H_{2k+1}(M;\pi_1(T),\cdots,\pi_{s-2}(T),s_\alpha(T)]} \right)^{(-1)^k}.$$

By analytic continuation in $r_\alpha(x)$ we have for fixed $\alpha$,

$$ord_0[p(x,\alpha)/q(x,\alpha)] = ord_0[p(x,\alpha)] - ord_0[q(x,\alpha)]$$

$$= \sum_{k=0}^{s-1}(-1)^k\ dim\ Root\ space\ [r_\alpha(T)\,|\,H_k(M;\pi_1(T),\cdots,\pi_{s-2}(T),s_\alpha(T))]$$

$$= \sum_{k=0}^{s-2}(-1)^k[dim\ Root\ space\ [r_\alpha(T)\,|\,ker\ s_\alpha(T)\,|\,H_k(M;\pi_1(T),\cdots,\pi_{s-2}(T))]$$

$$- dim\ Root\ space\ [r_\alpha(T)\,|\,coker\ s_\alpha(T)\,|\,H_k(M;\pi_1(T),\cdots,\pi_{s-2}(T))].$$

Since $\alpha \in \Lambda$, this integer is independent of $\alpha$. Now, since $V_1 \cap \pi_1^{-1}(0) \cap \cdots \cap \pi_{s-2}^{-1}(0) = W_1$ is locally irreducible and regular at zero, and since $\{w_\alpha\}$ is excellent for $W_1$, the Weierstrass preparation theorem gives us an analytic function $f$ such that for $x \in \bigcap_{i=1}^{s-2} ker\ \pi_i^{-1}(0)$,

$$p(x,\alpha) = u(x,\alpha)[r_\alpha(x) - f(s_\alpha(x))]^d \quad , \ u(0,\alpha) \neq 0$$

and

$$q(x,\alpha) = v(x,\alpha)[r_\alpha(x) - f(s_\alpha(x))]^e,\ v(0,\alpha) \neq 0$$

where $d = ord_0[p(x,\alpha)]$, $e = ord_0[q(x,\alpha)]$ and $p$ and $q$ are polynomials in $r_\alpha(x)$. For $x \in \bigcap_{i=1}^{s-2} ker \pi_i$, we have near zero,

$$D_{p(\cdot,\alpha)} = d[W_1],\ D_{q(\cdot,\alpha)} = e[W_1].$$

Consequently, for such $\alpha$,

$$D_{p(\cdot,\alpha)/q(\cdot,\alpha)}$$

is independent of $\alpha$.

Theorem 1.1 is now proved for pairs of tuples having the form $\pi = \pi(\pi_1,\cdots,\pi_s)$ and $\rho = (\pi_1,\cdots,\pi_{s-2},\rho_{s-1},\rho_s)$. To complete the proof we consider general pairs of tuples. For this purpose we introduce an equivalence relation.

Let $G$ denote the set of $s$ - tuples of independent linear functionals $\pi = (\pi_1,\cdots,\pi_s)$ for which $(\pi_1(T),\cdots,\pi_{s-1}(T))$ is Fredholm. We will say $\pi \in G$ is equivalent to $\rho \in G$ provided $\psi_\pi(x)/\psi_\rho(x)$ has a never vanishing holomorphic extension to a neighborhood of zero.

Now we will make an inductive argument.

For $l = 0,1,2, \cdots$, let $P_r(l)$ denote the proposition: $\pi$ is equivalent to $\rho$ if cardinality $\{\pi_1, \cdots, \pi_{s-1}\} \cap \{\rho_1, \cdots, \rho_{s-1}\}$

$$= \begin{cases} s - l - 1 & l < s \\ 0 & l \geq s. \end{cases}$$

We shall prove the validity of $P_r(l)$ for all $l$. Suppose, to begin, that $l = 0$. Then $P_r(0)$ is a special case of the results already proved for tuples of the form $(\pi_1, \cdots, \pi_s)$ and $(\pi_1, \cdots, \pi_{s-2}, \rho_{s-1}, \rho_s)$. Assume now that $P(l)$ holds for $l \leq n$. Suppose that $l = n + 1$. If $l = s$, there is nothing to prove, so assume that $l < s$. By rearranging subscripts we can take $\pi_{s-1} \notin \{\rho_1, \cdots, \rho_{s-1}\}$ and $\rho_{s-1} \notin \{\pi_1, \cdots, \pi_{s-1}\}$.

We will prove in the next technical lemma that we can increase the cardinality of the intersection of the tuples by modifying $\pi_{s-1}$ and $\rho_{s-1}$.

**LEMMA 4.1.** *Suppose that $(\pi_1(T), \cdots, \pi_{s-1}(T))$ and $(\rho_1(T), \cdots, \rho_{s-1}(T)$ are Fredholm $(s-1)$ - tuples. Then there exists a linear functional $\tau$ so that $(\pi_1,(T), \cdots, \pi_{s-2}(T), \tau(T))$ and $(\rho_1(T), \cdots, \rho_{s-2}(T), \tau(T))$ are also Fredholm.*

**PROOF.**

Let $X = \bigcap_{i=1}^{s-2} ker\, \pi_i$ and $Y = \bigcap_{i=1}^{s-2} ker\, \rho_i$. To prove the lemma it will suffice for us to find a linear functional $\tau$ on the span $X + Y$ which does not vanish on $[\sigma_{ess}(T) \cap X] \cup [\sigma_{ess}(T) \cap Y]$. Note that $ker\, \pi_{s-1} \cap \sigma_{ess}(T) \cap X$ and $ker\, \rho_{s-1} \cap \sigma_{ess}(T) \cap Y$ are both empty. Thus, if $X$ and $Y$ are independent we may take $\tau = \pi_{s-1}|_X + \rho_{s-1}|_Y$. On the other hand if $X = Y$ put $\tau = \pi_{s-1}$ or $\tau = \rho_{s-1}$. Finally, we have the case where $X \cap Y$ is one dimensional.

Let $l$ be a non-zero vector common to both spaces, and pick vectors $v$ in $X$ and $w$ in $Y$ so that $\{v, l, w\}$ is a base for $X + Y$ and $\rho_{s-2}(w) \neq 0$.

If $\rho_{s-1}(w) \neq 0$ put

$$\tau = \begin{cases} \pi_{s-1} & \text{on } X \\ c\, \rho_{s-1} & \text{on } \{w\} \end{cases}$$

where

$$c = \begin{cases} 1 & \text{if } \pi_{s-1}(l) = 0 \\ \dfrac{\pi_{s-1}(l)}{\rho_{s-1}(l)} & \text{if } \pi_{s-1}(l) \neq 0. \end{cases}$$

If $\rho_{s-1}(l) = 0$ put

$$\tau = \begin{cases} \rho_{s-1} & \text{on } Y \\ \pi_{s-1} & \text{on } \{v\}. \end{cases}$$

The construction of $\tau$ when $\rho_{s-1}(l)\neq 0$ is made as follows:

For $p \in X \cap \sigma_{ess}(T)$, we set $\tau(p)=\pi_{s-1}(p)\neq 0$.

For $p \in [Y \cap \sigma_{ess}(T)]\setminus X$, $p=\alpha(p)\,l+\beta(p)\,w$ with $\beta(p)\neq 0$. Thus $\tau(p)=\alpha(p)\,\pi_{s-1}(p)+\beta(p)\,\rho_{s-1}(w)\cdot c$.

If $\pi_{s-1}(l)=0$, then $\tau(p)=\beta(p)\,\rho_{s-1}(w)\neq 0$, while if $\pi_{s-1}(l)\neq 0$ we have

$$\tau(p)=[\alpha(p)\,\rho_{s-1}(l)+\beta(p)\,\rho_{s-1}(w)]\,\frac{\pi_{s-1}(l)}{\rho_{s-1}(l)}$$

$$=\rho_{s-1}(p)\cdot\frac{\pi_{s-1}(l)}{\rho_{s-1}(l)}\neq 0.$$

Next, suppose that $\rho_{s-1}(l)=0$. If $p \in Y \cap \sigma_{ess}(T)$, then $\tau(p)=\rho_{s-2}(p)\neq 0$, and if $p \in [X \cap \sigma_{ess}(T)]\setminus Y$, then $p=\gamma(p)\,v+\alpha(p)\,l$ where $\gamma(p)\neq 0$. Consequently $\tau(p)=\gamma(p)\,\pi_{s-1}(v)+\alpha(p)\,\rho_{s-1}(l)=\gamma(p)\,\pi_{s-1}(v)\neq 0$. We have therefore constructed $\tau$ so that $\tau(p)\neq 0$ for

$$p \in [X \cap \sigma_{ess}(T)] \cup [Y \cap \sigma_{ess}(T)].$$

It follows that $(\pi_1, \pi_2, \cdots, \pi_{s-2}, \tau)\neq 0$ on $\sigma_{ess}(T)$ and therefore $(\pi_1(T), \cdots, \pi_{s-2}(T), \tau(T))$ is a Fredholm $(s-1)$ - tuple. Also $(\rho_1(T), \cdots, \rho_{s-2}(T), \tau(T))$ is a Fredholm $s-1$ tuple. The lemma is proved.

We proceed with the induction. We now know that there is a linear functional $\tau$ on $\mathbb{C}^s$ so that $\pi_\tau\equiv(\pi_1, \cdots, \pi_{s-2}, \tau, \pi_s)$ and $\rho_\tau\equiv(\rho_1, \cdots, \rho_{s-2}, \tau, \rho_s)$ are both in $G$. But cardinality

$$(\pi_1, \cdots, \pi_{s-1}, \tau) \cap (\rho_1, \cdots, \rho_{s-2}, \tau)=s-(l-1).$$

Accordingly, the induction hypothesis implies that $\pi_\tau$ and $\rho_\tau$ are equivalent. But we can also obtain the conclusion immediately that $\pi$ and $\pi_\tau$ are equivalent and that $\rho$ and $\rho_2$ are equivalent. Thus $\pi$ is equivalent to $\rho$, and $P_r(n+1)$ is established. We have thus proved that $P_r(l)$ is true for all $l$. This concludes our proof of the cocycle property.

## 5. PROOF OF THE STABILITY THEOREM

We shall now prove Theorem 1.5. Note first that it is easy to see that $ind\,(T,\pi)=0$ for all $\pi$ if $dim\ Sp(M,T)\leq s-2$. Thus, suppose $Sp_0(M;T)=V_1\cup\cdots\cup V_t\cup$ lower dimensional pieces. Let $\pi(T)=(\pi_1(T), \cdots, \pi_{s-1}(T))$ be a Fredholm $(s-1)$ - tuple such that $ker\ \pi$ is excellent for $V_1\cup\cdots\cup V_t$. Let $\pi_1^*, \cdots, \pi_{s-1}^*$ be dual vectors for $\pi_1, \cdots, \pi_{s-1}$ respectively, and define $\pi_s$ to be the linear functional associated to the projection of $\mathbb{C}^s$ onto $ker\ \pi$ along $Ran\,\pi$. Then with $\tau=(\pi,\pi_s)$, and $\psi_\tau(x)=p(x)/q(x)$, we have

$$D_{\psi_\tau}=D_p-D_q=\sum_{i=1}^{t} m_i[V_i]-\sum_{i=1}^{t} n_i[V_i].$$

Now

$$p(x) = \sum_{k=0}^{r} \pi_s(x)^k \, a_k(\pi(x))$$

$$q(x) = \sum_{k=0}^{r} \pi_s(x)^k \, b_k(\pi(x))$$

and both functions restricted to $ker\ \pi$ have the form $c\ \pi_s(x)^d$ + higher powers with $c \neq 0$, $d \neq 0$.

Furthermore, the difference of these initial powers for $p(x)$ and $q(x)$ equals $ind\ (T,\pi)$.

Let $w_i$ denote the Weierstrass polynomial for $V_i$ with respect to the coordinates $\tau(x) = (\pi(x), \pi_s(x))$. Then

$$w_i(x) = \pi_s(x)^{k_i} + a_{1,i}(\pi(x))\pi_s(x)^{k_i - 1} + \ldots + a_{k_{i,i}}(\pi(x)),$$

where $a_{j,i}(\pi(0)) = 0$ and

$$k_i = \mu(V_i,\ 0,\ ker\ \pi).$$

But the Weierstrass preparation theorem gives us

$$p(x) = u(x) \prod_{i=1}^{t} w_i(x)^{m_i}$$

$$q(x) = v(x) \prod_{i=1}^{t} w_i(x)^{n_i}$$

with $u(0)$ and $v(0)$ both non-zero. Consequently,

$$ind\ (T,\pi) = \sum_{i=1}^{t} \mu([V_i,\ 0,\ ker\ \pi])(m_i - n_i).$$

But the cocycle theorem shows that $m_i - n_i$ is independent of the choice of $\pi$, and if $ker\ \pi$ is excellent $\mu(V_i,\ 0,\ ker\ \pi) = \mu(V_i, 0)$ by Theorem 1.4.

## 6. GLOBALIZATION

As the cocycle theorem above is concerned with smoothness properties of ratios of Lefschetz numbers it is of local character. However, if the $2(s-1)$ - dimensional Hausdorff measure of the joint essential spectrum $Sp(\mathcal{a},T)$ is zero, we can obtain global results. For a theorem due to Shiffman [35] says that the set

$$\{\pi \in \mathbf{P}^{s-1}(\mathbb{C}) \mid \pi^{\perp} \cap [Sp(\mathcal{a},T) - z] = \emptyset\}$$

has full measure whenever $z \notin Sp(\mathcal{a},T)$. Consequently, by the spectral mapping theorem, for each such point $z$ there is a projection $\pi\colon \mathbb{C}^s \to \mathbb{C}^{s-1}$ so that $\pi(T-z)$ is a Fredholm $(s-1)$ - tuple.

Let $\Omega_{\pi,z}$ denote the component of $\mathbb{C}^{s-1} \setminus Sp(\mathcal{a},\pi(T))$ which contains $\pi(z)$, and put $U_{\pi,z} = \pi^{-1}(\Omega_{\pi,z})$. The choice of a Fredholm $(s-1)$ - tuple of operators for each $z$ gives an open covering $\{U_{\pi,z}\}$ of $X = \mathbb{C}^s \setminus Sp(\mathcal{a},T)$. By Theorem 1.1 we can assign a $\theta^*$ function ($\theta^*$ denotes the sheaf of non-vanishing holomorphic functions on $X$) to each ordered nonempty intersection $U_{\pi,z} \cap U_{\rho,y}$:

$$g_{\pi,\rho} : U_{\pi,z} \cap U_{\rho,y} \rightarrow \mathbb{C}^*$$

by taking

$$g_{\pi,\rho} = \psi(\pi^{\perp};\pi)/\psi(\rho^{\perp};\rho).$$

The transition functions $g_{\pi,\rho}$ satisfy the compatibility conditions

$$g_{\pi,\rho} \cdot g_{\rho,\tau} \cdot g_{\tau,\pi} = 1 \quad \text{on} \quad U_{\pi,z} \cap U_{\rho,y} \cap U_{\tau,w}$$

and

$$g_{\pi,\pi} = 1 \quad \text{on } U_{\pi,z}$$

Consequently, there is a holomorphic line bundle $E_T \mapsto X$ having these transition functions, and the collection of Lefschetz numbers $(\psi(\pi^{\perp};\pi),\ U_{\pi,z})$ gives an element $\psi$ in the vector space of meromorphic cross sections of $E_T$. The associated divisor then gives an analytic cycle in $X$ whose local degree at $z$ is the maximal ideal index. Moreover, it is clear from these considerations that if $T'$ is another $s$ - tuple with the same joint essential spectrum then

$$E_{T \oplus T'} = E_T \otimes E_{T'}.$$

Also, since the Koszul complex is self-dual, we have $E_T t = -E$ provided $s$ is even. Here $t$ denotes the transpose map.

## 7. INTERSECTION FORMULA FOR LOCAL INDICES

For the proof of Theorem 1.6 we shall need some results involving the calculus of local residues. We shall follow the very nice treatment given in Griffiths-Harris [14, Chap. 5]. The residue is defined analytically as an integral and may be alternatively interpreted as a cohomology class. We shall state several of its properties and note some alternative interpretations via topology and local algebra.

Let $U_\epsilon$ be the open ball in $\mathbb{C}^n$ centered at 0 with radius $\epsilon$. Suppose $(f_1, \cdots, f_n)$ are analytic functions in the closure $\overline{U}_\epsilon$ which have the origin as an isolated common zero. For $g$ holomorphic in $\overline{U}_\epsilon$ the residue is given by

$$Res_{\{0\}} w = \int_\Gamma w$$

where $\Gamma$ is the real $n$-cycle defined by $\{z : |f_i(z)| = \epsilon\}$ and oriented by $d(arg\, f_1) \wedge \cdots \wedge d(arg\, f_n) \geq 0$ and $w$ is the meromorphic $n$-form

$$\frac{g(z)\, dz_1 \wedge \cdots \wedge dz_n}{f_1(z) \cdots f_n(z)}.$$

The residue depends only on the homology class of $\Gamma \in H_n(U_\epsilon \setminus \underset{i}{U} f_i^{-1}(0),\ Z)$ and the de Rham cohomology class $[w] \in H_{DR}^n(U \setminus \underset{i}{U} f_i^{-1}(0))$ of $w$. It is linear in $g$ and alternating in the $f_i$.

For $\delta$ small enough $f^{-1}(w)$ is a discrete set of points in $U_\epsilon$ for $\|w\| < \delta$. With $w = f(z)$, denote by $K = \frac{dw_1}{w_1} \wedge \cdots \wedge \frac{dw_n}{w_n}$, the Cauchy kernel and put $w(f) = f^*K = \frac{df_1}{f_1} \wedge \cdots \wedge \frac{df_n}{f_n}$.

The *local intersection number* is defined by

$$(D_1 \cap \cdots \cap D_n)_{\{0\}} = Res_{\{0\}}\ w(f_1, \cdots, f_n).$$

We list some interpretations:

(1) The topological degree of $f : U_\epsilon \setminus \{0\} \to \mathbb{C}^n \setminus \{0\}$

(2) The sheet number of $f$

(3) If $\theta$ is the local ring at the origin and $I \subset \theta$ the ideal generated by the $f_i$, then $(D_1 \cap \cdots \cap D_n)_{\{0\}} = dim_{\mathbb{C}}(\theta / I)$.

If the divisors $D_i$ meet at a finite number of points $P_v$ interior to $U_\epsilon$, the *total number of intersections* of the $D_i$ in $V$ is defined by

$$(D_1 \cap \cdots \cap D_n)_{U_\epsilon} = \sum_v (D_1 \cap \cdots D_n)_{\{P_v\}}$$

**PROPOSITION 7.1** *The total intersection number is invariant under continuous deformation of the $D_i$. Thus for $\|w\| < \delta$ the equation $f(z) = w$ will have exactly $d = (D_1 \cap \cdots \cap D_n)_{U_\epsilon}$ solutions $z_v(w)$ (counting multiplicity).*

**PROPOSITION 7.2** *If $f$ is holomorphic in $U_\epsilon$, then symmetric functions in the values $f(z_1(w)), \cdots, f(z_d(w))$ are holomorphic in $w$.*

Throughout this section we assume that $T = (T_1, \cdots, T_s)$ is an $s$-tuple of commuting operators on a Banach space $M$ and that $\Lambda_{2s-2}(\sigma_{ess}(T)) = 0$, where $\Lambda_m$ is $m$-dimensional Hausdorff measure. Under this assumption we have already shown how to construct the analytic cycle $[V]$. Our main concern now is the proof of a result which gives the index of a Fredholm $(s-1)$-tuple of functions $F(T)$ where $F = (F_1, \cdots, F_{s-1})$ is defined and holomorphic in a neighborhood of $Sp(M;T)$ and non-vanishing on $\sigma_{ess}(T)$. We will show that

$$ind(F(T)) = D_{F_1} \cap D_{F_2} \cap \cdots \cap D_{F_{s-1}} \cap [V].$$

We begin with a preliminary result on spectral inclusion.

**LEMMA 7.3** *Suppose $T = (T_1, \cdots, T_s)$ is an $s$-tuple of commuting operators on a Banach space $M$ and suppose $L = (L_1, \cdots, L_p)$ is a Fredholm $p$-tuple of* *commuting operators in the commutant of T. Then,*

$$\bigcup_{i=0}^{p} Sp(H_i(M;L),T) \subseteq Sp(M,T).$$

**PROOF.** The inclusion will follow from the projection mapping property for the Taylor spectrum and the fact that on a finite dimensional space the point spectrum of a tuple $T$ equals the spectrum [36].

Suppose $z \in Sp(H_i(M;L),T)$ for some $i$. We may suppose $z=0$. Then, since $T$ is singular on $H_i(M;L)$ and $L$ is Fredholm it follows that $coker\ T \mid H_i(M;L)$ is not the zero space. Consequently, from the long exact sequence of homology theorem [29]

$$H_i(M;T_1,L) \cong coker\ T_1 \mid H_i(M;L) \oplus ker\ T_1 \mid H_{i-1}(M;L)$$

we see that $H_i(M;T_1,L)$ is non-zero and moreover, $coker\ T_2 \mid H_i(M;T_1,L)$ is non-zero. Continuing in this way we see that $H_i(M;T,L)$ is non-zero, i.e., $(T,L)$ is singular on $M$. Therefore, by the projection property we have $0 \in Sp(M,T)$.

For the proof of Theorem 1.6 we shall use induction on the number of linear functionals in $F$.

First, suppose $F$ is an $(s-1)$-tuple of linear functionals. Thus, $F=(\pi_1,\cdots,\pi_{s-1})$. We may assume that $\pi_1,\cdots,\pi_{s-1}$ are independent, otherwise $ind(F(T))=0$, while $[V]=0$ in a neighborhood of the common zeros of $\pi_1,\cdots,\pi_{s-1}$. Now

$$ind(T-x,\ F(T)) = \sum_{j=0}^{s-1} (-1)^k \dim H_j(M;F(T),x)$$

where $H_j(M;F(T),x)$ is the spectral subspace of $T$ acting on $H_j(M;F(T))$ corresponding to $x$. Hence $ind(T-x,\ F(T)) = (D_{F_1} \cap \cdots \cap D_{F_s} \cap [V])_{\{x\}}$ by the cocycle Theorem 1.1 proved for linear functionals.

Next, suppose the result is valid for all $F=(F_1,\cdots,F_i,\pi_{i+1},\cdots,\pi_{s-1})$ where $\pi_j$ is linear for $j=i+1,\cdots,s-1$ and consider $F=(F_1,\cdots,F_i,F_{i+1},\pi_{i+2},\cdots,\pi_{s-1})$. It suffices to fix our attention to a point $x$ such that $F(x)=0$. By translation we may take $x=0$.

We first suppose that 0 is a manifold point for $V$. Consequently, near 0 we have $[V]=n_1[V_1]$ where $V_1$ is locally a complex submanifold of $\mathbb{C}^s$ and $n_1$ is some integer.

Denote by $\hat{F}$ the map obtained from $F$ by deleting $F_{i+1}$ and for $w \in \mathbb{C}^s$ let $\hat{w}$ be the point in $\mathbb{C}^{s-2}$ gotten by deleting $w_{i+1}$. By Federer's coarea formula [13, Theorem 3.2.22],

$$0 = \int_{\sigma_{ess}(T)} app\ J_{2s-4}(\hat{F})\, d\Lambda_{2s-2}$$

$$= \int_{B_1(0)} \Lambda_2(\sigma_{ess}(T) \cap \hat{F}^{-1}(y))\, d\Lambda_{2s-4}(y)$$

where $app\ J_{2s-4}(\hat{F})$ is the approximate Jacobian of $\hat{F}$ and $B_1(0)$ is the unit ball in $\mathbb{C}^{s-2}$ about 0, and $\Lambda_m$ denotes Hausdorff measure of dimension $m$.

Since 0 is a manifold point for $V$ Proposition 7.1 applies to the map $F$. Thus, there is a neighborhood $U \subset V$, $0 \in U$ such that for $y$ in $\mathbb{C}^s$, $\|y\| < \epsilon$ the number of solutions in $U$ (counting multiplicity) to $F(z) = w$ is constant. Moreover, if we choose $w$ outside the branch locus of $F$ the elements in $F^{-1}(w)$ will be distinct. As the branch locus is an analytic hypersurface, most choices of $w$ give distinct preimage points. We shall choose $w$ so that $F^{-1}(w) \cap U$ has distinct points $\{p_v(w)\}_{v=1}^{e}$ and at the same time $\hat{F}^{-1}(\hat{w}) \cap \sigma_{ess}(T)$ has $\Lambda_2$-measure equal to zero. Having made this choice for $w$, the Shiffman results cited above in section 6, tell us that we can find a linear fuctional $\tau$: $\mathbb{C}^s \to \mathbb{C}$ such that

(0) $\tau$ is excellent for $\hat{F}^{-1}(\hat{w}) \cap Sp(M,T)$ at $p_1(w)$

(1) $\tau$ separates the points $\{p_v(w)\}_{v=1}^{e}$

(2) The tuple $(\hat{F}(T) - \hat{w},\ \tau(T))$ is Fredholm.

For fixed $\hat{w} \in \mathbb{C}^{s-2}$ let $h = \hat{F} - \hat{w}$. For $y = (y_1, y_2) \in \mathbb{C}^{s-1}$, and, $y_2 \in \mathbb{C}$ such that $\|y\|$ is small and does not lie in the discriminant locus $D$ of $(h,\tau)$ we have

$$(h,\tau)^{-1}(y) = \{z_v(y)\}_{v=1}^{d}$$

where the $z_v(y)$ are distinct. Therefore for $y \notin D$,

$$\chi(F_{i+1}(T) - z;\ (h,\tau)(T) - y)$$
$$= \prod_{z_v(y) \in U} [F_{i+1}(z_v(y)) - z]^{m_v(y)} \cdot g(z,y)$$

where $g$ corresponds to homology eigenvalues of $T$ outside $U'$, a small neighborhood of $p_1(w)$. By the induction hypothesis, (each point, $z_v(y)$, being smooth)

$$m_v(y) = (D_{(h,\tau)-y} \cap [V])_{\{z_v(y)\}} = n$$

where $n$ is the local degree of $V$ at the origin, i.e., $n = ind\,(T,\pi)$ for excellent $\pi$. Consequently, by Proposition 7.2

$$\prod_{z_v(y) \in U} [F_{i+1}(z_v(y)) - w_{i+1}]^{m_v(y)}$$

is analytic in $y$ for all small $y$. Furthermore, by the cocycle property for $\psi(F_{i+1}(T);\ (h,\tau)(T))$ and

$$\chi(\tau(T) - y_2;\ (h(T) - y_1,\ F_{i+1}(T) - w_{i+1}) =$$
$$\prod_{f(p_v(w)) = w} [\tau(p_v(w + (y_1,0)) - y_2]^{n_v(w+(y_1,0))}$$

we have $n_1(w) = ord\ F_{i+1}(p_1(w)) \cdot (D_{(h,\tau)} \cap [V])_{\{p_1(w)\}} =$

$$(D_{(h,F_{i+1}-w_{i+1})} \cap [V])_{\{p_1(w)\}}.$$

In other words,

$$ind\,(T-p_1(w)\,|\,F(T)-w) = (D_{F-w} \cap [V])_{\{p_1(w)\}}.$$

Since $\{p_j(w)\}_{j=1}^{e}$ are regular points the same is true for 1 replaced by $j$. To finish the proof for regular points we take $w \mapsto 0$. Recall that for $\|w\|$ small and not in the discriminant locus of $F$ we have $F^{-1}(w) \cap U = \{p_v(w)\}_{v=1}^{e}$. Furthermore,

$$ind\,(T-p_v(w)\,|(F(T)-w) = \sum_{v=1}^{d} D_{F-w} \cap [V]_{\{p(w)\}}.$$

Now let $h$ be holomorphic in $\mathbb{C}^s$ such that $h$ separates the points in $\{x_l\}_{l=1}^{N} = \bigcup_{j=0}^{s-1} Sp(H_j(M;F(T)),T)$. Then for $w$ outside the branch locus of $F$ on $U$,

$$\chi(h(T)-z;\; F(T)-w) = \prod_{v=1}^{e} [h(p_v(w)-z]^n \cdot g(z,w)$$

where again $g$ corresponds to eigenvalues not in $U$. Taking $z$ large and letting $w \mapsto 0$ we get

$$\psi(h(T)-z;\; F(T)) = \prod_{l=1}^{N} [h(x_l)-z]^{n_l}$$

$$= [h(p_1(0))-z]^{en} \cdot g(z,0)$$

Consequently, $en = n_l$ where $x_l = 0$ so that $D_F \cap [V]_{\{0\}} = ind(T\,|\,F(T))$.

This completes the proof of Theorem 1.6 for the case of regular points.

Next we consider what happens for $x$ in the singular locus of $Sp(M,T) \setminus \sigma_{ess}(T)$. Again we may assume $x=0$. Thus, suppose $[V] = \sum_{j=1}^{t} n_j[V_j]$ in some neighborhood $\Omega$ of the origin in $\mathbb{C}^s$. Choose functions $h_1, \cdots, h_k$ holomorphic in $\Omega$ such that $D_{h_j} = |n_j|[V_j]$. Then, by linearity of the intersection number,

$$D_{F_1} \cap \ldots D_{F_{s-1}} \cap [V])_{\{0\}} =$$

$$\sum_{\alpha=1}^{k} sgn\; n_\alpha \cdot (D_{F_1} \cap \cdots \cap D_{F_{s-1}} \cap D_{h_\alpha})_{\{0\}}.$$

Let $w \in \mathbb{C}^{s-1}$ be chosen so that $(F,h_j)^{-1}(w,0)$ consists of distinct points in $\Omega$ which are regular for each $V_j$, $j=1, \cdots, k$. The set of such $w$, $\|w\|$ small , is a dense open set near 0. We write $(F,h_j)^{-1}(w,o) = \{z_v^{(j)}(w)\}_{v=1}^{d_j}$ where $d_j = (D_F \cap V_j)_{\{0\}}$ and $V_j$ is the subvariety without the weight $n_j$. Again, choose $h$ holomorphic in $\mathbb{C}^s$ and separating the zeros of $F$ in $Sp(M,T)$. Then, for large $z$,

$$\psi(h(T)-z; F(T)-w) =$$

$$\prod_{j=1}^{t}\prod_{v=1}^{d_j}[h(z_v^{(j)}(w))-z]^{n_j}\cdot g(z,w)$$

where $g$ is holomorphic and consequently, by continuity, i.e, Proposition 7.2 applied to each $(F,h_j)$, we have

$$\psi(h(T)-z;F(T))=[h(0)-z]^{\sum_{j=1}^{k}d_jn_j}\cdot g(z,o).$$

Accordingly,

$$ind\,(T,F(T))=\sum_{j=1}^{t}d_jn_j=(D_F\cap[V])_{\{0\}}.$$

This completes the proof of Theorem 1.6.

Corollary 1.7 now follows since

$$ind\,(F(T))=\sum_{x\in F^{-1}(0)\cap Sp(M,T)} ind\,(T-x,F(T)).$$

Corollaries 1.8 and 1.9 follow from $\det e^A=e^{trace\,A}$.

## 8. PROOF OF THE STRUCTURE THEOREM

In this section we prove the structure theorem which explains the relationship between the fundamental trace form and the analytic cycle $[V]$. This result is analogous to the case of planar algebras except that the support of $[V]$ may now have nondiscrete singularities and the fact that maximal complexity of the boundary becomes an important geometric feature which is not present in the one dimensional case.

We shall work in the context of cryptointegral algebras. Such algebras are modeled on pseudo-differential operators and defined via a commutator filtration.

Suppose $A$ is a self-adjoint algebra of operators on a complex Hilbert space. Let $A_1$ denote the commutator ideal of $A$ and let $A_2$ denote the smallest ideal in $A_1$ containing all commutators of elements in $A$ with elements in $A_1$. In general let $A_n$ be the smallest ideal in $A$ containing commutators of elements in $A_k$ with elements in $A_{n-k+1}$, $k=0,\cdots,n-1$. It follows that $[A_j,A_k]\subset A_{j+k+1}$, and moreover $A_iA_j\subset A_{i+j}$ [see 19]. The complete antisymmetric sum $[T_1,\cdots,T_m]$ is $\sum_{\sigma\in S_m}\epsilon(\sigma)\,T_{\sigma(1)}\cdots T_{\sigma(m)}$, where $S_m$ is the symmetric group on $(1,2,\cdots,m)$ and $\epsilon(\sigma)$ is the signum of $\sigma$.

**DEFINITION 8.1** *The self-adjoint algebra $A$ is called cryptointegral of dimension $n$, $n>1$, provided that $A_{n+1}$ consists of trace-class operators and for any $2n$ - operators $T_1,\cdots,T_{2n}$ the full antisymmetric sum $[T_1,\cdots,T_{2n}]$ is a trace class operator.*

Since $A_1^{n+1}\subset A_{n+1}$, it follows that the commutator ideal $A_1$ is contained in the Schatten ideal $L^p(H)$ for $p=n+1$.

Suppose that the operators $L_1, \cdots, L_s$ generate a cryptointegral algebra $A(L)$ of dimension $n$. Then there is a linear function $\rho: C_0^\infty(\mathbb{C}^s) \to A(L)$ such that the composition with the canonical epimorphism $A(L) \to A(L)/A(L)_1$ is multiplicative. For $f \in C_0^\infty(\mathbb{C}^s)$ let $f(L)$ denote the operator $\rho(f)$.

**THEOREM 8.2** *Suppose $A$ is a cryptointegral algebra of dimension $n$ with generators $L=(L_1, \cdots, L_s)$. Then there is a closed $(2n-1)$ - current $C$ in $\mathbb{C}^s$ having support in $\sigma_{ess}(L)$ so that*

$$(\sqrt{-1})^n \, Tr[f_1(L), f_2(L), \cdots, f_{2n}(L)] = C(f_1 df_2 \wedge \cdots \wedge df_{2n})$$

(The factor $(\sqrt{-1})^n$ is chosen to make $C$ real).

**PROOF.** The fact that $C$ is a linear functional of the differential forms $f_1 df_2 \wedge \cdots \wedge df_{2n}$ follows from the condition

$$Tr[f_0(L), f_1(L)f_2(L), \cdots, f_{2n}(L)] = Tr[f_0(L)f_1(L), f_2(L), \cdots, f_{2n}(L)] + Tr[f_0(L)f_2(L), f_1(L), \cdots, f_{2n}(L)].$$

See the remarks in Lemma 45 of [8]. Next, if $\eta$ is a $(2n-2)$ form then $dC(\eta) = C(d\eta) = 0$ since $Tr[1, f_2(L), \cdots, f_{2n}] = 0$ for any choice of functions $f_2, \cdots, f_{2n}$. Thus $C$ is closed. The continuity and support properties follow by Propositions 3.5 and 3.7 of [19].

The case $n=2$ is almost in [19] except they do not consider $C$. They show that

$$Tr[f_1(L), \cdots, f_4(L)] = l(df_1 \wedge \cdots \wedge df_4)$$

for some continuous linear functional $l$. Note however, that $l$ is not a current since it is only defined on exact forms. The fact that traces of commutators define closed currents seems to have first been observed by the authors in [4] where applications of the geometric measure theory consequences of this observation were studied for planar algebras.

Our formulation of the connection of $C$ with index is based upon a consideration of Bott-type operator matrices.

Suppose $A=(A_1, \cdots, A_n)$ are elements in $A(L)$. To such a tuple one assigns the Bott operator $\hat{A} \in L(H) \otimes M_{2^{n-1}}(\mathbb{C}) \cong L(\underbrace{H \oplus \cdots \oplus H}_{2^{n-1} \text{ copies}})$ (see [9] and [40]), where $M_k(\mathbb{C})$ stands for the ring of $k$ by $k$ matrices with coefficients in $\mathbb{C}$. The tuple $A$ is then said to be Fredholm if $\hat{A}$ is Fredholm and one has

$$index\,(A) \equiv_{def} index\,(\hat{A}).$$

For instance, if $n=2$

$$\hat{A}=\begin{pmatrix} A_1 & A_2 \\ -A_2^* & A_1^* \end{pmatrix}$$

and $n=3$

$$\hat{A}=\begin{pmatrix} A_1 & A_2 & A_3 & 0 \\ A_1^* & -A_2^* & 0 & A_3 \\ A_3^* & 0 & A_1^* & A_2 \\ 0 & -A_3^* & A_2^* & -A_1 \end{pmatrix}$$

This definition of $\hat{A}$ and index is given in [9] and [40] where *index* $(A)$ is also studied in terms of an associated Koszul system. When the operators $A_i$ are commuting $-$*index* $(A)$ agrees with the Euler characteristic of the standard Koszul complex associated to $A$. The motivation for considering $\hat{A}$ can be seen at the symbol level where one obtains a map to the general linear group $Gl(\mathbb{C}^{2^{n-1}})$ which can be deformed to $S^{2n-1} \cong U(2^{n-1})/U(2^{n-1}-1)$ where $U(N)$ denotes the unitary subgroup. The index of $\hat{A}$ is then given as a multiple (which depends on the extension) of the topological degree of that map.

**THEOREM 8.3**

$$index\,(A) = Tr[\sqrt{S}\,A_1, \sqrt{S}\,A_1^*, \sqrt{S}\,A_2, \sqrt{S}A_2^*, \ldots, \sqrt{S}\,A_n, \sqrt{S}\,A_n^*]$$

*where $S$ is any nonegative regularizer in $A(L)$ for $\sum_{i=1}^{n} A_i^* A_i$.*

**PROOF.** Since $\hat{A} \in A(L) \otimes M_{2^{n-1}}(\mathbb{C})$ it follows that the self-adjoint operator $\sum_{i=1}^{n} A_i^* A_i$ is Fredholm. Let $S \geq 0$ be any regularizer so that $S \sum_{i=1}^{n} A_i^* A_i - 1 \in A(L)_1$. Put $\tilde{A}_i = \sqrt{S}\,A_i$ and $B = \hat{\tilde{A}}$ $(\tilde{A} = (\tilde{A}_1, \cdots, \tilde{A}_n))$. Then *index* $B =$ *index* $\hat{A}$, and $B^*B - 1$ and $BB^* - 1 \in A(L)_1 \otimes M_{2^{n-1}}(\mathbb{C})$. Next choose a regularizer $R$ in $A(L) \otimes M_{2^{n-1}}(\mathbb{C})$ so that $RB - 1$ and $BR - 1 \in A(L)_{n+1} \otimes M_{2^{n-1}}(\mathbb{C})$. Such regularizers certainly exist. Using a result of A. Calderön (see Lemma 7.1 of [20]) we have

$$index\,(B) = Tr[B, R].$$

Now

$$(1 - B^*B)^n - (1 - BB^*)^n =$$

$$\sum_{k=0}^{n} \frac{n!}{k!(n-k)!} (-1)^k ((B^*B)^k - (BB^*)^k) = [B, Q],$$

$$(1 - B^*B)^n = 1 - QB, \quad (1 - BB^*)^n = 1 - BQ$$

where

$$Q = \sum_{k=1}^{n} \frac{n!}{k!(n-k)!} (-1)^k (B^*B)^{k-1} B^*.$$

Consequently, $Q$ is a regularizer for $B$ modulo $A(L)_n \otimes M_{2^{n-1}}(\mathbb{C})$. Note also that $R - Q \in A(L)_n \otimes M_{2^{n-1}}(\mathbb{C})$. We then have

$$index\,(A) = Tr\,[B,R] = Tr([B,Q] + [B,\ R - Q]).$$

Now the trace functional applied to a matrix of operators is the ordinary trace on $L(H)$ composed with the operator valued matrix trace $\tau_e$ which means to form the sum of the diagonal entries. But by Proposition 1 of [11] we have

$$\tau_e[B,Q] = [B_1, B_1^*, B_2, B_2^*, \cdots, B_n, B_n^*].$$

Also, observe that $\tau_e\,[B,\ R-Q]$ is a sum of commutators each term of which has the form $[X,Y]$ with $X \in A(L)$ and $Y$ self-adjoint in $A(L)_n$. Therefore $Tr\,(\tau_e[B,\ R-Q]) = 0$. Consequently,

$$\begin{aligned} ind\,(\hat{A}) &= Tr(\tau_e\,([B,Q] + [B,\ R-Q]) \\ &= Tr\,[B_1, B_1^*, B_2, B_2^*, \cdots, B_n, B_n^*]. \end{aligned}$$

and the proof is complete.

We see in the proof that the requirement of having a totally antisymmetric form in trace class is superfluous; it is a consequence of the fact that $A$ is a Fredholm tuple and $A(L)_{n+1}$ consists of trace class operators.

We note that R. Douglas and D. Voiculescu [11] sought to connect antisymmetric forms with index under certain hypotheses on commutators, i.e., given an $n$-tuple $A = (A_1, \cdots, A_n)$ they require that $[A_i, A_j]\,[A_i, A_j^*]$, $1 - A_i A_i^*$ and $1 - A_i^* A_i$ belong to the Schatten $n$-class for $1 \leq i \leq j \leq n$. They then showed $index\,(A) = Tr\,[A_1, A_1^*, \cdots, A_n, A_n^*]$. However, they stated they were not able to decide if such operator tuples existed which carried a non-zero index and we shall show as a corollary to the proof of Theorem 8.3 that such operator tuples do not exist.

A parallel difficulty is overcome in the work of A. Connes [8]. In [8] Proposition 15, a cocycle $\tau \in Z_\lambda^{2m-1}(B)$ is defined which later enters into a bilinear pairing between $K_1(B)$ and $H_\lambda^{odd}(B)$. Connes begins with a Hilbert space $E$ and a linear map $\rho$ from his symbol algebra $B$ to $L(E)$ which is required to be a homomorphism modulo $L^{p/2}(E)$. He requires that $m \geq p/2$, but if we consider the crytointegral algebra of dimension $n$ generated by pseudo-differential operators on a compact $n$-manifold, we get commutators which lie in $L^{n+\epsilon}(E)$, $\epsilon > 0$. Thus, $2m - 1 \geq 2(n + \epsilon) - 1 = 2n - 1 + 2\epsilon$. Hence, the cyclic cocycle $\tau$ constructed by Connes is in $Z_\lambda^{2n+1}(B)$ rather than $Z_\lambda^{2n-1}(B)$. Accordingly, the associated totally antisymmetric forms map to vanishing currents but Connes shows there is a cyclic cocycle $\phi$ in $Z_\lambda^{2n-1}(B)$ which goes to $\tau$ under the periodicity map. Theorem 8.3 above then identifies the antisymmetrization of $\phi$ as the fundamental trace form which also gives the full index theorem when all the lower homology classes of $\sigma_{ess}(A)$ vanish. Similiar considerations apply to Toeplitz extensions of Boutet de Monvel [2]. See also H. Upmeier [38].

As a corollary to Theorem 8.3 we get that *the* $L^n(H)$ *- smooth cryptointegral extensions of* $C(S^{2n-1})(n \geq 2)$ *are trivial.* This improves Proposition 3 of [11] and shows that the hypotheses of [11] are unsatisfactory.

To see that these extensions are trivial let $T=(T_1, \cdots, T_n)$ define an $L^n(H)$ - smooth extension (i.e., commutators $[T_i,T_j]$, $[T_i,T_j^*]$ lie in $L^n(H)$), so that $\Sigma T_i^* T_i - 1 \in L^n(H)$. It suffices to prove *index* $(\hat{T})=0$. For this purpose we proceed as above by choosing $R$ so that $R\hat{T}-1$ and $\hat{T}R-1 \in L^1(H)$ and write

$$(1-\hat{T}^*\hat{T})^{n-1}-(1-\hat{T}\hat{T}^*)^{n-1}=[\hat{T},Q].$$

where $Q$ is defined as above with $n$ replaced by $n-1$. Then $R-Q \in L^{1+\frac{1}{n-1}}(H) \otimes M_{2^{n-1}}(\mathbb{C})$ and we have

$$\textit{index}\,(T)=Tr[\hat{T},R]=Tr([\hat{T},Q]+[\hat{T},R-Q])=Tr(\tau_e([\hat{T},Q]+[\hat{T},R-Q]))=0$$

since $\tau_e[\hat{T},Q]=0$ by Proposition 1 of [11] and $Tr(\tau_e[\hat{T},R-Q])=0$ since $\tau_e[\hat{T},R-Q]$ is again a sum of commutators $[X,Y]$ with $Y$ self-adjoint in $L^{1+1/n}(H)$ and $[X,Y] \in L^1(H)$.

**PROPOSITION 8.4** *Suppose* $T=(T_1, \cdots, T_s)$ *is an* $s$*-tuple of commuting operators which generate a cryptointegral algebra* $A(L)$ *of dimension* $n$. *Then the current* $C$ *defined in Theorem 8.2 is a real MC - cycle.*

(Real means that $\overline{C(\eta)} = C(\overline{\eta})$).

The notion of a real MC - cycle was introduced by R. Harvey and B. Lawson in their work [17], [18] characterizing those closed odd-dimensional submanifolds of $\mathbb{C}^s$ which bound a complex subvariety. In the context of operator algebras the role of the subvariety is played by the cycle $[V]$.

Suppose $X$ is a complex manifold with Dolbeault decomposition $E_p(X)=\bigoplus_{r+s=p}E_{r,s}(X)$ and dual decomposition $E'_p(X)=\bigoplus_{r+s=p}E'_{r,s}(X)$. Given a current $T \in E'_p(X)$ we will denote the component of $T$ in the space $E'_{r,s}(X)$ by $T_{r,s}$. Note that $E_{r,s}(X)$ consists of forms (in local coordinates) $f(z)dz_{\alpha(1)}\wedge \cdots dz_{\alpha(r)}\wedge d\overline{z}_{\beta(1)}\wedge \cdots d\overline{z}_{\beta(s)}$ where $f$ is in $C_0^\infty(X)$.

**DEFINITION 8.5** Let $M$ be a $(2n-1)$-current with compact support on $X$. Then

(i) $M$ is maximally complex if the Dolbeault components $M_{r,s}=0$ for $|r-s|>1$, i.e., $M=M_{n,n-1}+M_{n-1,n}$.

(ii) $M$ satisifies the moment condition if $M(w)=0$ for all $\bar{\partial}$-closed $(n, n-1)$ forms $w$ on $X$.

For $n > 1$, (i) implies (ii) (see [17] Proposition 3.6).

**DEFINITION 8.6** A $(2n-1)$-current $M$ is called an MC-cycle if it is closed and for $n > 1$ is maximal complex, or if $n=1$, it satisfies the moment condition.

The propery of being a real MC-cycle is preserved under holomorphic maps $F$, i.e., if $M$ is a real MC-cycle so is $F_*(M)$.

With these remarks we turn to the proof of Proposition 8.4. By definition

$$C(f_1\, df_2 \wedge \cdots \wedge df_{2n}) = (\sqrt{-1})^n\, Tr[f_1(T), f_2(T), \cdots, f_{2n}(T)].$$

Let $N$ be the subgroup of the symmetric group $S_{2n}$ on $\{1,2, \cdots, 2n\}$ generated by the elements which interchanges the pairs $\{2j-1, 2j\}$. Then by part (c) of Proposition 1.1 of [19]

$$[A_1, A_2, \cdots, A_{2n}] = \sum_\sigma \epsilon(\sigma)[A_{\sigma(1)}, A_{\sigma(2)}]\ldots[A_{\sigma(2n-1)}, A_{\sigma(2n)}]$$

where $\sigma$ runs over a sequence of coset representatives for $N$ in $S_{2n}$.

Let $\eta$ be a test form in $E_{r,s}(\mathbb{C}^s)$ where $r+s=2n-1$. A typical term looks like $f\, dz_{\alpha(1)} \wedge \cdots dz_{\alpha(r)} \wedge d\bar{z}_{\beta(1)} \wedge \cdots \wedge d\bar{z}_{\beta(s)}$. For such forms

$$\begin{aligned} C(\eta) &= (\sqrt{-1})^n\, Tr[f(T), T_{\alpha(1)}, \cdots, T_{\alpha(r)}, T^*_{\beta(1)}, \cdots, T^*_{\beta(s)}] \\ &= (\sqrt{-1})^n\, Tr\Big(\sum_{\sigma \in S_{2n}/N} [\,,\,]\ldots[\,,\,]\Big). \end{aligned}$$

Suppose $n > 1$. If $|r-s| > 1$ then at least one simple commutator $[\,,\,]$ in each term of the above sum must be zero since the $T_\alpha{}'_s$ and $T^*_\beta{}'_s$ commute amongst themselves. Consequently, $C(\eta)=0$. Thus, for $|r-s| > 1$ the Dolbeault components $C_{r,s}$ vanish and therefore $C$ is maximally complex. If $n=1$, the moment condition is also easily checked [4]. Hence, $C$ is an MC - cycle. Finally, the reality of $C$ follows by taking adjoints:

$$\begin{aligned} \overline{(\sqrt{-1})^n\, Tr\,[A_1, \cdots, A_{2n}]} &= (-1)^n(\sqrt{-1})^n\, Tr([A_1, \cdots, A_{2n}]^*) \\ &= (\sqrt{-1})^n\, Tr\,[A_1^*, \cdots, A_{2n}^*]. \end{aligned}$$

When the joint essential spectrum is a smooth manifold $Y$ we can identify the totally antisymmetric form as the weak boundary of $[V]$ extended as a current to a neighborhood of $Sp(H,T)$. Since the pull back to $Y$ of the Bochner-Martinelli form under the map $f=(f_1, \cdots, f_{s-1})$ represents the characteristic class for the Bott matrix, we shall use the the Harvey-King projection method, Invent. Math. 15 (1972), 47-52, and the homotopy equation for the $\bar{\partial}$ operator in order to identify $C$ as the boundary of $[\tilde{V}]$.

We first observe an extension theorem of [18] which is based upon Shiffman's proof of the Remmert-Stein Theorem [35].

**THEOREM 8.7** *Let $W = Y \cup S$ be a compact set in $\mathbb{C}^s$ where $Y$ is an oriented, $C^1$-submanifold of dimension $2p-1$ having finite volume in an open subset $U$ of $\mathbb{C}^s$ and suppose $S$ is closed and $\Lambda_{2p-1}(S)=0$. Let $M$ be a holomorphic $p$-chain in $U \setminus W$. Then the mass of $M$ on $K$ is finite for each compact set $K$ of $U$. Therefore $M$ has a (unique) extension to a locally rectifiable current $M$ on $U$, and $d\tilde{M} = \Sigma c_j [Y_j]$ where $c_j \in Z$ and $Y_j$ is a connected component of $Y$ for each $j$.*

Consequently when $T=(T_1, \cdots, T_s)$ has $\sigma_{ess}(T)$ a scarred $C^1$-manifold of $\mathbb{C}^s$, $V$ has a unique current extension $[\tilde{V}]$ to a neighborhood $U$ of $Sp(M,T)$. The notation $[Y_j]$ above refers to the current of integration over the manifold $Y_j$ with the stated orientation. Using this extension theorem the argument which follows also proves Theorem 1.10.

**PROOF OF THEOREM 1.13** By Theorem 8.7 we know the cycle $[V]$ extends to a current $[\tilde{V}]$ in $U$ and $d[\tilde{V}]$ has the form $\Sigma y_\alpha [Y_\alpha]$ where $y_\alpha \in Z$. The identification of $d[\tilde{V}]$ with $C$ will depend on our two expressions for the index of an $(s-1)$-tuple $F(T)=(F_1(T), \cdots, F_{s-1}(T))$ when $F$ is holomorphic in $U$.

We shall use the notations

$$d = \partial + \bar{\partial}$$
$$d^c = \frac{\sqrt{-1}}{4\pi}(\bar{\partial} - \partial)$$
$$dd^c = \frac{\sqrt{-1}}{2\pi}\partial\bar{\partial}$$
$$\theta_l = (dd^c \log \|z\|^2)^l$$
$$\theta Ⓗ_l = \log \|z\|^2 \theta_l$$

If $F: U \to \mathbb{C}^{s-1}$ is a holomorphic mapping of a complex manifold $U$ then $F^*\theta_l = (dd^c \log \|F\|^2)^l$ and $F^* Ⓗ_l = \log \|F\|^2 F^*\theta_l$.

The generalization of the Poincaré - Lelong equation to vector valued functions states [15]:

**PROPOSITION 8.11** (Poincaré - Martinelli formula)

$$dd^c F^* Ⓗ_{s-2} = W$$

and

$$dd^c F^* \theta_l = 0$$

if $l < s-2$ *where $W = F^{-1}(0)$ is counted with suitable algebraic multiplicities.*

Now suppose $F: U \to \mathbb{C}^{s-1}$ is holomorphic in a neighborhood $U$ of $Sp(M,T)$ and gives rise to a Fredholm $(s-1)$ - tuple. Then we can express the index of $F(T)$ in two ways: first in terms of the completely antisymmetric form, and second in terms of our intersection formula involving the analytic cycle $[V]$. Comparing these formulas gives $F_*(\frac{2\pi)^{s-1}}{s-1} C + d[\tilde{V}]) = 0$. To see this let

$$\Phi(\xi) = d\xi_1 \wedge \cdots \wedge d\xi_{s-1}, \quad \Phi_j(\xi) = (-1)^{j-1}\xi_j \, d\xi_1 \wedge \ldots \wedge \widehat{d\xi_j} \wedge \cdots \wedge d\xi_{s-1}$$

where the symbol $\hat{}$ means to delete the term $d\xi_j$.

By Theorem 8.3 we have, with $G = F/\|F\|$

$$ind\,(F(T)) = \frac{(\sqrt{-1})^{s-1}}{s-1} C \left( G^* \left( \frac{\sum_{j=1}^{s-1} \Phi_j \wedge \bar{\Phi}}{\|\cdot\|^{2(s-1)}} \right) \right).$$

Since $F$ is nonvanishing on $\sigma_{ess}(T)$ there is a neighborhood $U'$ of $\sigma_{ess}(T)$ such that $F: U' \mapsto \mathbb{C}^{s-1} \setminus \{0\}$. Consequently, since $F$ and $G$ are homotopic in $U'$, and $C$ is closed and has support in $U'$ we have

$$C\left( F^* \left( \frac{\sum_{j=1}^{s-1} \Phi_j \wedge \bar{\Phi}}{\|\cdot\|^{2(s-1)}} \right) \right) = C\left( G^* \left( \frac{\sum_{j=1}^{s-1} \Phi_j \wedge \bar{\Phi}}{\|\cdot\|^{2(s-1)}} \right) \right).$$

Furthermore, since $C$ is real,

$$F^* \left( \frac{\sum_{j=1}^{s-1} \Phi_j \wedge \bar{\Phi}}{\|\cdot\|^{2(s-1)}} \right) = \partial \log \|F\|^2 \wedge (\partial\bar{\partial} \log \|F\|^2)^{s-2}$$

(see p. 372 of [14]), we have

$$\begin{aligned} ind\,(F(T)) &= \frac{(\sqrt{-1})^{s-1}}{s-1} C\,(\partial \log \|F\|^2 \wedge (\partial\bar{\partial} \log \|F\|^2)^{s-2}) \\ &= -\frac{(\sqrt{-1})^{s-1}}{s-1} C\,(\bar{\partial} \log \|F\|^2 \wedge (\partial\bar{\partial} \log \|F\|^2)^{s-2}) \\ &= -\frac{(2\pi)^{s-1}}{s-1} C\,(d^c F^* \textcircled{H}_{s-2}). \end{aligned}$$

On the other hand by Corollary 1.7 and Federer's generalization of Stokes' theorem for flat currents [13, section 4.3.20] we have, since $F^{-1}(0) \cap \sigma_{ess}(T) = \emptyset$,

$$\begin{aligned} ind\,(F(T)) &= D_{F_1} \cap D_{F_2} \cap \cdots \cap D_{F_{s-1}} \cap [V] \\ &= (dd^c F^* \textcircled{H}_{s-2}) \cap [\tilde{V}](1) \end{aligned}$$

$$= d[\tilde{V}] \cap d^c F^* \textcircled{H}_{s-2})(1) - d\left([\tilde{V}] \cap d^c F^* \textcircled{H}_{s-2}\right)(1)$$

$$= d[\tilde{V}](d^c F^* \textcircled{H}_{s-2})$$

where 1 denotes a test function which is equal to the constant one in a neighborhood of $Sp(M,T)$ and the symbol $\cap$ denotes intersection of flat currents [13]. Consequently,

$$F_*(d[\tilde{V}] + \frac{(2\pi)^{s-1}}{(s-1)} C)(d^c \textcircled{H}_{s-2}) = 0.$$

Since $d[\tilde{V}] + \frac{(2\pi)^{s-1}}{s-1} C$ is real it follows that

$$F_*[d[\tilde{V}] + \frac{(2\pi)^{s-1}}{s-1} C](\partial \textcircled{H}_{s-2}) = F_*[d[\tilde{V}] + \frac{(2\pi)^{s-1}}{s-1} C](k_0^{BM}) = 0$$

since $\partial \textcircled{H}_{s-2}$ is a scalar multiple of the Bochner-Martinelli $(s-1,\ s-2)$ - form $k_0^{BM}(\xi)$.

Replacing $F$ by $F-z$ for any $z \notin F(\sigma_{ess}(T))$ gives

$$F_*(d[\tilde{V}] + \frac{(2\pi)^{s-1}}{s-1} C)(k_z^{BM}) = 0.$$

At this point we need the fact that $C$ is flat. By the support theorem, $C = \Sigma r_j [Y_j]$ where $r_j \in \mathbb{R}$. Let $R = F_*(d[\tilde{V}] + \frac{(2\pi)^{s-1}}{s-1} C)$. Then $R$ is a real MC-cycle in $\mathbb{C}^{s-1}$, $R = R_{s-1,s-2} + R_{s-2,s-1}$, $R_{s-1,s-2} = \overline{R}_{s-2,s-1}$ and $\overline{\partial} R_{s-1,s-2} = 0$. Applying the homotopy equation for the $\overline{\partial}$ operator we have

$$R_{s-1,s-2} = (\overline{\partial} \circ K^{BM} + K^{BM} \overline{\partial}) R_{s-1,s-2} = \overline{\partial} \circ K^{BM} R_{s-1,s-2}$$

where $K^{BM}$ is the Bochner-Martinelli kernel

$$K^{BM}(z) = \frac{\beta_{s-1}}{\|z\|^{2s-2}} \sum_{j=1}^{s-1} \overline{z}_j \frac{\partial}{\partial \overline{z}_j}$$

where $\beta_{s-1} = (-1)^{(s-1)(s-2)}(s-2)!/(2i\pi)^{s-1}$ (see [17]). Since $R$ has *measure coefficients, i.e., C is flat,*

$$K^{BM} R_{s-1,s-2}(\eta) = \int_{z \in \mathbb{C}^{s-1}} R_{s-1,s-2}(k_z^{BM}) \wedge \eta(z) = 0$$

since $R_{s-1,s-2}(k_z^{BM}) = 0$ for all $z \notin F(\sigma_{ess}(T))$, i.e., for $\Lambda_{2s-2}$ - almost all $z$. Consequently, $\overline{\partial} K^{BM} R_{s-1,s-2} = R_{s-1,s-2} = 0$ and therefore $R = 0$.

Now from the geometric Lemmas 3.4 and 3.5 of [18] we deduce that there are enough nice projections $\phi$ so that by pulling back to $\mathbb{C}^s$, we have $d[\tilde{V}] + \frac{(2\pi)^{s-1}}{s-1} C = 0$.

**COROLLARY 8.12** *If h is holomorphic in a neighborhood of $Sp(M,T)$, then for any Fredholm tuple $(F_1(T), \cdots, F_{s-1}(T)) = F(T)$,*

$$-\sum_{k=0}^{s-1}(-1)^k \, Tr[h(T) \mid H_k(M,F(T))] =$$

$$\frac{(s-2)!}{(s-1)}(-1)^{\frac{(s-1)(s-2)}{2}} \sum_{j=1}^{s-1}(-1)^{j-1} \, Tr\,[h(T)\|F(T)\|^{-2(s-1)} F_j(T), F_1(T), \cdots, \hat{F}_j(T), \cdots, F_{s-1}(T), F_1(T)^*, \cdots, F_{s-1}(T)^*]$$

## 9. Appendix

In this appendix we show how ratios of Lefschetz numbers can be expressed as an alternating product of Steinberg symbols, (i.e. Lemma 9.1).

Suppose

$$(A = (A_1, \cdots, A_{s-2}), B, C)$$

is a commutative $s$ - tuple of bounded operators, and the $(s-1)$ - tuples $(A,B)$ and $(A,C)$ are Fredholm. Let $H_i(C,A)$ denote the $i^{th}$ homology module of the Koszul complex $E(M;(A,C))$. $B$ induces an endomorphism on $H_i(C,A)$ because both the kernel and ranges of the relevent boundary operators are invariant subspaces for $B$. We may therefore define a multiplicative Lefschetz number

$$\psi(B;(C,A)) \equiv \prod_{j=0}^{s-1}[det(B \mid H_j(C;A)]^{(-1)^j}$$

provided the determinants in the denominators are not equal to zero. By interchanging the roles of $B$ and $C$, we can also consider $\psi(C;(B,A))$.

The homology modules $H_i(A)$ of $E(M,A)$ need not be finite dimensional under our hypothesis. But $B$ and $C$ induce linear operators $b$ and $c$ on $H_i(A)$ which are algebraically Fredholm.

Let $R_i$ be the unital subring generated by $b$ and $c$ together with $F$, the ideal of operators having finite rank, and the regularizers of $b$ and $c$ with respect to $F$ on $H_i(A)$. Suppressing $i$ we note that the quotient $R/F$ is commutative and unital and there is a bicharacter

$$K_1(R/F) \otimes K_1(R/F) \to \mathbb{C}^*$$

given by composition

$$K_1(R/F) \otimes K_1(R/F) \xrightarrow{\{,\}} K_2(R/F) \xrightarrow{\partial} K_1(R/F) \xrightarrow{det_*} \mathbb{C}^*$$

where $K_1$ denotes the Whitehead group defined by Bass, $K_2$ is the Milnor group and $\{,\}$ is the Steinberg symbol.

Let $\{b,c;\, H_i(A)\}$ denote the Steinberg symbol of the 2 - tuple $(b,c)$ on $H_i(A)$.

Our purpose in this appendix is to isolate the proof of the following lemma, which has intrinsic interest because of its geometric content.

**SLICING LEMMA 9.1**

$$\psi(B;(C,A)) = \left( \prod_{i=0}^{s-2} det_* \partial \{b;c;\, H_i(A)\}^{(-1)^i} \right) \psi(C;(B,A)) \text{ provided } 0 \notin Sp(M;(A,B,C))$$

**PROOF.**

From the long exact sequence of homology

$$\cdots H_{\mu+1}(C,A) \to H_\mu(A) \to H_\mu(A) \to H_\mu(C,A) \to \cdots$$

it follows that

$$H_{\mu+1}(C,A) \cong coker\ C \mid H_{\mu+1}(A) \oplus ker\ C\ H_\mu(A).$$

But, if the rows are exact in the following commutative diagram, where the entries are free modules of finite dimension

$$\begin{array}{ccccccccc} 0 & \to & E' & \xrightarrow{\tilde\alpha} & E & \xrightarrow{\tilde\beta} & E'' & \to & 0 \\ & & \downarrow\alpha & & \downarrow\beta & & \downarrow\gamma & & \\ 0 & \to & E' & \xrightarrow{\tilde\alpha} & E & \xrightarrow{\tilde\beta} & E'' & \to & 0 \end{array}$$

and $\alpha,\beta,\gamma$ are linear maps, then $det\ \beta = det\ \alpha\ \det\gamma$ ( cf. th. 4.7 in [23]).

Consequently,

$$det\ B \mid H_{j+1}(C,A) = det\ B \mid coker\ C\ H_{j+1}(A) \cdot det\ B \mid ker\ C \mid H_j(A) \qquad (9.2)$$

as well as

$$det\ C \mid H_{j+1}(B,A) = det\ C \mid coker\ B\ H_{j+1}(A) \cdot det\ C \mid ker\ B \mid H_j(A). \qquad (9.3)$$

Accordingly, since

$$\frac{\psi(B;(C,A))}{\psi(C;(B,A))} = \frac{det\,(B \mid\mid H_0(C,A)}{det(C) \mid H_0(B,A))} \cdot \frac{det\,(C \mid H_1(B,A) \mid}{det\,(B \mid H_1(C,A))}$$

$$\cdots \left[ \frac{det\,(B \mid H_{s-1}(C,A))}{det\,(C \mid H_{s-1}(B,A))} \right]^{(-1)^{s-1}}$$

by grouping terms appropriately and using (9.2) and (9.3) above the right hand side becomes

$$\prod_{i=0}^{s-2} \left[ \frac{det\,(B \mid H_i(A) / C\, H_i(A))}{det\,(B \mid ker\ C \mid H_i(A))} \right]^{(-1)^i} \cdot \left[ \frac{det\ C \mid ker\ B \mid H_i(A)}{\det C \mid H_i(A)/BH_i(A)} \right]^{(-1)^i}$$

But, we have proved in [3] that

$$\frac{det\, B \mid ker\; C \mid H_i(A)}{det\, B \mid coker\; C \mid H_i(A)}$$
$$= det_* \circ \partial\{b,c;H_i(A)\} \frac{det\, C \mid ker\; B \mid H_i(A)}{det\, C \mid coker\; B \mid H_i(A)}$$

so that the results follows by substitution. Note that in the process of proving Lemma 9.1 we have also obtained a proof of Proposition 1.2 of the introduction.

**REFERENCES**

[1] L.G. Brown, R.G. Douglas, P.A. Fillmore, *Extensions of C* - algebras and K-homology,* Ann. of Math **105** (1977), 265-324.

[2] L. Boutet de Monvel, *On the index of Toeplitz operators of several complex variables,* Invent. Math **50,** (1979), 249-272.

[3] R.W. Carey and J.D. Pincus, *An invariant for certain operator algebras,* Proc. Nat. Acad. Sci. U.S.A. **71** (1974), 1952-1956.

[4] ______________________, *Principal functions, index theory, geometric measure theory, and function algebras,* Integral Eq. and Operator Theory **2** (1979), 441-483.

[5] ____________________, *Operator theory and boundaries of complex curves,* preprint 1982.

[6] ____________________, *Reciprocity for Fredholm operators,* Integral Eq. and Operator Theory **9** (1986), 469-501.

[7] ____________________, *Principal currents,* Integral Eq. and Operator Theory **8** (1985), 614-640.

[8] A. Connes, *Non-commutative differential geometry,* Inst. des Hautes Études Sci. Publ., Math. No. **62** (1985), 41-144.

[9] R.E. Curto, *Fredholm and invertible n-tuples of operators. The deformation problem,* Trans. Amer. Math. Soc., **266** (1981), 129-159.

[10] ________________, *Applications of several complex variables to multidimensional spectral theory,* Indiana University Operator Theory year, Pitman Research Notes, to appear.

[11] R.G. Douglas and D. Voiculescu, *On the smoothness of sphere extensions,* J. Operator Theory **6** (1981), 103-111.

[12] A.S. Fainstein and V.S. Shul'man, *Fredholm complexes in Banach spaces (Russian),* Funct. Analysis and Appl. **14** (1980), 87-88.

[13] H. Federer, *Geometric Measure Theory,* Die Grundlehren der math. Wissenschaften Band 153, Springer-Verlag, New York, 1969.

[14] P. Griffiths and J. Harris, *Principles of Algebraic Geometry,* Wiley, New York, 1978.

[15] P. Griffiths and J. King, *Nevanlinna theory and holomorphic maps between algebraic varieties,* Acta. Math **130** (1973), 145-220.

[16] V. Guillemin, *Toeplitz operators in n-dimensions,* Integral Eq. and Operator Theory **7** (1984), 145-205.

[17] F.R. Harvey and H.B. Lawson, Jr., *On boundaries of complex analytic varieties, I,* Ann. of Math. **102** (1975), 223-290.

[18] F.R. Harvey *Holomorphic chains and their boundaries,* Proceedings of Symposia in Pure Mathematics, **30 :** 1. A.M.S., Providence R.I. (1977), 309-382.

[19] J.W. Helton and R. Howe, *Traces of commutators of integral operators,* Acta Math. **135** (1975) no. 3-4, 271-305.

[20] L. Hormander, *The Weyl calculus of pseudo-differential operators,* Acta. Math., **32** (1979) 359-443.

[21] J. Janas, *Examples of cryptointegral algebras, (Russian)* Bull. Acad. Polon. Sci. Sër. Sci. Math **27** (1979) no. 9, 695-704.

[22] G.G. Kasparov, *Generalized index of elliptic operators,* Functional Analysis **7** (1973), 82-83.

[23] S. Lang, *Algebra,* 2nd Edition, Addison - Wesley, Menlo Park, CA., 1984.

[24] P. Lelong, *Integration sur un ensemble analytique complexes,* Bull. Soc. Math. France, **85** (1957), 239-262.

[25] R. Levy, *Cohomological invariants for essentially commuting systems of operators, (Russian)* Funct. Analysis and Appl. **17** (1983), 79-80.

[26] M.S. Livsic, *Cayley-Hamilton theorem, vector bundles and divisors of commuting operators,* Integral Eq. and Operator Theory **6** (1983), 250-273.

[27] A. Markoe, *Analytic families of differential complexes,* Journal Funct. Analy. **9** (1972), 181-188.

[28] M. Nagata, *Local Rings,* Krieger, Huntington, N.Y., 1975.

[29] D.G. Northcott, *Lessons on Rings,* Modules and Multiplicities, Cambridge Univ. Press, London, 1968.

[30] J.D. Pincus, *On the trace of commutators in the algebra of operators generated by an operator with trace-class self-commutator,* August (1972) preprint.

[31] ————, *On the integrality of principal functions,* Coll. Math. Soc. Janos Bolyai **35** (1980), 967-975.

[32] M. Putinar, *Base change and the Fredholm index,* Integral Eq. and Operator Theory **8** (1985), 674-692.

[33] ————, *Spectral theory and sheaf theory. II,* Math. Z. **192** (1986), 473-490.

[34] M. Putinar and F. - H. Vasilescu, *Continuous and analytic invariants for deformations of Fredholm complexes.* J. Operator Theory, **9** (1983), 3-26.

[35] B. Shiffman, *On the removal of singularities of analytic sets,* Michigan Math J., **15** (1968), 111-120.

[36] J.L. Taylor, *A joint spectrum for several commuting operators,* J. Functional Analysis **(6)** (1970), 172-191.

[37] ____________, *The analytic-functional calculus for several commuting operators,* Acta. Math., **125** (1970), 1-38.

[38] H. Upmeier, *Index theory for Toeplitz operators on bounded symmetric domains,* Bull. A.M.S. **16** (1987), 109-112.

[39] F.-H. Vasilescu, *A characterization of the joint spectrum in Hilbert spaces,* Rev. Roumaine Math. Pures Appl., **32** (1977), 1003-1009.

[40] ______________, *Stability of the index of a complex of Banach spaces,* J. Operator Theory **1** (1979), 187-205.

[41] ______________, *Fredholm operators and the continuity of the Lefschetz number,* J. Operator Theory **6** (1981), 143-153.

[42] ______________, *Analytic Functional Calculus and Spectral Decomposition,* Ed. Academei and D. Reidel Co., Bucharest and Dordrecht 1982.

[43] H. Whitney, *Complex Analytic Varieties,* Addison-Wesley, Menlo Park, Ca., 1972.

R.W. Carey, Department of Mathematics, University of Kentucky,
Lexington, KY 40506

J.D. Pincus, Department of Mathematics, State University of New York,
Stony Brook, NY 11794

---

This work is supported by grants from the National Science Foundation
Submitted: March 3. 1987

Operator Theory:
Advances and Applications, Vol. 29 


# COMPLETING A MATRIX SO AS TO MINIMIZE THE RANK

Chandler Davis*

(Dedicated to my respected mentor and friend M.S. Livšic)

The problem of choosing the missing entry in the partial matrix $\begin{bmatrix} A & C \\ B & ? \end{bmatrix}$ so as to minimize the rank, which had earlier been solved only under a somewhat restrictive hypothesis, is here given a general solution, with description of the full solution set.

## 1. OVERVIEW

Throughout the paper, A , B , and C are given linear transformations on finite-dimensional spaces, such that the problem of completing $\begin{bmatrix} A & C \\ B & ? \end{bmatrix}$ makes sense. More explicitly, there are given finite-dimensional spaces $H_i$ and $K_i$ $(i = 1,2)$, and linear transformations $A : H_1 \to K_1$, $B : H_1 \to K_2$, $C : H_2 \to K_1$; we may choose $D : H_2 \to K_2$ freely, resulting in $T(D) = \begin{bmatrix} A & C \\ B & D \end{bmatrix} : H \to K$ (here $H = H_1 \oplus H_2$ and $K = K_1 \oplus K_2$) ; it may be demanded that the choice be such as to give T(D) some extremal property.

For example, one such problem has all spaces Hilbert spaces and the objective is to minimize $\|T(D)\|$ . This problem is treated in [5] and other papers; the history is summarized in [6], Sec. 8.

In the present paper, the spaces have only the structure of finite-dimensional linear spaces and the objective

* The author thanks NSERC of Canada for financial support, and the Indian Statistical Institute Delhi Centre, where this work was begun.

is to minimize rank(T(D)) . A complete description of all solutions is given.

This problem was solved in the special case called "complementable" by G. Marsaglia and G.P. Styan [7], following preliminary results by others [4]; see also [3]. The answers in the general case can be cast in a similar form. The key concept is the "Schur compression" introduced by T. Ando [1], building on ideas of E.V. Haynsworth.

## 2. STATEMENT OF RESULTS

The point of the theorem to be presented is the same as in the case treated by Marsaglia and Styan: we observe in the example $\begin{bmatrix} 1 & 1 \\ 1 & 1 \end{bmatrix}$ that $\operatorname{rank}\left(\begin{bmatrix} A & C \\ B & D \end{bmatrix}\right)$ can be strictly less than $\operatorname{rank}\left(\begin{bmatrix} A & C \\ B & 0 \end{bmatrix}\right)$, and we seek to keep track of the extent of such reduction.

For simplicity, the following will be assumed throughout.

CONVENTION. *Assume* $\operatorname{null}(A) \cap \operatorname{null}(B) = 0$ . *Assume* $\operatorname{range}(A) + \operatorname{range}(C) = H_1$ .

I said I would solve the problem in general, and this Convention may seem to be reneging on that promise. Not so: the null-space of $\begin{bmatrix} A \\ B \end{bmatrix}$, even if non-zero, lies in null(T(E)) for all E , so it has no bearing on the problem; similarly for the eventuality that range([A C]) might be less than all of $H_1$ . It is a different sort of restriction which has significance, and I now name it.

DEFINITION 2.1. *The problem* $\begin{bmatrix} A & C \\ B & ? \end{bmatrix}$ *is 'complementable' in case* $\operatorname{range}(C) \subseteq \operatorname{range}(A)$ *and* $\operatorname{null}(B) \supseteq \operatorname{null}(A)$ .

The complementable case, then, is that in which Bnull(A) is zero and $C^{-1}\operatorname{range}(A)$ is total. The present treatment, in which the assumption of complementability is not made, involves keeping track of the two possibly proper subspaces

$B\,\mathrm{null}(A) \subseteq K_2$ and $C^{-1}\mathrm{range}(A) \subseteq H_1$ .

DEFINITION 2.2. *Given a linear transformation* $X : L \to M$ , *a transformation* $Y : M \to L$ *is called a 'relative inverse' of* $X$ *in case* $XYX = X$ , *and then it may be written* $Y = X^{\dagger}$ .

I avoid the term "generalized inverse" because it has too many meanings; this is the one sometimes called "{1} generalized inverse" [2], pp. 117-118. The term "relative" in this connection is suggested by usage going back to J. von Neumann, e.g., [8], Sec. 3.

Starting from the set-up described above, the most natural definition of Schur compression is this:

DEFINITION 2.3. *We say that* $D : K_1 \to K_2$ *is a 'Schur compression' of* $\begin{bmatrix} A & C \\ B & ? \end{bmatrix}$ *in case* $D = BA^{\dagger}C$ *for some relative inverse* $A^{\dagger}$ *of* $A$ .

PROPOSITION 2.1. *If* $D$ *is a Schur compression of* $\begin{bmatrix} A & C \\ B & ? \end{bmatrix}$ *and if* $M$ *and* $N$ *are linear transformations* $H_2 \to K_2$ *such that*

$$\mathrm{null}(M) \supseteq \mathrm{null}(C) \qquad \mathrm{null}(N) \supseteq C^{-1}\mathrm{range}(A)$$

$$\mathrm{range}(M) \subseteq B\,\mathrm{null}(A) \qquad \mathrm{range}(N) \subseteq \mathrm{range}(B) ,$$

*then* $D + M + N$ *is a Schur compression too.*

*For* $D$ *to be a Schur compression it is necessary and sufficient that*

(i) $\mathrm{null}(D) \supseteq \mathrm{null}(C)$ ,

(ii) $\mathrm{range}(D) \subseteq \mathrm{range}(B)$ , *and*

(iii) *the relation* $Ax = Cy$ *implies* $Dy = Bx \bmod B\,\mathrm{null}(A)$ .

It is already clear from the definitions that any Schur compression has properties (i), (ii), (iii). The other statements of the Proposition could be proved at once, and they embody the main ideas to be used. However, since I will not need to invoke the conclusions below, I omit these proofs; the ideas will reappear in the proof of (vi) => (iii) in Theorem 2.1.

The principal content of this theorem may be summed up very simply. The rank of $T(D)$ is minimized when $D$ is a Schur compression, any Schur compression. The optimizing $D$ is "essentially" unique — which means, as was hinted above, that it is unique on $C^{-1}\text{range}(A)$, modulo $B\text{null}(A)$. But the statement of the results as given in the Theorem and in supplementary propositions later, is longer and more complicated, due to including explicit details, alternative formulations, and some supplementary information.

THEOREM 2.1. *Given* $\begin{bmatrix} A & C \\ B & ? \end{bmatrix}$, *the following conditions on* $D$ *are equivalent:*

(i) $\text{rank}(T(D)) \leqq \text{rank}(T(E))$ *for all* $E$ ;

(ii) *for no* $E$ *is* $\text{null}(T(E)) \supsetneqq \text{null}(T(D))$ ;

(iii) *for a pre-assigned relative inverse* $A^{\dagger}$ *of* $A$, *there exist* $M$ *and* $N$ *such that*

$$\text{range}(M) \subseteq B\text{null}(A) \qquad \text{null}(N) \supseteq C^{-1}\text{range}(A)$$
$$D = BA^{\dagger}C + M + N \; ; \tag{2.1}$$

(iv) *there exists a relative inverse* $A^{\dagger}$ *of* $A$ *and there exist* $M$ *and* $N$ *such that* (2.1) *holds;*

(v) *for any* $x$, $y$ *such that* $Ax = Cy$ *there exists* $z$ *such that* $Az = Ax$, $Dy = Bz$ ;

(vi) *the relation* $Ax = Cy$ *implies* $Dy = Bx \bmod B\text{null}(A)$ ;

(vii) *for any* $\begin{bmatrix} x \\ y \end{bmatrix} \in \text{null}([A \;\; C])$ *there is a* $v \in \text{null}(A)$ *such that* $\begin{bmatrix} x+v \\ y \end{bmatrix} \in \text{null}\left(\begin{bmatrix} A & C \\ B & D \end{bmatrix}\right)$.

Other equivalent conditions could be adduced. Indeed, most of the conditions stated are not self-dual, but (i) is, so the duals of the others would also be equivalent.

PROPOSITION 2.2. *Under the hypotheses of Theorem* 2.1,

*the minimal value is* $\operatorname{rank}(T(D)) = \operatorname{rank}\left(\begin{bmatrix} A \\ B \end{bmatrix}\right) + \operatorname{rank}([A \quad C])$ $- \operatorname{rank}(A)$ .

PROPOSITION 2.3. *In order for the minimizing choices of* D *in Theorem* 2.1 *to be exactly the Schur compressions, it is necessary and sufficient that* $\operatorname{null}(C) = 0$ *and* $\operatorname{range}(B) = K_2$ .

The following gives an attractive strengthening of the assertion that conditions (ii) and its dual are among those equivalent to (i) in the Theorem.

PROPOSITION 2.4. *Given any* E *completing* $\begin{bmatrix} A & C \\ B & ? \end{bmatrix}$, *there exists* D *satisfying the equivalent conditions of Theorem* 2.1 *and such that* $\operatorname{null}(T(E)) \subseteq \operatorname{null}(T(D))$ , $\operatorname{range}(T(E)) \supseteq \operatorname{range}(T(D))$ .

## 3. PROOFS

PROOF OF THEOREM 2.1. It is immediate that (i) → (ii) and that (iii) => (iv). Condition (vi) is a mere rephrasing of (v), while (vii) differs only by renaming some vectors, therefore (v) <=> (vi) <=> (vii).

As to (iv) => (vi): Let $A^\dagger$ , M , N , x , y have the stated properties. Since $y \in C^{-1}\operatorname{range}(A)$ , then, $Ny = 0$ ; also $My = 0 \bmod B\operatorname{null}(A)$ . So to prove $Dy = Bx \bmod B\operatorname{null}(A)$ we have only to check that $BA^\dagger Cy - Bx \in B\operatorname{null}(A)$ . Now $BA^\dagger Cy = BA^\dagger Ax$ , and $A^\dagger Ax - x \in \operatorname{null}(A)$ by general properties of relative inverses; that does it.

The interest of the theorem is in the remaining three implications.

As to (ii) => (vii): Suppose that (vii) fails for a specific x , y , and let us concoct E violating (ii). Notice that there is no $w \in H_1$ making $\begin{bmatrix} w \\ y \end{bmatrix} \in \operatorname{null}(T(D))$ , for if there were we could set $v = w - x$ in (vii) and $v \in \operatorname{null}(A)$ would be automatic. That is, $y \notin \operatorname{span}(H_1, \operatorname{null}(T(D)))$ ; so we can require a rank-one transformation $H \to K_2$ to annihilate that subspace and still take y to a prescribed vector. Let, then, H be rank-one $H_2 \to K_2$ such that null([0 H]) $\supseteq$ null(T(D)) and Hy = Bx + Dy . Define E = D − H . Clearly null(T(E)) $\supseteq$ null(T(D)) ; on the other hand, $\begin{bmatrix} x \\ y \end{bmatrix} \in$ null(T(E))\ null(T(D)) . The construction has succeeded.

As to (v) => (i): Let $P$ be any complement to $C^{-1}$range(A) in $H_2$ ; then surely T(E) takes it one-one onto a complement to range(A) in range([A C]) . Thus for any E at all,

$$\text{(3.1)} \qquad \text{range}(T(E)) \supseteq \text{range}\left(\begin{bmatrix} A \\ B \end{bmatrix}\right) \dot{+} T(E)P ,$$

with dimensionalities on the right not being dependent on choice of E , i.e.,

$$\text{rank}(T(E)) \geqq \text{rank}(A) + \dim(B\text{null}(A)) + \dim P .$$

It will now be enough to show that equality holds in (3.1) if E is taken to be D for which (v) holds.

Accordingly, consider an arbitrary element $\begin{bmatrix} A & C \\ B & D \end{bmatrix}\begin{bmatrix} x \\ y \end{bmatrix}$ of range(T(D)) . By construction, we can take $w \in P$ so that Cw = Ax + Cy mod range(A) , which in turn means we can take $u \in H_1$ so that Cw = A(x+u) + Cy . Apply the hypothesized condition (v) to vectors x+u , w−y : There exists z such that Az = A(x+u) = C(w−y) , Bz = D(w−y) . We have obtained

$$\begin{bmatrix} A & C \\ B & D \end{bmatrix}\begin{bmatrix} x \\ y \end{bmatrix} = \begin{bmatrix} A \\ B \end{bmatrix}(x-z) + T(D)\begin{bmatrix} 0 \\ w \end{bmatrix} ,$$

and the latter sum is of the sort represented on the right in (3.1). This was the aim.

As to (vi) => (iii): Given $A^\dagger$ , and given D satisfying (vi), we are to examine the difference $D - BA^\dagger C$ . Call it Δ . The point is to prove that Δ takes $C^{-1}$range(A) into Bnull(A) ; for then, letting again $P$ denote any complement to $C^{-1}$range(A) in $H_2$ , we have only to set N = 0 on $C^{-1}$range(A) and N = Δ on $P$ and then set M = Δ − N , and with these specifications $D = BA^\dagger C + M + N$ will meet the requirements.

To this end, let $y \in C^{-1}$range(A) and let us see where Δy lies. We choose x so Cy = Ax ; by general properties of relative inverses, we are free to choose $x \in \text{range}(A^\dagger)$, and then $BA^\dagger Cy = BA^\dagger Ax = Bx$. But we assumed (vi): $Dy = Bx \bmod B\,\text{null}(A)$. That means exactly that the difference $\Delta y$ is in $B\,\text{null}(A)$ as required.

The theorem is proved.

PROOF OF PROPOSITION 2.2. Let us define integers $r_A$, $r_{AB}$, ... by looking at dimensionalities of increasing subspaces of $K_1$, $H_1$, and $H_2$. (The reader who goes through this will appreciate my choice of subscripts, so I will not pause to motivate it.)

Let $r_B = \dim \text{null}(A)$. Let $r_{AC} = \dim(\text{range}(C) \cap A\,\text{null}(B))$, which also equals $\dim(A^{-1}\text{range}(C) \cap \text{null}(B))$. Let $r_A + r_{AC} = \dim \text{null}(B)$. Let $r_{ABC} + r_{AC} = \dim(\text{range}(A) \cap \text{range}(C))$. Let $r_{AB} = \dim \text{range}(B) - \dim(BA^{-1}\text{range}(C))$. Finally, let $r_C = \dim H_2 - \dim(C^{-1}\text{range}(A))$.

One checks (somewhat laboriously) without using the Theorem that

$$\text{rank}(A) = r_A + r_{AB} + r_{AC} + r_{ABC}$$

$$\text{rank}\left(\begin{bmatrix} A \\ B \end{bmatrix}\right) = r_A + r_B + r_{AB} + r_{AC} + r_{ABC}$$

$$\text{rank}([A \quad C]) = r_A + r_{AB} + r_C + r_{AC} + r_{ABC}.$$

Then using the description of minimizing $D$ given by the Theorem, one calculates that

$$\text{rank}(T(D)) = r_A + r_B + r_{AB} + r_C + r_{AC} + r_{ABC},$$

in agreement with the formula stated.

REMARK. In this notation, $\text{rank}\left(\begin{bmatrix} A & C \\ B & 0 \end{bmatrix}\right)$ exceeds this minimal value by $r_{ABC}$.

PROOF OF PROPOSITION 2.3. This will not be written out. One compares the choices available for Schur compressions according to Proposition 2.1 with the choices available for minimizing $D$ according to Theorem 2.1(iii), and it turns out that $\text{null}(C)$ and $K_2/\text{range}(B)$ are the only places there can be any difference.

PROOF OF PROPOSITION 2.4. Given $E : H_2 \to K_2$, here is a construction of a $D : H_2 \to K_2$ with the properties called for.

Let $G_2$ be any complement to $G_1 = C^{-1}\text{range}(A)$ in $H_2$. Let $L_1$ be any complement to $L_2 = B\text{null}(A)$ in $K_2$. It will be convenient to decompose $T(E) = \begin{bmatrix} A & C \\ B & E \end{bmatrix}$ further according to this decomposition of the spaces, writing $\begin{bmatrix} A & C_1 & C_2 \\ B_1 & E_{11} & E_{12} \\ B_2 & E_{21} & E_{22} \end{bmatrix}$, and likewise for $T(D)$. From the theorem, $D_{11}$ is determined, but (2.1) shows that we are free to choose $D_{12} = E_{12}$, $D_{21} = E_{21}$, $D_{22} = E_{22}$, and we do.

Now we consider an arbitrary vector in $\text{null}(T(E))$. Because it is in $\text{null}([A \ \ C])$, its third component is zero, so let us write it $\begin{bmatrix} -x \\ y \\ 0 \end{bmatrix}$. We know about it that

$$Ax = C\begin{bmatrix} y \\ 0 \end{bmatrix} = C_1 y$$

$$B_1 x = E_{11} y$$

$$B_2 x = E_{21} y = D_{21} y \ .$$

We need to show it is a null-vector of $T(D)$, and for that it remains only to show that $B_1 x = D_{11} y$. But property (vi) allows us to infer from $Ax = C\begin{bmatrix} y \\ 0 \end{bmatrix}$ that $D\begin{bmatrix} y \\ 0 \end{bmatrix} = Bx \bmod L_2$, which is precisely $D_{11} y = B_1 x$.

The last conclusion of the Proposition is that $\text{range}(T(E)) \supseteq \text{range}(T(D))$. For this I will use duality (only thus can I get the benefit of the work done in studying Theorem 2.1(vi)). So consider an arbitrary left null-vector of $T(E)$. Its third component is zero, because $\text{range}(T(E)) \supseteq B\text{null}(A)$. Write it $[-\ell \ \ m \ \ 0]$; by the dual of (vi) or (vii), we can infer from $\ell A = mB$ the existence of $j$ such that $jA = 0$ and $mD_{11} = (\ell + j)C_1$. We need to show we have a left null-vector of $T(D)$, and for that it remains only to show that $mD_{11} = \ell C_1$, i.e., that $jC_1 = 0$, i.e., that $jCG_1 = 0$. But by definitions $CG_1 \subseteq \text{range}(A)$, and we know $jA = 0$; the proof is complete.

REFERENCES

1. T. Ando: Generalized Schur complements. Linear Alg. Appl. 27 (1979), 173-186.

2. A. Berman & R.J. Plemmons: Nonnegative Matrices in the Mathematical Sciences. New York, Academic Press: 1979.

3. D. Carlson & E.V. Haynsworth: Complementable and almost definite matrices. Linear Alg. Appl. 52/53 (1983), 157-176.

4. D. Carlson & E.V. Haynsworth & T. Markham: A generalization of the Schur complement by means of the Moore-Penrose inverse. SIAM J. Appl. Math. 26 (1974), 169-175.

5. Ch. Davis: An extremal problem for extensions of a sesquilinear form. Linear Alg. Appl. 13 (1976), 91-102.

6. Ch. Davis: Some dilation and representation theorems. In Proceedings Second International Symposium Functional Analysis. Kumasi (1982).

7. G. Marsaglia & G.P. Styan: Equalities and inequalities for ranks of matrices. Linear Multilinear Alg. 2 (1974), 269-292.

8. C.E. Rickart: Banach algebras with an adjoint operation. Ann. of Math. (2) 47 (1946), 528-550.

After submitting this paper I learned of extensive independent related work by I. Gohberg, M.A. Kaashoek and H.J. Woerdeman.

Department of Mathematics
University of Toronto
Toronto, Canada
M5S 1A1

Submitted: February 19, 1987

Operator Theory:
Advances and Applications, Vol. 29




# THE GENERALIZED SCHUR ALGORITHM: APPROXIMATION AND HIERARCHY

P. Dewilde and E.F.A. Deprettere

*Dedicated to Prof. M.S. Livsic on his birthday.*

The generalized Schur algorithm as applied on a (full and large) strictly positive definite matrix yields an approximative inverse, which is block-band structured (has block-band support), and is such that its inverse coincides with the original matrix on the band. In this paper we explore approximation properties of the inverse, as well as a hierarchical extension of the algorithm that leads to approximants which are more general than block-band.

## 1. INTRODUCTION

We consider a hermitian positive definite matrix $C$ of dimension $(n+1)^*(n+1)$:

$$C = \begin{bmatrix} C_{00} & C_{01} & \cdots & C_{0n} \\ C_{10} & C_{11} & \cdots & C_{1n} \\ & & \cdots & \\ C_{n0} & C_{n1} & \cdots & C_{nn} \end{bmatrix}$$

Typically $n$ will be large, and in particular situations - e.g. when $C$ is a finite element matrix - its elements will be computable but not yet computed. Desired will be an inverse $C_a^{-1}$ which approximates $C^{-1}$, and is based only on a small but judiciously chosen collection of elements in $C$. A first type of approximation which we shall explore further in this paper will have $C_a$ coinciding with $C$ on the chosen set of elements and $C_a^{-1}$ zero on their complement. Such a solution may be called an "extension" of the given set (both $C$ and $C_a$ have to positive). It has been studied by several authors in the past. In [1] the extension problem was considered for the case where the set of elements chosen has a block-band structure and the existence of solutions was considered. Since the matrix we are considering is strictly positive define, the conditions of [1] which state that certain principal submatrices must be nonsingular, will be trivially satisfied, and for any given band of data, a unique solution will exist. The solution can even be expressed in terms of entries of some of the principal submatrices and their inverses.

* This research has received partial support by the Commission of the EEC under the ESPRIT 991 program and by the IOP-IC program TEL45.009.

In this paper we shall consider the properties of factors of the inverse of $C_a$, $C_a^{-1} = L_a^{-*} L_a^{-1} = M_a^{-1} M_a^{-*}$ which have support on a "staircase set", i.e. a set of upper-triangular indices such that if $(i,j)$ belongs to it, then so do also indices of the type $(i-k, j+l)$ with $k \geqslant 0$, $l \geqslant 0$ and $j+l \geqslant i-k$. Such factors can be obtained by an algorithm which is an extension of the recursive Levinson algorithm familiar in estimation theory, in its so-called "Schur" or elimination version. The algorithm was known to Schur [2] as a careful reading of this 1917 paper will indicate, and has now found wide acceptance in the estimation context (for an early account see [3]). Its relevance for matrix inversion has been discussed by several authors [4, 5, 6, 7, 8], who have presented extensions of either its Levinson or Schur version to fit the more general context. The same algorithm, when only partially executed will yield factorizations of an extension $C_a$ and $C_a^{-1} = L_a^{-*} L_a^{-1} = M_a^{-1} M_a^{-*}$ as was shown in [9].

In the subsequent sections, we give a review of the extended Schur algorithm in its most simple expression (section 2), and proceed next to derive norm formulas relating the approximants to the original matrices (section 3).

It has been shown in the litterature [10, 11 ] that the extensions mentioned are in fact "maximal entropy' extensions w.r. to the original matrix interpreted as a covariance matrix. This result is independent of the location of the chosen elements (e.g. not block-band). Unfortunately, there is no known algorithm to compute the extension efficiently that works well for non block-band matrices. The more general case is, however, of great practical importance, e.g. for finite element analysis. In section 4 we shall relax the maximum-entropy requirement and propose a "hierarchical" extension of the extended Schur algorithm which will produce an efficient and correct approximant to $C^{-1}$.

The fact that many results from classical estimation theory or from classical interpolation theory have an equivalent matrix theory formulation should not be surprising in view of the central role that shift invariant spaces play in the two contexts. This point has been thoroughly investigated in [12]. Although we do not have to use the results of that paper explicitly, it will be clear that there are strong connections.

In order to avoid an unwielding proliferation of indices, we shall freely use signal processing diagrams which represent cascade applications of operators as illustrated in fig. 1.1

Concerning notations: matrices will generally be indicated with upper case Roman or Greek letters, their elements with the same lower case letters. Sets and spaces are generally printed in fat.

## 2. PRELIMINARIES

With the original positive definite matrix $C_g = [C_{ij}]$, $i = 0 \ldots n$, $j = 0 \ldots n$, we define the diagonal matrix $D = [C_{00} + C_{11} + \cdots + C_{nn}]$ and the normalization

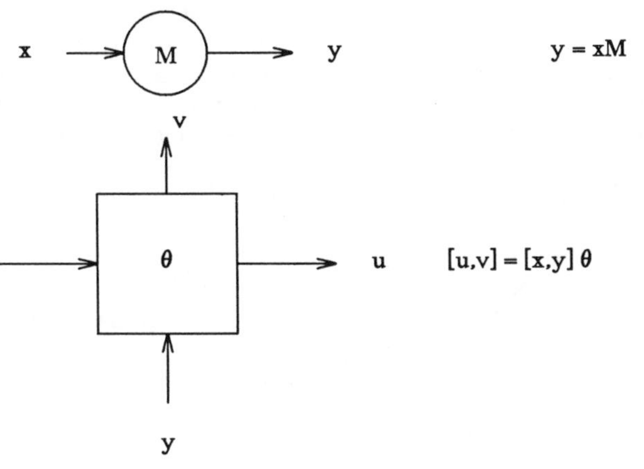


**Fig. 1.1. Illustrating the use of signal processing diagrams.**

$$C = D^{-1/2} C_g D^{-1/2} \tag{1.1}$$

We shall always suppose that the diagonal elements of $C_g$ belong to the set of elements that have to be extended, so that $D$ is well known. The computation of $C^{-1}$ is of course equivalent to the computation of $C_g^{-1}$. While this normalization is not strictly necessary, it will ease the subsequent development. Any matrix obtained as an approximation of $C$ will become an approximation to $C_g$ after denormalization with the diagonal matrices $D^{1/2} \cdots D^{1/2}$.

Next, given an $(n+1)*2(n+1)$ matrix $[\Gamma \quad \Delta]$, we shall say that it is (strictly) *admissible* if $\Gamma$ is invertible and $\Gamma\Gamma^* - \Delta\Delta^*$ is (strictly) positive definite. $[\Gamma \quad \Delta]$ will be admissible, if $S = \Gamma^{-1}\Delta$ is (strictly) contractive. Let

$$G = \begin{bmatrix} 1 & 2c_{01} & 2c_{02} & \cdots 2c_{0n} \\ 0 & 1 & 2c_{12} & \cdots 2c_{1n} \\ 0 & 0 & 1 & \cdots 2c_{2n} \\ \cdot & \cdot & \cdot & \cdots \cdot \\ 0 & 0 & 0 & \cdots 1 \end{bmatrix} \tag{2.2}$$

then

$$[\Gamma_0 \quad \Delta_0] \stackrel{\Delta}{=} \begin{bmatrix} \frac{G+1}{2} & \frac{G-1}{2} \end{bmatrix} \tag{2.3}$$

will be strictly admissible, since

$$\Gamma\Gamma^* - \Delta\Delta^* = \frac{G+G^*}{2} = C . \tag{2.4}$$

In the set of indices $[0..n] \times [0..n]$ we define the set of $\mathbf{U}$ of upper indices as

$$\mathbf{U} = \{(i,j) : j \geq i\}$$

A subset $\mathbf{S} \subset \mathbf{U}$ will be said to be a *staircase set* if it has the property that $(i+k, j-l) \in \mathbf{S}$ whenever $(i,j)$ does, $k \geq 0$, $l \geq 0$ and $i+k \leq j-l$. The complement $\mathbf{U} \backslash \mathbf{S}$ will be called $\mathbf{T}$. A staircase set and its related sets are shown in fig. 2.1.

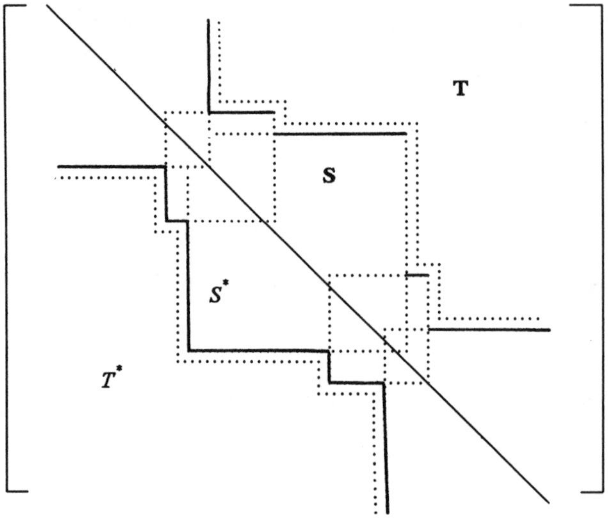


**Fig. 2.1 Staircase and related sets.**

**The Generalized Schur Algorithm.**

The generalized Schur algorithm starts up with $[\Gamma_0 \quad \Delta_0]$ and an initial staircase set which reduces to the diagonal. It proceeds recursively as follows:

Let $[\Gamma_{k-1} \quad \Delta_{k-1}]$ be strictly admissible with $\Gamma_{k-1}$ and $\Delta_{k-1}$ upper triangular and such that the support of $\Delta_{k-1}$ is on $\mathbf{T}_{k-1} = \mathbf{U} \backslash \mathbf{S}_{k-1}$ the complement of some staircase set. Let $\mathbf{S}_k$ be a staircase that is one element larger than $\mathbf{S}_{k-1}$: $\mathbf{S}_{k-1} \subset \mathbf{S}_k$ and $\mathbf{S}_k \backslash \mathbf{S}_{k-1} = (i,j)$. Let

$$\rho_i^j = -\frac{\delta_{ij}^{(k-1)}}{\gamma_{ii}^{(k-1)}} \tag{2.5}$$

then $|\rho_i^j| < 1$ because

(1) $\gamma_{ii}^{(k-1)}$ is non-zero since it is a diagonal entry of an invertible upper-triangular matrix, and

(2) $\delta_{ij}^{(k-1)}/\gamma_{ii}^{(k-1)}$ is the $(i,j)^{\text{th}}$ entry in $S_{k-1} = \Gamma_{k-1}^{-1}\Delta_{k-1}$ which is strictly contractive by hypothesis.

Consider the $2(n+1)*2(n+1)$ matrix $\theta_i^j$ defined by:

$$(\theta_i^j)_{ii} = \frac{1}{\sqrt{1-|\rho_i^j|^2}}, \quad (\theta_i^j)_{i,n+j} = \frac{\rho_i^j}{\sqrt{1-|\rho_i^j|^2}} \tag{2.6a}$$

$$(\theta_i^j)_{n+j,i} = \frac{(\rho_i^j)^*}{\sqrt{1-|\rho_i^j|^2}}, \quad (\theta_i^j)_{n+j,n+j} = \frac{1}{\sqrt{1-|\rho_i^j|^2}} \tag{2.6b}$$

$$(\theta_i^j)_{k,l} = 0 \text{ for } k \neq l \text{ otherwise} \tag{2.6c}$$

$$(\theta_i^j)_{k,k} = 1 \text{ otherwise} \tag{2.6d}$$

and let

$$[\Gamma_k \quad \Delta_k] = [\Gamma_{k-1} \quad \Delta_{k-1}]\theta_i^j. \tag{2.7}$$

$$J = \begin{bmatrix} I_n & 0 \\ 0 & -I_n \end{bmatrix} \tag{2.8}$$

with $I_n$ the $(n+1)*(n+1)$ unit matrix. Then:

(1) $\theta_i^j$ is J-unitary, i.e.

$$\theta_i^j J (\theta_i^j)^* = J \tag{2.9}$$

(2) $[\Gamma_k \quad \Delta_k]$ is strictly admissible with $\Gamma_k$ and $\Delta_k$ upper triangular.

(3) The support of $\Delta_k$ is on $\mathbf{T}_k$.

$\theta_i^j$ is in fact an "embedding" of the elementary J-unitary matrix

$$\frac{1}{\sqrt{1-|\rho_i^j|^2}} \begin{bmatrix} 1 & \rho_i^j \\ (\rho_i^j)^* & 1 \end{bmatrix}, \quad J = \begin{bmatrix} 1 & 0 \\ 0 & -1 \end{bmatrix}. \tag{2.10}$$

It eliminates $\delta_{ij}^{(k-1)}$ against $\gamma_{ii}^{(k-1)}$. Due to the staircase structure of $\Delta_{k-1}$, this elimination process will not produce any new fill-ins and the resulting $[\Gamma_k \quad \Delta_k]$ is ready for a new step in the procedure. After some $k$ steps of the algorithm, an overall elimination matrix $\Theta_k$ results which is such that:

$$[\Gamma_0 \quad \Delta_0]\,\Theta_k = [\Gamma_k \quad \Delta_k] \tag{2.11}$$

$$\Theta_k = \vec{\Pi}\,\theta_i^j. \tag{2.12}$$

Let

$$\Theta_k = \begin{bmatrix} \theta_{11} & \theta_{12} \\ \\ \theta_{21} & \theta_{22} \end{bmatrix} \tag{2.13}$$

be a block decomposition of $\Theta_k$ into $(n+1)*(n+1)$ blocks. Then the following properties hold:

1. $\Theta_k$ is J-unitary as a product of J-unitary elementary matrices.
2. supp $\theta_{11} \subset \mathbf{S}_k^*$, supp $\theta_{21} \subset \mathbf{S}_k^*$, supp $\theta_{12} \subset \mathbf{S}_k$, supp $\theta_{22} \subset \mathbf{S}_k$.
3. $\theta_{11}$ and $\theta_{22}$ are invertible.
4. Diagonal elements in $\theta_{12}$ and $\theta_{21}$ are zero.

(A proof of properties 2-4 follows immediately from the recursive step described above). A matrix $\Theta_k$ which has properties (1)-(4) we shall call $\mathbf{S}_k$ *-based*. We shall need the following characterization for it:

**Proposition 1.** Let $\theta$ be J-unitary, then the block-decomposition of $\theta$ into $(n+1)*(n+1)$ blocks has the following form:

$$\theta = \begin{bmatrix} \frac{1+G^*}{2} L^{-*} & \frac{1-G}{2} M^{-1} \\ \\ \frac{1-G^*}{2} L^{-*} & \frac{1+G}{2} M^{-1} \end{bmatrix} \tag{2.14}$$

where $\frac{G+G^*}{2} = LL^* = M^*M$ is strictly positive definite. If, in addition, $\theta$ is $\mathbf{S}$-based, then $G$, $L$, $M$ are upper triangular, the diagonal entries of $G$ are 1, and supp $L^{-1} \subset \mathbf{S}$, supp $M^{-1} \subset \mathbf{S}$.

**Proof.** We first establish that $\theta_{11} + \theta_{21}$ and $\theta_{22} + \theta_{12}$ are non-singular. For any vector $x \in C^{n+1}$ we have

$$\|(\theta_{11} + \theta_{21})x\| \geqslant \Big| \|\theta_{11}x\| - \|\theta_{12}x\| \Big|$$

by the triangle inequality for Euclidean norms and next, because of J-unitary

$$\|(\theta_{11} + \theta_{21})x\| \leqslant \Big| \sqrt{\|x\|^2 + \|\theta_{12}x\|^2} - \|\theta_{12}x\| \Big|$$

The latter expression can be zero only when $\|x\| = 0$. This shows that $(\theta_{11} + \theta_{21})$ is non-singular. A similar proof applies to $(\theta_{22} + \theta_{12})$. The rest of assertions is now immediate in view of the hypothesis, and some elementary algebra. In particular, we have

$$L_k^{-*} = (\theta_{11} + \theta_{21}) \, , M_k^{-1} = (\theta_{12} + \theta_{22})$$

from which the assertions about the supports follow. See [9] for a similar proof in a different context.

□

We summarize the results of the generalized Schur algorithm in the following theorem:

**Theorem 1.** Let $[\Gamma_0 \quad \Delta_0] = \left[ \frac{G+1}{2} \quad \frac{G-1}{2} \right]$, and let $\mathbf{T}_k = \mathbf{U} \backslash \mathbf{S}_k$ be a staircase set. Then there exists a J-unitary matrix

$$\theta_k = \begin{bmatrix} \frac{1+G_k^*}{2} L_k^{-*} & \frac{1-G_k}{2} M_k^{-1} \\ \\ \frac{1-G_k^*}{2} L_k^{-*} & \frac{1+G_k}{2} M_k^{-1} \end{bmatrix} \tag{2.15}$$

such that

$$(1) \quad [\Gamma_0 \quad \Delta_0]\theta_k = [\Gamma_k \quad \Delta_k] \tag{2.16}$$

is admissible with $\Gamma_k, \Delta_k$ upper triangular and supp $\Delta_k \subset \mathbf{T}_k$.

(2) supp $L_k^{-1} \subset \mathbf{S}_k$, supp $M_k^{-1} \subset \mathbf{S}_k$, and $G_k$ is upper triangular with diagonal entries 1 (i.e. $\theta_k$ is $\mathbf{S}_k$ - based ).

□

**Theorem 2.** Let $G$ , $G_k$ , $\mathbf{S}_k$ be as in Theorem 1. Then for all $(i,j) \in \mathbf{S}_k$ we have that $(G-G_k)_{i,j} = 0$.

**Proof.** From (2.17) we have

$$\left[ \frac{G_k+1}{2} \quad \frac{G_k-1}{2} \right] \theta_k = [L_k \quad 0] \tag{2.17}$$

Subtracting (2.17) from (2.16) we obtain:

$$\left( \frac{G-G_k}{2} \right) [L_k^{-*} \quad M_k^{-1}] = [\Gamma_k - L_k \quad \Delta_k] \tag{2.18}$$

and hence:

$$G-G_k = 2\Delta_k M_k \tag{2.19}$$

In the product $\Delta_k M_k$ the two matrices are upper-triangular, and hence also the result. Since the entries of $\Delta_k$ are zero on $\mathbf{S}_k$, they will remain so after multiplication with the upper triangular matrix $M_k$.

□

Let

$$C_k = \frac{1}{2}(G_k + G_k^*) \tag{2.20}$$

then by theorem 2, $C$ and $C_k$ coincide on $\mathbf{S}_k \cup \mathbf{S}_k^*$. Moreover

$$C_k^{-1} = L_k^{-*}L_k^{-1} = M_k^{-1}M_k^{-*} \tag{2.21}$$

so that supp $C_k^{-1} \subset \mathbf{S}_k \cup \mathbf{S}_k^*$. It follows that $C_k$ is an extension for $C$ as defined in the introduction.

## 3. APPROXIMATION THEORY

The approximation theory for $L_k$ and $C_k$ follows closely and generalizes in certain respects the theory for the classical Schur algorithm as discussed in [13]. Let us suppose that we have reached the stage characterized by the hypotheses of theorems 1 and 2:

$$[\Gamma_0 \quad \Delta_0]\theta_k = [\Gamma_k \quad \Delta_k] \tag{3.1}$$

with supp $\Delta_k \subset \mathbf{T}_k = \mathbf{U}\backslash\mathbf{S}_k$ and $\theta_k$ a $\mathbf{S}_k$-based matrix, given by (2.15). Assume the following definitions:

$\mathbf{H}_k$ the linear space of upper triangular matrices with support on $\mathbf{S}_k$

$\mathbf{M}_k$ the linear space of upper triangular matrices with support on $\mathbf{T}_k$

$P_0$ an operator on $(n+1)*(n+1)$ matrices which projects a matrix on its diagonal: $P_0A = a_{00} \oplus a_{11} \oplus \cdots \oplus a_{nn}$ with $\oplus$ the direct sum of entries.

$<F_1,F_2>_C$ the "matrix inner product" defined by $<F_1,F_2>_C = P_0(F_1CF_2^*)$ for two $(n+1)*(n+1)$ matrices $F_i$.

$(F_1,F_2)_C$ $= \frac{1}{(n+1)}$ trace $(F_1CF_2^*)$ an inner product on the linear space of $(n+1)*(n+1)$ matrices.

Notice that, with $C = LL^*$, $\|F\|_C$ is actually the Hilbert-Schmidt or Frobenius-norm of $FL$:

$$\|F\|_C = \|FL\|_{\text{Frob}} = \|FL\|_I \;. \tag{3.2}$$

We have the following sequence of propositions:

**Proposition 2.** $\mathbf{M}_k$ is invariant for pre- and postmultiplication with upper-triangular matrices.

**Proof.** consider e.g. $RA$ where $R$ is uppertriangular and $A \in \mathbf{M}_k$. The i$^{th}$ row of $RA$ is given by:

$$[RA]_{i.} = \sum_{k=i}^{n} r_{ik} A_{k.}$$

and hence:

$$\text{supp}[RA]_{i.} \subset \bigcup_{k=i}^{n} \text{supp}\, A_{k.} \subset \text{supp}\, A_{i.}$$

□

**Remark:** For any element $(i,j) \in \mathbf{T}$ define the horizontal distance to $\mathbf{S}$ as:

$$h(i,j) = \max\{j-k \; : \; (i,k) \in \mathbf{T}\}$$

and vertical distance to $\mathbf{S}$ as:

$$v(i,j) = \max\{k-i \; : \; (k,j) \in \mathbf{T}\}$$

and let the *characteristic matrix* $T$ of $\mathbf{T}$ be defined as follows: if $h(i,j) = v(i,j)$ then $t_{ij} = 1$ else $t_{ij} = 0$. Then $T$ generates $\mathbf{M}$ (the linear space of matrices with support on $\mathbf{T}$) in the sense that any matrix $A \in \mathbf{M}$ can be represented by $A = R_1 T R_2$ with $R_1$ and $R_2$ upper triangular matrices. In fact, any space of triangular matrices which is invariant for right and left multiplication with upper triangular matrices can be so represented.

**Proposition 3.** For all $F_1, F_2 \in \mathbf{H}_k$ one has

$$<F_1, F_2>_C = <F_1, F_2>_{C_k} \tag{3.3}$$

and hence a fortiori

$$(F_1, F_2)_C = (F_1, F_2)_{C_k}. \tag{3.4}$$

**Proof.**

$$<F_1, F_2>_C - <F_1, F_2>_{C_k} = P_0 F_1 \Delta_k M_k F_2^* + P_0(F_2 \Delta_k M_k F_1^*)^*$$

By proposition 2, $F_1 \Delta_k M_k \in \mathbf{M}_k$. When multiplied with $F_2^*$ whose support is on

$\mathbf{S}_k^*$, the diagonal entries will be zero due to the complementarity of the supports. Similarly for the second term.

□

**Corollary:** $\|L_k^{-1}\|_C = 1$.

**Proposition 4.** (Reproducing Kernel Property). For any $F \in \mathbf{H}_k$ it holds that

$$<F\ ,(P_0 L_k^{-1})L_k^{-1}>_C = P_0 F. \tag{3.5}$$

**Proof:** by proposition 3:

$$<F ,(P_0 L_k^{-1})L_k^{-1}>_C = <F\ ,(P_0 L_k^{-1})L_k^{-1}>_{C_k}$$

$$= P_0(F\ C_k\ L_k^{-*}(P_0 L_k^{-1})) = P_0(F\ L_k(P_0\ L_k^{-1}))$$

Since all factors are now upper-triangular, the latter evaluates to $P_0 F$.

□

Let $\Pi_k$ be the orthonormal projection on $\mathbf{H}_k$ w.r. to the $(\ .\ )_C$.

**Proposition 5.** Let $F$ be upper triangular and let $G \in \mathbf{H}_k$. Then one has:

$$<F\ ,G>_C = <\Pi_k F\ ,G>_C \tag{3.6}$$

(as would be the case for the usual I.P.).

**Proof.** Let $R = F - \Pi_k F$. For all $H \in \mathbf{H}_k$ we have then $(R ,H)_C = 0$. Specialize $H$ to $e_{ij}$ with $(i,j) \in \mathbf{S}_k$ and

$$(e_{ij})_{ij} = 1\ ,\ \text{zero otherwise.}$$

It follows that $(RC)_{ij} = 0$. Hence $RC = L_s^* + \Delta$ for some strictly upper $L_S$ and a $\Delta$ with support on $\mathbf{T}_k$. We now have:

$$<R\ ,G>_C = P_0\ L_s^*\ G^* + P_0\ \Delta G^* = 0 \tag{3.7}$$

because the first term is obviously strictly lower triangular, and the diagonal elements of the second are zero since the support of $G$ is complementary to the support of $\Delta$.

□

**Theorem 2.** Of all the matrices in $\mathbf{H}_k$, $(P_0 L_k^{-1})L_k^{-1}$ is the closest to $(P_0 L^{-1})L^{-1}$ in $\|.\|_C$. The error is given by:

$$<E\ ,E>_C \;=\; P_0L^{-2} - P_0L_k^{-2} \tag{3.8}$$

where $E = (P_0L^{-1})L^{-1} - (P_0L_k^{-1})L_k^{-1}$.

**Proof.** We show that

$$\Pi_k(P_0L^{-1})L^{-1} = (P_0L_k^{-1})L_k^{-1} \tag{3.9}$$

Since both sides are in $\mathbf{H}_k$, it suffices to show that for all $F \in \mathbf{H}_k$ it is true that

$$(\Pi_k(P_0L^{-1})L^{-1}\ ,F)_C = ((P_0L_k^{-1})L_k^{-1}\ ,F)_C$$

By proposition 5

$$\begin{aligned} <\Pi_k(P_0L^{-1})L^{-1}\ ,F>_C &= <(P_0L^{-1})L^{-1}\ ,F>_C \\ &= (P_0L^{-1})P_0(L^*F^*) \\ &= P_0F^* \end{aligned}$$

Since the diagonal entries of $L$ are real. By proposition 4, the second member evaluates to the same quantity.

□

As a consequence of Theorem 2, the Frobenius norm of the relative approximation error

$$\| I - (P_0L)(P_0L_k^{-1})L_k^{-1}L \|_{\text{Frob}}$$

can now easily be evaluated. Let, for each row $i$, $k_i$ be the largest index such that $(i, k_i) \in \mathbf{S}_k$. We have from the Schur algorithm:

$$(L_k^{-1})_{ii} = \prod_{j=i+1}^{k_i} \frac{1}{\sqrt{1-|\rho_i^j|^2}} \tag{3.10}$$

If the Schur algorithm is continued until all entries in the $\Delta_k$ matrix have been eliminated (say after $N$ steps), then $\Delta_N = 0$ and

$$[\Gamma_0 \quad \Delta_0]\Theta_N = [\Gamma_N \quad 0] \tag{3.11}$$

so that $C = \Gamma_N\Gamma_N^* = L_N L_N^*$, and hence

$$\Gamma_N = L_N = L\ . \tag{3.12}$$

It follows that

$$L_{ii}^{-1} = \prod_{j=i+1}^{n} \frac{1}{\sqrt{1 - |\rho_i^j|^2}} \tag{3.13}$$

where the $\{\rho_i^j\}$ now form a complete Schur parametrization of $C$. We have:

$$\frac{L_{ii}^2}{(L_k)_{ii}^2} = \prod_{j=(k_i+1)}^{n} (1 - |\rho_i^j|^2) \tag{3.14}$$

and finally:

$$< I - (P_0 L)(P_0 L_k^{-1}) L_k^{-1} L >_I = \bigoplus_{j=k_i+1}^{n} (1 - |\rho_i^j|^2) \tag{3.15}$$

$$\| I - (P_0 L)(P_0 L_k^{-1}) L_k^{-1} L \|_{\text{Frob}} = \sqrt{1 - \frac{1}{(n+1)} \sum_{i=1}^{n} \prod_{j=k_i+1}^{n} (1 - |\rho_i^j|^2)} \tag{3.16}$$

Since the $\rho_i^j$ that have been neglected are presumably small, the error will be small as well. It can be shown easily that using $L_k$ as an approximant to $L$ will result in a close approximation of $C_k$ to $C$ as well (it is better to approximate the square root of a positive definite matrix than to approximate the matrix itself directly).

### Matrix Fraction Descriptions

Let

$$\Theta_k^{-1} = \begin{bmatrix} A_k & B_k \\ C_k & D_k \end{bmatrix}. \tag{3.17}$$

Then the following holds:

**Theorem 3.** Let $S$ be an arbitrary contractive matrix with support on $\mathbf{T}_k$ and let

$$S_i = [A_k + S\, C_k]^{-1} [B_k + S\, D_k] \tag{3.18}$$

$$G_S = (I + S_i)(I - S_i)^{-1} \tag{3.19}$$

then $C_S = \dfrac{G_S + G_S^*}{2}$ is a positive definite extension of $C$ on $\mathbf{S}$. Conversely, any such extension can be represented in this way.

**Proof.** Since $\Theta_k^{-1} = J \Theta_k^* J$ we have that supp $(A_k) =$ supp $(B_k) = \mathbf{S}_k$ and supp $(C_k) =$ supp $(D_k) = \mathbf{S}_k^*$. Hence $S_k C_k$ and $S_k D_k$ are strictly upper-triangular, and $A_k + S_k C_k$ is seen to be invertible, since the diagonal of $A_k$ is free of zeros. From J-orthogonality of $\Theta_k^{-1}$, it follows that $A_k C_k^* = B_k D_k^*$ and hence:

$$S_i = A_k^{-1} B_k + A_k^{-1}(1 + SC_k A_k)^{-1} S_k D_k^{-*} \tag{3.20}$$

$$= (G_k + 1)^{-1}(G_k - 1) + \Delta_1 \tag{3.21}$$

where supp $\Delta_1 \subset \mathbf{T}_k$, since supp $S_k \subset \mathbf{T}_k$ and the right and left factors of $S_k$ in (3.20) are upper triangular. Hence:

$$G_S - G_k = \Delta_2 \tag{3.22}$$

with $\Delta_2 \in \mathbf{T}_k$, in fact:

$$\Delta_2 = (G_k + 1)[1 - \Delta_1 \frac{G_k + 1}{2}]^{-1} \Delta_1 \left( \frac{G_k + 1}{2} \right). \tag{3.23}$$

This shows that $G_S$ coincides with $G_k$ and hence with $G$ on $\mathbf{S}$. Hence also $C$ and $C_S$ will coincide on $\mathbf{S}_k \cup \mathbf{S}_k^*$.

Conversely, it will suffice to take

$$S = S_k = \Gamma_k^{-1} \Delta_k^{-1} \tag{3.24}$$

to obtain $G = G_S$ by (3.18) and (3.19). The Schur algorithm yields a parametrization that is only dependent on the elements of $C$ that lay in $\mathbf{S}_k$. Hence, any extension of $G$ will give the same elimination matrix $\Theta_k$, and remainders $\Gamma_k$ . $\Delta_k$ for which (3.24) will be contractive.

□

## 4. HIERARCHICAL REDUCTION

A close look at the elimination algorithm of section 2 shows that the Schur approximation $C_a$ to a given matrix $C$ necessarily will be based on a staircase set $\mathbf{T}$ and will give an extension of the elements of $C$ defined on a set of type $\mathbf{U} \backslash \mathbf{T}$. Very often, however, the desired form of the approximation will not have a bandstructure. It has been shown [10] that the general maximum entropy approximation for that case will still have the corresponding entries in $C_a$ matching with $C$ and the complementary entries in $C_a^{-1}$ zero. It will not be possible to obtain this approximation with a straightforward algorithm like the extended Schur algorithm presented earlier. It has been shown [14] that a solution to the general case may even fail to exist.

Experience with the Toeplitz case indicates that finding general extensions is indeed very hard. In order to obtain solutions with low complexity for the more general case, we shall have to be satisfied with close approximations, which, however, will not be of the maximum entropy type. An extension of the theory developed so far will provide for the necessary machinery.

In order not to burden the exposition with unnecessary detail, we shall deal with a prototype case that in itself has already a high degree of generality. Suppose that the entries in $C$ are clustered first in blocks in such a way that only blocks on the main block-diagonal and the first off-diagonal blocks are relevant. Next, suppose that between adjacent blocks of type $C_{ii}$ , $C_{i,i+1}$ , $C_{i+1,i+1}$ a reordering of rows and columns is again possible such that after reordering only elements close to the main diagonal will be significant. (This case will occur e.g. when the matrix $C$ represents entries for a finite element modelling problem where the finite elements are scattered in a two dimensional plane. It will not be possible to index the elements in such a way that closeby elements also have close indices. However, the two dimensional space can first be subdivided into, say, vertical stripes so that only elements in adjacent stripes have a significant influence on each other. The indexing scheme will assign indices to such elements so that stripes correspond to blocks in the matrix. Between adjacent stripes, however, a reordering will be necessary in order to account for horizontal proximity).

Let $C = [C_{ij}]_{i,j=0..n}$ be a positive definite block matrix (with diagonal entries equal to one). Let $C_{ii} = L_i L_i^* = M_i^* M_i$ be upper/lower respect. lower/upper triangular factorizations of the (positive definite) diagonal block-entries of $C$ and let $C_{ii}$ be decomposed as

$$C_{ii} = U_{ii} + Y_{ii}^* \tag{4.1}$$

where $U_{ii}$ is upper triangular and $Y_{ii}$ strictly upper triangular. Consider as before

$$[\Gamma_0 \quad \Delta_0] = \left[\begin{array}{cccc|cccc} U_{00} & C_{01} & \cdots & C_{0n} & Y_{00} & C_{01} & \cdots & C_{0n} \\ 0 & U_{11} & \cdots & C_{1n} & 0 & Y_{11} & \cdots & C_{1n} \\ . & . & \cdots & . & . & . & \cdots & . \\ 0 & 0 & \cdots & U_{nn} & 0 & 0 & \cdots & Y_{nn} \end{array}\right] \tag{4.2}$$

The first fase in the elimination process will consist in eliminating the $Y_{ii}$ entries with the usual Schur algorithm:

$$[\Gamma_0 \quad \Delta_0]\Theta_1 = \left[\begin{array}{cccc|cccc} L_0 & C_{01}L_1^{-*} & \cdots & C_{0n}L_n^{-*} & 0 & C_{01}M_1^{-1} & \cdots & C_{0n}M_n^{-1} \\ 0 & L_1 & \cdots & C_{1n}L_n^{-*} & 0 & 0 & \cdots & C_{1n}M_n^{-1} \\ . & . & \cdots & . & . & . & \cdots & . \\ 0 & 0 & \cdots & L_n & . & . & \cdots & 0 \end{array}\right] \tag{4.3}$$

$$\Theta_1 = \left[\begin{array}{c|c} \theta_{11} & \theta_{12} \\ \hline \theta_{21} & \theta_{22} \end{array}\right] \tag{4.4}$$

with: $\theta_{11} = U_{00}^* L_0^{-*} \oplus U_{11}^* L_1^{-*} \oplus \cdots \oplus U_{nn}^* L_n^{-*}$

$$\theta_{21} = Y_{00}^* L_0^{-*} \oplus Y_{11}^* L_1^{-*} \oplus \cdots \oplus U_{nn}^* L_n^{-*}$$

$$\theta_{12} = Y_{00} M_0^{-1} \oplus Y_{11} M_1^{-1} \oplus \cdots \oplus Y_{nn} M_n^{-1}$$

$$\theta_{22} = U_{00} M_0^{-1} \oplus U_{11} M_1^{-1} \oplus \cdots \oplus U_{nn} M_n^{-1}.$$

Proceeding further, one could eliminate the second block-diagonal in $\Delta$ using elementary block-type J-unitary rotations. These have the form:

$$\Theta(P) = \begin{bmatrix} I & P \\ P^* & I \end{bmatrix} \begin{bmatrix} S^{-*} & \\ & T^{-1} \end{bmatrix} \tag{4.5}$$

with

$$I - PP^* = SS^* \tag{4.6a}$$

$$I - P^* P = T^* T \tag{4.6b}$$

and whereby $S$ and $T$ are upper-triangular. The elimination of $C_{i,i+1} M_{i+1}^{-1}$ against $L_i$ would necessitate a

$$P_i = - L_i^{-1} C_{i,i+1} M_{i+1}^{-1} \tag{4.7}$$

and would produce a global $\Theta_2$ given by:

$$\Theta_2 = \left[\begin{array}{cccccc|ccc} S_0^{-*} & 0 & \dots & 0 & 0 & & (P_0)T_0^{-1} & \dots & 0 \\ 0 & S_1^{-*} & \dots & 0 & 0 & & 0 & \dots & 0 \\ \cdot & \cdot & \dots & \cdot & \cdot & & \cdot & \dots & \cdot \\ 0 & 0 & \dots & I & 0 & & 0 & \dots & 0 \\ & & & & & & & & \\ 0 & 0 & \dots & 0 & I & & 0 & \dots & 0 \\ (P_0)^* S_0^* & 0 & \dots & 0 & 0 & & T_0^{-1} & \dots & 0 \\ \cdot & \cdot & \dots & \cdot & \cdot & & \cdot & \dots & \cdot \\ 0 & 0 & \dots & 0 & 0 & & 0 & \dots & T_{n-1}^{-1} \end{array}\right] \tag{4.8}$$

which would give the (complete) Schur solution depicted in fig. 4.1.

However, before proceeding to this second stage, we may wish to neglect a number of elements in the 2*2 block matrices

$$C_i^{i+1} \overset{\Delta}{=} \begin{bmatrix} C_{ii} & C_{i,i+1} \\ C_{i+1,i} & C_{i+1,i+1} \end{bmatrix} \tag{4.9}$$

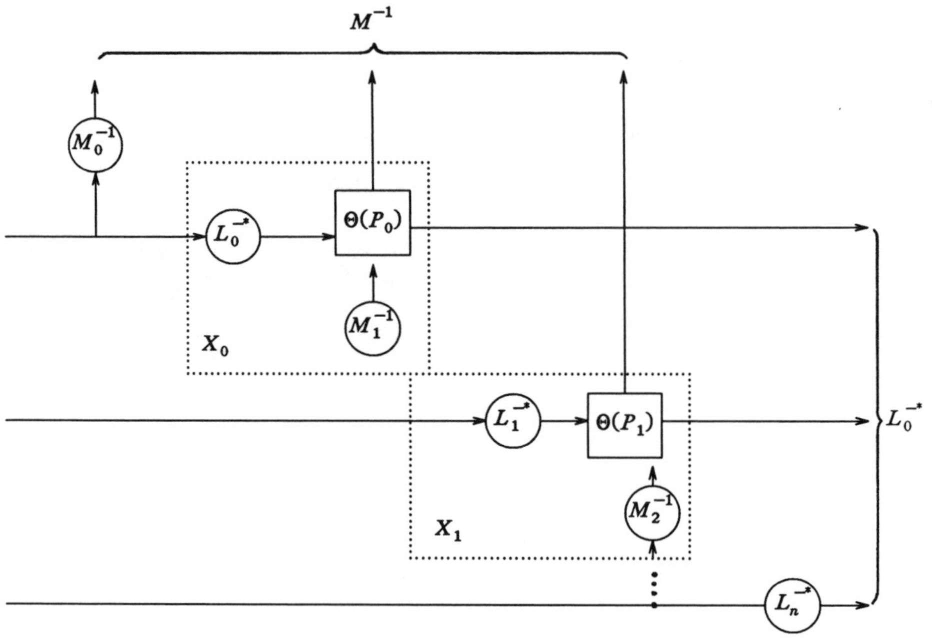


**Fig. 4.1 Exact Schur model for the 1st block diagonal case**

which give rise to $L_i$ , $M_{i+1}$ and $P_i$. This can be done by performing a "local" approximation on (4.9). Presumably (4.9) can be reordered by merging the indices of block $(ii)$ and block $(i+1,i+1)$ in such a way that all relevant entries now appear clustered around the main diagonal, thereby defining a staircase set on which a regular Schur approximation can be performed.

Let $\pi_S$ be the permutation matrix that defines the merge operation and let the local approximation produce hatted quantities:

$$\pi_S \, C_i^{i+1} \, \pi_S^* \approx \hat{C}_s = \hat{L}_s \hat{L}_s^* = \hat{M}_s^* \hat{M}_s \tag{4.10}$$

($\hat{L}_s^{-1}$ and $\hat{M}_s^{-1}$ are banded upper-triangular matrices; note that all quantities are implicitely indexed by $i$).

Restoring the original order will result in a factorization for the approximation

$$[\hat{C}_i^{i+1}]^{-1} = \pi_s^* \hat{C}_s^{-1} \pi_s \tag{4.11a}$$

$$= (\pi_s^* \hat{L}_s^{-*} \pi_s)(\pi_s^* \hat{L}_s^{-1} \pi_s) \tag{4.11b}$$

$$= (\pi_s^* \hat{M}_s^{-1} \pi_s)(\pi_s^* \hat{M}_s^{-*} \pi_s) \tag{4.11c}$$

Let

$$[\pi_s^* L_s^{-*} \pi_s \mid \pi_s^* \hat{M}_s^{-1} \pi_s] \stackrel{\Delta}{=} [\hat{\Gamma} \mid \hat{\Delta}] \stackrel{\Delta}{=} \left[\begin{array}{c|c|c|c} \hat{\Gamma}_{00} & \hat{\Gamma}_{01} & \hat{\Delta}_{00} & \hat{\Delta}_{01} \\ \hline \hat{\Gamma}_{10} & \hat{\Gamma}_{11} & \hat{\Delta}_{10} & \hat{\Delta}_{11} \end{array}\right] \tag{4.12}$$

Since the shuffled order of $\hat{C}_s$ is nothing but the merge of the original orders in the $i^{th}$ and $(i+1)^{th}$ diagonal blocks, we shall have that $\hat{\Delta}_{00}$ and $\hat{\Delta}_{11}$ are upper triangular, $\hat{\Gamma}_{00}$ and $\hat{\Gamma}_{11}$ lower triangular and all matrices will be (close to ) banded.

The strategy now consists in replacing $X_i$ by the $\hat{X}_i$ which come from the hat approximation.

Let $(\hat{C}_i^{i+1})^{-1} \stackrel{\Delta}{=} \hat{A}\hat{A}^* = \hat{B}\hat{B}^*$ (dropping indices for convenience) and our previous convention be lower/upper respect. upper/lower factorizations and let

$$[\hat{A} \quad \hat{B}] \stackrel{\Delta}{=} \left[\begin{array}{c|c|c|c} \hat{A}_{00} & 0 & \hat{B}_{00} & \hat{B}_{01} \\ \hline \hat{A}_{10} & \hat{A}_{11} & 0 & \hat{B}_{11} \end{array}\right] \tag{4.13}$$

then it is easy to see that

$$\hat{X} = \left[\begin{array}{c|c} \hat{A}_{00} & \hat{B}_{01} \\ \hline \hat{A}_{10} & \hat{B}_{11} \end{array}\right] \tag{4.14}$$

since the original scheme applied on $\hat{C}_i^{i+1}$ would yield a diagram like fig. 4.1 but with only two block entries.

Hence, the problem is reduced to computing the relevant entries in (4.13) from the entries in (4.12) in an efficient way. Since now $\hat{A}\hat{A}^* = \hat{\Gamma}\hat{\Gamma}^*$ and $\hat{B}\hat{B}^* = \hat{\Delta}\hat{\Delta}^*$, we have:

$$\hat{X} = \left[\begin{array}{c|c} \hat{A}_{00} & \hat{\Delta}^a \hat{B}_{11}^{-*} \\ \hline \hat{\Gamma}^a \hat{A}_{00}^{-*} & \hat{B}_{11} \end{array}\right] \tag{4.15}$$

where: (1) $\hat{A}_{00}\hat{A}^*_{00} = \Gamma_{00}\Gamma^*_{00} + \Gamma_{01}\Gamma^*_{01}$ (4.16a)

(2) $\Gamma^a = [\Gamma_{10}\Gamma^*_{00} + \Gamma_{11}\Gamma^*_{01}]$ (4.16b)

(3) $\Delta^a = [\Delta_{00}\Delta^*_{10} + \Delta_{01}\Delta^*_{11}]$ (4.16c)

(4) $\hat{B}_{11}\hat{B}^*_{11} = \Delta_{10}\Delta^*_{10} + \Delta_{11}\Delta^*_{11}$ (4.16d)

Since all the entries of the right hand side in (4.16) are banded, the entries of the left hand side can be computed efficiently. Indeed, (4.16a) and (4.16d) can be obtained by a straight banded Cholesky factorization, while (4.16b) and (4.16c) amount to mere multiplications of banded matrices. The result shown in (4.15) is such that all matrices displayed are banded. Two inverses occur, and they cannot be computed efficiently: they must remain as stated. Multiplication of $\hat{X}$ with a vector $x = [x_1 \;\; x_2]$ results in efficient operations because the product of a vector $x$ with the inverse of a banded matrix can be executed efficiently. E.g. $y = (x_1\Delta^a)\hat{B}^{-*}_{11}$ can be written as:

$$y\, B^*_{11} = (x_1\Delta^a)$$

and the vector $y$ can be computed from $(x_1\Delta^a)$ using $n.b$ operations where $n$ is the size of the vector and $b$ the average size of the band.

The resulting scheme is displayed in fig. 4.2. It produces approximating factors $L_a$ and $M_a$ for $C$. Notice that because of the approximation technique used it is not true anymore that $M_a^* M_a = L_a L_a^*$. However, if the $\hat{X}_i$ approximate the $X_i$ closely, then this will also be true for the $L_a$ with $L$ and $M_a$ with $M$ due to the feed forward nature of the diagram. An error analysis of the scheme given is beyond the scope of this paper and will be presented elsewhere. It may suffice to state that since the approximation is done directly on factors of $C_a^{-1}$, the resulting approximation properties should be very good.

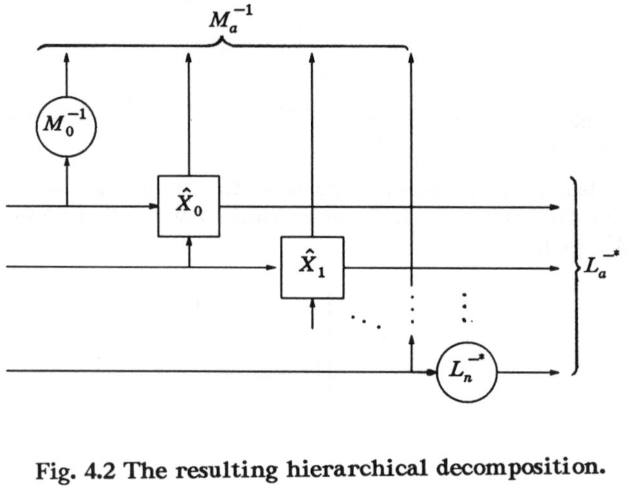


Fig. 4.2 The resulting hierarchical decomposition.

**References**

1. H. Dym and I. Gohberg, "Extensions of Band Matrices with Band Inverses," *Linear Algebra and its Applications*, pp. 1-24 Elsevier, (1981).

2. J. Schur, "Uber Potenzreihen, die im Innern des Einheitskreises beschrankt sind," *J. fur die Riene und Angewandte Math.* **147** pp. 205-232 (Sept 1917). (in German)

3. P. Dewilde, A. Vieira, and T. Kailath, "On a Generalized Szego-Levinson Realization Algorithm for Optimal Linear Predictors based on a Network Theoretic Approach," *IEEE Trans. CAS* **CAS-25**(9) pp. 663-675 (Sept. 1978).

4. Ph. Delsarte, Y. Genin, and Y. Kamp, "A Method of Matrix Inverse Triangular Decomposition, Based on Contiguous Principal Submatrices," *J. Linear Algebra and its Applications* **31** pp. 199-212 (June 1980).

5. M. Morf and J.M. Delosme, "Matrix Decompositions and Inversions Via Elementary Signature-Orthogonal Transformations," *ISMM Int'l Symp. on Mini and Microcomputers in Control and Measurement* **San Francisco, California**(May, 1981).

6. J.M. Delosme, "Algorithms for Finite Shift-Rank Processes," *Ph.D. Dissertation* **Stanford University**(September, 1982).

7. E. Deprettere, "Mixed Form Time-Variant Lattice Recursions," pp. 545-562 in *Outils et Modèles Mathèmatiques pour l'Automatique, l'Analyse de systèmes et le traitement du signal*, CNRS, Paris (1981).

8. H. Lev-Ari and T. Kailath, "Schur and Levinson Algorithms for Nonstationary Processes," *Proceedings ICASSP*, (1981).

9. P. Dewilde and E. Deprettere, "Approximate Inversion of Positive Matrices with Applications to Modelling," *Nato ASI Series* **Modelling, Robustness and Sensitivity Reduction in Control Systems**(1987).

10. H. Lev-Ari, "Multidimensional Maximum-Entropy Covariance Extension," *Proceedings ICASSP*, pp. 21.7.1-21.7.4 (1985).

11. Y. Kamp, "Some Results on Constrained Maximum Likelihood Estimation," *Proceedings ICASSP*, pp. 27.16.1-3 (1986).

12. J. Ball and I. Gohberg, "Shift Invariant Subspaces, Factorization and Interpolation of Matrices. I. The Canonical Case," *Lin. Algebra and its Appl.* **74** pp. 87-150 (1986).

13. P. Dewilde and H. Dym, "Lossless Chain Scattering Matrices and Optimum Linear Prediction: The Vector Case," *Intl. J. Circuit Theory and Appln.* 9 pp. 135-175 (1981).

14. R. Grone, Ch.R. Johnson, E.M. Sa, and H. Wolkowicz, "Positive Definite Completions of Partial Hermitian Matrices," *Linear Algebra and its Applications* 58 pp. 109-124 (1984).

P. Dewilde and E.F.A. Deprettere
Delft University of Technology
Department of Electrical Engineering
Mekelweg 4, 2628 CD Delft
The Netherlands

Submitted: October 20, 1987

Operator Theory:
Advances and Applications, Vol. 29



# A NEW CLASS OF CONTRACTIVE INTERPOLANTS AND MAXIMUM ENTROPY PRINCIPLES

**Harry Dym and Israel Gohberg**

To Moshe Livšic, the founding father of the theory
of Characteristic Operator Functions, on the occasion
of his seventieth birthday, with admiration and affection.

A general class of strictly contractive block matrix valued functions $g(\zeta) = [g_{ij}(\zeta)]$ , $i,j = 1,\cdots,k$ , whose block entries $g_{ij}$ are completely specified for $j < i+\tau$ (i.e., for $g_{ij}$ below the $\tau$'th block diagonal of $g$) and partially specified for $j = i+\tau$ (i.e., for $g_{ij}$ on the $\tau$'th block diagonal of $g$) is analyzed. Necessary and sufficient conditions for this class of "interpolants" to be nonempty are deduced. A linear fractional description of this class is then obtained and used to establish a maximum entropy principle. In particular it is shown that when this class is nonempty, then it contains exactly one interpolant which achieves the maximum entropy. This maximum entropy interpolant is also characterized as the "band" interpolant.

## CONTENTS

## 0. NOTATION.

Throughout this paper we shall let $\mathbb{C}$ denote the complex numbers, $\mathbb{D}$ the open unit disc and $\mathbb{T}$ its boundary :

$$\mathbb{D} = \{\zeta \in \mathbb{C} : |\zeta| < 1\}, \qquad \mathbb{T} = \{\zeta \in \mathbb{C} : |\zeta| = 1\} .$$

If $A$ is a matrix then $|A|$ stands for the maximum singular number of $A$. The symbol $W_{j\times k}$ denotes the Wiener space of continuous $j \times k$ matrix valued functions

$$g(\zeta) = \sum_{i=-\infty}^{\infty} g_i \zeta^i$$

with $j \times k$ matrix valued coefficients $g_i$ which are subject to the constraint

$$\sum_{i=-\infty}^{\infty} |g_i| < \infty \ ;$$

$$\begin{aligned}
(W_{j\times k})_+ &= \{g \in W_{j\times k} : g_i = 0 \ \text{ for } \ i < 0\} \ , \\
(W_{j\times k})_- &= \{g \in W_{j\times k} : g_i = 0 \ \text{ for } \ i > 0\} \ , \\
(W_{j\times k})^0_\pm &= \{g \in (W_{j\times k})_\pm : g_0 = 0\} \ .
\end{aligned}$$

The symbols $\underline{\underline{p}}$ and $\underline{\underline{q}}$ denote the projectors which are defined by the rules

$$\underline{\underline{p}}\left\{\sum_{i=-\infty}^{\infty} f_i\zeta^i\right\} = \sum_{i=0}^{\infty} f_i\zeta^i \ \text{ and } \ \underline{\underline{q}}\left\{\sum_{i=-\infty}^{\infty} f_i\zeta^i\right\} = \sum_{i=-\infty}^{0} f_i\zeta^i \ ;$$

$$\underline{\underline{q}}' = I - \underline{\underline{p}} \ \text{ and } \ \underline{\underline{p}}' = I - \underline{\underline{q}} \ .$$

For the mostpart these projectors will be applied in $W_{j\times 1}$ or in the Hilbert space $L_j^2$ of $j \times 1$ vector valued functions on the circle with square summable entries. In order to keep the notation simple, the domains of these projectors are not indicated in the notation. Finally, $\ell_j^2$ denotes the space of $j \times 1$ vector valued sequences $\{\xi_0, \xi_1, \cdots\}$ with $\sum_{i=0}^{\infty} |\xi_i|^2 < \infty$ .

## 1. INTRODUCTION.

Let $\varphi_0, \varphi_1, \cdots$ be a given sequence of $m \times n$ matrices with

$$\sum_{j=0}^{\infty} |\varphi_j| < \infty$$

and let

$$\mathcal{G}(\varphi) = \{g = \sum_{j=-\infty}^{\infty} g_j \zeta^j \text{ in } W_{m\times n} : g_j = \varphi_j \text{ for } j = 0, 1, \cdots$$
$$\text{and } I_m - g(\zeta)g(\zeta)^* > 0 \text{ for } \zeta \in \mathbb{T}\} .$$

In a previous paper [DG2] it was shown that $\mathcal{G}(\varphi)$ is nonempty if and only if the Hankel operator which maps

$$\{\xi_0, \xi_1, \cdots\} \in \ell_n^2 \longrightarrow \{\eta_0, \eta_1, \cdots\} \in \ell_m^2$$

by the rule

$$\eta_j = \sum_{k=0}^{\infty} \varphi_{j+k} \xi_k , \qquad j = 0, 1, \cdots,$$

is a strictly contractive map of $\ell_n^2$ into $\ell_m^2$ . This is a Wiener space version of the well known generalization to matrix valued functions by Adamyan, Arov and Krein [AAK] of the Nehari theorem. In particular it was shown in [DG2] that if $\mathcal{G}(\varphi)$ is nonempty, then there exists a unique element therein which maximizes the entropy integral

$$\mathcal{E}(g) = \frac{1}{2\pi} \int_0^{2\pi} \log \det\{I_m - g(e^{i\theta})g(e^{i\theta})^*\} d\theta \tag{1.1}$$

and a number of characterizations of this minimizing element were given.

In the present paper we shall develop analogous results for the more general class $B$ of $k \times k$ block matrix valued functions

$$b(\zeta) = \begin{bmatrix} b_{11}(\zeta) & \cdots & b_{1k}(\zeta) \\ \vdots & & \vdots \\ b_{k1}(\zeta) & \cdots & b_{kk}(\zeta) \end{bmatrix}$$

with $b_{ij} \in W_{\mu_i \times \nu_j}$ , where $\mu_1, \cdots, \mu_k$ and $\nu_1, \cdots, \nu_k$ are positive integers such that

$$\mu_1 + \cdots + \mu_k = m \qquad \text{and} \qquad \nu_1 + \cdots + \nu_k = n \ .$$

The space $B$ admits a direct sum decomposition

$$B = (B_\tau)_+ \dot{+} (B_\tau)_-^0$$

along the $\tau$'th (block) diagonal $-k < \tau < k$ , in which $(B_\tau)_+$[resp $(B_\tau)_-^0$] denotes the set of $b \in B$ with $b_{ij} = 0$ for $j > i+\tau$ [resp. $j < i+\tau$] and $b_{ij} \in (W_{\mu_i \times \nu_j})_+$ [resp. $(W_{\mu_i \times \nu_j})_-^0$] for $j = i+\tau$. Now for a given $\varphi \in (B_\tau)_+$ let

$$\mathcal{G}_\tau(\varphi) = \{g \in B : g - \varphi \in (B_\tau)_-^0 \text{ and } I_m - g(\zeta)g(\zeta)^* > 0 \text{ for } \xi \in \mathbb{T}\} .$$

We shall refer to the elements of $\mathcal{G}_\tau(\varphi)$ as strictly contractive interpolants of $\varphi$ . If $k = 1$, then $\tau = 0$ and $\mathcal{G}_\tau(\varphi)$ coincides with the class $\mathcal{G}(\varphi)$ mentioned earlier. If $k = 2$ and $\tau = 1$, then this class (and mild variations thereof) appear in the theory of $H^\infty$ control; see Doyle [Do1], [Do2] and Ball and Cohen [BC]. Necessary and sufficient conditions for these variants to be nonempty were obtained via the Sz. Nagy-Foias commutant lifting theorem by Feintuch and Francis [FF1], [FF2].

In this paper we obtain necessary and sufficient conditions for the class $\mathcal{G}_\tau(\varphi)$ to be nonempty for general $\tau$ and $k$ in terms of $k - |\tau|$ Hankel like operators which are based on the given data. The problem of finding a strictly contractive interpolant $g$ of the data $\varphi$ is converted into the equivalent problem of finding a positive extension

$$\begin{bmatrix} I_m & g \\ g^* & I_n \end{bmatrix} \text{ of the "band" data } \begin{bmatrix} I_m & \varphi \\ \varphi^* & I_n \end{bmatrix} .$$

This seemingly innocuous change of view has far reaching consequences. It enables us to invoke the abstract theory of band extensions, which was developed earlier in [DG1] and applied to the case $k = 1$ and $\tau = 0$ in [DG2], in order to introduce the concept of band interpolants in $\mathcal{G}_\tau(\varphi)$ : We shall say that $g \in \mathcal{G}_\tau(\varphi)$ is a band interpolant if the 12 block of $\begin{bmatrix} I_m & g \\ g^* & I_n \end{bmatrix}^{-1}$ belongs to $(B_\tau)_+$ . It turns out that each nonempty $\mathcal{G}_\tau(\varphi)$ space contains exactly one band interpolant $g^o$ and that it can be expressed via a pair of Wiener-Hopf type factorizations

$$\begin{aligned} \begin{bmatrix} I_m & g^o \\ g^{o*} & I_n \end{bmatrix} &= \begin{bmatrix} a^* & -c^* \\ 0 & I_n \end{bmatrix}^{-1} \begin{bmatrix} a & 0 \\ -c & I_n \end{bmatrix}^{-1} \\ &= \begin{bmatrix} I_m & 0 \\ -b^* & d^* \end{bmatrix}^{-1} \begin{bmatrix} I_m & -b \\ 0 & d \end{bmatrix}^{-1} \end{aligned}$$

the entries of which are suitably normalized solutions of a set of equations based on the given data $\varphi$; see Section 3 for the details and Section 2 for the abstract theory of band extensions in a form which is amenable to the present setting. Adapting an argument from the forthcoming monograph [D] which is based on a comparison of two such factorizations we then show in Section 4 that

$$\Theta(\zeta) = \begin{bmatrix} a(\zeta) & b(\zeta) \\ c(\zeta) & d(\zeta) \end{bmatrix}$$

is $J$ unitary on $\mathbb{T}$ with respect to the signature matrix $J = I_m \oplus -I_n$ and identify $\mathcal{G}_\tau(\varphi)$ as the set of linear fractional transformations

$$T_\Theta[h] = (ah+b)(ch+d)^{-1}$$

as $h$ runs through the set of strictly contractive elements on $\mathbb{T}$ which belong to $(B_\tau)_-^0$. This representation is then used in Section 5 to show that for every $g \in \mathcal{G}_\tau(\varphi)$, the entropy integral defined in (1.1) is subject to the inequality

$$\mathcal{E}(g) \le \mathcal{E}(g^o)$$

with equality if and only if $g$ is equal to the band interpolant $g^o$ .

## 2. BAND EXTENSIONS

In this section we shall develop a general theory of band extensions in a form which is suitable for the problem at hand. The discussion is adapted from the abstract treatment which was presented in [DG1] and its subsequent application in [DG2]. The latter is particularly relevant because this section essentially amounts to the observation that the formalism developed in Section 2 of [DG2] is applicable to the Banach algebra of block matrices of the form

$$f(\zeta) = \begin{bmatrix} a(\zeta) & b(\zeta) \\ c(\zeta) & d(\zeta) \end{bmatrix}$$

with $a \in W_{m\times n}$, $b \in W_{m\times n}$, $c \in W_{n\times m}$ and $d \in W_{n\times n}$ but with more general splittings of its components than the classical ones (in terms of $(W_{j\times k})_\pm$ and $(W_{j\times k})_\pm^0$) which were employed there.

In order to maximize the future applicability of the main theorems of this section we shall work in the general setting of a block Banach algebra

$$F = \left\{ f = \begin{bmatrix} a & b \\ c & d \end{bmatrix} : a \in A, \quad b \in B, \quad c \in C \text{ and } d \in D \right\} \quad ,$$

where $A$ and $D$ are Banach algebras with identities $I_a$ and $I_d$, respectively, and $B$ and $C$ are Banach spaces, such that for every choice of $a \in A,\ b \in B,\ c \in C$ and $d \in D$ :

(1) $bc \in A$ and $\|bc\|_A \le \|b\|_B \ \|c\|_C$

(2) $ab \in B$ and $\|ab\|_B \le \|a\|_A \ \|b\|_B$

(3) $bd \in B$ and $\|bd\|_B \le \|b\|_B \ \|d\|_D$

(4) $ca \in C$ and $\|ca\|_C \le \|c\|_C \ \|a\|_A$

(5) $dc \in C$ and $\|dc\|_C \le \|d\|_D \ \|c\|_C$

(6) $cb \in D$ and $\|cb\|_D \le \|c\|_C \ \|b\|_B$ .

Then $F$ is readily seen to be a Banach algebra with identity with respect to the natural rules for matrix multiplication and addition, with norm

$$\|f\|_F = \max\{\|a\|_A + \|b\|_B, \qquad \|c\|_C + \|d\|_D\} \ .$$

We further assume that the algebras $A$ and $D$ admit direct sum decompositions

$$A = A_-^0 \dot{+} A_0 \dot{+} A_+^0 \ , \quad D = D_-^0 \dot{+} D_0 \dot{+} D_+^0$$

in which all six of the newly indicated spaces are closed subspaces which are also algebras and are such that

$$I_a \in A_0 \ , \qquad I_d \in D_0$$

and the inclusions

$$A_0 A_\pm^0 \subset A_\pm^0 \ , A_\pm^0 A_0 \subset A_\pm^0 \ , D_0 D_\pm^0 \subset D_\pm^0 \ , D_\pm^0 D_0 \subset D_\pm^0$$

are in force. It is then readily checked that

$$A_\pm = A_\pm^0 \dot{+} A_0 \text{ and } D_\pm = D_\pm^0 \dot{+} D_0$$

are all algebras :

$$A_\pm A_\pm \subset A_\pm \text{ and } D_\pm D_\pm \subset D_\pm \ ,$$

and moreover that if $a \in A_0$ [resp. $d \in D_0$] and is invertible, then $a^{-1} \in A_0$ [resp. $d^{-1} \in D_0$]. Finally we suppose that the Banach spaces $B$ and $C$ admit direct sum decompositions of the form

$$B = B_+ \dot{+} B_-^0 \quad \text{and} \quad C = C_+^0 \dot{+} C_-$$

such that

$$\begin{aligned} B_\pm D_\pm &\subset B_\pm\ , & A_\pm B_\pm &\subset B_\pm\ , \\ C_\pm B_\pm &\subset D_\pm\ , & B_\pm C_\pm &\subset A_\pm\ , \\ C_\pm A_\pm &\subset C_\pm\ , & D_\pm C_\pm &\subset C_\pm\ , \end{aligned}$$

with the understanding that $B_- = B_-^0$, $C_+ = C_+^0$ and that if a superscript zero appears in one of the terms on the lefthand side of an inclusion, then it also appears on the right.

Now let us introduce the following subspaces of $F$ :

$$F_1 = \begin{bmatrix} 0 & B_-^0 \\ 0 & 0 \end{bmatrix} = \left\{ \begin{bmatrix} a & b \\ c & d \end{bmatrix} : a = 0,\ b \in B_-^0,\ c = 0 \text{ and } d = 0 \right\} ,$$

$$F_2 = \begin{bmatrix} A_- & B_+ \\ 0 & D_- \end{bmatrix} = \left\{ \begin{bmatrix} a & b \\ c & d \end{bmatrix} : a \in A_-,\ b \in B_+,\ c = 0 \text{ and } d \in D_- \right\} ,$$

$$F_3 = \begin{bmatrix} A_+ & 0 \\ C_- & D_+ \end{bmatrix} = \left\{ \begin{bmatrix} a & b \\ c & d \end{bmatrix} : a \in A_+,\ b = 0,\ c \in C_- \text{ and } d \in D_+ \right\} ,$$

$$F_4 = \begin{bmatrix} 0 & 0 \\ C_+^0 & 0 \end{bmatrix} = \left\{ \begin{bmatrix} a & b \\ c & d \end{bmatrix} : a = 0,\ b = 0,\ c \in C_+^0 \text{ and } d = 0 \right\} ,$$

$$F_+ = F_1 \dot{+} F_2,\ F_c = F_2 \dot{+} F_3,\ F_- = F_3 \dot{+} F_4 \qquad \text{and}$$

$$F_\pm^0 = \left\{ \begin{bmatrix} a & b \\ c & d \end{bmatrix} \in F_\pm : a \in A_\mp^0 \text{ and } d \in D_\mp^0 \right\} .$$

Clearly $F_\pm^0$ are subalgebras of $F$ and $F_\pm$ are subalgebras with identity. Moreover, the "central band"

$$F_c = F_2^0 \dot{+} F_3 = F_2 \dot{+} F_3^0 ,$$

where the superzero indicates that the block diagonal spaces have been replaced by their superzero counterparts, the full space

$$F = F_1 \dot{+} F_c \dot{+} F_4$$

and it is readily checked that if $f \in F_i$ and $g \in F_j$ then $fg$ belongs to the intersection of the $F_i$ row and the $F_j$ column in the following table :

| | $F_1$ | $F_2$ | $F_3$ | $F_4$ |
|---|---|---|---|---|
| $F_1$ | 0 | $F_1$ | $F_+^0$ | $F_c$ |
| $F_2$ | $F_1$ | $F_+$ | $F_c$ | $F_-^0$ |
| $F_3$ | $F_+^0$ | $F_c$ | $F_-$ | $F_4$ |
| $F_4$ | $F_c$ | $F_-^0$ | $F_4$ | 0 |

We shall say that $f \in F$ admits a canonical left [resp. right] factorization with respect to $F_\pm$ if

$$f = f_+ f_- \qquad \text{[resp. } f = f_- f_+\text{]}$$

where $f_+$ and $f_-$ are invertible elements in $F$ such that $(f_+)^{\pm 1} \in F_+$ and $(f_-)^{\pm 1} \in F_-$

Similarly we shall say that $a \in A$ and $d \in D$ admits a canonical left [resp. right] factorization with respect to $A_\pm$ if the corresponding factorization formulas hold with $a_\pm$ invertible in $A_\pm$ and $d_\pm$ invertible in $D_\pm$.

We shall say that $f \in F$ is an extension of $h \in F_c$ if

(1) $f - h \in F_1 \dot{+} F_4$ .

We shall say that $f \in F$ is a band extension of $h \in F_c$ if, in addition to (1),

(2) $f$ is invertible in $F$ and

(3) $f^{-1} \in F_c$ .

Furthermore, we shall say that a band extension $f$ of $h \in F_c$ is a type I [resp. type II] extension if $f$ admits a canonical left [resp. right] factorization with respect to $F_\pm$.

These definitions are adapted from Section 4 of [DG1]. The apparent discrepencies in formulation are because, unlike $F$, the algebras considered there do not necessarily contain an identity.

We next state four lemmas which will be useful in the proof of the main theorems. The proofs are omitted because the first two are elementary and the latter two are easily adapted from the proofs of the corresponding Lemmas in [DG2].

**LEMMA 2.1.** *Let*

$$u = \begin{bmatrix} u_{11} & 0 \\ u_{21} & u_{22} \end{bmatrix}$$

*belong to $F_-$ . Then $u$ is invertible in $F_-$ if and only if $u_{11}$ is invertible in $A_+$ and $u_{22}$ is invertible in $D_+$.*

**LEMMA 2.2.** *Let*

$$v = \begin{bmatrix} v_{11} & v_{12} \\ 0 & v_{22} \end{bmatrix}$$

*belong to $F_+$ . Then $v$ is invertible in $F_+$ if and only if $v_{11}$ is invertible in $A_-$ and $v_{22}$ is invertible in $D_-$.*

**LEMMA 2.3.** *Let*

$$f = \begin{bmatrix} a & b \\ c & d \end{bmatrix}$$

*belong to $F$. Then $f$ admits a canonical right factorization with respect to $F_\pm$ if and only if $a$ and $d - ca^{-1}b$ admit canonical left factorizations with regard to $A_\pm$ and $D_\pm$, respectively.*

**LEMMA 2.4.** *Let $f$ be as in Lemma 2.3. Then $f$ admits a canonical left factorization with respect to $F_\pm$ if and only if $d$ and $a - bd^{-1}c$ admit canonical right factorizations with regard to $D_\pm$ and $A_\pm$, respectively.*

**THEOREM 2.1.** *Let*

$$k = \begin{bmatrix} k_{11} & k_{12} \\ k_{21} & k_{22} \end{bmatrix}$$

*belong to $F_c$ . Then $k$ admits a type I extension if and only if there exists a set of solutions $u_{ij}$ to the system of equations*

$$P_{A_+}(k_{11}u_{11} + k_{12}u_{21}) = I_a \tag{2.1a}$$

$$P_{C_-}(k_{21}u_{11} + k_{22}u_{21}) = 0 \tag{2.1b}$$

$$P_{D_+}(k_{22}u_{22}) = I_d \tag{2.1c}$$

*and a set of solutions $v_{ij}$ to the system of equations*

$$P_{A^0_-}(v_{11}k_{11} + v_{12}k_{21}) = 0 \tag{2.2a}$$

$$P_{B_+}(v_{11}k_{12}+v_{12}k_{22})=0 \tag{2.2b}$$

$$P_{D^0_-}(v_{22}k_{22})=0 \tag{2.2c}$$

*such that* $u_{11}$ *is invertible in* $A_+$ , $u_{22}$ *is invertible in* $D_+$, $u_{21}\in C_-$, $v_{11}$ *is invertible in* $A_-$, $v_{22}$ *is invertible in* $D_-$, $v_{12}\in B_+$, $v_{11}-I_a\in A^0_-$ *and* $v_{22}-I_d\in D^0_-$ .

*Moreover, if* $u_{ij}$ *and* $v_{ij}$ *are such a solution set, then*

$$u=\begin{bmatrix} u_{11} & 0 \\ u_{21} & u_{22}\end{bmatrix} \quad \text{and} \quad v=\begin{bmatrix} v_{11} & v_{12} \\ 0 & v_{22}\end{bmatrix} \tag{2.3}$$

*are invertible in* $F_-$ *and* $F_+$, *respectively, and*

$$f=v^{-1}u^{-1} \tag{2.4}$$

*is a type I extension of* $k$. *Conversely, every type I extension* $f$ *of* $k$ *can be expressed in the form (2.4), where the entries* $u_{ij}$ *and* $v_{ij}$ *in* $u$ *and* $v$ *are solutions of (2.1) and (2.2) which sit in the indicated spaces and satisfy the stated invertibility and normalization conditions.*

**PROOF.** The proof is essentially the same as the proof of Theorem 2.1 of [DG2], since the general splittings enjoy the same salient features that the classical splittings employed in [DG2] do and the requisite Lemmas are still in force.

□

**THEOREM 2.2.** *Let*

$$k=\begin{bmatrix} k_{11} & k_{12} \\ k_{21} & k_{22}\end{bmatrix}$$

*belong to* $F_c$ . *Then* $k$ *admits a type II extension if and only if there exists a set of solutions* $x_{ij}$ *to the system of equations*

$$P_{A_+}(x_{11}k_{11})=I_a \tag{2.5a}$$

$$P_{C_-}(x_{21}k_{11}+x_{22}k_{21})=0 \tag{2.5b}$$

$$P_{D_+}(x_{21}k_{12}+x_{22}k_{22})=I_d \tag{2.5c}$$

*and a set of solutions* $y_{ij}$ *to the system of equations*

$$P_{A^0_-}(k_{11}y_{11})=0 \tag{2.6a}$$

$$P_{B_+}(k_{11}y_{12}+k_{12}y_{22})=0 \tag{2.6b}$$

$$P_{D^0_-}(k_{21}y_{12}+k_{22}y_{22})=0 \tag{2.6c}$$

*such that* $x_{11}$ *is invertible in* $A_+$, $x_{22}$ *is invertible in* $D_+$, $x_{21}\in C_-$, $y_{11}$ *is invertible in* $A_-$, $y_{22}$ *is invertible in* $D_-$, $y_{12}\in B_+$, $y_{11}-I_a\in A^0_-$ *and* $y_{22}-I_d\in D^0_-$ .

*Moreover, if* $x_{ij}$ *and* $y_{ij}$ *are such a solution set, then*

$$x=\begin{bmatrix} x_{11} & 0 \\ x_{21} & x_{22} \end{bmatrix} \quad and \quad y=\begin{bmatrix} y_{11} & y_{12} \\ 0 & y_{22} \end{bmatrix} \tag{2.7}$$

*are invertible in* $F_-$ *and* $F_+$ *, respectively, and*

$$f=x^{-1}y^{-1} \tag{2.8}$$

*is a type II extension of* $k$. *Conversely, every type II extension* $f$ *of* $k$ *can be expressed in the form (2.8), where the entries* $x_{ij}$ *and* $y_{ij}$ *in* $x$ *and* $y$ *are solutions of (2.5) and (2.6) which sit in the indicated spaces and satisfy the stated invertibility and normalization conditions.*

**PROOF.** This is verified in much the same way as Theorem 2.1.

□

**THEOREM 2.3.** *If* $k\in F_c$ *admits a type I extension* $f$ *and a type II extension* $g$, *then* $f=g$ *and there are no other type I or type II extensions.*

**PROOF.** See the proof of Theorem 2.3 of [DG2].

□

## 3. CONTRACTIVE INTERPOLANTS.

In this section we shall apply the general theorems of Section 2 to the specific Banach Algebra $F=W_{(m+n)\times(m+n)}$ with blocks $A=W_{m\times m}$, $B=W_{m\times n}$, $C=W_{n\times m}$ and $D=W_{n\times n}$, which are each further divided into sub-blocks as follows:

$$\begin{aligned} A&=\{[a_{ij}], \quad i,j=1,\cdots,k: \quad a_{ij}\in W_{\mu_i\times\mu_j}\} \\ B&=\{[b_{ij}], \quad i,j=1,\cdots,k: \quad b_{ij}\in W_{\mu_i\times\nu_j}\} \\ C&=\{[c_{ij}], \quad i,j=1,\cdots,k: \quad c_{ij}\in W_{\nu_i\times\mu_j}\} \\ D&=\{[d_{ij}], \quad i,j=1,\cdots,k: \quad d_{ij}\in W_{\nu_i\times\nu_j}\} \ , \end{aligned}$$

where $\mu_i$ and $\nu_i$ and positive integers such that

$$\mu_i + \cdots + \mu_k = m \qquad \text{and} \qquad \nu_1 + \cdots + \nu_k = n \ .$$

We now set

$$A_- = \{a \in A : a_{ij} = 0 \ \text{ for } \ i > j \ \text{ and } \ a_{ii} \in (W_{\mu_i \times \mu_i})_- \ \text{ for } \ i = 1, \cdots, k\} \ ,$$

$$A_+ = \{a \in A : a_{ij} = 0 \ \text{ for } \ i < j \ \text{ and } \ a_{ii} \in (W_{\mu_i \times \mu_i})_+ \ \text{ for } \ i = 1, \cdots, k\} \ ,$$

$$A_\pm^0 = \{a \in A_\pm : a_{ii} \in (W_{\mu_i \times \mu_i})_\pm^0 \ \text{ for } \ i = 1, \cdots, k\} \ ,$$

$$A_0 = \{a \in A : a_{ij} = 0 \ \text{ for } \ i \neq j \ \text{ and } \ a_{ii} \in \mathbb{C}^{\mu_i \times \mu_i} \ \text{ for } \ i = 1, \cdots, k\} \ ,$$

$$D_- = \{d \in D : d_{ij} = 0 \ \text{ for } \ i > j \ \text{ and } \ d_{ii} \in (W_{\nu_i \times \nu_i})_- \ \text{ for } \ i = 1, \cdots, k\} \ ,$$

$$D_+ = \{d \in D : d_{ij} = 0 \ \text{ for } \ i < j \ \text{ and } \ d_{ii} \in (W_{\nu_i \times \nu_i})_+ \ \text{ for } \ i = 1, \cdots, k\} \ ,$$

$$D_\pm^0 = \{d \in D_\pm : d_{ii} \in (W_{\nu_i \times \nu_i})_\pm^0 \ \text{ for } \ i = 1, \cdots, k\} \ ,$$

$$D_0 = \{d \in D : d_{ij} = 0 \ \text{ for } \ i \neq j \ \text{ and } \ d_{ii} \in \mathbb{C}^{\nu_i \times \nu_i} \ \text{ for } \ i = 1, \cdots, k\},$$

and for a fixed integer $\tau$, $-k \leq \tau \leq k$ , we take

$$(B_\tau)_-^0 = \{b \in B : b_{ij} = 0 \ \text{ for } \ j < i + \tau \ \text{ and } \ b_{ij} \in (W_{\mu_i \times \nu_j})_-^0 \ \text{ for } \ j = i + \tau\}$$

$$(B_\tau)_+ = \{b \in B : b_{ij} = 0 \ \text{ for } \ j > i + \tau \ \text{ and } \ b_{ij} \in (W_{\mu_i \times \nu_j})_+ \ \text{ for } \ j = i + \tau\}$$

$$(C_\tau)_- = \{c \in C : c_{ij} = 0 \ \text{ for } \ j < i - \tau \ \text{ and } \ c_{ij} \in (W_{\mu_i \times \nu_j})_- \ \text{ for } \ j = i - \tau\}$$

$$(C_\tau)_+^0 = \{c \in C : c_{ij} = 0 \ \text{ for } \ j > i - \tau \ \text{ and } \ c_{ij} \in (W_{\mu_i \times \nu_j})_+^0 \ \text{ for } \ j = i - \tau\} \ .$$

Thus, for example if $k = 2$ and $\tau = 1$ , then the splittings have the form indicated schematically below :

$$A_+, D_+ : \begin{bmatrix} W_+ & 0 \\ W & W_+ \end{bmatrix} \qquad A_-, D_- : \begin{bmatrix} W_- & W \\ 0 & W_- \end{bmatrix}$$
$$(B_\tau)_+ \quad : \begin{bmatrix} W & W_+ \\ W & W \end{bmatrix} \qquad (B_\tau)_-^0 \quad : \begin{bmatrix} 0 & W_-^0 \\ 0 & 0 \end{bmatrix}$$
$$(C_\tau)_+^0 \quad : \begin{bmatrix} 0 & 0 \\ W_+^0 & 0 \end{bmatrix} \qquad (C_\tau)_- \quad : \begin{bmatrix} W & W \\ W_- & W \end{bmatrix} ,$$

where the spaces $W$, $W_\pm$ and $W_\pm^0$ are of the appropriate size, in accordance with the block decomposition of $A$, $B$, $C$ and $D$ which was explained earlier.

It is now readily checked that the requisite inclusions set forth in Section 2 are met and hence that Theorems 2.1 and 2.2 are applicable. We shall utilize them to show that, if $\varphi \in (B_\tau)_+$ , then

$$\mathcal{G}_\tau(\varphi) = \{g \in B : g - \varphi \in (B_\tau)_-^0 \text{ and } I_m - g(\zeta)g(\zeta)^* > 0 \text{ on } \mathbb{T}\}$$

is nonempty if and only if the Hankel like operators

$$\Gamma_{ij} = P_i \Phi Q_j , \qquad i, j = 1, \cdots, k ,$$

are strictly contractive mappings of $L^2_{\nu_1} \oplus \cdots \oplus L^2_{\nu_k}$ into $L^2_{\mu_1} \oplus \cdots \oplus L^2_{\mu_k}$ for every choice of $i, j = 1, \cdots, k$ on the $\tau$'th diagonal, i.e., with $j - i = \tau$. Here $\Phi$ designates the operator of multiplication by $\varphi$,

$$\begin{aligned} P_1 &= \underline{\underline{p}} \oplus I_{\mu_2} \oplus I_{\mu_3} \oplus \cdots \oplus I_{\mu_{k-1}} \oplus I_{\mu_k} \\ P_2 &= 0 \oplus \underline{\underline{p}} \oplus I_{\mu_3} \oplus \cdots \oplus I_{\mu_{k-1}} \oplus I_{\mu_k} \\ &\vdots \\ P_k &= 0 \oplus 0 \oplus \cdots \oplus 0 \oplus \underline{\underline{p}} \end{aligned}$$

are orthogonal projections on $L^2_{\mu_1} \oplus \cdots \oplus L^2_{\mu_k}$ and

$$Q_1 = \underline{\underline{q}} \oplus 0 \oplus 0 \oplus \cdots \oplus 0$$
$$Q_2 = I_{\nu_1} \oplus \underline{\underline{q}} \oplus 0 \oplus \cdots \oplus 0$$
$$\vdots$$
$$Q_k = I_{\nu_1} \oplus I_{\nu_2} \oplus \cdots \oplus I_{\nu_{k-1}} \oplus \underline{\underline{q}}$$

are orthogonal projections on $L^2_{\nu_1} \oplus \cdots \oplus L^2_{\nu_k}$ . It will also prove convenient to introduce the auxiliary projections

$$P_j = I_m \text{ for } j \le 0, \qquad Q_j = 0 \text{ for } j \le 0$$
$$P_j = 0 \text{ for } j > k, \qquad Q_j = I_n \text{ for } j > k$$

and accordingly to define $\Gamma_{ij}$ for every pair of integers $i, j$ . We shall use the symbol $\|\Gamma_{ij}\|_2$ to indicate the operator norm of $\Gamma_{ij}$ between the two $L^2$ spaces.

It turns out that the proof of the necessity of the conditions $\|\Gamma_{ij}\|_2 < 1$ for $\mathcal{G}_\tau(\varphi)$ to be nonempty reduces to an easy estimate, whereas the proof of sufficiency is considerably more involved. The present strategy is to show that if $\|\Gamma_{ij}\|_2 < 1$ for $ij$ on the $\tau$'th diagonal, then

$$h = \begin{bmatrix} I_m & \varphi \\ \varphi^* & I_n \end{bmatrix}$$

(which belongs to $F_c$) admits an extension

$$f = \begin{bmatrix} I_m & g \\ g^* & I_n \end{bmatrix}$$

which is both type I and type II because the equations in Theorems 2.1 and 2.2 admit solution sets of the requisite form. In fact there is only one such extension $f$, it is positive definite on $\mathbb{T}$ : $f(\zeta) > 0$ for every point $\zeta \in \mathbb{T}$ , and the corresponding $g$ belongs to $\mathcal{G}_\tau(\varphi)$. We shall refer to this particular $g$ as the band interpolant. It will play a central role in the ensuing drama.

The main burden of the proof is carried by the next two theorems. We begin with a preliminary lemma.

**LEMMA 3.1.** *If $\varphi \in (B_\tau)_+$ and if $\|\Gamma_{ij}\|_2 < 1$ for $i, j = 1, \cdots, k$ with $j = i + \tau$, then $\|\Gamma_{ij}\|_2 < 1$ for every choice of $i, j$ with $j = i + \tau$ .*

**PROOF.** Since $\Gamma_{ij} = 0$ if either $i > k$ or if $j < 0$ , it suffices to show that

$$\|\Gamma_{i-1,j-1}\|_2 \leq \|\Gamma_{ij}\|_2 \quad \text{if} \quad i \leq 1 \tag{3.1}$$

and

$$\|\Gamma_{ij}\|_2 \geq \|\Gamma_{i+1,j+1}\|_2 \quad \text{if} \quad j \geq k \tag{3.2}$$

To begin with let us introduce the orthogonal projectors

$$E_j = \begin{cases} 0 & \text{for} \quad j \leq 0 \\ I_{\nu_1} \oplus \cdots \oplus I_{\nu_j} \oplus 0 \oplus \cdots \oplus 0 & \text{for} \quad 1 \leq j \leq k \\ I_n & \text{for} \quad k < j \end{cases}$$

on $L^2_{\nu_1} \oplus \cdots \oplus L^2_{\nu_k}$ and

$$F_j = \begin{cases} I_m & \text{for} \quad j \leq 0 \\ 0 \oplus \cdots 0 \oplus I_{\mu_j} \oplus \cdots \oplus I_{\mu_k} & \text{for} \quad 1 \leq j \leq k \\ 0 & \text{for} \quad k < j \end{cases}$$

on $L^2_{\mu_1} \oplus \cdots \oplus L^2_{\mu_k}$ . Then, since

$$P_i \geq P_{i+1} \quad \text{and} \quad Q_i \leq Q_{i+1} \ ,$$

it is readily seen that

$$Q_j \geq E_{j-1} \geq Q_{j-1}$$

and hence that for $i \leq 1$

$$\|P_{i-1}\Phi Q_{j-1}\|_2 = \|\Phi Q_{j-1}\|_2 \leq \|\Phi E_{j-1}\|_2 \ .$$

But now as

$$\begin{aligned} \|\Phi E_t\|_2 &\geq \|P_1 \Phi E_t\|_2 \\ &\geq \| \begin{bmatrix} \underline{\underline{p}} & & \\ & \ddots & \\ & & \underline{\underline{p}} \end{bmatrix} \Phi E_t\|_2 \\ &= \|\Phi E_t\|_2 \ , \end{aligned}$$

it follows that

$$\|P_{i-1}\Phi Q_{j-1}\|_2 \leq \|P_1\Phi Q_j\|_2 = \|P_i\Phi Q_j\|$$

for $i \leq 1$ , which establishes (3.1).

Next, since

$$P_{j-1} \geq F_j \geq P_j \ ,$$

it is readily seen in much the same way that if $j \geq k$ , then

$$\begin{aligned}\|P_i\Phi Q_j\|_2 &\geq \|F_{i+1}\Phi Q_j\|_2 \\ &= \|F_{i+1}\Phi\|_2 \\ &= \|F_{i+1}\Phi Q_{j+1}\|_2 \\ &\geq \|P_{i+1}\Phi Q_{j+1}\|_2 \ ,\end{aligned}$$

which proves (3.2). □

**THEOREM 3.1.** *Let $\alpha \in W_{s_1\times t_1}$, $\beta \in W_{s_1\times t_2}$, $\gamma \in W_{s_2\times t_1}$, $\delta \in W_{s_2\times t_2}$ and suppose that the operator*

$$\Gamma = \begin{bmatrix} \underline{\underline{p}}\alpha & \underline{\underline{p}}\beta\underline{\underline{q}}' \\ \gamma & \delta\underline{\underline{q}}' \end{bmatrix}$$

*is a strictly contractive map of $L^2_{t_1} \oplus L^2_{t_2}$ into $L^2_{s_1} \oplus L^2_{s_2}$. Then*

$$\Delta = \begin{bmatrix} I_{s_1+s_2} & \Gamma \\ \Gamma^* & I_{t_1+t_2} \end{bmatrix}$$

*is an invertible map of $\mathcal{W} = W_{s_1} \oplus W_{s_2} \oplus W_{t_1} \oplus W_{t_2}$ onto itself.*

**PROOF.** It is readily seen that $\Delta$ is a 1:1 map of $L^2_{s_1+s_2} \oplus L^2_{t_1+t_2}$ onto itself, because $\|\Gamma\|_2 < 1$. Therefore, since the kernel of $\Delta$ acting on $\mathcal{W}$ is a subspace of $L^2_{s_1+s_2} \oplus L^2_{t_1+t_2}$, $\Delta$ is also 1:1 on $\mathcal{W}$. Thus, in order to complete the proof, it is enough to show that for every choice of $u \in W_{s_1}$, $v \in W_{s_2}$, $x \in W_{t_1}$ and $y \in W_{t_2}$ there is at least one choice of $e \in W_{s_1}$, $f \in W_{s_2}$, $g_+ \in W_{t_1}$ and $h \in W_{t_2}$ such that

$$\Delta \begin{bmatrix} e \\ f \\ g \\ h \end{bmatrix} = \begin{bmatrix} u \\ v \\ x \\ y \end{bmatrix} ,$$

or equivalently, that for every choice of $u_+ \in (W_{s_1})_+$ , $v_- \in (W_{s_2})^0_-$ , $v_+ \in (W_{s_2})_+$ , $x_- \in (W_{t_1})^0_-$ , $x_+ \in (W_{t_1})_+$ and $y_- \in (W_{t_2})^0_-$ there exists at least one choice of $e_+ \in (W_{s_1})_+$ , $f_- \in (W_{s_2})^0_-$ , $f_+ \in (W_{s_2})_+$ , $g_- \in (W_{t_1})^0_-$ , $g_+ \in (W_{t_1})_+$ and $h_- \in (W_{t_2})^0_-$ such that

$$\begin{bmatrix} I_{s_1} & 0 & 0 & \underline{\underline{p}}\alpha\underline{\underline{q}}' & \underline{\underline{p}}\alpha\underline{\underline{p}} & \underline{\underline{p}}\beta\underline{\underline{q}}' \\ 0 & I_{s_2} & 0 & \underline{\underline{q}}'\gamma\underline{\underline{q}}' & \underline{\underline{q}}'\gamma\underline{\underline{p}} & \underline{\underline{q}}'\delta\underline{\underline{q}}' \\ 0 & 0 & I_{s_2} & \underline{\underline{p}}^{\gamma}\underline{\underline{q}}' & \underline{\underline{p}}\gamma\underline{\underline{p}} & \underline{\underline{p}}\delta\underline{\underline{q}}' \\ \underline{\underline{q}}'\alpha^*\underline{\underline{p}} & \underline{\underline{q}}'\gamma^*\underline{\underline{q}}' & \underline{\underline{q}}'\gamma^*\underline{\underline{p}} & I_{t_1} & 0 & 0 \\ \underline{\underline{p}}\alpha^*\underline{\underline{p}} & \underline{\underline{p}}\gamma^*\underline{\underline{q}}' & \underline{\underline{p}}\gamma^*\underline{\underline{p}} & 0 & I_{t_1} & 0 \\ \underline{\underline{q}}'\beta^*\underline{\underline{p}} & \underline{\underline{q}}'\delta^*\underline{\underline{q}}' & \underline{\underline{q}}'\delta^*\underline{\underline{p}} & 0 & 0 & I_{t_2} \end{bmatrix} \begin{bmatrix} e_+ \\ f_- \\ f_+ \\ g_- \\ g_+ \\ h_- \end{bmatrix} = \begin{bmatrix} u_+ \\ v_- \\ v_+ \\ x_- \\ x_+ \\ y_- \end{bmatrix}$$

In particular it is enough to show that the preceding operator is Fredholm with index zero. But since this property is preserved under compact perturbations it is clearly more than enough to show that the preceding equation with all the terms involving both a $\underline{\underline{p}}$ and a $\underline{\underline{q}}'$ in the operator replaced by zero is uniquely solvable in $\mathcal{W}$ for every right hand side which belongs to $\mathcal{W}$. But then the resulting system of equations is readily seen to decouple into the pair of systems

$$\begin{bmatrix} I_{s_1} & 0 & \underline{\underline{p}}\alpha\underline{\underline{p}} \\ 0 & I_{s_2} & \underline{\underline{p}}\gamma\underline{\underline{p}} \\ \underline{\underline{p}}\alpha^*\underline{\underline{p}} & \underline{\underline{p}}\gamma^*\underline{\underline{p}} & I_{t_1} \end{bmatrix} \begin{bmatrix} e_+ \\ f_+ \\ g_+ \end{bmatrix} = \begin{bmatrix} u_+ \\ v_+ \\ x_+ \end{bmatrix} \tag{3.3}$$

and

$$\begin{bmatrix} I_{s_2} & \underline{\underline{q}}'\gamma\underline{\underline{q}}' & \underline{\underline{q}}'\delta\underline{\underline{q}}' \\ \underline{\underline{q}}'\gamma^*\underline{\underline{q}}' & I_{t_1} & 0 \\ \underline{\underline{q}}'\delta^*q^* & 0 & I_{t_2} \end{bmatrix} \begin{bmatrix} f_- \\ g_- \\ h_- \end{bmatrix} = \begin{bmatrix} v_- \\ x_- \\ y_- \end{bmatrix} . \tag{3.4}$$

But now by the presumed strict contractiveness of $\Gamma$ with respect to the $L^2$ norm it follows that the two indicated sets of equations are uniquely solvable in the appropriately sized $L^2$ spaces for every right hand side. Thus by Theorem 5.1 on page 201 of Gohberg-Feldman [GF] the symbol

$$x(\zeta) = \begin{bmatrix} I_{s_1} & 0 & \alpha(\zeta) \\ 0 & I_{s_2} & \gamma(\zeta) \\ \alpha(\zeta)^* & \gamma(\zeta)^* & I_{t_1} \end{bmatrix}$$

of the operator which intervenes in the system of equations (3.3) admits a canonical left factorization

$$x(\zeta) = x_-(\zeta)x_+(\zeta)$$

and hence it follows that the system is uniquely solvable in the appropriately sized $W_+$ space. In fact the solution

$$\begin{bmatrix} e_+ \\ f_+ \\ g_+ \end{bmatrix} = x_+^{-1}\underline{\underline{P}}\left\{ x_-^{-1} \begin{bmatrix} u_+ \\ v_+ \\ x_+ \end{bmatrix}\right\} ,$$

with the usual conventions. Similar considerations apply to the system (3.4) and so the proof is complete. □

**THEOREM 3.2.** *If $\varphi \in (B_\tau)_+$ and if $\|\Gamma_{ij}\|_2 < 1$ for the $k - |\tau|$ choices of $i, j = 1, \cdots, k$ with $j = i + \tau$, then there exists a unique solution pair $\alpha \in A_+$ and $\gamma \in (C_\tau)_-$ of the system of equations*

$$\alpha + P_{A_+}\varphi\gamma = I_m \tag{3.5a}$$

$$P_{C_-}\varphi^*\alpha + \gamma = 0 \tag{3.5b}$$

*and a unique solution pair $\beta \in (B_\tau)_+$ and $\delta \in D_-$ of the system of equations*

$$\beta + P_{B_+}\varphi\delta = 0 \tag{3.6a}$$

$$P_{D_-}\varphi^*\beta + \delta = I_n \ , \tag{3.6b}$$

*where $C_-$ is short for $(C_\tau)_-$ in (3.5b) and $B_+$ is short for $(B_\tau)_+$ in (3.6a).*

**PROOF.** Let $\alpha_j$, $\gamma_j$ and $\varepsilon_j$ denote the $j$'th block column (of width $\mu_j$) of $\alpha$, $\gamma$ and $I_m = I_{\mu_1} \oplus \cdots \oplus I_{\mu_k}$, respectively. Then the system of equations (3.5) splits into the $k$ systems of equations

$$\alpha_i + \Gamma_{i,i+\tau}\gamma_i = \varepsilon_i$$

$$\Gamma^*_{i,i+\tau}\alpha_i + \gamma_i = 0 \quad ,$$

$i = 1, \cdots, k$ . By Lemma 3.1 and the prevailing assumptions, $\|\Gamma_{i,i+\tau}\|_2 < 1$ for $i = 1, \cdots, k$. Therefore, by Theorem 3.1, there exists a unique solution pair $\alpha_i$, $\gamma_i$ for every $i = 1, \cdots, k$ where the columns of $\alpha_i$ belong to $W_m$ and the columns of $\gamma_i$ belong to $W_n$. Moreover, since

$$\begin{aligned}\alpha_i &= (I - \Gamma_{i,i+\tau}\Gamma^*_{i,i+\tau})^{-1}\varepsilon_i \\ &= \varepsilon_i + \Gamma_{i,i+\tau}\Gamma^*_{i,i+\tau}(I - \Gamma_{i,i+\tau}\Gamma^*_{i,i+\tau})^{-1}\varepsilon_i\end{aligned} \tag{3.7}$$

and

$$\gamma_i = -\Gamma^*_{i,i+\tau}\alpha_i \quad ,$$

it is readily seen that $\alpha = [\alpha_1 \cdots \alpha_k]$ belongs to $A_+$ and $\gamma = [\gamma_1 \cdots \gamma_k]$ belongs to $(C_\tau)_-$

The proof for the existence of a unique solution pair $\beta \in (B_\tau)_+$ and $\delta \in D_-$ to the system of equations (3.6) goes through in much the same way upon splitting $\beta$ and $\delta$ into the block columns $\beta_i$ and $\delta_i$ (of width $\nu_i$) and letting $\psi_i$ denote the $i$'th block column of $I_n = I_{\nu_1} \oplus \cdots \oplus I_{\nu_k}$. This leads to the $k$ systems

$$\beta_i + \Gamma_{i-\tau,i}\delta_i = 0$$

$$\Gamma^*_{i-\tau,i}\beta_i + \delta_i = \psi_i \quad ,$$

$i = i, \cdots, k$ , which are readily seen to be uniquely solvable in the appropriately sized Wiener spaces just as above. The corresponding matrices $\beta = [\beta_1 \cdots \beta_k]$ and $\delta = [\delta_1 \cdots \delta_k]$ are the unique solution pair of (3.6) with $\beta \in (B_\tau)_+$ and $\delta \in D_-$ .

□

**THEOREM 3.3.** *If $\varphi \in (B_\tau)_+$ and if $\|\Gamma_{ij}\|_2 < 1$ for the $k - |\tau|$ choices of $i, j = 1, \cdots, k$ with $j = i + \tau$, then $\begin{bmatrix} I_m & \varphi \\ \varphi^* & I_n \end{bmatrix}$ admits a band extension $\begin{bmatrix} I_m & g \\ g^* & I_n \end{bmatrix}$ which is both type I and type II, i.e.,*

$$\begin{bmatrix} I_m & g \\ g^* & I_n \end{bmatrix} = \begin{bmatrix} a^* & -c^* \\ 0 & I_n \end{bmatrix}^{-1} \begin{bmatrix} a & 0 \\ -c & I_n \end{bmatrix}^{-1} \tag{3.8}$$

*and*

$$\begin{bmatrix} I_m & g \\ g^* & I_n \end{bmatrix} = \begin{bmatrix} I_m & 0 \\ -b^* & d^* \end{bmatrix}^{-1} \begin{bmatrix} I_m & -b \\ 0 & d \end{bmatrix}^{-1} , \tag{3.9}$$

*where $a$ is invertible in $A_+$ , $b \in (B_\tau)_+$ , $c \in (C_\tau)_-$ and $d$ is invertible in $D_-$ .*

**PROOF.** The proof is divided into steps. Therein the symbol $\|\Gamma_{ij}\|_W$ is used to denote the operator norm of $\Gamma_{ij}$ with respect to the appropriately sized Wiener spaces.

**STEP 1.** *If, in addition to the imposed constraints,*

$$\max\{\|\Gamma_{ij}\|_W \ , \ \|\Gamma_{ij}^*\|_W\} < 1/\sqrt{2}$$

*for every choice of $i, j$ with $j = i + \tau$ , then the solution $\alpha$ of the system (3.5) is invertible in $A_+$ and the solution $\delta$ of the system (3.6) is invertible in $D_-$ .*

**PROOF OF STEP 1.** It follows readily from (3.7) that the $i$'th block row $a_{ii}$ (of height $\mu_i$) of $\alpha_i$ is given by the formula

$$\begin{aligned} \alpha_{ii} &= \varepsilon_i^* \alpha_i \\ &= I_{\mu_i} + \varepsilon_i^* \Gamma_{i,i+\tau} \Gamma_{i,i+\tau}^* (I - \Gamma_{i,i+\tau} \Gamma_{i,i+\tau}^*)^{-1} \varepsilon_i \end{aligned} \tag{3.10}$$

for $i = 1, \cdots, k$ . Therefore, since

$$\varepsilon_i^* \Gamma_{i,i+\tau} \Gamma_{i,i+\tau}^* (I - \Gamma_{i,i+\tau} \Gamma_{i,i+\tau}^*)^{-1} \varepsilon_i \in (W_{\mu_i \times \mu_i})_+$$

and its norm in that algebra is strictly less than one, $\alpha_{ii}$ is invertible in $(W_{\mu_i \times \mu_i})_+$ for $i = 1, \cdots, k$ . Hence $\alpha$ is invertible in $A_+$ .

In much the same way, it follows from the formula

$$\delta_i = \psi_i + \Gamma_{i-\tau,i}^* \Gamma_{i-\tau,i} (I - \Gamma_{i-\tau,i}^* \Gamma_{i-\tau,i})^{-1} \psi_i$$

that the corresponding $i$'th block row (of height $\nu_i$)

$$\delta_{ii} = \psi_i^* \delta_i = I_{\nu_i} + \psi_i^* \Gamma_{i-\tau,i}^* (I - \Gamma_{i-\tau,i} \Gamma_{i-\tau,i}^*)^{-1} \Gamma_{i-\tau,i} \psi_i \tag{3.11}$$

is invertible in $(W_{\nu_i \times \nu_i})_-$ and hence that $\delta$ is invertible in $D_-$. This completes the proof of Step 1.

**STEP 2.** *Let $\alpha^\varepsilon$ and $\gamma^\varepsilon$ denote the solutions of (3.5) with $\varphi$ replaced by $\varepsilon\varphi$, where $\varepsilon$ is a complex constant which is subject to the bound*

$$|\varepsilon| < \rho = (\max\{\|\Gamma_{i,i+\tau}\|_2 : i = 1, \cdots, k\})^{-1} \quad . \tag{3.12}$$

*Then*

$$M_\varepsilon = \operatorname{diag}\{\alpha_{11}^\varepsilon(0), \cdots, \alpha_{kk}^\varepsilon(0)\}$$

*is positive definite (and hence invertible),*

$$a^\varepsilon = \alpha^\varepsilon M_\varepsilon^{-1/2} \in A_+ \quad and \quad c^\varepsilon = -\gamma^\varepsilon M_\varepsilon^{-1/2} \in (C_\tau)_+$$

*for all such $\varepsilon$. Moreover, if $\varepsilon$ is subject to the more stringent condition*

$$|\varepsilon| < \min\{\rho, (2^{1/2}\|\varphi\|_W)^{-1}\} \ , \tag{3.13}$$

*then $a^\varepsilon$ is invertible in $A_+$ and*

$$k_\varepsilon = \begin{bmatrix} I_m & \varepsilon\varphi \\ \varepsilon^*\varphi^* & I_n \end{bmatrix}$$

*admits a type I extension*

$$\begin{bmatrix} I_m & g^\varepsilon \\ g^{\varepsilon *} & I_n \end{bmatrix} = \begin{bmatrix} a^{\varepsilon *} & -c^{\varepsilon *} \\ 0 & I_n \end{bmatrix}^{-1} \begin{bmatrix} a^\varepsilon & 0 \\ -c^\varepsilon & I_n \end{bmatrix}^{-1} \quad . \tag{3.14}$$

**PROOF OF STEP 2.** By formula (3.10),

$$\alpha_{ii}^\varepsilon(0) = \frac{1}{2\pi}\int_0^{2\pi} \alpha_{ii}^\varepsilon(e^{i\theta})d\theta \geq I_{\mu_i} \ .$$

Therefore, the block diagonal matrix $M\varepsilon$ is positive definite for $|\varepsilon| < \rho$ (and hence in particular for $|\varepsilon| \leq 1$). Moreover, by Step 1, $\alpha^\varepsilon$ is invertible in $A_+$ for $\varepsilon$ subject to the more stringent condition (3.13). Now, since $\alpha^\varepsilon$ and $\gamma^\varepsilon$ solve (3.5) with $\varphi$ replaced by $\varepsilon\varphi$, it is readily checked that $u_{11} = \alpha^\varepsilon$, $u_{21} = \gamma^\varepsilon$, $u_{22} = I_n$ , is a solution set of

(2.1) with $k_{11} = I_m$, $k_{12} = \varepsilon\varphi$, $k_{21} = (\varepsilon\varphi)^*$ and $k_{22} = I_n$ which meets the requisite invertibility and normalization conditions and that $v_{11} = (\alpha^\varepsilon M_\varepsilon^{-1})^*$ is invertible in $A_-$ , $v_{12} = (\gamma M_\varepsilon^{-1})^*$ belongs to $(B_\tau)_+$ and $v_{22} = I_n$ is invertible in $D_\pm$ . Moreover, since

$$(\alpha^\varepsilon - I_m)M_\varepsilon^{-1} + \varepsilon\varphi\gamma^\varepsilon M_\varepsilon^{-1} \in A_-^0$$

by (3.5a), the conjugate transpose,

$$v_{11} - (M_\varepsilon^{-1})^* + v_{12}\varepsilon^*\varphi^* \quad ,$$

belongs to $A_+^0$ . Therefore

$$v_{11} + P_{A_-}v_{12}\varepsilon^*\varphi^* = (M_\varepsilon^{-1})^* = M_\varepsilon^{-1} \; .$$

Next, since

$$\varepsilon^*\varphi^*\alpha^\varepsilon M_\varepsilon^{-1} + \gamma^\varepsilon M_\varepsilon^{-1} \in (C_\tau)_+^0$$

by (3.5b), its conjugate transpose

$$v_{11}\varepsilon\varphi + v_{12} \in (B_\tau)_-^0 \quad ,$$

which in turn implies that

$$P_{B_+}v_{11}\varepsilon\varphi + v_{12} = 0 \quad .$$

Thus $v_{11}$, $v_{12}$ and $v_{22} = I_n$ is a solution set of the system of equations (2.2) with $k_{11} = I_m$, $k_{12} = \varepsilon\varphi$, $k_{21} = \varepsilon^*\varphi^*$ and $k_{22} = I_n$ which meets the requisite invertibility and normalization conditions. Consequently, by Theorem 2.1,

$$\begin{bmatrix} v_{11} & v_{12} \\ 0 & v_{22} \end{bmatrix}^{-1} \begin{bmatrix} u_{11} & 0 \\ u_{21} & u_{22} \end{bmatrix}^{-1} = \begin{bmatrix} (\alpha^\varepsilon)^* & (\gamma^\varepsilon)^* \\ 0 & I_n \end{bmatrix}^{-1} \begin{bmatrix} M_\varepsilon^* & 0 \\ 0 & I_n \end{bmatrix} \begin{bmatrix} \alpha^\varepsilon & 0 \\ \gamma^\varepsilon & I_n \end{bmatrix}^{-1}$$

is a type I extension of $k_\varepsilon$ . But this is the same as the right hand side of (3.14) and so the proof of Step 2 is complete.

**STEP 3.** *Let $\beta^\varepsilon$ and $\delta^\varepsilon$ denote the solutions of (3.6) with $\varphi$ replaced by $\varepsilon\varphi$, where $\varepsilon$ is a complex constant which satisfies the bound (3.12). Then*

$$N_\varepsilon = diag\{\delta_{11}^\varepsilon(\infty), \cdots, \delta_{kk}^\varepsilon(\infty)\}$$

*is positive definite (and hence invertible),*

$$b^\varepsilon = -\beta^\varepsilon N_\varepsilon^{-1/2} \in (B_\tau)_+ \quad \text{and} \quad d^\varepsilon = \delta^\varepsilon N_\varepsilon^{-1/2} \in D_-$$

*for all such $\varepsilon$ . Moreover, if $\varepsilon$ is subject to the more stringent condition (3.13), then $\delta^\varepsilon$ is invertible in $D_-$ and $k_\varepsilon$ admits a type II extension*

$$\begin{bmatrix} I_m & h^\varepsilon \\ h^{\varepsilon *} & I_n \end{bmatrix} = \begin{bmatrix} I_m & 0 \\ -b^{\varepsilon *} & d^\varepsilon \end{bmatrix}^{-1} \begin{bmatrix} I_m & -b^\varepsilon \\ 0 & d^\varepsilon \end{bmatrix}^{-1} . \tag{3.15}$$

**PROOF OF STEP 3.** To begin with, it follows from (3.11) that

$$\delta_{jj}(\infty) = \frac{1}{2\pi}\int_0^{2\pi} \delta_{jj}(e^{i\theta})d\theta \geq I_{\nu_j}$$

for $j = 1, \cdots, k$ and hence that $N_\varepsilon$ is positive definite for $|\varepsilon| < \rho$. Thus $b^\varepsilon$ and $d^\varepsilon$ are well defined for all such $\varepsilon$. Now, since $\beta^\varepsilon$ and $\delta^\varepsilon$ are solutions of (3.6) with $\varphi$ replaced by $\varepsilon\varphi$, it is readily checked that $x_{11} = I_m$, $x_{21} = \beta^{\varepsilon *}$ and $x_{22} = \delta^{\varepsilon *}$ are solutions of (2.5) and that $y_{11} = I_m$, $y_{12} = \beta^\varepsilon N_\varepsilon^{-1}$ and $y_{22} = \delta^\varepsilon N_\varepsilon^{-1}$ are solutions of (2.6) (with $k_{11} = I_m$, $k_{12} = \varepsilon\varphi$, $k_{21} = \varepsilon^*\varphi^*$ and $k_{22} = I_n$) which meet the requisite invertibility and normalization condition as set forth in Theorem 2.2, when $\varepsilon$ meets the bound (3.13). Therefore, by that theorem, $k_\varepsilon$ admits a type II extension

$$\begin{bmatrix} x_{11} & 0 \\ x_{21} & x_{22} \end{bmatrix}^{-1} \begin{bmatrix} y_{11} & y_{12} \\ 0 & y_{22} \end{bmatrix}^{-1} = \begin{bmatrix} I_m & 0 \\ \beta^{\varepsilon *} & \delta^{\varepsilon *} \end{bmatrix}^{-1} \begin{bmatrix} I_m & 0 \\ 0 & N_\varepsilon \end{bmatrix} \begin{bmatrix} I_m & \beta^\varepsilon \\ 0 & \delta^\varepsilon \end{bmatrix}^{-1} ,$$

which is readily seen to be the same as the right hand side of (3.15).

**STEP 4** *is to complete the proof of the theorem.*

**PROOF OF STEP 4.** The argument is adapted from the tail end of the proof of Theorem 4.1 in [DG2]. To begin with, if $\varepsilon$ is subject to (3.13), then $g^\varepsilon = h^\varepsilon$ by Theorem 2.3 and therefore

$$a^\varepsilon(\zeta)^* a^\varepsilon(\zeta) = I_m + c^\varepsilon(\zeta)^* c^\varepsilon(\zeta)$$

and

$$d^\varepsilon(\zeta)^* d^\varepsilon(\zeta) = I_n + b^\varepsilon(\zeta)^* b^\varepsilon(\zeta)$$

for every point $\zeta \in \mathbb{T}$ , as follows by computing the 11 block of (3.14) and the 22 block of (3.15), respectively. Since the functions $a^\varepsilon(\zeta)$, $b^\varepsilon(\zeta)$, $c^\varepsilon(\zeta)$, $d^\varepsilon(\zeta)$ and their adjoints are analytic for real $\varepsilon$ in the interval $-\rho < \varepsilon < \rho$, it follows that for each fixed point $\zeta \in \mathbb{T}$ these identities are valid for all real $\varepsilon$ with $|\varepsilon| < \rho$ (and hence in particular for $\varepsilon = 1$). Therefore

$$a^\varepsilon(\zeta)^* a^\varepsilon(\zeta) \geq I_m$$

and hence

$$|\det\{a_{11}^\varepsilon(\zeta) \cdots a_{kk}^\varepsilon(\zeta)\}| = |\det\, a^\varepsilon(\zeta)| \geq 1$$

for $-\varepsilon < \rho < \varepsilon$ and $\zeta \in \mathbb{T}$ . This insures that no zeros in det $a_{ii}^\varepsilon(\zeta)$, $i = i, \cdots, k$ , can "cross the boundary" $\mathbb{T}$ of $\mathbb{D}$ and thus since det $a_{ii}^\varepsilon(\zeta)$ is nonzero in $\bar{\mathbb{D}}$ for small $|\varepsilon|$, the same holds true for $\varepsilon = 1$. To make the argument precise fix $i$, $i = 1, \cdots, k$ and let

$$E_1 = \{\varepsilon \in (0, \rho) : \det\, a_{ii}^\varepsilon(\zeta) \text{ has a zero in } \mathbb{D}\}$$

and

$$E_2 = \{\varepsilon \in (0, \rho) : \det\, a_{ii}^\varepsilon(\zeta) \text{ has no zeros in } \mathbb{D}\}$$

Then, since $|\det\, a_{ii}^\varepsilon(\zeta)| > 0$ on $\mathbb{T}$ for $0 < \varepsilon < \rho$ , $E_1$ is open by Rouche's theorem. On the otherhand

$$E_2 = \{\varepsilon \in (0, \rho) : \det\, a_{ii}^\varepsilon(\zeta) \quad \textit{has no zeros in } \bar{\mathbb{D}}\} ,$$

which is open by continuity. Moreover, $E_1$ and $E_2$ are disjoint $E_1 \cup E_2 = (0, \rho)$ and $E_2$ is nonempty. Thus, since $(0, \rho)$ is connected, $E_2 = (0, \rho)$. In particular this implies that det $a_{ii}^\varepsilon(\zeta)$ is nonzero in $\bar{\mathbb{D}}$ and hence, by the matrix version of Wiener's theorem, that $\alpha_{ii}^\varepsilon(\zeta)$ is invertible in $(W_{\mu_i \times \mu_i})_+$ for $i = 1, \cdots, k$ and $0 < \varepsilon < \rho$ . Therefore $\alpha^\varepsilon(\zeta)$ is invertible in $A_+$ for $0 < \varepsilon < \rho$. By a similar argument, $d^\varepsilon(\zeta)$ is invertible in $D_-$ for $0 < \varepsilon < \rho$. Thus the analysis leading to formulas (3.14) and (3.15) is valid for $0 < \varepsilon < \rho$, as are the formulas themselves. The choice $\varepsilon = 1$ yields (3.7) and (3.8).

□

**THEOREM 3.4.** *If $\varphi \in (B_\tau)_+$ and if $\|\Gamma_{ij}\|_2 < 1$ for the $k - |\tau|$ choices of $i, j = 1, \cdots, k$ with $j = i + \tau$, then $\mathcal{G}_\tau(\varphi)$ contains exactly one band interpolant.*

**PROOF.** Under the stated conditions, Theorem 3.3 guarantees that $\mathcal{G}_\tau(\varphi)$ contains at least one band interpolant $g$. Therefore it remains to show that it contains at most one. Accordingly, let $h \in \mathcal{G}_\tau(\varphi)$ be a band interpolant. Then

$$\begin{bmatrix} I_m & h \\ h^* & I_n \end{bmatrix}^{-1} = \begin{bmatrix} \alpha & \beta \\ \beta^* & \delta \end{bmatrix} ,$$

where $\alpha \in A$ and $\delta \in D$ are both positive definite on $\mathbb{T}$ and $\beta \in (B_\tau)_+$. Thus the last block matrix admits a factorization of the form

$$\begin{bmatrix} I_m & h \\ h^* & I_n \end{bmatrix}^{-1} = \begin{bmatrix} I_m & 0 \\ \beta^*\alpha^{-1} & I_n \end{bmatrix} \begin{bmatrix} \alpha & 0 \\ 0 & \delta - \beta^*\alpha^{-1}\beta \end{bmatrix} \begin{bmatrix} I_m & \alpha^{-1}\beta \\ 0 & I_n \end{bmatrix} ,$$

where $\delta - \beta^*\alpha^{-1}\beta > 0$. But now, as $\alpha > 0$ on $\mathbb{T}$, it admits a block triangular factorization of the form

$$\alpha = \alpha_\ell \alpha_0 \alpha_\ell^* \ ,$$

where $\alpha_\ell$ is block lower triangular and $\alpha_0$ is block diagonal with $(\alpha_\ell)_{ii} = I_{\mu_i}$ and $(\alpha_0)_{ii} > 0$ for $i = i, \cdots, k$. Thus

$$\alpha_0 = zz^* \ ,$$

where $z$ is block diagonal with block entries $z_{ii} \in (W_{\mu_i \times \mu_i})_+$ and hence

$$\alpha = \alpha_+ \alpha_+^*$$

where $\alpha_+ = \alpha_\ell z$ is invertible in $A_+$.

Next, it is readily seen that

$$\delta - \beta^*\alpha^{-1}\beta = I_n$$

and hence that

$$\begin{bmatrix} I_m & h \\ h^* & I_n \end{bmatrix}^{-1} = \begin{bmatrix} I_m & 0 \\ \beta^*\alpha^{-1} & I_n \end{bmatrix} \begin{bmatrix} \alpha_+\alpha_+^* & 0 \\ 0 & I_n \end{bmatrix} \begin{bmatrix} I_m & \alpha^{-1}\beta \\ 0 & I_n \end{bmatrix}$$

$$= \begin{bmatrix} \alpha_+ & 0 \\ \beta^*(\alpha_+^*)^{-1} & I_n \end{bmatrix} \begin{bmatrix} \alpha_+^* & \alpha_+^{-1}\beta \\ 0 & I_n \end{bmatrix} .$$

Therefore, since $\alpha_+^{-1}\beta \in (B_\tau)_+$, this exhibits

$$\begin{bmatrix} I_m & h \\ h^* & I_n \end{bmatrix} \text{ as a type I extension of } \begin{bmatrix} I_m & \varphi \\ \varphi^* & I_n \end{bmatrix} .$$

Thus it must agree with the already exhibited type II (and type I) extension exhibited in Theorem 3.3, i.e., $h = g$. This establishes the asserted uniqueness.

□

## 4. LINEAR FRACTIONAL TRANSFORMATIONS

In this section we shall show that if $\varphi \in (B_\tau)_+$ and if $\|\Gamma_{ij}\|_2 < 1$ for the $k - |\tau|$ choices of $i, j = 1, \cdots, k$ with $j = i + \tau$ , then $\mathcal{G}_\tau(\varphi)$ is equal to the set of linear transformations

$$T_\Theta[h] = (ah + b)(ch + d)^{-1}$$

of the set of $h$ in $(B_\tau)_-^0$ which are strictly contractive on $\mathbb{T}$ , where $a$, $b$, $c, d$ are the entries in the factorization formulas (3.8) and (3.9).

It is perhaps well to recall at this point that these entries were obtained by normalizing the (unique) solutions $\alpha$ and $\gamma$ of (3.5) and the (unique) solutions $\beta$ and $\delta$ of (3.6) according to the recipies given in the statements of Steps 2 and 3 of the proof of Theorem 3.3. The specific normalizations which were imposed were chosen to achieve

$$aa^* = \alpha M^{-1}\alpha^* \ , cc^* = \gamma M^{-1}\gamma^* \ , \ bb^* = \beta N^{-1}\beta^* \ \text{ and } \ dd^* = \delta N^{-1}\delta^*$$

(here we have dropped the superscript $\varepsilon$ from the notation). We could just as well have written

$$M^{-1} = M^{-1/2}UU^*M^{-1/2} \ \text{ and } \ N^{-1} = N^{-1/2}VV^*N^{-1/2}$$

with $U$ and $V$ unitary, and then set $a = \alpha M^{-1/2}U$, $c = -\gamma M^{-1/2}U$, $b = -\beta N^{-1/2}V$ and $d = \delta N^{-1/2}V$ . This suggests that $a$, $b$, $c$ and $d$ are unique up to the indicated right constant unitary factors. This is indeed the case, as is explained from another point of view in the next two lemmas.

**LEMMA 4.1.** *If $a_i$ are invertible in $A_+$ and $c_i \in (C_\tau)_-$ for $i = 1,2$ and if*

$$\begin{bmatrix} a_1(\zeta)^* & -c_1(\zeta)^* \\ 0 & I_n \end{bmatrix}^{-1} \begin{bmatrix} a_1(\zeta) & 0 \\ -c_1(\zeta) & I_n \end{bmatrix}^{-1} = \begin{bmatrix} a_2(\zeta)^* & -c_2(\zeta)^* \\ 0 & I_n \end{bmatrix}^{-1} \begin{bmatrix} a_2(\zeta) & 0 \\ -c_2(\zeta) & I_n \end{bmatrix}^{-1}$$

*for every point* $\zeta \in \mathbb{T}$, *then there exists a constant (block diagonal) unitary matrix* $U$ *such that*

$$a_2 = a_1 U \quad \text{and} \quad c_2 = c_1 U \ .$$

**PROOF.** The identity implies that

$$\begin{bmatrix} a_1^{-1} & 0 \\ c_1 a_1^{-1} & I_n \end{bmatrix} \begin{bmatrix} a_2 & 0 \\ -c_2 & I_n \end{bmatrix} = \begin{bmatrix} a_1^* & -c_1^* \\ 0 & I_n \end{bmatrix} \begin{bmatrix} a_2^{*-1} & a_2^{*-1} c_2^* \\ 0 & I_n \end{bmatrix}$$

and hence that

$$a_1^{-1} a_2 = a_1^* a_2^{*-1}$$

and

$$c_1 a_1^{-1} a_2 = c_2 \ .$$

The first of these implies that

$$U = a_1^{-1} a_2 \in A_+ \cap A_- = A_0$$

is a constant block diagonal matrix which is unitary. This yields the first asserted formula; the second is plain from the second equation.

□

**LEMMA 4.2.** *If* $d_i$ *are invertible in* $D_-$ *and* $b_i \in (B_\tau)_+$ *for* $i = 1, 2$ *and if*

$$\begin{bmatrix} I_m & 0 \\ -b_1(\zeta)^* & d_1(\zeta)^* \end{bmatrix}^{-1} \begin{bmatrix} I_m & -b_1(\zeta) \\ 0 & d_1(\zeta) \end{bmatrix}^{-1} = \begin{bmatrix} I_m & 0 \\ -b_2(\zeta)^* & d_2(\zeta)^* \end{bmatrix}^{-1} \begin{bmatrix} I_m & -b_2(\zeta) \\ 0 & d_2(\zeta) \end{bmatrix}^{-1}$$

*for every point* $\zeta \in \mathbb{T}$ , *then there exists a constant (block diagonal) unitary matrix* $V$ *such that*

$$d_2 = d_1 V \quad \text{and} \quad b_2 = b_1 V \ .$$

**PROOF.** The identity implies that

$$\begin{bmatrix} I_m & b_1 d_1^{-1} \\ 0 & d_1^{-1} \end{bmatrix} \begin{bmatrix} I_m & -b_2 \\ 0 & d_2 \end{bmatrix} = \begin{bmatrix} I_m & 0 \\ -b_1^* & d_1^* \end{bmatrix} \begin{bmatrix} I_m & 0 \\ d_2^{*-1} b_2^* & d_2^{*-1} \end{bmatrix}$$

and hence that

$$d_1^{-1} d_2 = d_1^* d_2^{*-1}$$

and

$$b_1 d_1^{-1} d_2 = b_2 \quad .$$

The first of these implies that

$$V = d_1^{-1} d_2 \in D_- \cap D_+ = D_0$$

is a constant block diagonal unitary matrix. This yields the first asserted formula; the second is plain from the second equation.

□

It is now plain that if $a_i$, $b_i$, $c_i$ and $d_i$ meet the hypotheses of the preceding two lemmas, then

$$\begin{bmatrix} a_2(\zeta) & b_2(\zeta) \\ c_2(\zeta) & d_2(\zeta) \end{bmatrix} = \begin{bmatrix} a_1(\zeta) & b_1(\zeta) \\ c_1(\zeta) & d_1(\zeta) \end{bmatrix} \begin{bmatrix} U & 0 \\ 0 & V \end{bmatrix} \tag{4.1}$$

for every point $\zeta \in \mathbb{T}$ , where $U$ and $V$ are constant (block diagonal) unitary matrices.

**THEOREM 4.1.** *If $\varphi \in (B_\tau)_+$ and if $\|\Gamma_{ij}\|_2 < 1$ for the $k - |\tau|$ choices of $i, j = 1, \cdots, k$ which lie on the $\tau$'th diagonal, then the $(m+n) \times (m+n)$ matrix valued function*

$$\Theta(\zeta) = \begin{bmatrix} a(\zeta) & b(\zeta) \\ c(\zeta) & d(\zeta) \end{bmatrix}$$

*which is based on the entries in the factorizations (3.8) and (3.9) is $J$ unitary on $\mathbb{T}$ with respect to the signature matrix*

$$J = \begin{bmatrix} I_m & 0 \\ 0 & -I_n \end{bmatrix} \quad .$$

**PROOF.** The statement means that

$$\Theta(\zeta)^* J \Theta(\zeta) = J \tag{4.2}$$

for every point $\zeta \in \mathbb{T}$ . This amounts to checking the following three identities :

$$a(\zeta)^* a(\zeta) - c(\zeta)^* c(\zeta) = I_m \tag{4.3}$$

$$a(\zeta)^* b(\zeta) - c(\zeta)^* d(\zeta) = 0 \tag{4.4}$$

$$b(\zeta)^* b(\zeta) - d(\zeta)^* d(\zeta) = -I_n \tag{4.5}$$

The identity (4.3) is obtained by evaluating the 11 block of (3.8), while (4.5) is obtained by evaluating the 22 block of (3.9).

Next, upon matching the right hand sides of (3.8) and (3.9), it follows that

$$\begin{bmatrix} a & 0 \\ -c & I_n \end{bmatrix}^{-1} \begin{bmatrix} I_m & -b \\ 0 & d \end{bmatrix} = \begin{bmatrix} a^* & -c^* \\ 0 & I_n \end{bmatrix} \begin{bmatrix} I_m & 0 \\ -b^* & d^* \end{bmatrix}^{-1} ,$$

which is equivalent to the four identities

$$a(\zeta)^{-1} = a(\zeta)^* - c(\zeta)^* d(\zeta)^{*-1} b(\zeta)^* \tag{4.6}$$

$$c(\zeta)a(\zeta)^{-1} = d(\zeta)^{*-1} b(\zeta)^* \tag{4.7}$$

$$a(\zeta)^{-1} b(\zeta) = c(\zeta)^* d(\zeta)^{*-1} \tag{4.8}$$

$$d(\zeta) - c(\zeta)a(\zeta)^{-1} b(\zeta) = d(\zeta)^{*-1} \ , \tag{4.9}$$

which are valid for every point $\zeta \in \mathbb{T}$. Identity (4.7) is equivalent to (4.4).

□

**COROLLARY.** *The identities*

$$a(\zeta)a(\zeta)^* - b(\zeta)b(\zeta)^* = I_m \tag{4.10}$$

$$c(\zeta)a(\zeta)^* - d(\zeta)b(\zeta)^* = 0 \tag{4.11}$$

$$c(\zeta)c(\zeta)^* - d(\zeta)d(\zeta)^* = -I_n \tag{4.12}$$

*hold for every choice of* $\zeta \in \mathbb{T}$ .

**PROOF.** The cited identities are equivalent to the assertion that

$$\Theta(\zeta) J \theta(\zeta)^* = J$$

for every point $\zeta \in \mathbb{T}$ which in turn is an immediate consequence of (4.2).

□

**LEMMA 4.3.** *If* $\varphi \in (B_\tau)_+$ *and if* $\|\Gamma_{ij}\|_2 < 1$ *for the* $k - |\tau|$ *choices of* $i, j = 1, \cdots, k$ *with* $j = i + \tau$ *and if* $c$ *and* $d$ *are the entries which intervene in the factorization formula (3.9), then* $ch + d$ *is invertible in* $D_-$ *for every choice of* $h \in (B_\tau)^0_-$ *which is contractive on* $\mathbb{T}$ *(strictly or not).*

**PROOF.** Since $ch \in D_-^0$ and $d \in D_-$, $ch+d$ clearly belongs to $D_-$. Moreover, $d$ is invertible in $D_-$ and $d^{-1}c$ is strictly contractive on $\mathbb{T}$ by (4.12). Therefore, the $ii$ block (of size $\nu_i \times \nu_i$)

$$(d^{-1}ch)_{ii} = (d_{ii})^{-1}c_{i,i-\tau}h_{i-\tau,i}$$

belongs to $(W_{\nu_i \times \nu_i})_-^0$ and is strictly contractive on $\mathbb{T}$. Thus, by the maximum modulus principle, it is strictly contractive on $\{\zeta \in \mathbb{C} : | \leq |\zeta| \leq \infty\}$ and hence, by the matrix version of Wiener's theorem

$$I_{\nu_i} + (d^{-1}ch)_{ii} = d_{ii}^{-1}(d+ch)_{ii}$$

is invertible in $(W_{\nu_i \times \nu_i})_-$. But this in turn implies that $(d+ch)_{ii}$ is invertible in $(W_{\nu_i \times \nu_i})_-$ and hence that $d+ch$ is invertible in $D_-$, as claimed.

□

**THEOREM 4.2.** *If $\varphi \in (B_\tau)_+$ and $\|\Gamma_{ij}\|_2 < 1$ for the $k - |\tau|$ choices of $i,j = 1,\cdots,k$ with $j = i+\tau$, and if $\Theta$ is defined as in Theorem 4.1, then*

$$\mathcal{G}_\tau(\varphi) = \{T_\Theta[h] : h \in (B_\tau)_-^0 \text{ and } I_m - h(\zeta)h(\zeta)^* > 0 \text{ for every point } \zeta \in \mathbb{T}\}\,. \tag{4.13}$$

**PROOF.** Lemma 4.3 guarantees that $T_\Theta[h]$ is well defined for contractive $h$ in $(B_\tau)_-^0$. Moreover, the evaluation (on $\mathbb{T}$)

$$\begin{aligned}(ch+d)^*\{T_\Theta[h]^*T_\Theta[h] - I_n\}(ch+d) &= [h^* I_n]\Theta^* J\Theta \begin{bmatrix} h \\ I_n \end{bmatrix} \\ &= [h^* I_n]J \begin{bmatrix} h \\ I_n \end{bmatrix} \\ &= h^*h - I_n\end{aligned}$$

clearly implies that $T_\Theta[h]$ is strictly contractive on $\mathbb{T}$, since $h$ is.

Next, with the help of (4.6) and Lemma 4.3, it follows that

$$\begin{aligned}T_\Theta[h] - T_\Theta[0] &= (ah+b)(ch+d)^{-1} - bd^{-1} \\ &= \{ah + b - bd^{-1}(ch+d)\}(ch+d)^{-1} \\ &= (a - bd^{-1}c)h(ch+d)^{-1} \\ &= a^{*-1}h(ch+d)^{-1}\end{aligned} \tag{4.14}$$

belongs to $(B_\tau)_-^0$. Thus, since $bd^{-1} \in \mathcal{G}_\tau(\varphi)$, so does $T_\Theta[h]$. This proves that the righthand side of (4.13) is included inside $\mathcal{G}_\tau(\varphi)$.

Next, suppose that $g \in \mathcal{G}_\tau(\varphi)$ and let

$$h = T_{\Theta^{-1}}[g]$$

so that

$$g = T_\Theta\left[T_{\Theta^{-1}}[g]\right] = T_\Theta[h] \quad .$$

Now, since $\Theta^{-1}$ is $J$ unitary on $\mathbb{T}$ , it follows from the first few lines of the proof of this theorem that $h$ is strictly contractive on $\mathbb{T}$, because every $g \in \mathcal{G}_\tau(\varphi)$ is. Thus, in order to obtain the opposite inclusion to the one deduced in the previous paragraph and hence to complete the proof, it remains only to show that $h \in (B_\tau)^0_-$ . To this end observe first that

$$g - bd^{-1} = T_\Theta[h] - T_\Theta[0]$$

belongs to $(B_\tau)^0_-$ since both $bd^{-1}$ and $g$ belong to $\mathcal{G}_\tau(\varphi)$. Therefore, by (4.14),

$$a^{*-1}h(ch+d)^{-1} \in (B_\tau)^0_- \quad ,$$

as does $h(d^{-1}ch+I_n)$ . Now, $f = d^{-1}c$ belongs to $(C_\tau)_-$ and, thanks to (4.12), is strictly contractive on $\mathbb{T}$. Therefore $fh(fh+I_n)^{-1} \in D^0_-$ and $(I_n+fh)^{-1} = I_n - fh(I_n+fh)^{-1}$ belongs to $D_-$, as does

$$v = (I_n - fh)(I_n + fh)^{-1} \ .$$

But, since $fh$ is strictly contractive on $\mathbb{T}$, it is readily checked that

$$v(\zeta) + v(\zeta)^* > 0$$

for every point $\zeta \in \mathbb{T}$ . In particular,

$$v_{ii}(\zeta) + v_{ii}(\zeta)^* > 0$$

for every point $\zeta \in \mathbb{T}$ and therefore, as follows for example from the Poisson formula for the exterior of the disc,

$$v_{ii}(\zeta) + v_{ii}(\zeta)^* \geq 0$$

for $1 \leq |\zeta| \leq \infty$ . Thus $I_{\nu_i} + v_{ii}(\zeta)$ is invertible in $(W_{\nu_i \times \nu_i})_-$. But this in turn implies that

$$I_n + v = 2(I_n + fh)^{-1}$$

is invertible in $D_-$ and hence that

$$h = \{h(I_n + fh)\}(I_n + fh)^{-1} \qquad \text{belongs to } (B_\tau)^0_- \ .$$

## 5. MAXIMUM ENTROPY

In this section we shall show that as $g$ runs over $\mathcal{G}_\tau(\varphi)$ , the maximum value of the entropy integral $\mathcal{E}(g)$ is achieved by the band interpolant $bd^{-1} = a^*c^{*-1}$, only.

**THEOREM 5.1.** *If $\varphi \in (B_\tau)_+$ and $\|\Gamma_{ij}\|_2 < 1$ for the $k - |\tau|$ choices of $i, j = 1, \cdots, k$ with $j = i + \tau$, then*

$$\mathcal{E}(g) \leq -\frac{1}{2\pi}\int_0^{2\pi} \log\,\det\{d(e^{i\theta})^* d(e^{i\theta})\}d\theta \tag{5.1}$$

*for every choice of $g \in \mathcal{G}_\tau(\varphi)$ . Equality prevails in (5.1) if and only if $g$ is equal to the band interpolant, i.e., if and only if*

$$g = T_\Theta[0] = bd^{-1} = a^{*-1}c^* \ . \tag{5.2}$$

**PROOF.** Let $g \in \mathcal{G}_\tau(\varphi)$ . Then, by Theorem 4.2,

$$g = T_\Theta[h] = (ah + b)(ch + d)^{-1}$$

(on $\mathbb{T}$) for some $h \in B_-^0$ which is strictly contractive on $\mathbb{T}$. Therefore, by a straightforward calculation which takes advantage of (4.2), it is readily seen that

$$I_n - g^*g = \{d^* + h^*c^*\}^{-1}\{I_n - h^*h\}\{d + ch\}^{-1}$$

on $\mathbb{T}$ and hence that

$$\mathcal{E}(g) = \mathcal{E}(h) - \delta_h - \delta_h^* \ ,$$

where

$$\delta_h = \frac{1}{2\pi}\int_0^{2\pi} \log\,\det\{d(e^{i\theta})^* + h(e^{i\theta})^* c(e^{i\theta})^*\}d\theta \ .$$

But now, since $d^* \in D_+$ , $c^* \in C_+$ , $h^* \in C_+^0$ and $cd^{-1}$ is strictly contractive on $\mathbb{T}$, it follows that

$$\psi = h^*c^*d^{*-1}$$

is a strictly contractive member of $D_+^0$ and hence that

$$\log\,\det\{d^* + h^*c^*\} = \log\,\det\{I_n + \psi\} + \log\,\det\{d^*\}$$
$$= \sum_{i=1}^{k} \log\,\det\{I_{\nu_i} + \psi_{ii}\} + \sum_{i=1}^{k} \log\,\det\{d_{ii}^*\}\ .$$

Thus

$$\delta_h = \sum_{i=1}^{k} \log\,\det\{I_{\nu_i} + \psi_{ii}(0)\} + \frac{1}{2\pi}\int_0^{2\pi} \log\,\det\{d(e^{i\theta})^*\}d\theta\ .$$

The terms in the sum are all equal to zero because

$$\psi_{ii}(0) = 0\ .$$

Consequently $\delta_h$ is independent of $h$ and is equal to the indicated integral. The rest is plain since

$$\mathcal{E}(h) \le 0$$

with equality if and only if $h = 0$ .

□

**COROLLARY.** *If $g \in \mathcal{G}_\tau(\varphi)$ , then*

$$\mathcal{E}(g) \le \sum_{1}^{k} \log|\det\, d_{ii}(\infty)|^{-2} \tag{5.3}$$

*with equality if and only if $g$ is equal to the band interpolant.*

We remark that the bound (7.3) of [DG2] emerges from (5.3) in the special case that $k = 1$ (and hence $\tau = 0$).

## 6. REFERENCES

[AAK] Adamjan, V.M., D.Z. Arov and M.G. Krein: Infinite Hankelblock matrices and related extension problems, Izv. Akad. Nauk SSR. Ser. Math. **6** (1971), 87-112 [English transl.: Amer. Math. Soc. **111** (1978), 133-156].

[BC] Ball, J.A. and N. Cohen: Sensitivity minimization in an $H^{\infty}$ norm: parametrization of all suboptimal solutions, Int. J. Control **46** (1987), 785-816.

[Do1] Doyle, J.C.: Synthesis of robust controllers, Proc. IEEE Conf. Dec. Control, 1983.

[Do2] Doyle, J.C.: Lecture Notes in Advances in Multivariable Control, ONR/Honeywell Workshop, Minneapolis, 1984.

[ D ] Dym, H., J. Contractive Matrices, Reproducing Kernel Hilbert Spaces and Interpolation, in preparation.

[DG1] Dym, H. and I. Gohberg: Extension of kernels of Fredholm operators, J. d'Analyse Math. **42** (1982/83), 51-97.

[DG2] Dym, H. and I. Gohberg: A maximum entropy principle for contractive interpolants, J. Functional Analysis, **65** (1986), 83-125.

[FF1] Feintuch, A. and B.A. Francis: Uniformly optimal control of linear feedback systems, Automatica **21** (1985), 563-574.

[FF2] Feintuch, A. and B.A. Francis: Distance formulas for operator algebras arising in optimal control problems, This volume.

[GF ] Gohberg, I.C. and I.A. Feldman, Convolution equations and projection methods for their solution, Trans. Math. Monographs, Vol. 41, Amer. Math. Soc., Providence, R.I., 1974.

Department of Theoretical Mathematics
The Weizmann Institute of Science
Rehovot 76100, Israel.

Department of Mathematical Sciences
Tel Aviv University
Ramat Aviv 69978, Israel.

Submitted: July 9, 1987

Operator Theory:
Advances and Applications, Vol. 29



# DISTANCE FORMULAS FOR OPERATOR ALGEBRAS ARISING IN OPTIMAL CONTROL PROBLEMS

Avraham Feintuch and Bruce Francis

Dedicated to Professor Moshe Livsic,
a great scientist and a man of personal integrity and honour,
on the occasion of his seventieth birthday.

The paper considers extensions of Nehari's distance formula to more general situations arising in control theory. A formula is derived for the distance from a periodic operator to a certain subalgebra of operators.

## INTRODUCTION

The seminal paper by Zames [15] formulated a linear-quadratic optimal control problem where the exogenous signals are not fixed but belong to weighted balls in appropriate function spaces. One reason for the remarkable influence of this paper, especially on operator theorists interested in system-theoretic problems, is the fact that the mathematical formulation of this problem (given in Zames' paper [15] and developed further in other papers by himself and collaborators) was given in terms of classical results in interpolation theory and their modern operator-theoretic interpretations as they appeared in the work of Adamjan, Arov, Krein [1], [2], Sarason [13], Sz.-Nagy-Foias [14].

As a result of this, new interest was raised in these problems and the work in this area can be seen as proceeding in three major directions:

(1) Finding procedures for the actual computation of the norms of Hankel operators arising in these problems.

(2) Extending to more general situations which arise in control theory the classical Nehari formula for the distance from a bounded measurable function on the unit circle to the algebra $\mathbf{H}_\infty$.

(3) Characterizing the minimizing functions for which the Nehari distance formula is attained.

This paper proceeds in the second direction. We will define a very general distance problem which includes the problem considered by Davis *et al.* [4] on the one hand and that defined by Doyle [5] on the other. We will show how the various distance problems arising in control theory fit into this context and give a unified approach to the solutions in each case. This paper is based on our previous work [7], [8] on these problems and is our attempt to provide a single conceptual framework within which the relationship between the various problems is clarified. A special case ($\mathbf{H}_\infty$) of this problem has been discussed thoroughly by Doyle and Francis from an engineering point of view [6]. Since that paper contains a complete bibliography, we have restricted ourselves to references which are directly related to the results given here.

## A GENERAL DISTANCE PROBLEM

Let $\mathbf{H}$ be a complex Hilbert space and $\mathbf{A}$ a (weakly closed) operator algebra on $\mathbf{H}$ with the following property: if $T \in \mathbf{A}$ and has closed range, then $T$, $T^*$ have factorizations of the type

$$T = UA\,, \quad T^* = V^* B^*$$

where $A$, $A^{-1}$, $B$, $B^{-1} \in \mathbf{A}$, $U$ in $\mathbf{A}$ is an isometry on $\mathbf{H}$ with range that of $T$, and $V$ in $\mathbf{A}$ is an isometry on $\mathbf{H}$ such that $V^*$ has the same range as $T^*$.

The best known contexts where such factorizations exist are as follows:

(1) $\mathbf{A} = \mathbf{B}(\mathbf{H})$, the space of bounded linear operators on $\mathbf{H}$, and the factorizations are the polar decompositions of $T$ and $T^*$,

(2) $\mathbf{A} = \mathbf{H}_\infty$ and the factorizations are the classical inner-outer factorizations.

In this paper we consider these as well as their 'generalizations':

(3) The commutants of powers of the unilateral shift in which it has been shown in [8] that inner-outer factorizations exist.

(4) Discrete nest algebras, where the existence of such factorizations has been shown by Arveson [3].

The problem we will consider can now be formulated as follows: given an operator $T$ in $\mathbf{A}$ and operators $W_1$, $W_2$ in $\mathbf{A}$ with closed range, find

$$\mu := \inf\{\|T - W_1 Q W_2\| : Q \in \mathbf{A}\}$$

It is easily seen that this infimum is attained. The proof is essentially the same as that of [7], Theorem 1.

THEOREM 1. *There exists* $Q$ *in* $\mathbf{A}$ *such that* $\mu = \|T - W_1 Q W_1\|$.

PROOF. We can write

$$W_1 = UA$$

$$W_2 = BV$$

where $A^{-1}, B^{-1} \in \mathbf{A}$, $U^* U = I$ and $VV^* = I$. Thus

$$\|T - W_1 Q W_2\| = \|T - UAQBV\|$$

Now the mapping $Q \rightarrow AQB$ is bijective on $\mathbf{A}$. Thus

$$\inf\{\|T - W_1 Q W_2\| : Q \in \mathbf{A}\} = \inf\{\|T - UQV\| : Q \in \mathbf{A}\}$$

We claim that $U\mathbf{A}V$ is weakly closed. Indeed, suppose $\{X_\alpha\}$ is a net in $\mathbf{A}$ such that $\{UX_\alpha V\}$ converges weakly to $Y$ on $\mathbf{H}$. Since $U^* U = VV^* = I$, $X_\alpha$ converges weakly to $U^* YN^*$. Since $\mathbf{A}$ is weakly closed, $X := U^* YV^* \in \mathbf{A}$. Thus $\{UX_\alpha V\}$ converges weakly to $UXV \in U\mathbf{A}V$. Then $\mu = \text{dist}(T, U\mathbf{A}V)$ and there exists a sequence $\{Z_k\}$ in $U\mathbf{A}V$ such that $\|T - Z_k\| \rightarrow \mu$. Since $\{Z_k\}$ is bounded and thus weakly compact, there exists some subsequence converging weakly to some $Z$ in $U\mathbf{A}V$. Thus $Z = UQV$ for some $Q$ in $\mathbf{A}$ and

$$\mu = \|T - Z\| = \|T - UQV\| \quad \square$$

It will be useful to isolate $Q$ in the expression $\|T - UQV\|$. Here we use an idea found in [5] and [7].

Since $U$ and $V^*$ are isometries, so are

$$\begin{bmatrix} U^* \\ I - UU^* \end{bmatrix} \text{ and } [V^* \;\; I - V^* V]^*$$

Thus

$$\|T - UQV\| = \left\| \begin{bmatrix} U^* \\ I - UU^* \end{bmatrix} (T - UQV)[V^*, \;\; I - V^* V] \right\|$$

$$= \left\| \begin{bmatrix} A - Q & B \\ C & D \end{bmatrix} \right\|$$

where

$$\begin{bmatrix} A & B \\ C & D \end{bmatrix} := \begin{bmatrix} U^* \\ I - UU^* \end{bmatrix} T [V^* \;\; I - V^* V]$$

Observe that $A, B, C, D \in \mathbf{A} \bigcup \mathbf{A}^*$, the von Neumann algebra generated by **A**. We thus obtain that

$$\mu = \min\{\| \begin{bmatrix} A-Q & B \\ C & D \end{bmatrix} \| : Q \in \mathbf{A}\}$$

THE DAVIS-KAHAN-WEINBERGER-PARROTT THEOREM

The first result we discuss within the framework described above is one that seems to play a fundamental role in dilation theory. We choose $\mathbf{A}=\mathbf{B}(\mathbf{H})$. We are given operators $T, W_1, W_2$ in $\mathbf{B}(\mathbf{H})$ such that $W_1, W_2$ have closed range. We are required to find

$$\mu = \inf \{\|T - W_1 Q W_2\| : Q \in \mathbf{B}(\mathbf{H})\}$$

Using the above reduction we state the solution in the following familiar form.

THEOREM 2. [4, 11] *Let* $\mathbf{X}_i$, $\mathbf{Y}_i (i=1,2)$ *be Hilbert spaces and let*

$$\begin{bmatrix} A & B \\ C & D \end{bmatrix} : \mathbf{X}_1 \oplus \mathbf{X}_2 \to \mathbf{Y}_1 \oplus \mathbf{Y}_2$$

*be a linear operator. Then*

$$\inf \left\{ \| \begin{bmatrix} A-Q & B \\ C & D \end{bmatrix} \| : Q \in \mathbf{B}(\mathbf{X}_1, \mathbf{Y}_1) \right\} = \max \left\{ \| \begin{bmatrix} B \\ D \end{bmatrix} \|, \| [C \ D] \| \right\}$$

THE GENERALIZED NEHARI PROBLEM

Let $\mathbf{h}_2(\mathbf{C}^m)$ denote the Hilbert space of sequences $\{x_0, x_1, \ldots\}$ of m-dimensional complex vectors which are square summable, i.e.

$$\sum \|x_i\|^2 < \infty$$

Here the norm of $x_i$ is the usual Euclidean norm on $\mathbf{C}^m$ . Usually the dimension $m$ is irrelevant, and then we write simply $\mathbf{h}_2$ .

The Banach space of (bounded linear) operators from $\mathbf{h}_2(\mathbf{C}^m)$ to $\mathbf{h}_2(\mathbf{C}^n)$ is denoted $\mathbf{B}[\mathbf{h}_2(\mathbf{C}^m), \mathbf{h}_2(\mathbf{C}^n)]$, or just **B** when $m$ and $n$ are irrelevant. Each operator in $\mathbf{B}[\mathbf{h}_2(\mathbf{C}^m), \mathbf{h}_2(\mathbf{C}^n)]$ has a matrix representation with respect to the standard basis of $\mathbf{h}_2$ . Thus if

$$\text{mat } A = \begin{bmatrix} a_{00} & a_{01} & \cdot \\ a_{10} & a_{11} & \cdot \\ \cdot & \cdot & \end{bmatrix}$$

each entry $a_{ij}$ is a complex $n \times m$ matrix. Here and elsewhere a single dot indicates continuation of a row or column. The subspace of **B** of operators with lower triangular matrices is denoted by **C** (**C** is a subalgebra of **B** if $m=n$).

A distinguished operator in **B** is the unilateral shift $S$ whose action is

$$\{x_0, x_1, \ldots\} \rightarrow \{0, x_0, x_1, \ldots\}$$

An operator $A$ in **B** is Toeplitz if $S^* A S = A$; equivalently, its matrix is constant along diagonals:

$$\text{mat } A = \begin{bmatrix} a_0 & a_{-1} & a_{-2} & \cdot \\ a_1 & a_0 & a_{-1} & \cdot \\ a_2 & a_1 & a_0 & \cdot \\ \cdot & \cdot & \cdot & \end{bmatrix}$$

The subspace of **B** of Toeplitz operators will be denoted by $\mathbf{P}^1$. We consider the problem: given $T$, $W_1$, $W_2$ in $\mathbf{P}^1 \cap \mathbf{C}$, find

$$\min \{\|T - W_1 Q W_2\| \ : \ Q \in \mathbf{P}^1 \cap \mathbf{C}\}$$

We now turn to some facts concerning complex functions. The space of square-integrable functions defined on the unit circle and taking values in $\mathbf{C}^m$ is denoted by $\mathbf{L}_2(\mathbf{C}^m)$, or just $\mathbf{L}_2$. The closed subspace of $\mathbf{L}_2$ of functions having analytic continuations into the unit disc is the Hardy space $\mathbf{H}_2$. Its orthogonal complement is denoted by $\mathbf{H}_2^{\perp}$. It is a standard fact in the theory of Fourier series that $\mathbf{h}_2$ and $\mathbf{H}_2$ are isomorphic.

The set of essentially bounded functions defined on the unit circle and taking values in $\mathbf{C}^{n \times m}$ is denoted by $\mathbf{L}^{\infty}(\mathbf{C}^{n \times m})$, or $\mathbf{L}_{\infty}$. The norm on $\mathbf{L}_{\infty}$ is the one induced by that on $\mathbf{L}_2$: for $F$ in $\mathbf{L}^{\infty}$,

$$\|F\|_{\infty} = \sup\{\|Fg\|_2 : g \in \mathbf{L}_2, \|g\|_2 \leq 1\}$$

It can be proved that

$$\|F\|_{\infty} = \text{ess} \sup_{\theta} \|F(e^{i\theta})\|_{\infty}$$

the right hand norm being the one on $\mathbf{C}^{n\times m}$. The subset of $\mathbf{L}_\infty$ of matrices having analytic continuations into the unit disc is denoted by $\mathbf{H}_\infty$.

Finally, we consider the relevant connections between operators and complex functions. If $F \in \mathbf{P}^1$ and has matrix

$$\begin{bmatrix} F_0 & F_{-1} & \cdot \\ F_1 & F_0 & \cdot \\ \cdot & \cdot & \end{bmatrix}$$

define $\hat{F}(e^{i\theta}) = \sum_{-\infty}^{\infty} F_k e^{ik\theta}$. It is standard that $\hat{F} \in \mathbf{L}_\infty$ and that $\|F\| = \|\hat{F}\|_\infty$. If $F \in \mathbf{C} \cap \mathbf{P}^1$, then the above matrix of $F$ is lower block triangular and $\hat{F} \in \mathbf{H}_\infty$.

Thus, the problem given at the beginning of this section can be restated as: given $T, W_1, W_2$ in $\mathbf{H}_\infty$, find

$$\min \{\|T - W_1 Q W_2\|_\infty : Q \in \mathbf{H}_\infty\}$$

Using an inner-outer factorization for $W_1$, a *-inner-outer factorization for $W_2$, and the argument given after Theorem 1, we obtain the "generalized Nehari problem": given $A, B, C, D$ in $\mathbf{L}_\infty$, find

$$\mu = \inf \left\{ \left\| \begin{bmatrix} A-Q & B \\ C & C \end{bmatrix} \right\|_\infty : Q \in \mathbf{H}_\infty \right\}$$

Let $\mathbf{P}$ denote orthogonal projection from $\mathbf{L}^2 = \mathbf{H}_2^\perp \oplus \mathbf{H}_2$ onto $\mathbf{H}_2$ and define the bounded linear operator

$$\Gamma : \mathbf{H}_2 \oplus \mathbf{L}_2 \to \mathbf{H}_2^\perp \oplus \mathbf{L}_2$$

$$\Gamma \begin{bmatrix} f \\ g \end{bmatrix} = \begin{bmatrix} (I-P)(Af+Bg) \\ Cf+Dg \end{bmatrix}$$

for $f$ in $\mathbf{H}^2$, $g$ in $\mathbf{L}_2$. It is easily seen that $\mu \geq \|\Gamma\|$. Indeed, let $Q \in H_\infty$, $f \in \mathbf{H}_2$, $g \in \mathbf{L}_2$, $\left\| \begin{bmatrix} f \\ g \end{bmatrix} \right\| = 1$. Since $Qf \in \mathbf{H}_2$, $(I-P)Qf = 0$. Thus

$$\left\|\begin{bmatrix} A-Q & B \\ C & D \end{bmatrix}\right\| \geq \left\|\begin{bmatrix} A-Q & B \\ C & D \end{bmatrix}\begin{bmatrix} f \\ g \end{bmatrix}\right\|$$

$$\geq \left\|\begin{bmatrix} I-P & O \\ O & I \end{bmatrix}\begin{bmatrix} A-Q & B \\ C & D \end{bmatrix}\begin{bmatrix} f \\ g \end{bmatrix}\right\|$$

$$= \left\|\Gamma \begin{bmatrix} f \\ g \end{bmatrix}\right\|$$

Therefore, $\left\|\begin{bmatrix} A-Q & B \\ C & D \end{bmatrix}\right\| \geq \|\Gamma\|$, so the inequality $\mu \geq \|\Gamma\|$ follows. We show that in fact equality holds.

THEOREM 3 [7] $\mu = \|\Gamma\|$

PROOF. The proof is an application of a lifting theorem due to Sz.Nagy and Foias. In view of the already established inequality $\mu \geq \|\Gamma\|$, it suffices to show the existence of $Q$ in $\mathbf{H}^\infty$ such that

$$\left\|\begin{bmatrix} A-Q & B \\ C & D \end{bmatrix}\right\| = \|\Gamma\|$$

First, three additional operators are introduced. Define the scalar-valued $\mathbf{H}_\infty$-function $\hat{W}(e^{i\theta}) = e^{i\theta}$ and let $W$ denote the operator on $\mathbf{L}_2$ of multiplication by $\hat{W}$. Obviously, $W$ is unitary. Now define the operators

$$U : \mathbf{H}_2 \oplus \mathbf{L}_2 \longrightarrow \mathbf{H}_2 \oplus \mathbf{L}_2$$

$$U\begin{bmatrix} f \\ g \end{bmatrix} = \begin{bmatrix} Wf \\ Wg \end{bmatrix}, \quad f \in \mathbf{H}_2\,, \quad g \in \mathbf{L}_2$$

and

$$U_1 : \mathbf{H}_2^\perp \oplus \mathbf{L}_2 \longrightarrow \mathbf{H}_2^\perp \oplus \mathbf{L}_2$$

$$U_1\begin{bmatrix} f \\ g \end{bmatrix} = \begin{bmatrix} (I-P)\,Wf \\ Wg \end{bmatrix}, \quad f \in \mathbf{H}_2^\perp\,, \quad g \in \mathbf{L}_2$$

It is easily checked that Figure 1 is a commutative diagram. Also, commutativity of Figure 2 is immediate. Observe that the operator $\begin{bmatrix} W & 0 \\ 0 & W \end{bmatrix}$ is the minimal isometric dilation of $U_1$. The lifting theorem of Sz.-Nagy-Foias [14] now guarantees the existence of an operator $\Gamma_1$ such that $\|\Gamma_1\| = \|\Gamma\|$ and Figure 3 commutes.

It is a standard argument to prove that the equation

$$\begin{bmatrix} W & 0 \\ 0 & W \end{bmatrix}\Gamma = \Gamma_1 U$$

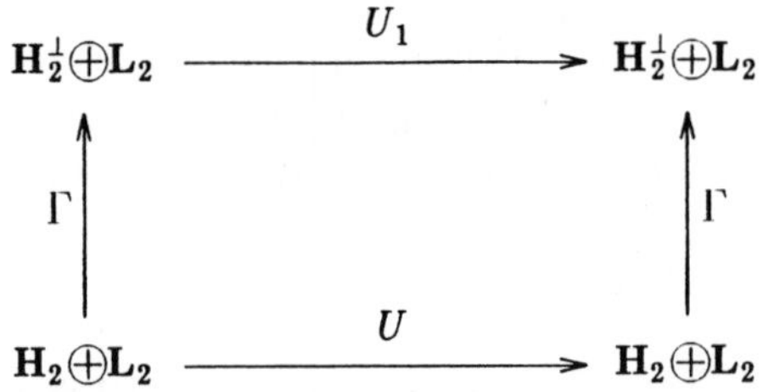


Figure 1

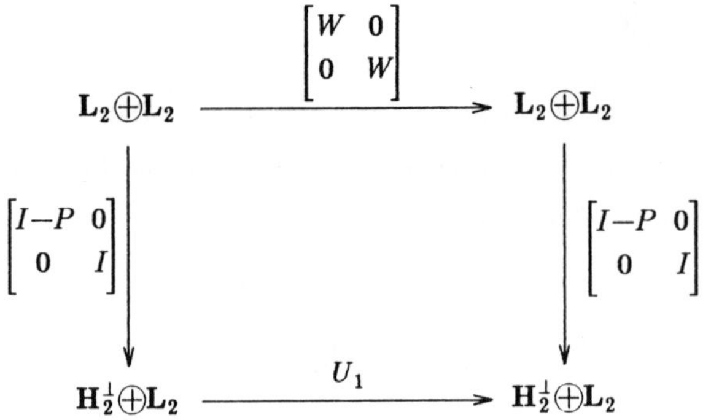


Figure 2

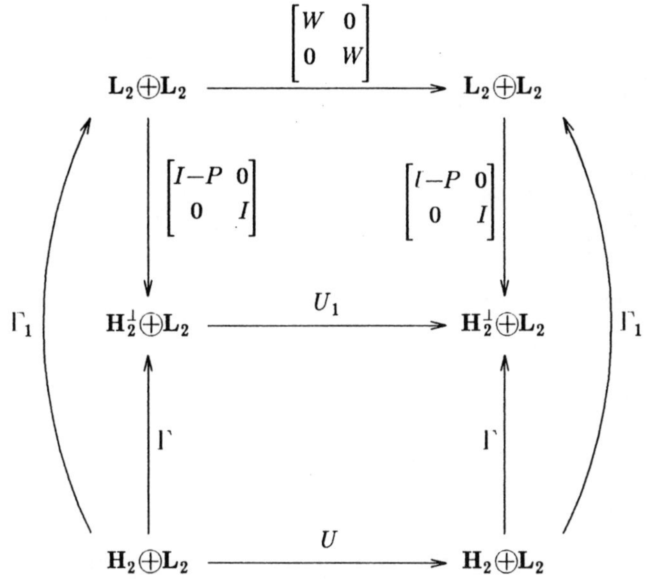
$\begin{bmatrix} W & 0 \\ 0 & W \end{bmatrix}$
$L_2 \oplus L_2$
$L_2 \oplus L_2$
$\begin{bmatrix} I-P & 0 \\ 0 & I \end{bmatrix}$
$\begin{bmatrix} I-P & 0 \\ 0 & I \end{bmatrix}$
$\Gamma_1$
$H_2^\perp \oplus L_2$
$U_1$
$H_2^\perp \oplus L_2$
$\Gamma_1$
$\Gamma$
$\Gamma$
$H_2 \oplus L_2$
$U$
$H_2 \oplus L_2$

Figure 3

implies that $\Gamma_1$ is a multiplication operator, i.e. there exist $A_1, B_1, C_1, D_1$ in $\mathbf{L}_\infty$ such that

$$\Gamma_1 \begin{bmatrix} f \\ g \end{bmatrix} = \begin{bmatrix} A_1 & B_1 \\ C_1 & D_1 \end{bmatrix} \begin{bmatrix} f \\ g \end{bmatrix}$$

Next, the equation

$$\begin{bmatrix} I-P & 0 \\ 0 & I \end{bmatrix} \Gamma_1 = \Gamma$$

and the definition of $\Gamma$ imply that

$$(I-P)(A_1-A)\mathbf{H}_2 = 0$$

$$(I-P)(B_1-B)\mathbf{L}_2 = 0$$

$$C_1 = C$$

$$D_1 = D$$

Thus $B_1 = B$ and $A_1 = A-Q$ for some $Q$ in $\mathbf{H}_\infty$. Finally, the equation $\|\Gamma_1\| = \|\Gamma\|$ implies

$$\|\Gamma\| = \left\| \begin{bmatrix} A-Q & B \\ C & D \end{bmatrix} \right\|$$

as required. □

The operator $\Gamma$ maps $\mathbf{H}_2 \oplus \mathbf{L}_2$ to $\mathbf{H}_2^\perp \oplus \mathbf{L}_2$. As such, its matrix has a natural partition into four blocks. We shall have occasion several times in the sequel to display such matrices. It is convenient to do it like this:

[ ] [ ]
[ ] [ ]

For example, mat $\Gamma$ is

$$\begin{bmatrix} \cdot & \cdot & \\ A_{-2} & A_{-3} & \cdot \\ A_{-1} & A_{-2} & \cdot \end{bmatrix} \begin{bmatrix} & \cdot & \cdot & \cdot & \\ \cdot & B_{-1} & B_{-2} & B_{-3} & \cdot \\ \cdot & B_0 & B_{-1} & B_{-2} & \cdot \end{bmatrix}$$

$$\begin{bmatrix} \cdot & \cdot & \\ C_{-1} & C_{-2} & \cdot \\ C_0 & C_{-1} & \cdot \\ C_1 & C_0 & \cdot \\ \cdot & \cdot & \end{bmatrix} \begin{bmatrix} & \cdot & \cdot & \cdot & \\ \cdot & D_0 & D_{-1} & D_{-2} & \cdot \\ \cdot & D_1 & D_0 & D_{-1} & \cdot \\ \cdot & D_2 & D_1 & D_0 & \cdot \\ & \cdot & \cdot & \cdot & \end{bmatrix}$$

A final remark on this problem: the solution to the classical Nehari problem can be easily derived from Theorem 2 (see [11]). It should be possible to derive Theorem 3 from there as well.

## ALGEBRAS OF PERIODIC OPERATORS

Evidently, Toeplitz operators correspond to time-invariant systems. Time-varying systems closely related to these are the N-periodic systems [8]. For an integer $N \geq 1$ and an operator $A$ in $\mathbf{B}[\mathbf{h}_2(\mathbf{C}^m), \mathbf{h}_2(\mathbf{C}^n)]$, $A$ is N-periodic if $(S^N)^* A S^N = A$. The matrix of $A$ is then block Toeplitz: it looks like

$$\text{mat } A = \begin{bmatrix} A_0 & A_{-1} & A_{-2} & \cdot \\ A_1 & A_0 & A_{-1} & \cdot \\ A_2 & A_1 & A_0 & \cdot \\ \cdot & \cdot & \cdot & \end{bmatrix}$$

where each block $A_i$ is $Nn \times Nm$. The subspace (subalgebra if $m = n$) of $\mathbf{B}$ of N-periodic operators is denoted (consistent with the previous section) $\mathbf{P}^N$. We observe for later use that mat $A$ is also the matrix of a Toeplitz operator $T_A$ in $\mathbf{B}[\mathbf{h}_2(\mathbf{C}^m), \mathbf{h}_2(\mathbf{C}^n)]$ [8]. We shall call $T_A$ the Toeplitz extension of $A$ and note that $A$ and $T_A$ have the same norms.

Note that $\mathbf{C} \cap \mathbf{P}^N$ is the algebra of lower triangular N-periodic operators. Thus $A \in \mathbf{C} \cap \mathbf{P}^N$ iff $A_i = 0$ for $i < 0$ and $A_0$ is lower triangular.

The distance problem can be stated as follows: given $T$, $W_1$, $W_2$ in $\mathbf{C} \cap \mathbf{P}^N$ such that $W_1$, $W_2$ have closed range, find

$$\mu = \inf \{\|T - W_1 Q W_2\| : Q \in \mathbf{C} \cap \mathbf{P}^N\}$$

Using the fact that operators in $\mathbf{C} \cap \mathbf{P}^N$ have inner-outer factorizations, whose factors are in $\mathbf{C} \cap \mathbf{P}^N$ [8], and the argument used above, we can reformulate this problem in a, by now, standard form: find

$$\mu = \inf \left\{ \| \begin{bmatrix} A-Q & B \\ C & D \end{bmatrix} \| \ : \ Q \in \mathbf{C} \cap \mathbf{P}^N \right\}$$

with $A, B, C, D$ in $\mathbf{P}^N$.

Recall that $T_A$ denotes the Toeplitz extension of $A$; let $\hat{T}_A$ denote its natural Laurent extension to $\mathbf{l}^2 = \mathbf{h}_2^\perp \oplus \mathbf{h}_2$. Identifying an operator in $\mathbf{C} \cap \mathbf{P}^N$ with its Toeplitz extension allows us to look at $\mathbf{C} \cap \mathbf{P}^N$ as a subspace (subalgebra) of $\mathbf{H}_\infty$. Then,

$$\mu = \inf \left\{ \| \begin{bmatrix} T_A - T_Q & T_B \\ T_C & T_D \end{bmatrix} \| \ : \ Q \in \mathbf{C} \cap \mathbf{P}^N \right\}$$

The matrix of this operator whose norm is to be minimized is

$$\begin{bmatrix} \begin{bmatrix} A_0 - Q_0 & A_{-1} & \cdot \\ A_1 - Q_1 & A_0 - Q_0 & \cdot \\ \cdot & \cdot & \end{bmatrix} & \begin{bmatrix} B_0 & B_{-1} & \cdot \\ B_1 & B_0 & \cdot \\ \cdot & \cdot & \end{bmatrix} \\ \begin{bmatrix} C_0 & C_{-1} & \cdot \\ C_1 & C_0 & \cdot \\ \cdot & \cdot & \end{bmatrix} & \begin{bmatrix} D_0 & D_{-1} & \cdot \\ D_1 & D_0 & \cdot \\ \cdot & \cdot & \end{bmatrix} \end{bmatrix}$$

Note that the infimum is taken over all sequences $Q_i$ with $\sum_{i=0}^{\infty} Q_i z^i \in \mathbf{H}_\infty$ and $Q_0$ lower triangular.

We compute the infimum in two stages. Fix $Q_0$ and take the infimum over all appropriate sequences $\{Q_1, Q_2, \ldots\}$. But (after shifting up a row) this is just the problem solved in the previous section. Thus $\mu$ equals the infimum over all lower triangular $Q_o$'s of the norm of the operator whose matrix is

$$\begin{bmatrix} \cdot & \cdot & \\ A_{-1} & A_{-2} & \cdot \\ A_0-Q_0 & A_{-1} & \cdot \end{bmatrix} \begin{bmatrix} & \cdot & \cdot & \cdot & \\ \cdot & B_0 & B_{-1} & B_{-2} & \cdot \\ \cdot & B_1 & B_0 & B_{-1} & \cdot \end{bmatrix}$$

$$\begin{bmatrix} \cdot & \cdot & \\ C_{-1} & C_{-2} & \cdot \\ C_0 & C_{-1} & \cdot \\ C_1 & C_0 & \cdot \\ \cdot & \cdot & \end{bmatrix} \begin{bmatrix} & \cdot & \cdot & \cdot & \\ \cdot & D_0 & D_{-1} & D_{-2} & \cdot \\ \cdot & D_1 & D_0 & D_{-1} & \cdot \\ \cdot & D_2 & D_1 & D_0 & \cdot \\ & \cdot & \cdot & \cdot & \end{bmatrix}$$

Call this matrix $M$.

We are now ready to prove the main result of this section, which generalizes the result of [8]. Let $P$ denote the orthogonal projection from $\mathbf{h}_2^\perp \oplus \mathbf{h}_2$ onto $\mathbf{h}_2$.

THEOREM 4. $\mu = \max\{\delta_i \ : \ 0 \le i \le N-1\}$ *where* $\delta_i$ *is the norm of*

$$\begin{bmatrix} I-P & O \\ O & I \end{bmatrix} \begin{bmatrix} T_{S^{*i}AS^i} & T_{S^{*i}B} \\ T_{CS^i} & T_D \end{bmatrix} \begin{bmatrix} P & O \\ O & I \end{bmatrix}$$

PROOF. For simplicity, the proof will be given in the case $N=2$. The same arguments apply in general. In this case all block matrices in $T_A$, etc. are $2\times2$ block matrices:

$$A_i = \begin{bmatrix} a_{2i} & w_{2i-1} \\ a_{2i+1} & w_{2i} \end{bmatrix} \qquad B_i = \begin{bmatrix} b_{2i} & x_{2i-1} \\ b_{2i+1} & x_{2i} \end{bmatrix}$$

$$C_i = \begin{bmatrix} c_{2i} & y_{2i-1} \\ c_{2i+1} & y_{2i} \end{bmatrix} \qquad D_i = \begin{bmatrix} d_{2i} & z_{2i-1} \\ d_{2i+1} & z_{2i} \end{bmatrix}$$

$$Q_0 = \begin{bmatrix} q_0 & 0 \\ q_1 & r_0 \end{bmatrix}$$

Thus matrix $M$ is

$$\begin{bmatrix} \cdot & \cdot & \\ a_0-q_0 & w_{-1} & \cdot \\ a_1-q_1 & w_0-r_0 & \cdot \end{bmatrix} \begin{bmatrix} & \cdot & \cdot & \\ \cdot & b_0 & x_{-1} & \cdot \\ \cdot & b_1 & x_0 & \cdot \end{bmatrix}$$

$$\begin{bmatrix} \cdot & \cdot & \\ c_0 & y_{-1} & \cdot \\ c_1 & y_0 & \cdot \\ \cdot & \cdot & \end{bmatrix} \begin{bmatrix} & \cdot & \cdot & \\ \cdot & d_0 & z_{-1} & \cdot \\ \cdot & d_1 & z_0 & \cdot \\ & \cdot & \cdot & \end{bmatrix}$$

$\mu$ equals the infimum norm of this matrix over all $q_0$, $q_1$, $r_0$. This minimization is done using Theorem 2.

First, choose $q_0$ to minimize the norm of the submatrix of $M$ obtained by deleting the row containing $q_0$ and $r_0$; by Theorem 2, the minimum equals max $\{\delta_0, \delta_1\}$. Second, choose $r_0$ to minimize the norm of the submatrix of $M$ obtained by deleting the left-most column; again by Theorem 2, the minimum equals max $\{\delta_0, \delta_1\}$. Finally, having chosen $q_0$ and $r_0$ in this way, choose $q_1$ to minimize the norm of $M$. The minimum equals the maximum of the norms of the submatrices just considered. But these latter norms both equal max $\{\delta_0, \delta_1\}$. □

## A GENERALIZED ARVESON FORMULA

Let $\mathbf{C}$ denote the family of operators in $\mathbf{B}[\mathbf{h}_2(\mathbf{C}^m),\mathbf{h}_2(\mathbf{C}^n)]$ whose matrix representation with respect to the standard orthonormal basis is block lower triangular. $\mathbf{C}$ is a weakly closed subspace (subalgebra, if $n=m$) of $\mathbf{B}$, and by [3] an operator $T$ in $\mathbf{C}$ with closed range has factorizations of the required type. Thus if $T_1, W_1, W_2 \in \mathbf{C}$

$$\mu := \inf \{\|T-W_1 U W_2\| : U \in \mathbf{C}\}$$

can be expressed as

$$\inf \left\{ \left\| \begin{bmatrix} A-U & B \\ C & D \end{bmatrix} \right\| : U \in \mathbf{C} \right\}$$

where $A, B, C, D$ are given operators in $\mathbf{B}$.

We remark that the case $B=C=D=0$ is the well-known Arveson distance formula given in [3]. We also note that

$$\mathbf{P}^1 \subset \mathbf{P}^2 \subset \cdots \subset \mathbf{C} =: \mathbf{P}^\infty$$

Let $\{Q_k : k \geq 0\}$ be the standard family of truncation projections on $\mathbf{h}_2$; i.e. $Q_k$ maps the sequence $\{x_0, x_1, \ldots\}$ into the sequence $\{x_0, \ldots, x_k, 0, \ldots\}$. Let $Q_{-1}$ and $Q_\infty$ be defined as the zero operator and identity operator, respectively. Finally, define a family $\{\Gamma_k : k \geq -1\}$ of operators in $\mathbf{B}$,

$$\Gamma_k := \begin{bmatrix} Q_k & 0 \\ 0 & I \end{bmatrix} \begin{bmatrix} A & B \\ C & D \end{bmatrix} \begin{bmatrix} I-Q_k & 0 \\ 0 & I \end{bmatrix}$$

If $U \in \mathbf{C}$, then $Q_k U(I-Q_k) = 0$, so that

$$\begin{bmatrix} Q_k & 0 \\ 0 & I \end{bmatrix} \begin{bmatrix} A-U & B \\ C & D \end{bmatrix} \begin{bmatrix} I-Q_k & 0 \\ 0 & I \end{bmatrix} = \Gamma_k$$

This implies that

$$\left\| \begin{bmatrix} A-U & B \\ C & D \end{bmatrix} \right\| \geq \|\Gamma_k\|$$

which in turn leads to the inequality

$$\mu \geq \sup\{\|\Gamma_k\| : k > -1\}$$

In fact equality holds.

THEOREM 5. $\mu = \sup\ \{\|\Gamma_k\| : k \geq -1\}$

The proof is given in two steps. The first step considers only a finite number of truncation projections, and is similar to the proof of Arveson's theorem [12]. Let

$$\{-1 = i_{-1} < i_0 < \cdots < i_{n-1}\}$$

be a finite collection of integers and let $i_n = \infty$. Denote by $\mathbf{S}$ the finite collection of truncation projections

$$\{Q_{i_j} : j = -1, \ldots, n\}$$

Finally, let $\mathbf{C_S}$ denote those operators $H$ in $\mathbf{B}$ which satisfy

$$QH(I-Q) = 0\ , \qquad Q \in \mathbf{S}$$

Defining $\Delta Q_j = Q_{i_j} - Q_{i_{j-1}}$ , $j = 0, \ldots, n$, we have the direct sum decomposition

$$\mathbf{h}_2 = \Delta Q_0 \mathbf{h}_2 \oplus \cdots \oplus \Delta Q_n \mathbf{h}_2$$

With respect to this decomposition, the matrix representation of an operator in $\mathbf{C_S}$ is lower triangular.

LEMMA 6.

$$\inf\left\{\left\|\begin{bmatrix} A-U & B \\ C & D \end{bmatrix}\right\| : U\in \mathbf{C_S}\right\} =$$

$$= \max\left\{\left\|\begin{bmatrix} Q & 0 \\ 0 & I \end{bmatrix}\begin{bmatrix} A & B \\ C & D \end{bmatrix}\begin{bmatrix} I-Q & 0 \\ 0 & I \end{bmatrix}\right\| \ : \ Q\in \mathbf{S}\right\} \tag{1}$$

PROOF. The proof is by induction on $n$. Consider the case $n=1$, and take matrix representations with respect to the above decompositions. The left-hand side of (1) equals the infimum norm of

$$\begin{bmatrix} A_{00}-U_{00} & A_{01} & B_0 \\ A_{10}-U_{10} & A_{11}-U_{11} & B_1 \\ C_0 & C_1 & D \end{bmatrix} \tag{2}$$

where the infimum is over all $U_{ij}$ in $\mathbf{B}$. From Theorem 1, this equals the maximum of (i) the norm of

$$\begin{bmatrix} B_0 \\ B_1 \\ D \end{bmatrix}$$

and (ii) the infimum norm of

$$\begin{bmatrix} A_{00}-U_{00} & A_{01} & B_0 \\ C_0 & C_1 & D \end{bmatrix}$$

But Theorem 1 implies that the latter infimum equals the maximum norm of

$$\begin{bmatrix} A_{01} & B_0 \\ C_1 & D \end{bmatrix}, \ [C_0 \ \ C_1 \ \ D]$$

Thus the infimum norm of (2) equals the maximum norm of the three matrices

$$\begin{bmatrix} B_0 \\ B_1 \\ D \end{bmatrix}, \quad \begin{bmatrix} A_{01} & B_0 \\ C_1 & D \end{bmatrix}, \quad [C_0 \ \ C_1 \ \ D]$$

These norms equal those of

$$\begin{bmatrix} Q_{i_j} & 0 \\ 0 & I \end{bmatrix}\begin{bmatrix} A & B \\ C & D \end{bmatrix}\begin{bmatrix} I-Q_{i_j} & 0 \\ 0 & I \end{bmatrix}, \ j=-1,0,1$$

This proves the lemma for $n=1$.

In the general case, the left-hand side of (1) equals the infimum norm of

$$\begin{bmatrix} A_{00}-U_{00} & A_{01} & \cdot & A_{0n} & B_0 \\ A_{10}-U_{10} & A_{11}-U_{11} & \cdot & A_{1n} & B_1 \\ \cdot & \cdot & \cdot & \cdot & \cdot \\ A_{n0}-U_{n0} & A_{n1}-U_{n1} & \cdot & A_{nn}-U_{nn} & B_n \\ C_0 & C_1 & \cdot & C_n & D \end{bmatrix}$$

An application of Theorem 1 and the induction hypothesis imply that this infimum equals the maximum norm of

$$\begin{bmatrix} B_0 \\ \cdot \\ B_n \\ D \end{bmatrix}$$

and

$$\begin{bmatrix} Q_{i_j} & 0 \\ 0 & I \end{bmatrix} \begin{bmatrix} A & B \\ C & D \end{bmatrix} \begin{bmatrix} I-Q_{i_j} & 0 \\ 0 & I \end{bmatrix}, \ -1 \leq j < n$$

But the two matrices

$$\begin{bmatrix} B_0 \\ \cdot \\ B_n \\ D \end{bmatrix}, \quad \begin{bmatrix} Q_{i_n} & 0 \\ 0 & I \end{bmatrix} \begin{bmatrix} A & B \\ C & D \end{bmatrix} \begin{bmatrix} I-Q_{i_n} & 0 \\ 0 & I \end{bmatrix}$$

have equal norm. □

PROOF OF THEOREM 5. Let $\mathbf{F}$ denote the family of all finite sets $\mathbf{S}$ of truncation projections. Then, from the definition of $\Gamma_k$,

$$\sup\{\|\Gamma_k\| : k \geq -1\}$$
$$= \sup_{\mathbf{S}\in\mathbf{F}} \max_{\mathbf{Q}\in\mathbf{S}} \left\| \begin{bmatrix} Q & 0 \\ 0 & I \end{bmatrix} \begin{bmatrix} A & B \\ C & D \end{bmatrix} \begin{bmatrix} I-Q & 0 \\ 0 & I \end{bmatrix} \right\|$$

Thus from the lemma

$$\sup\{\|\Gamma_k\| : k \geq -1\} = \sup_{\mathbf{S}\in\mathbf{F}} \inf_{U\in\mathbf{C_S}} \left\| \begin{bmatrix} A-U & B \\ C & D \end{bmatrix} \right\|$$

So to prove the theorem it remains to show that

$$\mu = \sup_{\mathbf{S}\in\mathbf{F}} \inf_{U\in\mathbf{C_S}} \left\| \begin{bmatrix} A-U & B \\ C & D \end{bmatrix} \right\|$$

This is equivalent to showing that

$$\inf \{\|T - W_1 U W_2\| : U \in \mathbf{C}\} = \sup_{\mathbf{S}\in\mathbf{F}} \inf_{U\in\mathbf{C_S}} \|T - W_1 U W_2\|$$

Since $\mathbf{C} \subset \mathbf{C_S}$ for every $\mathbf{S}$ in $\mathbf{F}$, the left side of the expression is greater than or equal to the right side. To show the reverse inequality, let $\sigma$ denote the supremum on the right-hand side and fix $\epsilon > 0$. For each $\mathbf{S}$ in $\mathbf{F}$ choose $U_\mathbf{S} \in \mathbf{C_S}$ such that

$$\|T - W_1 U_\mathbf{S} W_2\| \leq \sigma + \epsilon$$

Then $\{W_1 U_\mathbf{S} W_2\}$ is a bounded set. Since $\mathbf{F}$ is a directed set (partially ordered by inclusion), by weak compactness there exists a net $\{\mathbf{S}_\alpha\}$ in $\mathbf{F}$ such that $W_1 U_{\mathbf{S}_\alpha} W_2$ converges weakly. Since $W_1 = SA$ with $S^*S = I$ and $A^{-1} \in \mathbf{C}$ and $W_2 = BT$ with $TT^* = I$ and $B^{-1} \in \mathbf{C}$, it follows that $\{U_{\mathbf{S}_\alpha}\}$ converges to an operator $U_1$ which belongs to $\mathbf{C}_{\mathbf{S}_\alpha}$ for all $\alpha$. Since $\bigcap_\alpha \mathbf{C}_{\mathbf{S}_\alpha} = \mathbf{C}$, $Q_1 \in \mathbf{C}$. Thus

$$\inf \{\|T - W_1 U W_2\| : U \in \mathbf{C}\| \leq \|T - W_1 U_1 W_2\| \leq \sigma + \epsilon$$

Since $\epsilon$ was arbitrary, we conclude that the left side is less than or equal to $\sigma$. □

## REMARKS

(1) We have obtained formulas for the distance of an operator

$$\begin{bmatrix} A & B \\ C & D \end{bmatrix}$$

to the algebra

$$\left\{ \begin{bmatrix} U & 0 \\ 0 & 0 \end{bmatrix} : U \in \mathbf{P}^i \right\} =: \mathbf{P}^i \oplus 0$$

where $A, B, C, D \in \mathbf{P}^i \cup \mathbf{P}^{i^*}$. Suppose $A, B, C, D \in \mathbf{P}^i \cup \mathbf{P}^{i^*}$ and $j > i \geq 1$. Then $\mathbf{P}^i \subset \mathbf{P}^j$ and

$$\operatorname{dist}\left( \begin{bmatrix} A & B \\ C & D \end{bmatrix}, \mathbf{P}^j \oplus 0 \right) \leq \operatorname{dist}\left( \begin{bmatrix} A & B \\ C & D \end{bmatrix}, \mathbf{P}^i \oplus 0 \right)$$

It is easy to show that in fact equality exists. This implies that the Nehari formula is in fact a special case of the Arveson formula and has interesting system-theoretic implications.

(2) In this paper we have concerned ourselves only with obtaining distance formulas. In application it is important to be able to compute these formulas. Foias, Tannenbaum, and Zames in a series of papers (see [9]) have developed algorithms for doing this for the classical Nehari problem. Hopefully, these algorithms can be extended to the generalized formulas given here.

## REFERENCES

1 Adamjan, V.M., D.Z. Arov, M.G. Krein, "Analytic properties of Schmidt pairs for a Hankel operator and the generalized Schur-Takagi problem, Math. USSR Sbornik 15 (1971), 31-73.

2 Adamjan, V.M., D.Z. Arov, M.G. Krein, "Infinite Hankel block matrices and related extension problems", A.M.S. Translations (2)111 (1978), 133-156.

3 Arveson, W. "Interpolation problems in nest algebras", J. Funct. Anal. 20 (1975) 208-233.

4 Davis, C., W.M. Kahan, H.F. Weinberger, "Norm-preserving dilations and their applications to optimal error bounds", SIAM J. Num. Anal. 19 (1982), 445-469.

5 Doyle, J., Notes, ONR/Honeywell Workshop on Advances in Multivariable Control (1984).

6 Francis, B.A., J. Doyle, "Linear control theory with an $\mathbf{H}_\infty$ optimality criterion", SIAM J. Cont. Optim., to appear.

7 Feintuch, A., B.A. Francis, "Uniformly Optimal Control of Linear Feedback Systems", Automatica 21 (1985), 563-574.

8 Feintuch, A., P. Khargonekar, A. Tannenbaum, "On the sensitivity minimization problem for linear periodic systems", SIAM J. Cont. and Opt. (1986), to appear.

9 Foias, C., A. Tannenbaum, G. Zames, "Sensitivity minimization for arbitrary SISO distributed plants", System and Control Letters, to appear.

10 Khargonekar, P., K. Poolla, A. Tannenbaum, "Robust control of linear time-varying plants using periodic compensation", IEEE Trans. Auto. Cont. AC-30 (1985), 1088-1098.

11 Parrott, S., "On the quotient norm and the Sz. Nagy-Foias lifting theorem", J. Funct. Anal. 30 (1978), 311-328.

12 Power, S.C., "The distance to upper triangular operators", Math. Proc. Cambridge Phil. Soc. 88 (1980), 327-329.

13 D. Sarason, "Generalized interpolation in $\mathbf{H}_\infty$", Trans. A.M.S. (1967), 179-203.

14 Sz. Nagy, B., C. Foias, "Harmonic analysis of operators in Hilbert space", North Holland, 1970.

15 Zames, G., "Feedback and optimal sensitivity", IEEE Trans. Aut. Control, AC-26, (1981) 301-320.

Avraham Feintuch
Department of Mathematics
Ben-Gurion University
of the Negev
Beersheva
Israel

Bruce Francis
Department of Elect. Eng.
University of Toronto
Toronto, Ont.
Canada M5S 1A4

Submitted: November 17, 1986

Operator Theory:
Advances and Applications, Vol. 29




# ON THE SCHUR REPRESENTATION IN THE COMMUTANT LIFTING THEOREM II.

Ciprian Foias and Arthur E. Frazho

This note is a continuation of [4]. Here we present a short proof of the fact that the Schur representation formula presented in [4] yields all contractive intertwining dilations in the Commutant Lifting Theorem.

We dedicate this note to Professor M.S. Livsic on the occassion of his 70th birthday. He was the first to use linear functional representations in modelling operators.

## 1. INTRODUCTION.

In this note we follow the notation and terminology established in [4]. The orthogonal projection onto a Hilbert space $H$ is denoted by $P_H$. If A is a contraction then $D_A$ is the positive square root of $(I-A^*A)$ and $\mathcal{D}_A$ is the closed range of $D_A$. The unilateral shift on $l^2(\mathcal{D})$ is denoted by S. We use S regardless of the space $\mathcal{D}$.

Throughout T on $H$ and $T'$ on $H'$ and A mapping $H$ into $H'$ are all contractions with the following intertwining property: $T'A = AT$. The minimal isometric dilations of T and $T'$ are denoted by U on $K$ and $U'$ on $K'$, respectively. In fact the minimal isometric dilation $U'$ of $T'$ is given by

$$U' = \begin{bmatrix} T' & 0 \\ D_{T'} & S \end{bmatrix} \text{ on } K' = H' \oplus l^2(\mathcal{D}_{T'}) . \tag{1.1}$$

Recall that B is a *contractive intertwining dilation* of A if B is a contraction mapping $K$ into $K'$ satisfying

$$U'B = BU \text{ and } P_{H'}B = AP_H . \tag{1.2}$$

The Commutant Lifting Theorem [1,3,4,5,6] states that there exists a contractive intertwining dilation B of A.

In [4] we have shown that the set of all contractions B(W) where W is a Schur contraction defines a family of contractive intertwining dilations of A. (The contraction B(W) is defined in Equation (1.8) below.) Reference [1] uses some rather involved techniques to prove that this family of contractions B(W) provides all contractive intertwining dilations of A. Here we will use the geometric techniques in [4] to give a direct proof of this result.

To simplify notation we will always assume that $T = U$ is an isometry on $H$, that is, T is its own minimal isometric dilation. If this is not the case then one can replace A by $AP_H$ and replace T by U. Then B is a contractive intertwining dilation of A with respect to T and $T'$ if and only if B is a contractive intertwining dilation of $AP_H$ with respect to U and $T'$. Therefore, obtaining all contractive intertwining dilations of A is equivalent to obtaining all contractive intertwining dilations of $AP_H$. So for convenience we always assume that $T = U$.

In this setting, the unitary operator $\omega$ in [4] mapping

$$F = \{D_A Th : h \epsilon H\}^- \text{ onto } F' = \{D_A h \oplus D_{T'} Ah : h \epsilon H\}^-$$

is defined by

$$\omega(D_A Th) = D_A h \oplus D_{T'} Ah \qquad (h \epsilon H)\,. \tag{1.3}$$

Clearly $\omega$ has a unique unitary extension (also denoted by $\omega$) mapping $l^2(F)$ onto $l^2(F')$ and commuting with the unilateral shift. This unitary extension is generated by $\omega S^n f = S^n \omega f$ where f is in $F$ and $n \geq 0$. Recall that W is a *Schur contraction* if W is a contraction mapping $l^2(D_A)$ into $l^2(D_A \oplus D_{T'})$ commuting with the unilateral shift ($SW = WS$) and $W | F = \omega$.

As in [4] the linear space of formal series with values in a Hilbert space $D$ is denoted by $l(D)$. For example f in $l(D)$ admits a formal series expansion of the form

$$f = (f_o, f_1, f_2, \cdots) = \sum_o^\infty f_n z^n$$

where f is in $D$ for all $n \geq 0$. Let W be a Schur contraction with formal (power) series expansion of the form $W = \sum_o^\infty W_n z^n$. Then W defines a linear operator mapping $l(D_A)$ into $l(D_A \oplus D_{T'})$ by convolution:

$$Wf = \sum_{n=0}^\infty \sum_{i=0}^n W_{n-i} f_i z^n\,. \tag{1.4}$$

Since $T = U$ the space $N$ in [4] becomes:

$$N = H \oplus l(D_A) \oplus l(D_{T'})\,.$$

If W is a Schur contraction then the linear space $M(W)$ is defined by

$$M(W) = \{(h \oplus d \oplus f') \epsilon N : W(D_A h \oplus d) = d \oplus f'\} \tag{1.5}$$

The projection from $N$ onto $H$ is denoted by $P_H$. By Lemma 3.1 in [4] every h in $H$ uniquely determines a $\varsigma$ in $M(W)$ such that $h = P_H \varsigma$.

Let $W^{(n)}$ be the square matrix operator mapping $\overset{n}{\underset{o}{\oplus}} D_A$ into $\overset{n}{\underset{o}{\oplus}} (D_A \oplus D_{T'})$ defined by

$$W^{(n)} = \begin{bmatrix} W_o & 0 & 0 & \cdots & 0 & 0 \\ W_1 & W_o & 0 & \cdots & 0 & 0 \\ W_2 & W_1 & W_o & \cdots & 0 & 0 \\ . & . & . & \cdots & . & . \\ . & . & . & \cdots & . & . \\ . & . & . & \cdots & W_o & . \\ W_n & W_{n-1} & W_{n-2} & \cdots & W_1 & W_o \end{bmatrix} \tag{1.6}$$

Obviously W is a Schur contraction if and only if $W^{(n)}$ is a contraction for all $n \geq 0$ and $W_o | F = \omega$. By convolution, $h \oplus d \oplus f'$ is in $M(W)$ if and only if

$$W^{(n)}(D_A h \oplus (\overset{n-1}{\underset{o}{\oplus}} d_i)) = \overset{n}{\underset{o}{\oplus}} (d_i \oplus f_i') \tag{1.7}$$

for all $n \geq 0$. Here $d = (d_i)_{i=0}^{\infty}$ and $f' = (f_i')_{i=0}^{\infty}$. In this case $W_o D_A h = d_o \oplus f_o'$. So $d_o$ and $f_o'$ are uniquely determined by h and $W_o$. The lower triangular structure of $W^{(n)}$ shows that $d_n \oplus f_n'$ is uniquely determined by h and the previous $d_i$ for $i < n$, which in turn depend on h linearly, that is, $d_i = d_i(h)$ and $f_i' = f_i'(h)$ are linear operators mapping $H$ into $D_A$ and $H$ into $D_{T'}$ respectively, for all i. Therefore h and $W^{(n)}$ recursively and uniquely determines the first $n+1$ components $\overset{n}{\underset{o}{\oplus}} d_i$ and $\overset{n}{\underset{o}{\oplus}} f_i'$ of d and $f'$ in $M(W)$, respectively.

Let W be a Schur contraction. The operator B(W) mapping $H$ into $H' \oplus l(D_{T'})$ is defined by

$$B(W)h = Ah \oplus f' = Ah \oplus (f_i')_{i=0}^{\infty} \quad (h \in H) \tag{1.8}$$

where $\varsigma = h \oplus d \oplus f'$ is the unique element in $M(W)$ satisfying $h = P_H \varsigma$. Reference [4] shows that B(W) is a contractive intertwining dilation of A. Equation (1.7) can be used to recursively calculate the components $f_i'$ of $f'$. Here we will use the results in [4] to give a direct proof of the following result.

THEOREM 1.1 ([1]). *The set of all contractive intertwining dilations* B *of* A *is given by* B = B(W) *where* W *is a Schur contraction. Moreover the mapping* W → B(W) *is one to one. In particular there is a one to one correspondence between the set of all contractive intertwining dilations* B *of* A *and the set of all Schur contractions.*

As noted earlier [4] shows that each B(W) is a contractive intertwining dilation of A. Moreover [4] also shows that the mapping W → B(W) is one to one. So to complete the proof we will show that every contractive intertwining dilation B of A produces a

Schur contraction W such that B = B(W).

## 2. PRELIMINARY RESULTS.

In this section we will present several preliminary results which will be used in proving the unfinished part of the previous theorem. To this end consider the operator

$$M = \begin{bmatrix} E & F \\ D & G \end{bmatrix} : H_1 \oplus H_2 \to H_1' \oplus H_2' \,. \tag{2.1}$$

LEMMA 2.1 ([5]; see also [2]). *Let* [D,G] *and* $[F^*, G^*]^*$ *in* (2.1) *both be contractions. Then there exists an operator* E *such that* M *is a contraction.*

LEMMA 2.2. *Let* B *be a contractive intertwining dilation of* A. *Then* B *admits a decomposition of the form:*

$$Bh = Ah \oplus CD_Ah = Ah \oplus f' \quad (h \in H) \tag{2.2}$$

*where* $C$ *is a contraction mapping* $D_A$ *into* $l^2(D_{T'})$ *satisfying*

$$CD_ATh = D_{T'}Ah \oplus CD_Ah \quad (h \in H)\,. \tag{2.3}$$

PROOF. The second equation in (1.2) and T = U implies that B admits a decomposition of the form Bh = Ah ⊕ Zh where Z is a contraction mapping $H$ into $l^2(D_{T'})$. Since B is a contraction

$$||D_Ah||^2 = ||h||^2 - ||Ah||^2 \geq ||Zh||^2 \quad (h \in H)\,.$$

This implies that there exists a contraction C mapping $D_A$ into $l^2(D_{T'})$ satisfying $Z = CD_A$. This proves (2.2). Equations (1.1) and (2.2) give:

$$ATh \oplus CD_ATh =$$

$$BTh = U'(Ah \oplus CD_Ah) = T'Ah \oplus (D_{T'}Ah \oplus CD_Ah)\,.$$

This yields (2.3) and completes the proof.

Let B be a contractive intertwining dilation of A and C its corresponding contraction in Lemma 2. Throughout the contraction $C_n$ from $D_A$ to $\bigoplus_o^n D_{T'}$ is the compression of C to $\bigoplus_o^n D_{T'}$, that is, if $CD_Ah = (f_i')_{i=0}^{\infty}$ then $C_nD_Ah = \bigoplus_o^n f_i'$. According to the previous Lemma

$$C_iD_ATh = D_{T'}Ah \oplus C_{i-1}D_Ah \quad (h \in H \text{ and } i \geq 0)\,. \tag{2.4}$$

(We set $C_{-1} = 0$.)

LEMMA 2.3. *Let* $C_n$ *be a contraction satisfying* (2.4) *for* $i = n$, *and* $W^{(n)}$ *be a contraction of the form* (1.6) *where* $W_o|F = \omega$. *Assume that* $h \oplus (\bigoplus_o^n d_i(h)) \oplus C_n D_A h$ *is the unique element in* $H \oplus (\bigoplus_o^n D_A) \oplus (\bigoplus_o^n D_{T'})$ *solving*

$$W^{(n)}(D_A h \oplus (\bigoplus_o^{n-1} d_i(h))) = (\bigoplus_o^n d_i(h)) \oplus C_n D_A h\ . \tag{2.5}$$

*Then*

$$d_o(Th) = D_A h \text{ and } d_{i+1}(Th) = d_i(h) \quad (0 \le i < n \text{ and } h \in H)\ . \tag{2.6}$$

PROOF. Using (2.4) and $W_o|F = \omega$ we have

$$W^{(n)} \begin{bmatrix} D_A Th \\ D_A h \\ d_o(h) \\ \cdot \\ \cdot \\ \cdot \\ d_{n-2}(h) \end{bmatrix} = \begin{bmatrix} D_A h \oplus D_{T'} A h \\ W^{(n-1)} \begin{bmatrix} D_A h \\ d_o(h) \\ \cdot \\ \cdot \\ \cdot \\ d_{n-2}(h) \end{bmatrix} \end{bmatrix} =$$

$$\begin{bmatrix} D_A h \\ d_o(h) \\ d_1(h) \\ \cdot \\ \cdot \\ \cdot \\ d_{n-1}(h) \end{bmatrix} \oplus \begin{bmatrix} D_{T'} A h \\ C_{n-1} D_A h \end{bmatrix} = \begin{bmatrix} D_A h \\ d_o(h) \\ d_1(h) \\ \cdot \\ \cdot \\ \cdot \\ d_{n-1}(h) \end{bmatrix} \oplus C_n D_A Th\ . \tag{2.7}$$

However $Th \oplus (\bigoplus_o^n d_i(Th)) \oplus C_n D_A Th$ is the unique solution of

$$W^{(n)}\begin{bmatrix} D_A Th \\ d_o(Th) \\ d_1(Th) \\ \cdot \\ \cdot \\ \cdot \\ d_{n-1}(Th)\end{bmatrix} = \begin{bmatrix} d_o(Th) \\ d_1(Th) \\ \cdot \\ \cdot \\ \cdot \\ d_n(Th)\end{bmatrix} \oplus C_n D_A Th \,.$$

Comparing this with (2.7) yields (2.4) and completes the proof.

## 3. PROOF OF THEOREM 1.1

To prove the remaining part of Theorem 1.1, assume that B is a contractive intertwining dilation of A. Throughout $Bh = Ah \oplus f'$ where h is in $H$ and $CD_Ah = f' = (f_o, f_1, f_2, \ldots)$ is in $l^2(D_{T'})$. Consulting (1.6) (1.7) (1.8) and (2.2) we see that $B = B(W)$ for some Schur contraction W if and only if there exists a set of operators $\{W_i\}_o^\infty$ mapping $D_A$ into $D_A \oplus D_{T'}$ such that for all $n \geq 0$

$$\|W^{(n)}\| \leq 1 \text{ and } W_o|F = \omega \quad \text{and}$$

$$W^{(n)}(D_Ah \oplus (\bigoplus_o^{n-1} d_i(h))) = (\bigoplus_o^{n} d_i(h)) \oplus C_nD_Ah \ \ (\text{for all } n \geq 0)\,. \tag{3.1}$$

As noted earlier the lower triangular structure of $W^{(n)}$ guarantees that $d_n$ in $D_A$ is recursively determined by h and the previous $d_i$'s. The proof of Theorem 3.5 in [4] shows that the $d_n$ is uniquely determined by h and $\{f_i'\}_o^n$.

We proceed by induction. The conditions in (3.1) for $W_o$ become:

$$\|W_o\| \leq 1, \ W_o|F = \omega \quad \text{and} \quad P_{D_{T'}}W_o = C_o\,. \tag{3.2}$$

This is equivalent to the existence of a contraction of the form

$$W_o = \begin{bmatrix} E & F \\ D & G\end{bmatrix} : R \oplus F \to D_{T'} \oplus D_A \tag{3.3}$$

satisfying

$$[D,G] = P_{D_{T'}}W_o = C_o \text{ and } W_o|F = \omega, \text{ i.e. } [F^*,G^*]^* = \omega\,, \tag{3.4}$$

where $R = D_A \ominus F$. Equation (1.3) (2.4) and $W_o|F = \omega$ give:

$$P_{D_{T'}}W_oD_AT = D_{T'}A = C_oD_AT\,.$$

Thus $F = P_{D_{T'}}W_o|F = C_o|F$ and $P_{D_{T'}}W_o$ and $C_o$ are compatible on $F$. Since $C_o$ and $\omega$ are both contractions, (3.4) with Lemma 2.1 shows that there exists an E such that

$W_o$ is a contraction. Theorem 3.5 in [4] proves that this $W_o$ is unique. This completes the construction of $W_o = W^{(o)}$ satisfying (3.1).

Now we proceed by induction and assume that $W^{(n)}$ is a contraction satisfying (3.1). We will use Lemma 2.1 to construct a $W^{(n+1)}$ satisfying (3.1) for $n+1$. Lemmas 2.2 and 2.3 with (2.6) readily yield the following useful result for $0 \leq j \leq n$ and h in $H$:

$$D_A T^{j+1}h \oplus \cdots \oplus D_A Th \oplus d_o(Th) \oplus d_1(Th) \oplus \cdots \oplus d_{n-j}(Th) =$$

$$D_A T^{j+1}h \oplus d_o(T^{j+1}h) \oplus d_1(T^{j+1}h) \oplus \cdots \oplus d_n(T^{j+1}h)\,. \tag{3.5}$$

Let Q be the orthogonal projection from

$$\overset{n+1}{\underset{o}{\oplus}} (D_A \oplus D_{T'}) \text{ onto } (\overset{n}{\underset{o}{\oplus}} (D_A \oplus D_{T'})) \oplus (\{0\} \oplus D_{T'})$$

and $f_j(h)$ the element in $\overset{n+1}{\underset{o}{\oplus}} D_A$ defined by

$$f_j(h) = D_A T^{j+1}h \oplus D_A T^j h \oplus \cdots \oplus D_A Th \oplus 0 \oplus \cdots \oplus 0\,.$$

Let $g = \overset{n+1}{\underset{o}{\oplus}} g_i$ be in $\overset{n+1}{\underset{o}{\oplus}} D_A$. For a fixed $W^{(n+1)}$ extending $W^{(n)}$ we set $\tilde{g}$ equal to the $D_{T'}$ component in the last row of $W^{(n+1)}g$. Using

$$g'' = \overset{n+1}{\underset{o}{\oplus}} g_i'' = \overset{n+1}{\underset{o}{\oplus}} P_R g_i \quad \text{and} \quad g' = \overset{n+1}{\underset{o}{\oplus}} g_i' = \overset{n+1}{\underset{o}{\oplus}} P_F g_i$$

with the fact that the last component of $f_j(h)$ is zero we have:

$$||g+f_j(h)||^2 - ||QW^{(n+1)}(g+f_j(h))||^2 =$$

$$||g+f_j(h)||^2 - ||W^{(n)}((\overset{n}{\underset{o}{\oplus}} g_i)+f_j(h))||^2 - ||\tilde{g}||^2 =$$

$$||g''||^2 + ||g'+f_j(h)||^2 - ||W^{(n)}(\overset{n}{\underset{o}{\oplus}} g_i'')||^2 - ||\tilde{g}||^2 - ||(\overset{n}{\underset{o}{\oplus}} \omega)((\overset{n}{\underset{o}{\oplus}} g_i')+f_j(h))||^2 =$$

$$||g''||^2 + ||g_{n+1}'||^2 - ||W^{(n)}(\overset{n}{\underset{o}{\oplus}} g_i'')||^2 - ||\tilde{g}||^2 =$$

$$||g''||^2 + ||g'||^2 - ||W^{(n)}(\overset{n}{\underset{o}{\oplus}} (g_i''+g_i'))||^2 - ||\tilde{g}||^2 =$$

$$||g||^2 - ||QW^{(n+1)}g||^2\,. \tag{3.6}$$

Let $\hat{f}_j(h)$ be the element appearing in the left hand side of (3.5) and

$$\hat{f} = \begin{bmatrix} D_A h \\ d_o(h) \\ d_1(h) \\ \cdot \\ \cdot \\ \cdot \\ d_n(h) \end{bmatrix} + \hat{f}_o(h_o) + \cdots + \hat{f}_n(h_n) = \begin{bmatrix} D_A \hat{h} \\ d_o(\hat{h}) \\ d_1(\hat{h}) \\ \cdot \\ \cdot \\ \cdot \\ d_n(\hat{h}) \end{bmatrix} \tag{3.7}$$

where h and $h_i$ are all in $H$ and $\hat{h} = h + \sum_o^n T^{j+1} h_j$. The last equality follows from (3.5) and the definition of $\hat{h}$. The last equation in (3.1) (for n + 1 instead of n) with (3.7) and the fact $C_{n+1}$ is a contraction yields:

$$\|\hat{f}\|^2 - \|QW^{(n+1)}\hat{f}\|^2 \geq 0 . \tag{3.8}$$

Applying (3.6) n+1 times for $g = g_j$, $h = -h_j$ $(0 \leq j \leq n)$ with $g_o = \hat{f}$, $g_{j+1} = g_j + f_j(-h_j)$ and $g_{n+1} = \tilde{f}$, where

$$\tilde{f} = \begin{bmatrix} D_A h \\ d_o(h) \\ d_1(h) \\ \cdot \\ \cdot \\ \cdot \\ d_n(h) \end{bmatrix} + (\hat{f}_o(h_o) - f_o(h_o)) + \cdots + (\hat{f}_n(h_n) - f_n(h_n)) ,$$

we deduce from (3.7)(3.8) that

$$\|\tilde{f}\|^2 - \|QW^{(n+1)}\tilde{f}\|^2 \geq 0 . \tag{3.9}$$

A simple calculation shows that

$$\tilde{f} = \begin{bmatrix} D_A h \\ D_A h_o + \delta_o \\ D_A h_1 + \delta_1 \\ \cdot \\ \cdot \\ \cdot \\ D_A h_n + \delta_n \end{bmatrix}$$

where $\delta_i$ is a linear combination of h, $h_o$, ..., $h_{i-1}$ with range in $D_A$. Thus $\tilde{f}$ runs through a dense set in $\overset{n+1}{\underset{o}{\oplus}} D_A$. This, (3.1) for n+1 and (3.9) show that $QW^{(n+1)}$ is a well defined contraction for all choices of $W_{n+1}$. Lemma 2.1 with

$$[D,G] = QW^{(n+1)} \text{ and } [F^*,G^*]^* = W^{(n)}$$

implies that there exists a contraction $W_{n+1}$ such that $W^{(n+1)}$ is a contraction. The proof of Theorem 3.5 in [4] shows that this $W_{n+1}$ is unique. This completes the induction and the proof of Theorem 1.1.

ACKNOWLEDGEMENTS

This research was supported in part by a grant from the National Science Foundation No. ECS 8419354 and by the Research Fund of Indiana University.

REFERENCES

1. Arsene, Gr., Z. Ceausescu, and C. Foias. On intertwining dilations VIII. *J. Operator Theory, 4* (1980), pp. 55-91.

2. Arsene, Gr. and A. Gheondea. Completing matrix contractions. *J. Operator Theory,* 7 (1982) pp. 179-189.

3. Foias, C. Contractive intertwining dilations and waves in layered media. *Proceedings on the International Congress of Mathematicians.* Helsinki (1978), Vol. 2, pp. 605-613.

4. Foias, C. and A.E. Frazho. On the Schur representation in the Commutant Lifting Theorem I. Operator Theory Advances and Applications I. *Schur Methods in Operator Theory and signal processing* Edited by I. Gohberg (1986), pp. 207-217.

5. S. Parrott, On a quotient norm and the Sz.-Nagy-Foias lifting theorem, *J. Funct. Analysis,* 30 (1978), pp. 311-328.

6. Sz.-Nagy, B. and C. Foias. *Harmonic analysis of operators on Hilbert space,* Amsterdam-Budapest, 1970.

7. Sz.-Nagy, B. and C. Foias. Dilation des communtants. *C.R. Acad. Sci. Paris, Serie A,* 266 (1968) pp. 493-495.

Indiana University
Department of Mathematics
Bloomington, Indiana 47401

Purdue University
School of Aeronautics and Astronautics
West Lafayette, Indiana 47907

Submitted: November 2, 1986

Operator Theory:
Advances and Applications, Vol. 29




# NODES AND REALIZATION OF RATIONAL MATRIX FUNCTIONS: MINIMALITY THEORY AND APPLICATIONS

I. Gohberg, M.A. Kaashoek and L. Lerer (1)

*Dedicated to Moshe Livšic, on the occasion of his seventieth birthday, with great respect and gratitude. We owe him much of the modern understanding of the connections between operators and systems.*

This paper contains a unified minimality theory for systems with several state space operators. It includes the theorems of minimality for time-invariant boundary value systems, for partial realization, for various classes of N-D-systems, and also for systems governed by certain partial differential equations.

## 0. INTRODUCTION

Let $M_1, M_2, \ldots$ be a given sequence of $m \times p$ matrices. A triple $\Sigma = (A,B,C)$ of linear operators, $A : X \to X$, $B : \mathbb{C}^p \to X$ and $C : X \to \mathbb{C}^m$, is called a *realization* of $M_1, M_2, \ldots$ if

(0.1) $$M_j = CA^{j-1}B, \quad j = 1,2,\ldots .$$

Here X is a finite dimensional linear space, which is called the *state space* of the realization $\Sigma$. In connection with the notion of realization four problems appear in a natural way. The first is the existence problem and concerns the question when a given sequence admits a realization. The second is the minimality problem, i.e., the problem to find criteria for the state space dimension to be as small as possible. The third is the reduction problem, namely how to reduce a given realization to a minimal one. The fourth is the uniqueness problem for minimal realizations and asks to what extent a realization with minimal state space dimension is unique.

In the classical theory of time invariant causal systems (see

---

(1) The work of this author is supported by the Fund of Promotion of Research of the Technion - Israel Institute of Technology.

[16,30] and the books [15,18,26]) these four problems are completely solved in the following way. A sequence $M_1, M_2, \ldots$ admits a realization if and only if

$$(0.2) \qquad \max_{k\geq 1} \operatorname{rank} \begin{bmatrix} M_1 & M_2 & \cdots & M_k \\ M_2 & M_3 & \cdots & M_{k+1} \\ \vdots & \vdots & & \vdots \\ M_k & M_{k+1} & \cdots & M_{2k-1} \end{bmatrix} < \infty ,$$

and the integer defined by the left hand side of (0.2) is the smallest possible state space dimension of a realization of $M_1, M_2, \ldots$. Furthermore, a realization $\Sigma = (A,B,C)$ of $M_1, M_2, \ldots$ is minimal (i.e., has smallest possible state space dimension) if

$$(0.3) \qquad N(\Sigma) := \operatorname{Ker} \begin{bmatrix} C \\ CA \\ \vdots \\ CA^{n-1} \end{bmatrix} = (0),$$

$$(0.4) \qquad R(\Sigma) := \operatorname{Im} [B \;\; AB \;\; \ldots \;\; A^{n-1}B] = X,$$

where $n = \dim X$. If the conditions (0.3) and (0.4) are not both fulfilled, then the realization $\Sigma = (A,B,C)$ may be reduced to a minimal one in the following way. Put $X_1 = N(\Sigma)$, let $X_0$ be a direct complement of $X_1 \cap R(\Sigma)$ in $R(\Sigma)$, and choose $X_2$ such that $X = X_1 \oplus X_0 \oplus X_2$. Then relative to the decomposition $X = X_1 \oplus X_0 \oplus X_2$ the operators A,B and C partition as follows:

$$A = \begin{bmatrix} * & * & * \\ 0 & A_0 & * \\ 0 & 0 & * \end{bmatrix}, \quad B = \begin{bmatrix} * \\ B_0 \\ 0 \end{bmatrix}, \quad C = [0 \;\; C_0 \;\; *],$$

and $(A_0, B_0, C_0)$ is a minimal realization of $M_1, M_2, \ldots$ . Finally, we mention that a minimal realization $\Sigma = (A,B,C)$ of a given sequence is unique up to similarity, which means that any other minimal realization $\Sigma_1 = (A_1, B_1, C_1)$ of the same sequence is of the form

$$A_1 = SAS^{-1}, \quad B_1 = SB, \quad C_1 = CS^{-1},$$

where S is some invertible operator.

The four problems mentioned above also appear if only a finite or infinite part of the sequence $M_1, M_2, \ldots$ is given. For example, take the partial realization problem when just $M_1, \ldots, M_r$ are supposed to be fixed (for some positive integer r). In this case the triple $\Sigma = (A,B,C)$ is said to be a realization if

$$M_j = CA^{j-1}B, \quad j = 1, \ldots, r.$$

In this context the first problem is trivial, the second and the third were only recently solved (in [13]), and for the fourth problem only partial solutions are known (see [13] and the references there in).

Different problems in various areas of mathematical systems theory (e.g., concerning boundary value systems and N-D-systems) lead to multi-indexed versions of the four problems. The triple (A,B,C) is now replaced by a node $(A_1, \ldots, A_k; B, C)$ of which the main operators $A_1, \ldots, A_k$ act on the state space X, and B and C are as before. In one version of the multi-indexed analogues the role of the sequence $M_1, M_2, \ldots$ is taken over by the set of all moments

$$M_{(\gamma_1, \ldots, \gamma_\ell)} = CA_{\gamma_1}A_{\gamma_2} \cdots A_{\gamma_\ell}B,$$

where $(\gamma_1, \ldots, \gamma_\ell)$ runs over the set $\Gamma_k$ of all $\ell$-tuples, $\ell$ arbitrary, with entries from $\{1, 2, \ldots, k\}$. In other versions one does not start with all moments but with a restriced set of moments, while at the same time the four problems have to be considered only for nodes with certain additional properties. In this case we speak about *nodes and minimality with restrictions*. For example, the problem of minimality, reduction and uniqueness may be considered in the set of nodes

$$\mathcal{D} = \{(A_1, A_2; B, C) \mid A_1A_2 - A_2A_1 = BC\}$$

with moments

$$CA_1^{k_1}A_2^{k_2}B, \ k_1 \geq 0, \ k_2 \geq 0,$$

in which case the set $\Gamma_2$ of all tuples with entries from $\{1,2\}$ is replaced by the smaller set of all tuples of the form $(1, \ldots, 1, 2, \ldots, 2)$. This particular type of minimality with restrictions appears in the infinite dimensional case in the theory of the Pincus determining function (see, e.g., [25],[4]) and it is related to Donaldson's description ot the Yang-Mills instantons ([5], also [14]).

In this paper we deal with the minimality problem, the reduction problem and the uniqueness problem. The multi-indexed existence problem is not considered in this paper. In Chapter I we solve the full unrestricted multi-indexed version. As a first application we prove in this framework the theorems in [12] about irreducibility of boundary value systems.

The second chapter concerns minimality with restrictions. We distinguish two types. For the first type the given moments have a certain property of domination, and in this case restricted minimality is the same as minimality without restrictions. To establish the property of domination is here the main difficulty. We give the solution for several examples. For the second type of restricted minimality, when the domination property is absent, we do not have a general theory. For two important examples of this type (one connected with the partial realization problem and the other with the problem of minimality for boundary value systems) the minimality and reduction problems are completely solved.

The third chapter concerns applications and is dedicated to minimality questions for some classes 2-D and N-D systems.

The four problems mentioned in the first paragraph can be restated in terms of realizations of rational matrix functions. For nodes with several main operators this approach is developed systematically in the last chapter. On the one hand we obtain in this way the minimality theory for realizations of several classes of rational matrix functions in several variables, and on the other hand we also extend the theory developed in the first two chapters. New examples, not covered by the theory of the earlier chapters, are included. They are related to 2-D systems and systems governed by partial differential equations.

It is a pleasure to dedicate this paper to Moshe Livšic, an outstanding mathematician and a good friend. He understood at a very early stage the connections between operator theory and systems, introduced a wonderful tool - the characteristic operator function - and proved one of the first minimality theorems. We mention with gratitude the impact his work has on the present authors.

The theory of colligations for (several) operators developed by M.S. Livšic is of particular relevance for the present paper. We mention [22,23,24], and also the papers [8] be H. Gauchman and [21] by S. Levin, which originated from his work.

## I. MINIMALITY OF NODES

In this chapter a general theory of minimality for nodes with several main operators is developed. The criterium of minimality is derived, the reduction of a node to a minimal one is described explicitly, and the necessary and sufficient conditions for similarity of minimal nodes is given. The general theory is illustrated on the problem of reduction for boundary value systems.

### I.1. Nodes and words

In what follows the term *node* is used for a (k+3)-tuple of the form

$$\Xi = (A_1,\dots,A_k;X;B,C),$$

where $A_i : X \to X$ $(i=1,\dots,k)$, $B : \mathbb{C}^p \to X$ and $C : X \to \mathbb{C}^m$ are linear operators acting between finite dimensional linear spaces X, $\mathbb{C}^m$ and $\mathbb{C}^p$. The operators $A_1,\dots,A_k$ are called the *main operators* of the node $\Xi$, while B and C will be referred to as the *input* and *output operators* of $\Xi$, respectively. The space X is called the *state space* of the node $\Xi$. The set of all nodes will be denoted by $N$ while $N_k$ stands for the set of all nodes with k main operators. Here and elsewhere the integers m and p are assumed to be fixed and they don't appear in our notations.

By $\Gamma_k$ we denote the union of the empty set $\emptyset$ with the collection of all $\ell$-tuples $\gamma = (\gamma_1,\dots,\gamma_\ell)$ $(\ell = 1,2,\dots)$ with $\gamma_i \in \{1,2,\dots,k\}$ $(i=1,2,\dots,\ell)$. If $A_1,A_2,\dots,A_k$ are linear operators acting on a linear space X and $\gamma = (\gamma_1,\dots,\gamma_\ell) \in \Gamma_k$ an expression of the form

$$\omega_\gamma(A_1,\dots,A_k) := A_{\gamma_1}A_{\gamma_2}\cdots A_{\gamma_\ell} \tag{1.1}$$

will be called a *word* in operators $A_1,\dots,A_k$. By definition

$$\omega_\emptyset(A_1,\dots,A_k) := I_X,$$

the identity operator on X. If the operators $A_1,\dots,A_k$ come from a node $\Xi = (A_1,\dots,A_k;X;B,C)$, then we shall also use the notation

$$\omega_\gamma(\Xi) := \omega_\gamma(A_1,\dots,A_k).$$

The integer $\ell$ will be called the *length of the word* (1.1), notationally, $|\omega_\gamma| := |\gamma| := \ell$. By definition $|\omega_\emptyset| = 0$.

Given a node $\Xi = (A_1,\dots,A_k,X;B,C)$, we introduce two subspaces of X:

$$R(\Xi) = \bigvee_{\gamma\in\Gamma_k} \operatorname{Im}\omega_\gamma(\Xi)B, \tag{1.2}$$

the *controllable subspace* of $\Xi$, and

(1.3) $N(\Xi) = \bigcap_{\gamma\in\Gamma_k} \operatorname{Ker} C\omega_\gamma(\Xi)$,

the *unobservable subspace* of $\Xi$. Here and in the sequel the notation $\bigvee_{\gamma\in\Gamma} Z_\gamma$ is used for the linear hull of the set $\bigcup_{\gamma\in\Gamma} Z_\gamma$.

Clearly, the subspaces $R(\Xi)$ and $N(\Xi)$ are invariant under each of the operators $A_1,\ldots,A_k$. In fact, as follows from the proof of Proposition 1.1 below the infinite intersection and sum in (1.2), (1.3) can be replaced by finite ones. More precisely, if n is the dimension of the state space X, then

(1.4) $R(\Xi) = \bigvee_{|\gamma|\le n-1} \operatorname{Im} \omega_\gamma(\Xi)B$,

(1.5) $N(\Xi) = \bigcap_{|\gamma|\le n-1} \operatorname{Ker} C\omega_\gamma(\Xi)$.

A node $\Xi = (A_1,\ldots,A_k;X;B,C)$ will be called *controllable* if $R(\Xi) = X$. Similarly, if $N(\Xi) = (0)$, then the node $\Xi$ is said to be *observable*.

The following characterization of the subspaces $R(\Xi)$ and $N(\Xi)$ will be useful.

PROPOSITION 1.1. *Given a node* $\Xi = (A_1,\ldots,A_k;X;B,C)$, *the space* $N(\Xi)$ *is the greatest common invariant subspace for* $A_1,\ldots,A_k$ *contained in* $\operatorname{Ker} C$.

PROOF. Introduce the spaces

$$N_\ell = \bigcap_{|\gamma|\le\ell} C\omega_\gamma(\Xi).$$

It is obvious that

(1.6) $N_0 \supset N_1 \supset N_2 \supset \ldots$

We claim that if $N_{s-1} = N_s$ for some s, then $N_{\alpha-1} = N_\alpha$ for all $\alpha \ge s$. Indeed, let $x \in N_s$, i.e. $C\omega_\gamma(A_1,\ldots,A_k)x = 0$ for any word $\omega_\gamma$ of length $\le s$. Then $A_1x, A_2x,\ldots,A_kx \in N_{s-1}$. By our assumption $N_{s-1} = N_s$, and hence $C\omega_\gamma(A_1,\ldots,A_k)A_jx = 0$ for any word $\omega_\gamma$ with $|\gamma| \le s$ and any $j = 1,\ldots,k$. This means that $x \in N_{s+1}$. So, the equality $N_{s-1} = N_s$ implies $N_s = N_{s+1}$. Proceeding in this way we conclude that $N_{\alpha-1} = N_\alpha$ for all $\alpha \ge s$. Using this fact and the inclusions (1.6) one deduces by a simple dimension argument that the smallest integer $s_0$ for which $N_{s_0+1} = N_{s_0}$ satisfies the estimation $s_0 \le n-1$. Note that this also proves formula (1.5).

Further, let us show that $N_{s_0}$ is invariant under each of the operators $A_j$ $(j = 1,\ldots,k)$. Indeed, let $x \in N_{s_0} = N_{s_0+1}$. Then $C\omega_\gamma(A_1,\ldots,A_k)A_jx = 0$ for all words $\omega_\gamma$ with $|\gamma| \le s_0$ and for $j = 1,\ldots,k$. In other words, $A_jx \in N_{s_0}$ $(j = 1,\ldots,k)$, i.e. the space $N_{s_0}$ is $A_j$-invariant for each $j = 1,\ldots,k$. Now, if

$M \subset \operatorname{Ker} C$ is any subspace which is invariant under each of the operators $A_j$ $(j = 1,\dots,k)$ and $x \in M$, then, clearly, $\omega_\gamma(A_1,\dots,A_k)x \in \operatorname{Ker} C$ for any word $\omega_\gamma$ and thus $M \subset N_{s_0}$. □

Using similar arguments (or by passing to the adjoint operators) one proves the following proposition.

PROPOSITION 1.2. *Given a node* $\Xi = (A_1,\dots,A_k;X;B,C)$, *the space* $R(\Xi)$ *is the smallest common invariant subspace for* $A_1,\dots,A_k$ *which contains* $\operatorname{Im} B$.

## I.2. Main minimality theorems

In this section we present the main theorems about minimal nodes. The proofs will be given in the next section.

Given a node $\Xi = (A_1,\dots,A_k;X;B,C) \in N_k$, the expression

$$M_\gamma(\Xi) := C\omega_\gamma(\Xi)B, \quad \gamma \in \Gamma_k$$

will be called a *moment* of $\Xi$ and $|\gamma|$ will be referred to as the length of the moment $M_\gamma(\Xi)$. By $M(\Xi)$ we denote the set of all moments of the node $\Xi$:

$$M(\Xi) = \{M_\gamma(\Xi) \mid \gamma \in \Gamma_k\}.$$

We say that two nodes $\Xi,\tilde{\Xi} \in M_k$ have the same moments and write $M(\Xi) \equiv M(\tilde{\Xi})$ if $M_\gamma(\Xi) = M_\gamma(\tilde{\Xi})$ for any $\gamma \in \Gamma_k$.

A node $\Xi \in N_k$ is called *minimal* if its state space dimension is as small as possible among all nodes in $N_k$ with the same moments as $\Xi$. Minimal nodes are characterized as follows.

THEOREM 2.1. *A node* $\Xi \in N_k$ *is minimal if and only if it is controllable and observable, i.e. if and only if* $N(\Xi) = (0)$ *and* $R(\Xi) = X$, *where* $X$ *is the state space of* $\Xi$.

To describe how to get a minimal node from a given one we need the following notions of reduction and dilation. We say that a node $\Xi_0 = (A_1^{(0)},\dots,A_k^{(0)};X_0;B_0,C_0) \in N_k$ is a *reduction* of the node $\Xi = (A_1,\dots,A_k;X;B,C)$ if the space $X$ admits a direct sum decomposition $X = X_1 \oplus X_0 \oplus X_2$ such that relative to this decomposition the following partitionings hold true

$$(2.1) \qquad A_i = \begin{pmatrix} * & * & * \\ 0 & A_i^{(0)} & * \\ 0 & 0 & * \end{pmatrix} \quad (i = 1,\dots,k), \quad B = \begin{pmatrix} * \\ B_0 \\ 0 \end{pmatrix}, \quad C = \begin{pmatrix} 0 & C_0 & * \end{pmatrix}.$$

In this case we say also that $\Xi$ is a *dilation* of $\Xi_0$.

Note that if $\Xi_0$ is a reduction of $\Xi$ then $M(\Xi_0) \equiv M(\Xi)$.

THEOREM 2.2. *Any node* $\Xi = (A_1,\ldots,A_k;X;B,C) \in N_k$ *is a dilation of a minimal node. Namely: put* $X_1 = N(\Xi)$, *let* $X_0$ *be a direct complement of* $X_1 \cap R(\Xi)$ *in* $R(\Xi)$, *and choose* $X_2$ *such that* $X = X_1 \oplus X_0 \oplus X_2$. *Then relative to this decomposition the partitionings* (2.1) *hold true and* $\Xi_0 = (A_1^{(0)},\ldots,A_k^{(0)};X_0;B_0,C_0)$ *is a minimal node.*

Next we discuss similarity of nodes. Two nodes $\Xi = (A_1,\ldots,A_k;X;B,C) \in M_k$ and $\tilde{\Xi} = (\tilde{A}_1,\ldots,\tilde{A}_k;\tilde{X};\tilde{B},\tilde{C}) \in M_k$ are said to be *similar* if

$$\tilde{A}_i = SA_iS^{-1} \ (i=1,\ldots,k), \quad \tilde{B} = SB, \quad \tilde{C} = CS^{-1},$$

with some invertible operator $S : X \to \tilde{X}$.

THEOREM 2.3. *Let* $\Xi, \tilde{\Xi} \in N_k$ *be minimal nodes. Then the nodes* $\Xi$ *and* $\tilde{\Xi}$ *are similar if and only if they have the same moments, i.e.*

$$(2.2) \qquad M_\gamma(\Xi) = M_\gamma(\tilde{\Xi}), \quad \gamma \in \Gamma_k$$

In fact, it is enough to check condition (2.2) for a finite number of $\ell$-tuples in $\Gamma_k$, as follows from the next result.

THEOREM 2.4. *If the nodes* $\Xi = (A_1,\ldots,A_k;X;B,C) \in N_k$ *and* $\tilde{\Xi} = (\tilde{A}_1,\ldots,\tilde{A}_k,\tilde{X};\tilde{B},\tilde{C}) \in N_k$ *satisfy the condition*

$$(2.3) \qquad M_\gamma(\Xi) = M_\gamma(\tilde{\Xi}), \quad \gamma \in \Gamma_k, \quad |\gamma| \le 2\max\{\dim X, \dim \tilde{X}\} - 1,$$

*then* (2.2) *holds true for any* $\gamma \in \Gamma_k$. *Here* $X$ *and* $\tilde{X}$ *are the state spaces of* $\Xi$ *and* $\tilde{\Xi}$, *respectively.*

## I.3. Proofs of the minimality theorems.

In this section we prove Theorems 2.1 - 2.4. It turns out to be convenient to give one chain of arguments, consisting of five parts, which yields the desired results.

Part 1. Let $\Xi = (A_1,\ldots,A_k;X;B,C)$ be a node in $N_k$ and make the decomposition $X = X_1 \oplus X_0 \oplus X_2$ as in Theorem 2.2. In this part we shall show that relative to the above state space decomposition the partitionings (2.1) hold true and that the reduction $\Xi_0 = (A_1^{(0)},\ldots,A_k^{(0)};X_0;B_0,C_0)$ is controllable and observable, i.e.

$$(3.1) \qquad N(\Xi_0) = (0), \quad R(\Xi_0) = X_0.$$

Indeed, from the definition of the subspaces $X_1$ and $X_0$ we see (cf. Propositions 1.1 and 1.2) that $X_1$ and $X_1 \oplus X_0$ are invariant under each $A_i$ $(i=1,\dots,k)$ which implies immediately the partitionings in (2.1) for the operators $A_i$. Since $X_1 \subset \operatorname{Ker} C$ and $\operatorname{Im} B \subset X_1 \oplus X_0$ the partitionings (2.1) for B and C are also clear.

Further, $N(\Xi_0) \subset \operatorname{Ker} C_0 \subset \operatorname{Ker} C$, and from the partitionings of $A_i$ we see that $A_i(N(\Xi_0)) \subset X_1 \oplus N(\Xi_0)$. Hence the subspace $X_1 \oplus N(\Xi_0)$ is contained in $\operatorname{Ker} C$ and it is $A_i$-invariant for all $i=1,2,\dots,k$. But by Proposition 1.2 the space $X_1$ is the largest common invariant subspace of $A_i$, $i=1,\dots,k$, contained in $\operatorname{Ker} C$, and hence $N(\Xi_0) = (0)$, i.e. $\Xi_0$ is observable.

To prove the controllability of $\Xi_0$ note that $R(\Xi) = (X_1 \cap R(\Xi)) \oplus X_0$. Put

$$M = (X_1 \cap R(\Xi)) \oplus R(\Xi_0).$$

Then $\operatorname{Im} B \subset (X_1 \cap R(\Xi)) \oplus \operatorname{Im} B_0 \subset M$. As $R(\Xi)$ and $R(\Xi_0)$ are invariant under $A_i$ and $A_i^{(0)}$, respectively, we have

$$A_i(R(\Xi_0)) \subset (X_1 \cap R(\Xi)) \oplus R(\Xi_0),$$

and hence

$$A_i M \subset A_i(X_1 \cap R(\Xi)) + A_i(R(\Xi_0)) \subset M \quad (i=1,\dots,k).$$

In other words, M is a common invariant subspace for $A_i$, $i=1,\dots,k$, and $M \supset \operatorname{Im} B$. But in view of Proposition 1.2 the space $R(\Xi) = (X_1 \cap R(\Xi)) \oplus X_0$ is the smallest common invariant subspace of $A_i$, $i=1,\dots,k$, which contains $\operatorname{Im} B$, and hence $R(\Xi_0) = X_0$. Thus $\Xi_0$ is controllable.

This first part also shows that in order to prove Theorem 2.2 it is enough to prove Theorem 2.1.

Part 2. The previous part shows that a minimal node is necessarily controllable and observable. Indeed, if $\Xi = (A_1,\dots,A_k;X;B,C)$ is a minimal node and if $N(\Xi) \neq (0)$ or $R(\Xi) \neq X$, then using Part 1 we can construct a reduction $\Xi_0$ of $\Xi$ whose state space dimension, $\dim X_0$, is strictly less than $\dim X$, which contradicts the minimality of $\Xi$, because, clearly, $\Xi$ and $\Xi_0$ have the same moments.

Part 3. Let $\Xi \in N_k$ be an observable and controllable node and let $\tilde{\Xi}$ be another node in $N_k$ with the same moments as $\Xi$. To prove Theorem 2.1 we have to show that $\dim X \leq \dim \tilde{X}$, where X and $\tilde{X}$ are the state spaces of $\Xi$ and $\tilde{\Xi}$, respectively. By applying Part 1 we may assume without loss of generality that

$N(\tilde{\Xi}) = (0)$ and $R(\Xi) = \tilde{X}$. We shall show that this implies that $\Xi$ and $\tilde{\Xi}$ are similar, and, in particular, $\dim X = \dim \tilde{X}$.

Part 4. Now we shall prove that if the nodes $\Xi = (A_1,\dots,A_k;X;B,C) \in N_k$ and $\tilde{\Xi} = (\tilde{A}_1,\dots,\tilde{A}_k;\tilde{X};\tilde{B},\tilde{C}) \in N_k$ are controllable and observable and have the same moments, then $\Xi$ and $\tilde{\Xi}$ are similar.

Set $q = \max\{\dim X, \dim \tilde{X}\}$ and choose some order in the set $G = \{\gamma \in \Gamma_k \mid |\gamma| \le q-1\}$, so that $G = \{\gamma^{(1)},\gamma^{(2)},\dots,\gamma^{(\omega)}\}$ with $\omega = (k^q-1)(k-1)^{-1}$. Introduce the matrices

$$\Gamma = \mathrm{col}\,(C\omega_{\gamma(i)}(\Xi))_{i=1}^{\omega}, \qquad \Lambda = \mathrm{row}\,(\omega_{\gamma(i)}(\Xi)B)_{i=1}^{\omega},$$

and let $\tilde{\Gamma}$ and $\tilde{\Lambda}$ denote the corresponding matrices for $\tilde{\Xi}$. Since $\Xi$ and $\tilde{\Xi}$ are observable, equality (1.5) implies that $\mathrm{Ker}\,\Gamma = \mathrm{Ker}\,\tilde{\Gamma} = (0)$, i.e. the matrices $\Gamma$ and $\tilde{\Gamma}$ are left invertible. Similarly, since $\Xi$ and $\tilde{\Xi}$ are controllable equality (1.4) yields the right invertibility of the matrices $\Lambda$ and $\tilde{\Lambda}$. Next, since $\Xi$ and $\tilde{\Xi}$ have the same moments we infer that

$$\Gamma\Lambda = \tilde{\Gamma}\tilde{\Lambda}. \tag{3.2}$$

Set $S := \tilde{\Gamma}^{+}\Gamma = \tilde{\Lambda}\Lambda^{+}$. Here and elsewhere the notation $M^{+}$ is used for onesided inverses of M. A direct computation shows that the map $S : X \to \tilde{X}$ is invertible and $S^{-1} = \Gamma^{+}\tilde{\Gamma} = \Lambda\tilde{\Lambda}^{+}$. Furthermore, using (3.2) we obtain the equalities

$$\begin{aligned} S\Lambda &= \tilde{\Gamma}^{+}\Gamma\Lambda = \tilde{\Gamma}^{+}\tilde{\Gamma}\tilde{\Lambda} = \tilde{\Lambda}, \\ \tilde{\Gamma}S &= \tilde{\Gamma}\tilde{\Lambda}\Lambda^{+} = \Gamma\Lambda\Lambda^{+} = \Gamma, \end{aligned} \tag{3.3}$$

which imply, in particular, that

$$\tilde{B} = SB, \qquad \tilde{C} = CS^{-1}.$$

Using again the assumption that $\Xi$ and $\tilde{\Xi}$ have the same moments we can also write

$$\Gamma A_j \Lambda = \tilde{\Gamma}\tilde{A}_j\tilde{\Lambda} \quad (j = 1,\dots,k). \tag{3.4}$$

From these equalities and (3.3) we obtain

$$\tilde{\Gamma}(\tilde{A}_j S - SA_j)\Lambda = \tilde{\Gamma}\tilde{A}_j\tilde{\Lambda} - \Gamma A_j\Lambda = 0 \quad (j = 1,\dots,k).$$

Since $\Lambda$ is right invertible and $\tilde{\Gamma}$ is left invertible, we see that $\tilde{A}_j = SA_jS^{-1}$ $(j = 1,\dots,k)$, which concludes Part 4.

Thus, Theorem 2.1 is proved. Note that Theorem 2.1 and Part 4 also provide a proof of Theorem 2.3.

Part 5. In this step we prove Theorem 2.4. Let $\Xi,\tilde{\Xi} \in N_k$ satisfy condition (2.3). Part 1 shows that there are controllably and observable reductions $\Xi_0$ and $\tilde{\Xi}_0$ of $\Xi$ and $\tilde{\Xi}$, respectively. Clearly, (2.3) implies that

(3.5) $$M_\gamma(\Xi_0) = M_\gamma(\tilde{\Xi}_0) \quad (\gamma \in \Gamma_k, |\gamma| \le 2\max\{\dim X_0, \dim \tilde{X}_0\} - 1).$$

This implies that equalities (3.2) and (3.4) hold true and using Step 4 we infer that $\Xi_0$ and $\tilde{\Xi}_0$ are similar. But then clearly $M_\gamma(\Xi_0) = M_\gamma(\tilde{\Xi}_0)$ for any $\gamma \in \Gamma_k$, and since $M_\gamma(\Xi) = M_\gamma(\Xi_0)$, $M_\gamma(\Xi) = M_\gamma(\tilde{\Xi}_0)$, Theorem 2.4 is proved. □

## I.4. A first application: irreducibility of boundary value systems

This section concerns the problem of reduction of time-invariant boundary value systems which we solved in [12]. Here we show that the irreducibility problem can be rephrased as a minimality problem of the type considered in the previous sections. This allows us to obtain the main irreducibility results of [12] as a corollary of the general theory developed in this chapter.

Consider a time-invariant boundary value system $\theta$ with state space representation

(4.1) $$\theta \begin{cases} \dot{x}(t) = Ax(t) + Bu(t), & a \le t \le b, \\ y(t) = Cx(t), & a \le t \le b, \\ N_1x(a) + N_2x(b) = 0. \end{cases}$$

Here $A : X \to X$, $N_i : X \to X$ $(i=1,2)$ are linear operators acting on a finite dimensional linear space $X$, called the *state space* of $\theta$, and $B : \mathbb{C}^p \to X$, $C : X \to \mathbb{C}^m$ are also linear operators. We shall denote the system $\theta$ by the quintet $\theta = (A,B,C;N_1,N_2)$.

Assume that the state space $X$ of $\theta = (A,B,C;N_1,N_2)$ decomposes into a direct sum $X = X_1 \oplus X_0 \oplus X_2$ such that relative to this decomposition the following partitionings hold

(4.2) $$A = \begin{pmatrix} * & * & * \\ 0 & A_0 & * \\ 0 & 0 & * \end{pmatrix}, \quad B = \begin{pmatrix} * \\ B_0 \\ 0 \end{pmatrix}, \quad C = \begin{pmatrix} 0 & C_0 & * \end{pmatrix},$$

(4.3) $$N_\nu = E\begin{pmatrix} * & * & * \\ 0 & N_\nu^{(0)} & * \\ 0 & 0 & * \end{pmatrix} \quad (\nu = 1,2).$$

Here the symbols $*$ denote unspecified entries and $E$ is some invertible operator on X. Given such partitionings we call the system $\theta_0 = (A_0,B_0,C_0;N_1^{(0)},N_2^{(0)})$ a *reduction* of $\theta$ and we refer to $\theta$ as a *dilation* of $\theta_0$. If $\dim X_0 < \dim X$ we say that the reduction $\theta_0$ of $\theta$ is *proper*. The system $\theta$ is called *irreducible* if $\theta$ does not admit a proper reduction.

Let $\theta = (A,B,C;N_1,N_2)$ and $\tilde{\theta} = (\tilde{A},\tilde{B},\tilde{C};\tilde{N}_1,\tilde{N}_2)$ be two boundary value systems. The systems $\theta$ and $\tilde{\theta}$ are said to be *similar* if there exist invertible operators $S,E : X \to \tilde{X}$ such that

$$(4.4) \qquad \tilde{A} = SAS^{-1}, \quad \tilde{B} = BS^{-1}, \quad \tilde{C} = SC,$$

$$(4.5) \qquad \tilde{N}_1 = EN_1S^{-1}, \quad \tilde{N}_2 = EN_2S^{-1}.$$

Throughout this section we always assume that the boundary conditions of $\theta$ are *well-posed*, i.e. the operator $N_1e^{aA}+N_2e^{bA}$ is invertible. The boundary conditions of a boundary value system $\theta = (A,B,C;N_1,N_2)$ with well-posed boundary conditions can be rewritten in the form

$$(I-P)x(a) + Pe^{(a-b)A}x(b) = 0,$$

where $P = e^{aA}\{(N_1e^{aA}+N_2e^{bA})^{-1}N_2e^{bA}\}e^{-aA}$ is the *canonical boundary value operator*.

Note that the class of well-posed boundary value systems is closed under the operations of reduction and similarity.

With each boundary value system $\theta = (A,B,C;N_1,N_2)$ with state space X and canonical boundary value operator P we shall associate the node $\Xi_\theta = (A,P;X;B,C)$. Observe that a system $\theta_0$ is a (proper) reduction of the system $\theta$ if and only if the node $\Xi_{\theta_0}$ is a (proper) reduction of the node $\Xi_\theta$. Indeed, if the partitionings (4.2) - (4.3) hold true for a system $\theta = (A,B,C;N_1,N_2)$, then the canonical boundary value operator P of $\theta$ is partitioned as follows

$$(4.6) \qquad P = \begin{pmatrix} * & * & * \\ 0 & P_0 & * \\ 0 & 0 & * \end{pmatrix},$$

and one easily sees that $P_0$ is the canonical boundary value operator of $\theta_0 = (A_0,B_0,C_0;N_1^{(0)},N_2^{(0)})$ defined by the partitionings (4.2) - (4.3). So, $\Xi_{\theta_0}$ is of the form $\Xi_{\theta_0} = (A_0,P_0;X_0;B_0,C_0)$ and is a reduction of $\Xi_\theta$. Conversely, if a node $\Xi_0 = (A_0,P_0;X_0;B_0,C_0)$ is a reduction of $\Xi_\theta$, i.e. (4.2) and (4.6) hold true, then setting $N_1^{(0)} = I-P_0$, $N_2^{(0)} = P_0e^{(a-b)A_0}$ and $E = N_1+N_2e^{(b-a)A}$ one checks that the system $\theta_0 = (A_0,B_0,C_0;N_1^{(0)},N_2^{(0)})$ is a reduction of $\theta$ (i.e. (4.3) also holds true) and $\Xi_0 = \Xi_{\theta_0}$.

Note also that two systems $\theta$ and $\tilde{\theta}$ are similar if and only if the nodes $\Xi_\theta$ and $\Xi_{\tilde{\theta}}$ are similar. This follows easily from the fact that equalities (4.5) are equivalent to the equality $\tilde{P} = SPS^{-1}$.

The proposition below shows that the irreducibility of a boundary value system $\theta$ is the same as the minimality of the node $\Xi_\theta$.

PROPOSITION 4.1. *Let* $\theta = (A,B,C;N_1,N_2)$ *be a boundary value system with state space* X *and canonical boundary value operator* P. *Then the system is irreducible if and only if the node* $\Xi_\theta = (A,P;X;B,C)$ *is minimal.*

PROOF. Let $\theta$ be irreducible and assume that the node $\Xi_\theta$ is not minimal. Then in view of Theorems 2.1 - 2.2 there is a proper reduction $\Xi_0 = (A_0,P_0;X_0;B_0,C_0)$ of $\Xi_\theta$ ($\dim X_0 < \dim X$). But then the system $\theta_0 := (A_0,B_0,C_0;I-P_0,P_0e^{(a-b)A_0})$ is a proper reduction of the system $\theta$ which contradicts the irreducibility of $\theta$.

Conversely, let the node $\Xi_\theta$ be minimal and assume that $\theta$ admits a proper reduction $\theta_0 = (A_0,B_0,C_0;N_1^{(0)},N_2^{(0)})$. Let $P_0$ be the canonical boundary value operator of $\theta_0$ and $X_0$ its state space. It is clear that $\Xi_{\theta_0} := (A_0,P_0;X_0;B_0,C_0)$ is a proper reduction of $\Xi_\theta$ which contradicts the minimality of the node $\Xi_\theta$. □

Using Proposition 4.1 we can apply now Theorems 2.1 - 2.4 in order to characterize irreducible systems.

THEOREM 4.2. *Let* $\theta = (A,B,C;N_1,N_2)$ *be a boundary value sytem. Let* X *be the state space of* $\theta$ *and* P *its canonical boundary value operator. Then* $\theta$ *is irreducible if and only if* $N(\theta) = (0)$ *and* $R(\theta) = X$, *where*

$$N(\theta) := \bigcap_{\substack{\alpha_1+\beta_1+\dots+\alpha_r+\beta_r\le n-1\\ \alpha_j\ge 0,\beta_j\ge 0,r\ge 0}} \operatorname{Ker} CA^{\alpha_1}P^{\beta_1}\dots A^{\alpha_r}P^{\beta_r}, \quad R(\theta) := \bigvee_{\substack{\alpha_1+\beta_1+\dots+\alpha_r+\beta_r\le n-1\\ \alpha_j\ge 0,\beta_j\ge 0,r\ge 0}} \operatorname{Im} A^{\alpha_1}P^{\beta_1}\dots A^{\alpha_r}P^{\beta_r}B \tag{4.7}$$

*and* $n = \dim X$.

This result follows immediately from Proposition 4.1, Theorem 2.1 and formulas (1.4) - (1.5).

THEOREM 4.3. *Let* $\theta = (A,B,C;N_1,N_2)$ *and* $\tilde{\theta} = (\tilde{A},\tilde{B},\tilde{C};\tilde{N}_1,\tilde{N}_2)$ *be two irreducible boundary value systems. Let* X *and* $\tilde{X}$ *denote the state spaces of* $\theta$ *and* $\tilde{\theta}$, *respectively, and let* $P,\tilde{P}$ *be the corresponding canonical boundary value operators. Then* $\theta$ *and* $\tilde{\theta}$ *are similar if and only if*

$$CA^{\alpha_1}P^{\beta_1}\dots A^{\alpha_r}P^{\beta_r}B = \tilde{C}\tilde{A}^{\alpha_1}\tilde{P}^{\beta_1}\dots\tilde{A}^{\alpha_r}\tilde{P}^{\beta_r}\tilde{B} \tag{4.8}$$

*for all non-negative integers* $\alpha_j, \beta_j, r$ *such that* $\sum_{j=1}^{r} \alpha_j + \sum_{j=1}^{r} \beta_j \le 2q-1$, *where* $q = \max\{\dim X, \dim \widetilde{X}\}$.

Note that (4.8) means in fact that the moments $M_\gamma(\Xi_\theta)$ and $M_\gamma(\Xi_{\widetilde{\theta}})$ are equal for $|\gamma| \le 2q-1$, and hence Theorem 4.3 follows from Proposition 4.1 and Theorems 2.3 - 2.4.

THEOREM 4.4. *A boundary value system* $\theta = (A,B,C;N_1,N_2)$ *is a dilation of an irreducible system* $\theta_0$ *which is obtained as follows: put* $X_1 = N(\theta)$, *let* $X_0$ *be a direct complement of* $X_1 \cap R(\theta)$ *in* $R(\theta)$ *and choose* $X_2$ *such that* $X = X_1 \oplus X_0 \oplus X_2$. *Then relative to this decomposition the partitionings* (4.2) - (4.3) *hold true and the system* $\theta_0 = (A_0,B_0,C_0;N_1^{(0)},N_2^{(0)})$ *is irreducible. Here* $N(\theta)$ *and* $R(\theta)$ *are defined by* (4.7).

This result follows immediately from Proposition 4.1 and Theorem 2.2.

II. MINIMALITY WITH RESTRICTIONS

In this chapter the theory of minimal nodes is extended and refined further. We study now minimality in a restricted class of nodes and for a restricted list of moments connected with the nodes. It turns out that in some cases the restricted minimality is the same as minimality without restrictions. Several examples of such cases are given. The minimality problem for partial realizations and for boundary value systems provide two important examples of restricted minimality essentially different from the minimality without restrictions.

II.1. Definitions

Let $\mathcal{D} \subset N_k$ and $\Gamma \subset \Gamma_k$ be non-empty subsets of $N_k$ and $\Gamma_k$, respectively. We say that a node $\Xi \subset N_k$ is $(\Gamma,\mathcal{D})$-*minimal* if $\Xi \in \mathcal{D}$ and the state space dimension of $\Xi$ is minimal among all nodes $\widetilde{\Xi} \in \mathcal{D}$ such that

$$M_\gamma(\Xi) = M_\gamma(\widetilde{\Xi}), \qquad \gamma \in \Gamma.$$

In the case when $\mathcal{D} = N_k$, a $(\Gamma,N_k)$-minimal node will be called $\Gamma$-*minimal*. It is clear that a $\Gamma$-minimal node is also $(\Gamma,\mathcal{D})$-minimal for any subset $\mathcal{D} \subset N_k$. The converse statement is not true generally speaking (see, for example, Sections 2.4 and 2.5). However the following holds true.

PROPOSITION 1.1. *If the set* $\mathcal{D} \subset N_k$ *is closed under reduction, then a* $(\Gamma,\mathcal{D})$-*minimal node* $\Xi \in \mathcal{D}$ *is a minimal node (and, in particular,* $\Gamma$-*minimal).*

PROOF. Let $\Xi = (A_1,\dots,A_k;X;B,C) \in \mathcal{D}$ be a $(\Gamma,\mathcal{D})$-minimal node, and assume that $\Xi$ is not minimal. Then Theorems I.2.1 - I.2.2 yield that there is a reduction $\Xi_0 = (A_1^{(0)},\dots,A_k^{(0)};X_0;B_0,C_0)$ of $\Xi$ such that $\dim X_0 < \dim X$. But $\mathcal{D}$ is closed under reduction and therefore $\Xi_0 \in \mathcal{D}$. Also, $M_\gamma(\Xi) = M_\gamma(\Xi_0)$, $\gamma \in \Gamma$. So, we get a contradiction with the $(\Gamma,\mathcal{D})$-minimality of $\Xi$. □

A subset $\mathcal{D} \subset N_k$ is called a *realization domain* if it is closed under similarity and reduction. In what follows $\mathcal{D}$ will be always assumed to be a realization domain.

Given a non-empty subset $\Gamma \subset \Gamma_k$ and a node $\Xi \in N_k$ we denote

$$M_\Gamma(\Xi) = \{M_\gamma(\Xi) \mid \gamma \in \Gamma\}.$$

We say that nodes $\Xi,\tilde{\Xi} \in N_k$ have the same moments with respect to the set $\Gamma$ and write $M_\Gamma(\Xi) \equiv M_\Gamma(\tilde{\Xi})$ if $M_\gamma(\Xi) = M_\gamma(\tilde{\Xi})$ for any $\gamma \in \Gamma$.

The central notion of this chapter is the following. Given non-empty sets $\Gamma$ ($\subset \Gamma_k$) and $\mathcal{D}$ ($\subset N_k$) we say that the pair $(\Gamma,\mathcal{D})$ is *dominating* if for any two nodes $\Xi,\tilde{\Xi} \in \mathcal{D}$ the equality $M_\Gamma(\Xi) \equiv M_\Gamma(\tilde{\Xi})$ implies $M(\Xi) \equiv M(\tilde{\Xi})$, in other words the pair $(\Gamma,\mathcal{D})$ is dominating if the fact that two nodes $\Xi,\tilde{\Xi} \in \mathcal{D}$ have the same moments with respect to $\Gamma$ yields that $M_\gamma(\Xi) = M_\gamma(\tilde{\Xi})$ for any $\gamma \in \Gamma_k$.

## 2.2. Examples of dominating pairs

In this section we present three examples of dominating pairs. First we consider the following subset of $\Gamma_2$:

$$\Gamma_2' = \{\gamma = (\underbrace{1,\dots,1}_{q},\underbrace{2,\dots,2}_{\ell-q}),\ q = 0,1,\dots,\ell;\ \ell = 1,2,\dots\} \cup \{\emptyset\}.$$

So, if $\Xi = (A_1,A_2;X;B,C)$ is a node in $N_2$ then

$$M_{\Gamma_2'} = \{CA_1^iA_2^jB\}_{i,j=0}^{\infty}$$

Next, we consider domains $\mathcal{D}$ consisting of nodes of which the main operators satisfy some Lie-type conditions. We say that $\mathcal{D}$ is a *Lie domain* in $N_k$ if there exist complex numbers $\ell_{ij}^{\nu}$ ($i,j,\nu = 1,\dots,k$), called *structural constants*, such that

$$\mathcal{D} = \{\Xi = (A_1,\dots,A_k;X;B,C) \in N_k \mid [A_i,A_j] = \sum_{\nu=1}^{k} \ell_{ij}^{\nu}A_\nu\ (i,j = 1,\dots,k)\}. \tag{2.1}$$

Here and in the sequel the symbol $[S,T]$ stands for the commutator of the operators $S$ and $T$, i.e., $[S,T] := ST - TS$. It is clear that a Lie domain is always a realization domain. The following commutator relations (see, e.g. [4], pg 67) will be intensively used in the proofs below.

(2.2) $$[S^{\alpha},T^{\beta}] = \sum_{0\le p\le\alpha-1} S^{p}\Big(\sum_{0\le q\le\beta-1} T^{q}[S,T]T^{\beta-q-1}\Big)S^{\alpha-p-1}, \quad \alpha\ge 1,\ \beta\ge 1.$$

PROPOSITION 2.1. *Let $\mathcal{D} = \mathcal{D}_L$ be a Lie domain in $N_2$. Then the pair $(\Gamma_2', \mathcal{D}_L)$ is dominating.*

PROOF. Let $\Xi = (A_1,A_2;X;B,C) \in \mathcal{D}_L$, $\widetilde{\Xi} = (\widetilde{A}_1,\widetilde{A}_2;\widetilde{X};\widetilde{B},\widetilde{C}) \in \mathcal{D}_L$, and assume that

(2.3) $$CA_1^{\beta_1}A_2^{\beta_2}B = \widetilde{C}\widetilde{A}_1^{\beta_1}\widetilde{A}_2^{\beta_2}\widetilde{B}, \quad \beta_i \ge 0,\ i=1,2.$$

We shall use induction on the length of words $\omega_\gamma$ to prove that

(2.4) $$C\omega_\gamma(A_1,A_2)B = \widetilde{C}\omega_\gamma(\widetilde{A}_1,\widetilde{A}_2)\widetilde{B}$$

for any word $\omega_\gamma$, $\gamma \in \Gamma_2$.

For a word $\omega_\gamma$ with $|\gamma| = 1$ the equality (2.4) is found among the equalities (2.3). Assume for the induction hypothesis that (2.4) holds true for any word $\omega_\gamma$ of length $\le \ell-1$. Take a word $\omega_\gamma$ with $|\gamma| = \ell$. If $\gamma = (\gamma_1,\dots,\gamma_\ell)$, set $\beta_1 := \#\{i \mid \gamma_i = 1\}$ and $\beta_2 := \#\{i \mid \gamma_i = 2\}$. Using the commutator relations (2.2) and the definition (2.1) of the Lie domain one sees that

(2.5) $$\omega_\gamma(A_1,A_2) = CA_1^{\beta_1}A_2^{\beta_2}B + \sum_{\alpha\in A} c_\alpha\omega_\alpha(A_1,A_2),$$

where $c_\alpha$ are some complex numbers and $A$ is a set of $(\ell-1)$-tuples $\alpha = (\alpha_1,\dots,\alpha_{\ell-1})$ with $\alpha_i \in \{1,2\}$, $i=1,\dots,\ell-1$. Hence by the induction hypothesis

$$C\omega_\gamma(A_1,A_2)B = \widetilde{C}\omega_\gamma(\widetilde{A}_1,\widetilde{A}_2)\widetilde{B}$$

for any $\alpha \in A$. From (2.5) it is clear that the last equalities and (2.3) immediately imply (2.4) for the given word $\omega_\gamma$. □

Next we consider the following two realization domains in $N_2$:

(2.6.a) $$\mathcal{D}^{(0)} = \{\Xi = (A_1,A_2;X;B,C) \in N_2 \mid A_1A_2 = A_2A_1\},$$

(2.6.b) $$\mathcal{D}_P = \{\Xi = (A_1A_2;X;B,C) \in N_2 \mid A_1A_2 - A_2A_1 = BC\}.$$

The domain $\mathcal{D}_P$ will be called a *Pincus domain*. In the infinite dimensional case such domains with certain additional selfadjointness conditions appear in the theory of the Pincus determining function (see, e.g., [25],[4]). The domain $\mathcal{D}_P$ also appears in Donaldson's description of Yang-Mills instantons (see [5], also [14]). A version of the next proposition can be found in [4].

PROPOSITION 2.2. *The pairs $(\Gamma_2', \mathcal{D}^{(0)})$ and $(\Gamma_2', \mathcal{D}_P)$ are dominating pairs.*

PROOF. We shall prove that the pair $(\Gamma_2', \mathcal{D}_P^{(a)})$, where

(2.6.c) $$\mathcal{D}_P^{(a)} = \{\Xi = (A_1,A_2;X;B,C) \in N_2 \mid A_1A_2 - A_2A_1 = aBC\},$$

is a dominating pair. Here a is an arbitrary complex number. Thus $\mathcal{D}_P^{(0)} = \mathcal{D}^{(0)}$ and $\mathcal{D}_P^{(1)} = \mathcal{D}_P$.

Now let $\omega_\gamma(A_1,A_2)$ be a word of length $|\gamma| = r$. Write the sequence $\gamma$ in the form

$$\gamma = (\underbrace{1,\dots,1}_{i_1},\underbrace{2,\dots,2}_{j_1},\underbrace{1,\dots,1}_{i_2},\underbrace{2,\dots,2}_{j_2},\dots,\underbrace{1,\dots,1}_{i_q},\underbrace{2,\dots,2}_{j_q})$$

where

$$0 \le i_1 \le r, \quad 0 \le j_q \le r, \quad i_k \ge 1\ (k=2,\dots,q),\ j_k \ge 1\ (k=1,\dots,q-1),$$

and put ind $\omega_\gamma := 0$ if $q = 1$ and

$$\text{ind}\ \omega_\gamma := j_1 + j_2 + \dots + j_{q-1},\ q > 1.$$

We shall use induction on ind $\omega_\gamma$ in order to prove that

$$\Xi = (A_1,A_2;X;B,C) \in \mathcal{D}_P^{(a)}, \quad \tilde{\Xi} = (\tilde{A}_1,\tilde{A}_2;\tilde{X};\tilde{B},\tilde{C}) \in \mathcal{D}_P^{(a)}$$

and

(2.7) $$CA_1^{\beta_1}A_2^{\beta_2}B = \tilde{C}\tilde{A}_1^{\beta_1}\tilde{A}_2^{\beta_2}\tilde{B}, \quad \beta_i \ge 0,\ i=1,2,$$

implies that

(2.8) $$C\omega_\gamma(A_1,A_2)B = \tilde{C}\omega_\gamma(\tilde{A}_1,\tilde{A}_2)\tilde{B}$$

for any word $\omega_\gamma$. If ind $\omega_\gamma = 0$, then $\gamma$ must be of the form $\gamma = (\underbrace{1,\dots,1}_{\beta_1},\underbrace{2,\dots,2}_{\beta_2})$ and $\omega_\gamma(A_1,A_2) = A_1^{\beta_1}A_2^{\beta_2}$. So, in this case (2.8) is just the same as (2.7). Next assume for the induction hypothesis that (2.8) holds true for any word $\omega_\gamma$ with ind $\omega_\gamma \le \ell-1$. Take a word $\omega_\gamma$ with ind $\omega_\gamma = \ell$ and represent it in the form

(2.9) $$\omega_\alpha(A_1,A_2) = \omega_{\alpha_0}(A_1,A_2)\cdot A_2^\delta A_1^\mu A_2^\nu,$$

where $\delta \ge 1$, $\mu \ge 1$, $\nu \ge 0$ are integers and the word $\omega_{\alpha_0}(A_1,A_2)$ is either of length zero or of the form $\omega_{\alpha_0}(A_1,A_2) = \omega_{\tilde{\alpha}_0}(A_1,A_2)\cdot A_1$. It is clear that

(2.10) $$\ell := \text{ind}\ \omega_\alpha = \text{ind}\ \omega_{\alpha_0} + \delta$$

Now apply the commutator relations (2.2) to the product $A_2^\delta A_1^\mu$ in (2.9) and use the definition (2.6.c) of the domain $\mathcal{D}_P^{(a)}$ to obtain

(2.11) $$C\omega_\alpha(A_1,A_2)B = C\omega_{\alpha_0}(A_1,A_2)A_1^\mu A_2^{\delta+\nu}B + \\ - a\sum_{0\le p\le\delta-1}\ \sum_{0\le q\le\mu-1} C\omega_{\alpha_0}(A_1,A_2)A_2^pA_1^qBCA_1^{\mu-q-1}A_2^{\delta-p-1+\nu}B.$$

Since $\operatorname{ind}[\omega_{\alpha_0}(A_1,A_2)A_1^{\mu}A_2^{\delta+\nu}] = \operatorname{ind}\omega_{\alpha_0}(A_1,A_2) < \ell$, we can apply the induction hypothesis to get

$$(2.12)\qquad C\omega_{\alpha_0}(A_1,A_2)A_1^{\mu}A_2^{\delta+\nu}B = \tilde{C}\omega_{\alpha_0}(\tilde{A}_1,\tilde{A}_2)\tilde{A}_1^{\mu}\tilde{A}_2^{\delta+\nu}\tilde{B}.$$

Further, it follows from (2.10) that

$$\operatorname{ind}\,[\omega_{\alpha_0}(A_1,A_2)A_2^{p}A_1^{q}] \le \operatorname{ind}\,\omega_{\alpha_0}(A_1,A_2)+p < \ell$$

for $p=0,1,\dots,\delta-1$ and $q=0,1,\dots,\mu-1$. Hence, by the induction hypothesis,

$$(2.13)\qquad C\omega_{\alpha_0}(A_1,A_2)A_2^{p}A_1^{q}B = \tilde{C}\omega_{\alpha_0}(\tilde{A}_1,\tilde{A}_2)\tilde{A}_2^{p}\tilde{A}_1^{q}\tilde{B}\quad (p=0,\dots,\delta-1;q=0,\dots,\mu-1)$$

The equalities (2.7) yield that for any $p=0,\dots,\delta-1$ and $q=0,\dots,\mu-1$:

$$(2.14)\qquad CA_1^{\mu-q-1}A_2^{\delta-p-1+\nu}B = \tilde{C}\tilde{A}_1^{\mu-q-1}\tilde{A}_2^{\delta-p-1+\nu}\tilde{B}$$

Substituting (2.12) - (2.14) in (2.11) and using the analogue of (2.11) for $\tilde{C}$, $\tilde{A}_1$, $\tilde{A}_2$ and $\tilde{B}$ we obtain (2.8) for $\omega_\alpha$. □

Next we consider a pair $(\Gamma,\mathcal{D})$ of which the realization domain consists of all nodes with a fixed upper bound for their state space dimension and the set $\Gamma$ depends on this bound as well. Namely, for a fixed positive integer $s \ge 2$ we denote

$$(2.15)\qquad \mathcal{D}_s = \{\Xi = (A_1,A_2;X;B,C) \in N_2 \mid \dim X \le \tfrac{1}{2}s\}$$

and we set

$$(2.16)\qquad \Gamma^{(s)} = (\underbrace{1,\dots,1}_{\alpha_1},\underbrace{2,\dots,2}_{\alpha_2},\underbrace{1,\dots,1}_{\alpha_3},\dots,\underbrace{\sigma(s),\dots,\sigma(s)}_{\alpha_s}) \in \Gamma_2 \mid \alpha_j \ge 0,\ j=1,\dots,s\} \cup \{\emptyset\},$$

where $\sigma(s) := \frac{1}{2}(3+(-1)^s)$. Clearly $\mathcal{D}_s$ is a realization domain. Note that $\Gamma^{(s)}$ consists of all $\ell$-tuples ($\ell = 0,1,\dots$) in $\Gamma_2$ of which the entries change from 1 to 2 or from 2 to 1 not more than s-1 times.

PROPOSITION 2.3. *The pair* $(\Gamma^{(s)},\mathcal{D}_s)$ *is dominating.*

PROOF. Let $\Xi = (A_1,A_2;X;B,C) \in \mathcal{D}_s$ and $\tilde{\Xi} = (\tilde{A}_1,\tilde{A}_2;\tilde{X};\tilde{B},\tilde{C}) \in \mathcal{D}_s$ be such that

$$(2.17)\qquad CA_1^{\beta_1}A_2^{\beta_2}\dots A_{\sigma(x)}^{\beta_s}B = \tilde{C}\tilde{A}_1^{\beta_1}\tilde{A}_2^{\beta_2}\dots\tilde{A}_{\sigma(s)}^{\beta_s}\tilde{B},\quad \beta_i \ge 0,\quad i=1,\dots,s.$$

We have to show that

$$(2.18)\qquad M_\gamma(\Xi) = M_\gamma(\tilde{\Xi})$$

for any $\gamma \in \Gamma_2$. Observe that in view of Theorem I.2.4 it is enough to establish (2.18) for $\gamma \in \Gamma_2$ with $|\gamma| \le 2\max\{\dim X, \dim\tilde{X}\} - 1$. Since in our case $\dim X \le \frac{s}{2}$, $\dim \tilde{X} \le \frac{s}{2}$, we have to prove (2.18) for any $\gamma \in \Gamma_2$ with $|\gamma| \le s-1$. So, let $\gamma = (\gamma_1,\ldots,\gamma_r) \in \Gamma_2$ and $r \le s-1$. Then the moment $M_\gamma(\Xi)$ can be written in the form

$$(2.19) \qquad M_\gamma(\Xi) = CA_1^{i_1}A_2^{i_2}\ldots A_{\sigma(p)}^{i_p}B$$

with $i_1 \ge 0$, $i_p \ge 0$, $i_k > 0$ $(k = 2,\ldots,p-1)$ and $p \le r+1$. Represent also $M_\gamma(\Xi)$ in the form (2.19) and observe that since $r+1 \le s$ the equalities (2.18) for $\gamma$ with $|\gamma| \le s-1$ are found among the equalities (2.17). □

## II.3 Minimality theory with dominating pairs

Let $\Gamma$ be a non-empty subset of $\Gamma_k$ and let $\mathcal{D}$ be a non-empty realization domain in $N_k$. In this section we show that if the pair $(\Gamma,\mathcal{D})$ is dominating then the $(\Gamma,\mathcal{D})$-minimality is the same as $(\Gamma_k,N_k)$-minimality.

THEOREM 3.1. *Let $(\Gamma,\mathcal{D})$ be a dominating pair and let $\Xi \in \mathcal{D}$. The following assertions are equivalent:*

(i) *$\Xi$ is a $(\Gamma,\mathcal{D})$-minimal node;*

(ii) *$\Xi$ is a minimal node;*

(iii) *$N(\Xi) = 0$ and $R(\Xi) = X$, where $X$ is the state space of $\Xi$.*

PROOF. To prove the implication (i) → (iii) assume that $N(\Xi) \ne (0)$ or $R(\Xi) \ne X$. Then using Part 1 in Section I.3 we obtain a reduction $\Xi_0$ of $\Xi$ whose state space dimension is strictly less than the dimension of $X$. Since $\mathcal{D}$ is a realization domain, $\Xi_0 \in \mathcal{D}$. Also, $M_\gamma(\Xi_0) = M_\gamma(\Xi)$ for any $\gamma \in \Gamma$. Thus we obtain a contradiction with the $(\Gamma,\mathcal{D})$-minimality of $\Xi$.

The implication (iii) → (ii) is stated in Theorem I.2.1. It remains to prove that (ii) implies (i). Let $\Xi = (A_1,\ldots,A_k;X;B,C) \in \mathcal{D}$ be a minimal node, and let $\tilde{\Xi} = (\tilde{A}_1,\ldots,\tilde{A}_k;\tilde{X};\tilde{B},\tilde{C})$ be any other node in $\mathcal{D}$ such that

$$M_\gamma(\tilde{\Xi}) = M_\gamma(\Xi), \qquad \gamma \in \Gamma.$$

Since the pair $(\Gamma,\mathcal{D})$ is dominating, the last equalities imply that $M_\gamma(\tilde{\Xi}) = M_\gamma(\Xi)$ for any $\gamma \in \Gamma_k$. But then in view of the minimality of the node $\Xi$ we infer that $\dim \tilde{X} \ge \dim X$. □

COROLLARY 3.2. *Let $(\Gamma,\mathcal{D})$ be a dominating pair. Two $(\Gamma,\mathcal{D})$-minimal nodes $\Xi$ and $\tilde{\Xi}$ are similar if and only if*

$$(3.1) \qquad M_\gamma(\Xi) = M_\gamma(\tilde{\Xi}), \qquad \gamma \in \Gamma.$$

PROOF. Since $(\Gamma,\mathcal{D})$ is a dominating pair, the equalities (3.1) imply that $M_\gamma(\Xi) = M_\gamma(\tilde{\Xi})$ for any $\gamma \in \Gamma_k$. In view of Theorem 3.1 the nodes $\Xi$ and $\tilde{\Xi}$ a are minimal. So, we can apply Theorem I.2.3 to conclude that $\Xi$ and $\tilde{\Xi}$ are similar. □

COROLLARY 3.3. *Let $(\Gamma,\mathcal{D})$ be a dominating pair. Two nodes $\Xi,\tilde{\Xi} \in \mathcal{D}$ are dilations of similar (minimal) nodes if and only if (3.1) holds true.*

This result follows readily from Theorem 3.1, Corollary 3.2 and Theorem I.2.2.

## II.4.1. Minimality in the partial realization problem

This section concerns the problem of minimality for partial realizations, which we solved in [13]. Here we show that this problem can be rephrased as a problem of $(\Gamma,\mathcal{D})$-minimality for a non-dominating pair $(\Gamma,\mathcal{D})$. It turns out that the minimality theorem for this case differs considerably from the one for dominating pairs. For the sake of completeness we give full proofs of the main theorems.

First let us recall the problem of partial realization: Given a finite sequence $M_1,\dots,M_r$ of $m\times p$ matrices, find a system $\theta = (A,B,C)$ of linear operators $A : X \to X$, $B : \mathbb{C}^p \to X$ and $C : X \to \mathbb{C}^m$ acting between finite dimensional spaces such that

$$(4.1) \qquad CA^{i-1}B = M_i, \quad i=1,\dots,r,$$

and the dimension of the *state space* X is as small as possible. A system $\theta = (A,B,C)$ that satisfies (4.1) is called a *realization* of $M_1,\dots,M_r$, and if the state space dimension of a realization $\theta$ is minimal among all realizations of $M_1,\dots,M_r$ the realization $\theta$ is called *minimal*. The above problem known as the *partial realization problem* was introduced and studied by R. Kalman in [17].

To put the partial realization problem in the framework of the present chapter define the subset $\Gamma^{(r)}$ of $\Gamma_1$ by

$$\Gamma^{(r)} = \{(\emptyset),(1),(1,1),\dots,(\underbrace{1,1,\dots,1}_{r})\}.$$

Furthermore, to each realization $\theta = (A,B,C)$ of $M_1,\dots,M_r$ with state space X we associate the node $\Xi_\theta = (A;X;B,C) \in \mathcal{N}_1$. Then a realization $\theta = (A,B,C)$ with state space X of $M_1,\dots,M_r$ is minimal if and only if the node $\Xi_\theta := (A;X;B,C)$ is a $(\Gamma^{(r)},\mathcal{N}_1)$-minimal node. Note that the pair $(\Gamma^{(r)},\mathcal{N}_1)$ is not dominating. Indeed, for two arbitrary nodes $\Xi = (A;X;B,C) \in \mathcal{N}_1$ and $\tilde{\Xi} = (\tilde{A};\tilde{X};\tilde{B},\tilde{C}) \in \mathcal{N}_1$ the equalities $CA^iB = \tilde{C}\tilde{A}^i\tilde{B}$, $i=0,1,\dots,r-1$, do not imply in general that

$CA^iB = \tilde{C}\tilde{A}^i\tilde{B}$ for $i \geq r$. So, the results of Section 3 are not applicable in the case under consideration. The next theorem gives the necessary and sufficient conditions for $(\Gamma^{(r)}, N_1)$-minimality which are specific for this case.

THEOREM 4.1. *A node* $\Xi = (A;X;B,C) \in N_1$ *is* $(\Gamma^{(r)}, N_1)$-*minimal if and only if the following conditions are satisfied:*

a) $$\operatorname{Ker}\begin{pmatrix} C \\ CA \\ \vdots \\ CA^{r-1} \end{pmatrix} = (0);$$

b) $$\operatorname{Im}\begin{pmatrix} B & AB \dots A^{r-1}B \end{pmatrix} = X;$$

c) $$\operatorname{Ker}\begin{pmatrix} C \\ CA \\ \vdots \\ CA^{j-1} \end{pmatrix} \subset \operatorname{Im}\begin{pmatrix} B & AB & \dots & A^{r-j-1} \end{pmatrix}, \quad j = 1,\dots,r-1.$$

PROOF. We shall use the following notations: $N_j(\Xi) = \bigcap_{k=0}^{j-1} \operatorname{Ker} CA^k$, $R_j(\Xi) = \bigvee_{k=0}^{j-1} \operatorname{Im} A^kB$, $j = 1,2,\dots$ . The proof is splitted into 4 steps.

Step 1. Fix an integer $1 \leq j \leq r-1$. In this first Step we show how to compress a given node $\Xi = (A;X;B,C) \in N_1$ to another node $\Xi_0 = (A_{00};X_0;B_0,C_0)$ such that $M_{\Gamma^{(r)}}(\Xi_0) \equiv M_{\Gamma^{(r)}}(\Xi)$, $\dim X_0 \leq \dim X$ and

(4.2) $$N_j(\Xi_0) \subset R_{r-j}(\Xi_0).$$

In particular, this will prove the necessity of condition c). To be more precise, choose a subspace $X_1$ in $N_j(\Xi)$ such that $X_1$ is a direct complement of $R_{r-j}(\Xi)$ in the space $R_{r-j}(\Xi) + N_j(\Xi)$ and let $X_0$ be a direct complement of $X_1$ in $X$ such that $X_0 \supset R_{r-j}(\Xi)$. Write the partitionings of A,B and C relative to the decomposition $X = X_1 \oplus X_0$:

(4.3) $$A = \begin{pmatrix} A_{11} & A_{10} \\ A_{01} & A_{00} \end{pmatrix}, \quad B = \begin{pmatrix} B_1 \\ B_0 \end{pmatrix}, \quad C = \begin{pmatrix} C_1 & C_0 \end{pmatrix}.$$

Then the node $\Xi_0 = (A_{00};X_0;B_0,C_0)$ satisfies (4.2) and $M_{\Gamma^{(r)}}(\Xi_0) \equiv M_{\Gamma^{(r)}}(\Xi)$.

Indeed, since $R_{r-j}(\Xi) \subset X_0$, we have $\operatorname{Im} B \subset X_0$, and hence $B_1 = 0$. Thus

$$AB = \begin{pmatrix} A_{10}B_0 \\ A_{00}B_0 \end{pmatrix},$$

and from the inclusions $\operatorname{Im} AB \subset R_{r-j}(\Xi) \subset X_0$ we infer that $A_{10}B_0 = 0$. Proceeding in this way we obtain

$$(4.4)\qquad A^\nu B = \begin{pmatrix} 0 \\ A_{00}^\nu B_0 \end{pmatrix}, \quad \nu = 0,\dots,r-j-1.$$

Next, since $X_1 \subset \operatorname{Ker} C$, we have $C_1 = 0$, and therefore $CA = \begin{pmatrix} C_0A_{01} & C_0A_{00} \end{pmatrix}$. From $X_1 \subset \operatorname{Ker} CA$ it follows that $C_0A_{01} = 0$, and hence $CA = \begin{pmatrix} 0 & C_0A_{00} \end{pmatrix}$. Proceeding in this way one obtains

$$(4.5)\qquad CA^\nu = \begin{pmatrix} 0 & C_0A_{00}^\nu \end{pmatrix}, \quad \nu = 0,\dots,j-1.$$

The equalities (4.4) and (4.5) imply that

$$C_0A_{00}^{\nu-1}B_0 = CA^{\nu-1}B, \quad \nu = 1,\dots,r-1,$$

$$\begin{aligned} C_0A_{00}^{r-1}B_0 &= \begin{pmatrix} 0 & C_0A_0^{j-1} \end{pmatrix} \begin{pmatrix} A_{11} & A_{10} \\ A_{01} & A_{00} \end{pmatrix} \begin{pmatrix} 0 \\ A_{00}^{r-j-1}B_0 \end{pmatrix} \\ &= CA^{j-1}AA^{r-j-1}B = CA^{r-1}B, \end{aligned}$$

i.e., $M_{\Gamma(r)}(\Xi_0) \equiv M_{\Gamma(r)}(\Xi)$.

It remains to prove (4.2). Take $x_0 \in N_j(\Xi_0)$. Then (4.5) implies that $\begin{pmatrix} 0 \\ x_0 \end{pmatrix} \in N_j(\Xi)$. But $N_j(\Xi) \subset R_{r-j}(\Xi) \oplus X_1$ and $R_{r-j}(\Xi) \subset X_0$. So $\begin{pmatrix} 0 \\ x_0 \end{pmatrix} \in R_{r-j}(\Xi)$, and (4.4) shows that $x_0 \in R_{r-j}(\Xi_0)$.

<u>Step 2</u>. In this step we make a compression of a given node $\Xi = (A;X;B,C) \in N_1$ to another node $\Xi_0 = (A_{00};X_0;B_0,C_0)$ such that $M_{\Gamma(r)}(\Xi_0)$ $M_{\Gamma(r)}(\Xi)$, $\dim X_0 \le \dim X$ and

$$(4.6)\qquad N_r(\Xi) = (0).$$

In particular, this proves the necessity of condition a). To be more precise, put $X_1 = N_r(\Xi)$ and let $X_0$ be a direct complement of $X_1$ in the state space $X$ of $\Xi$. Let (4.3) give the partitionings of $A$, $B$ and $C$ relative to the decomposition $X = X_1 \oplus X_0$. Then the node $\Xi_0 = (A_{00};X_0;B_0,C_0)$ satisfies (4.6) and $M_{\Gamma(r)}(\Xi_0) \equiv M_{\Gamma(r)}(\Xi)$.

Indeed, since $X_1 \subset \operatorname{Ker} CA^j$ $(j = 0,1,\dots,r-1)$, one sees as in Step 1 that

$$(4.7)\qquad CA^j = \begin{pmatrix} 0 & CA_{00}^j \end{pmatrix}, \quad j = 0,1,\dots,r-1.$$

Thus $CA^{j-1}B = C_0A_{00}^{j-1}B_0$ for $j = 1,\dots,r$, i.e. $M_{\Gamma(r)}(\Xi_0) \equiv M_{\Gamma(r)}(\Xi)$. Now, let $x_0 \in N_r(\Xi_0)$. Then (4.7) yields $CA^jx_0 = C_0A_{00}^jx_0 = 0$ for $j = 0,1,\dots,r-1$. Thus $x_0 \in X_1$. But $X_1 \cap X_0 = (0)$, and hence $x_0 = 0$.

Step 3. In this step we make a compression of a given node $\Xi = (A;X;B,C)$ to another node $\Xi_0 = (A_{00};X_0;B_0,C_0)$ such that $M_{\Gamma(r)}(\Xi_0) \equiv M_{\Gamma(r)}(\Xi)$, $\dim X_0 \le \dim X$ and

$$R_r(\Xi_0) = X_0. \tag{4.8}$$

In particular, this proves the necessity of condition b). To be precise, put $X_0 = R_r(\Xi)$ and let $X_1$ be a direct complement of $X_0$ in the state space $X$ of $\Xi$. Let (4.3) give the partitionings of $A$, $B$ and $C$ relative to the decomposition $X = X_1 \oplus X_0$. Then the node $\Xi_0 = (A_{00};X_0;B_0,C_0)$ satisfies (4.8) and $M_{\Gamma(r)}(\Xi_0) \equiv M_{\Gamma(r)}(\Xi)$.

Indeed, as in Step 1 one sees that the inclusions $\operatorname{Im} A^jB \subset X_0$ $(j = 0,\dots,r-1)$ imply that

$$A^jB = \begin{pmatrix} 0 \\ A_{00}^jB_0 \end{pmatrix}, \quad j = 0,1,\dots,r-1. \tag{4.9}$$

It follows that $C_0A_{00}^{j-1}B_0 = CA^{j-1}B$ for $j = 1,\dots,r$, i.e. $M_{\Gamma(r)}(\Xi_0) \equiv M_{\Gamma(r)}(\Xi)$. From $R_r(\Xi_0) \subset X_0$ and (4.9) we conclude that

$$X_0 := R_r(\Xi) = \operatorname{Im} \begin{pmatrix} 0 & 0 & \dots & 0 \\ B_0 & A_{00}B_0 & \dots & A_{00}^{r-1}B_0 \end{pmatrix},$$

which proves (4.8).

Step 4. It remains to prove the sufficiency of conditions a) - c). Let $\Xi = (A;X;B,C)$ satisfy conditions a) - c) and let $\tilde{\Xi} = (\tilde{A};\tilde{X};\tilde{B},\tilde{C})$ be another node in $N_1$ such that $M_{\Gamma(r)}(\tilde{\Xi}) \equiv M_{\Gamma(r)}(\Xi)$, i.e.

$$\tilde{C}\tilde{A}^{i-1}\tilde{B} = CA^{i-1}B \quad (i = 1,\dots,r). \tag{4.10}$$

We have to show that $\dim X \le \dim \tilde{X}$.

To this end introduce the matrices

$$H_{ij}(\Xi) = \begin{pmatrix} C \\ CA \\ \vdots \\ CA^{i-1} \end{pmatrix} \begin{pmatrix} B & AB & \dots & A^{j-1}B \end{pmatrix}, \quad i,j = 1,2,\dots , \tag{4.11}$$

and let $H_{ij}(\tilde{\Xi})$ denote the corresponding matrices for $\tilde{\Xi}$. Equalities (4.10) imply that

$$H_{ij}(\Xi) = H_{ij}(\tilde{\Xi}), \quad i+j \le r+1. \tag{4.12}$$

From the definition (4.11) it is clear that

$$\text{(4.13)} \qquad \operatorname{rank} H_{ij}(\Xi) = \dim\{R_j(\Xi) + N_i(\Xi)\} - \dim N_i(\Xi).$$

Now introduce the integer

$$\text{(4.14)} \qquad \rho(\Xi) := \sum_{i+j=r+1} \operatorname{rank} H_{ij}(\Xi) - \sum_{i+j=r} \operatorname{rank} H_{ij}(\Xi),$$

and let $\rho(\tilde{\Xi})$ be the corresponding integer for the node $\tilde{\Xi}$. Equalities (4.12) imply that

$$\text{(4.15)} \qquad \rho(\Xi) = \rho(\tilde{\Xi}).$$

Using (4.13) one easily checks that

$$\text{(4.16)} \qquad \rho(\tilde{\Xi}) = \dim\{R_r(\tilde{\Xi}) + N_1(\tilde{\Xi})\} - \dim N_r(\tilde{\Xi}) - \sum_{i=1}^{r-1} \dim \frac{R_{r-i}(\tilde{\Xi}) + N_i(\tilde{\Xi})}{R_{r-i}(\tilde{\Xi}) + N_{i+1}(\tilde{\Xi})},$$

which implies, in particular, that $\rho(\tilde{\Xi}) \le \dim \tilde{X}$. On the other hand, substituting $\Xi$ instead of $\tilde{\Xi}$ in (4.16) and using conditions a) - c) we readily see that

$$\text{(4.17)} \qquad \rho(\Xi) = \dim X,$$

which in view of (4.15) completes the proof of the theorem. □

For the partial realization problem as stated at the beginning of this section Theorem 4.1 can be summarized as follows (see [13]).

<u>THEOREM 4.2</u>. *A realization* $\theta = (A,B,C)$ *of* $M_1,\dots,M_r$ *(with state space* X*) is a minimal realization if and only if conditions* a) - c) *are fulfilled. The minimal state space dimension* $\delta(M_1,\dots,H_r)$ *(= the degree of* $M_1,\dots,M_r$*) is given by the formula*

$$\delta(M_1,\dots,M_r) = \sum_{i+j=r+1} \operatorname{rank} H_{ij} - \sum_{i+j=r} \operatorname{rank} H_{ij},$$

*where* $H_{ij}$ *are Hankel matrices defined by*

$$H_{ij} = \begin{pmatrix} M_1 & \cdots & M_j \\ \vdots & & \vdots \\ M_i & \cdots & M_{i+j-1} \end{pmatrix}, \qquad i+j \le r+1.$$

The last assertion of this theorem follows clearly from (4.14), (4.15) and (4.17). Furthermore, note that the operations on nodes (realizations) described in Steps 1 - 3 in the proof of Theorem 4.1 provide a compression algorithm for compressing an arbitrary realization of $M_1,\dots,M_r$ to a minimal one in a finite number of steps. Indeed, it is clear that a repeated application of these operations to a realization of $M_1,\dots,M_r$ will lead in a finite number of steps to a realization $\theta = (A,B,C)$ for which conditions a) - c) are fulfilled and this $\theta$ is minimal in view of Theorem 4.2. It is worth mentioning that a realization of $M_1,\dots,M_r$ is always available. For example, take the shift realization by setting $X = \overset{r}{\underset{i=1}{\oplus}} \mathbb{C}^m$ and

$$A = \begin{pmatrix} 0 & I & & \\ & & \ddots & \\ & & & I \\ 0 & 0 & \dots & 0 \end{pmatrix}, \quad B = \begin{pmatrix} M_1 \\ \vdots \\ M_r \end{pmatrix}, \quad C = \begin{pmatrix} I & 0 & \dots & 0 \end{pmatrix}.$$

For further details we refer to our paper [13].

## II.5. Minimality for boundary value systems

In this section we return to the boundary value systems considered in Section I.4. We show that the minimality problem for such systems, which we solved in [12], can be rephrased as a $(\Gamma',N_2)$-minimality problem for a certain set $\Gamma' \subset \Gamma_2$. The pair $(\Gamma',N_2)$ happens to be non-dominating. The main theorem of this section gives necessary and sufficient conditions for minimality for this specific non-dominating pair $(\Gamma',N_2)$.

First let us recall the minimality problem for time-invariant well-posed boundary value systems. Consider the system (I.4.1), i.e.

$$\theta \begin{cases} \dot{x}(t) = Ax(t) + Bu(t), & a \le t \le b, \\ y(t) = Cx(t), & a \le t \le b, \\ N_1x(a) + N_2x(b) = 0, \end{cases}$$

which we assume to be well-posed. For brevity we shall write $\theta = (A,B,C;N_1,N_2)$. The input/output behaviour of the system $\theta$ can be characterized by means of a well-defined input/output map, namely (see [11] Section I.6) the integral operator $T_\theta : L_2([a,b],\mathbb{C}^p) \to L_2([a,b],\mathbb{C}^m)$,

$$(5.1) \qquad y(t) = (T_\theta u)(t) = \int_a^b k_\theta(t,s)u(s)ds, \quad a \le t \le b,$$

of which the kernel $k_\theta$ is given by

$$(5.2) \qquad k_\theta(t,s) = \begin{cases} Ce^{(t-a)A}(I-P)e^{-(s-a)A}B, & a \le s < t \le b, \\ -Ce^{(t-a)A}Pe^{-(s-a)A}B, & a \le s < t \le b. \end{cases}$$

Here $P$ is the canonical boundary value operator of $\theta$ and $L_2([a,b],V)$ stands for the space of all (equivalence classes of) square integrable $V$-valued functions on $[a,b]$.

The system $\theta$ is called *minimal* if among all systems with the same input/output map as $\theta$ the dimension of the state space of $\theta$ is as small as possible.

Expanding $e^{(t-a)A}$ and $e^{(a-s)A}$ into power series in t-a and s-a, respectively, one sees from (5.1) - (5.2) that the input/output map $T_\theta$ of $\theta = (A,B,C;N_1,N_2)$ is uniquely determined by the operators

$$CA^iP^\nu A^jB \quad (i,j = 0,1,\dots;\nu = 0,1), \tag{5.3}$$

where P is the canonical boundary value operator of $\theta$. Hence $\theta$ is minimal if and only if the state space dimension of $\theta$ is less than or equal to the state space dimension of any other system $\tilde{\theta} = (\tilde{A},\tilde{B},\tilde{C};\tilde{N}_1,\tilde{N}_2)$ such that

$$\tilde{C}\tilde{A}^i\tilde{P}^\nu\tilde{A}^j\tilde{B} = CA^iP^\nu A^jB \quad (i,j = 0,1,\dots; \ = 0,1) \tag{5.4}$$

where $\tilde{P}$ stands for the canonical boundary value operator of $\tilde{\theta}$.

As in Section I.4 we associate with each system $\theta = (A,B,C;N_1,N_2)$ the node $\Xi_\theta = (A,P;X;B,C) \in N_2$, where X is the state space of $\theta$ and P stands for the canonical boundary value operator of $\theta$. Introduce the following subset $\Gamma'$ of $\Gamma_2$

$$\Gamma' = \{(\underbrace{1,1,\dots,1}_{\ell})|\ell = 1,2,\dots\} \cup \{(\underbrace{1,\dots,1}_{i},2,\underbrace{1,\dots,1}_{j})|i,j = 0,1,\dots\} \cup \{\emptyset\}. \tag{5.5}$$

Then equalities (5.4) are equivalent to equality of moments

$$M_\gamma(\Xi_\theta) = M_\gamma(\Xi_{\tilde{\theta}}), \qquad \gamma \in \Gamma', \tag{5.6}$$

where we set $A = A_1$, $P = A_2$ and $\tilde{A} = \tilde{A}_1$, $\tilde{P} = \tilde{A}_2$. So, in the above notations the system $\theta$ is minimal if and only if the node $\Xi_\theta$ is $(\Gamma',N_2)$-minimal.

So, we pass to the investigation of $(\Gamma',N_2)$ minimality. It is easily seen that the pair $(\Gamma',N_2)$ is not dominating, so we can not apply the results of Section 3. To state the necessary and sufficient conditions for a node $\Xi = (A_1,A_2;X;B,C) \in N_2$ to be $(\Gamma',N_2)$-minimal we need some additional notations:

$$\operatorname{Ker}(C|A_1) := \bigcap_{j=0}^{\infty} \operatorname{Ker} CA_1^j; \qquad \operatorname{Im}(A_1|B) := \bigvee_{j=0}^{\infty} \operatorname{Im} A_1^jB;$$

$$\operatorname{Ker}\Xi := \bigcap_{\nu=0}^{1} \bigcap_{i,j=0}^{\infty} \operatorname{Ker} CA_1^iA_2^\nu A_1^j; \quad \operatorname{Im}\Xi := \bigvee_{\nu=0}^{1} \bigvee_{i,j=0}^{\infty} \operatorname{Im} A_1^iA_2^\nu A_1^jB.$$

Taking into account the finite dimensionality of X one easily checks that the infinite sums and intersections in the notations introduced above can be replaced by finite ones:

$$\operatorname{Ker}(C|A_1) = \bigcap_{j=0}^{n-1} \operatorname{Ker} CA_1^j; \qquad \operatorname{Im}(A_1|B) = \bigvee_{j=0}^{n-1} \operatorname{Im} A_1^j B;$$

$$\operatorname{Ker} \Xi = \bigcap_{\nu=0}^{1} \bigcap_{i,j=0}^{n-1} \operatorname{Ker} CA_1^i A_2^\nu A_1^j; \qquad \operatorname{Im} \Xi = \bigvee_{\nu=0}^{1} \bigvee_{i,j=0}^{n-1} \operatorname{Im} A_1^i A_2^\nu A_1^j B.$$

THEOREM 5.1. *A node* $\Xi = (A_1,A_2;X;B,C) \in N_2$ *is* $(\Gamma',N_2)$*-minimal if and only if the following conditions are satisfied:*

(i) $\operatorname{Ker}(C|A_1) \subset \operatorname{Im}(A_1|B)$,

(ii) $\operatorname{Ker} \Xi = \{0\}$,

(iii) $\operatorname{Im} \Xi = X$.

The proof of Theorem 5.1 will be based on three lemmas.

LEMMA 5.2. *Given* $\Xi = (A_1,A_2;X;B,C) \in N_2$, *let* $X_1 \subset \operatorname{Ker}(C|A_1)$ *be chosen such that* $\operatorname{Im}(A_1|B) \oplus X_1 = \operatorname{Im}(A_1|B) + \operatorname{Ker}(C|A_1)$, *and let* $X_0$ *be a direct complement of* $X_1$ *in* $X$ *with* $\operatorname{Im}(A_1|B) \subset X_0$. *Write* $A_1,A_2,B,C$ *as operator matrices relative to the decomposition* $X = X_1 \oplus X_0$:

$$(5.7) \qquad A_i = \begin{pmatrix} (A_i)_{11} & (A_i)_{10} \\ (A_i)_{01} & (A_i)_{00} \end{pmatrix} \quad (i=1,2), \qquad B = \begin{pmatrix} B_1 \\ B_0 \end{pmatrix}, \qquad C = \begin{pmatrix} C_1 & C_0 \end{pmatrix}.$$

*Then the node* $\Xi_0 = ((A_1)_{00},(A_2)_{00};X_0;B_0,C_0)$ *satisfies*

$$(5.8) \qquad M_\gamma(\Xi_0) = M_\gamma(\Xi), \qquad \gamma \in \Gamma'$$

*and*

$$(5.9) \qquad \operatorname{Ker}(C_0|(A_1)_{00}) \subset \operatorname{Im}((A_1)_{00}|B_0).$$

PROOF. Since $\operatorname{Im}(A_1|B) \subset X_0$, we have $\operatorname{Im} B \subset X_0$, and hence $B_1 = 0$. The fact that $X_1 \subset \operatorname{Ker}(C|A_1)$ implies that $C_1 = 0$. Next, observe that

$$A_1B = \begin{pmatrix} (A_1)_{10}B_0 \\ (A_1)_{00}B_0 \end{pmatrix}, \qquad CA_1 = \begin{pmatrix} C_0(A_1)_{01} & C_0(A_1)_{00} \end{pmatrix}.$$

Now use the inclusions $\operatorname{Im} AB \subset X_0$, $X_1 \subset \operatorname{Ker} CA$. It follows that $(A_1)_{10}B_0 = 0$ and $C_0(A_1)_{01} = 0$. Proceeding in this way one finds that

$$(5.10) \qquad A_1^jB = \begin{pmatrix} 0 \\ (A_1)_{00}^jB_0 \end{pmatrix}, \quad CA_1^j = \begin{pmatrix} 0 & C_0(A_1)_{00}^j \end{pmatrix}, \quad j \geq 0.$$

In particular,

$$(5.11)\qquad CA_1^jB = C_0(A_1)_{00}^jB_0, \qquad j \geq 0.$$

Furthermore, for any $i,j \geq 0$

$$(5.12)\qquad CA_1^iA_2A_1^jB = \begin{pmatrix} 0 & C_0(A_1)_{00}^i \end{pmatrix}\begin{pmatrix} (A_2)_{10}(A_1)_{00}^jB_0 \\ (A_2)_{00}(A_1)_{00}^jB_0 \end{pmatrix} = C_0(A_1)_{00}^i(A_2)_{00}(A_1)_{00}^jB.$$

Equalities (5.11) and (5.12) show that (5.8) holds true. Thus, it remains to prove (5.9). Take $x_0 \in \mathrm{Ker}(C_0|(A_1)_{00})$. From (5.10) it follows that $\begin{pmatrix} 0 \\ x_0 \end{pmatrix} \in \mathrm{Ker}(C|A_1)$. But $\mathrm{Ker}(C|A_1) \subset \mathrm{Im}(A_1|B) \oplus X_1$ and $\mathrm{Im}(A_1|B) \subset X_0$. So $\begin{pmatrix} 0 \\ x_0 \end{pmatrix} \in \mathrm{Im}(A_1|B)$, and thus $x_0 \in \mathrm{Im}((A_1)_{00}|B_0)$. □

<u>LEMMA 5.3</u>. *Given* $\Xi = (A_1,A_2;X;B,C) \in N_2$, *put* $X_1 = \mathrm{Ker}\,\Xi$, *and let* $X_0$ *be a direct complement of* $X_1$ *in* $X$. *Let* (5.7) *give the partitioning of* $A_1,A_2,B,C$ *relative to the decomposition* $X = X_1 \oplus X_0$. *Then the node* $\Xi_0 = ((A_1)_{00},(A_2)_{00};X_0;B_0,C_0)$ *satisfies* (5.8) *and* $\mathrm{Ker}\,\Xi_0 = \{0\}$.

<u>PROOF</u>. Obviously, $A_1X_1 \subset X_1$ and hence $(A_1)_{01} = 0$. It follows that

$$(5.13)\qquad A_1^jB = \begin{pmatrix} * \\ (A_1)_{00}^jB_0 \end{pmatrix}, \qquad j \geq 0.$$

Further, $X_1 \subset \mathrm{Ker}\,C$, which implies that $C_1 = 0$, and hence

$$(5.14)\qquad C(A_1)^j = \begin{pmatrix} 0 & C_0(A_1)_{00}^j \end{pmatrix} \qquad j \geq 0.$$

Also, $CA_1^jA_2 = \begin{pmatrix} C_0(A_1)_{00}^j(A_2)_{01} & C_0(A_1)_{00}^j(A_2)_{00} \end{pmatrix}$ for $j \geq 0$. But $X_1 \subset \mathrm{Ker}\,CA_1^jA_2$. Thus $C_0(A_1)_{00}^j(A_2)_{01} = 0$ for $j \geq 0$. Hence

$$(5.15)\qquad CA_1^jA_2 = \begin{pmatrix} 0 & C_0(A_1)_{00}^j(A_2)_{00} \end{pmatrix}, \qquad j \geq 0.$$

From (5.13), (5.14) and (5.15), we conclude that

$$CA_1^jB = C_0(A_1)_{00}^jB_0, \qquad j \geq 0,$$

$$CA_1^iA_2A_1^jB = C_0(A_1)_{00}^i(A_2)_{00}(A_1)_{00}^jB_0 \qquad i,j \geq 0.$$

This shows that $\Xi_0$ satisfies (4.8). Now take $x_0 \in \mathrm{Ker}\,\Xi_0$. Note that

$$CA_1^iA_2^\nu A_1^jx_0 = C_0(A_1)_{00}^i(A_2)_{00}^\nu(A_1)_{00}^jx_0$$

for $\nu = 0,1$ and $i,j = 0,1,2,\ldots$ . So, $x_0 \in X_1$. But $X_1 \cap X_0 = \{0\}$ and hence $x_0 = 0$, which proves that $\mathrm{Ker}\,\Xi_0 = \{0\}$. □

LEMMA 5.4. *Given* $\Xi = (A_1,A_2;X;B,C) \in N_2$, *put* $X_0 = \operatorname{Im}\Xi$, *and let* $X_1$ *be a direct complement of* $X_0$ *in* X. *Let* (5.7) *give the partitionings of* $A_1,A_2$, B,C *relative to the decomposition* $X = X_1 \oplus X_0$. *Then* $\Xi_0 = ((A_1)_{00},(A_2)_{00};X_0;B_0,C_0)$ *satisfies* (5.8) *and* $\operatorname{Im}\Xi_0 = X_0$.

PROOF. Obviously, $A_1X_0 \subset X_0$ and hence $(A_1)_{10} = 0$. Further, $\operatorname{Im} B \subset X_0$, which implies $B_1 = 0$. It follows that

$$(5.16)\qquad A_1^jB = \begin{pmatrix} 0 \\ (A_1)_{00}^jB_0 \end{pmatrix}, \qquad j \geq 0,$$

$$(5.17)\qquad CA_1^j = \begin{pmatrix} * & C_0(A_1)_{00}^j \end{pmatrix}, \qquad j \geq 0.$$

From (5.16) we see that

$$A_2A_1^jB = \begin{pmatrix} (A_2)_{10}(A_1)_{00}^jB_0 \\ (A_2)_{00}(A_1)_{00}^jB_0 \end{pmatrix}, \qquad j \geq 0.$$

But $A_2A_1^jB \subset X_0$, and hence $(A_2)_{10}(A_1)_{00}^jB_0 = 0$. So

$$(5.18)\qquad A_2A_1^jB = \begin{pmatrix} 0 \\ (A_2)_{00}(A_1)_{00}^jB_0 \end{pmatrix}, \qquad j \geq 0.$$

From (4.16), (4.17) and (4.18) we conclude again that $\Xi_0$ satisfies (5.8).

From (4.20) and the fact that $(A_1)_{10} = 0$ it follows that

$$A_1^iA_2^\nu A_1^jB = \begin{pmatrix} 0 \\ (A_1)_{00}^i(A_2)_{00}^\nu(A_1)_{00}^jB_0 \end{pmatrix}$$

for all $\nu = 0,1$ and $i,j = 0,1,2,\dots$ . This implies that $\operatorname{Im}\Xi_0 = X_0$. □

PROOF of Theorem 5.1. Suppose that the node $\Xi = (A_1,A_2;X;B,C) \in N_2$ is $(\Gamma',N_2)$-minimal. Then it is clear from Lemmas 5.2 - 5.4 that (i), (ii) and (iii) are satisfied.

Conversely, assume that conditions (i), (ii) and (iii) are satisfied for the node $\Xi$. Let $\tilde\Xi = (\tilde A_1,\tilde A_2;\tilde X;\tilde B,\tilde C)$ be another node such that

$$(5.19)\qquad CA_1^jB = \tilde C\tilde A_1^j\tilde B, \qquad j \geq 0,$$

$$(5.20)\qquad CA_1^iA_2A_1^jB = \tilde C\tilde A_1^i\tilde A_2\tilde A_1^j\tilde B, \qquad j \geq 0.$$

We have to prove that $\dim X \leq \dim\tilde X$. By applying the compression procedure of Lemmas 5.2 - 5.4 it is clear that without loss of generality we may assume that for the realization $\tilde\Xi$ the condition (i), (ii) and (iii) are also satisfied.

Introduce $X_1 = \mathrm{Ker}(C|A_1)$, $X_0 \oplus \mathrm{Ker}(C|A_1) = \mathrm{Im}(A_1|B)$, $X_1 \oplus X_0 \oplus X_2 = X$, $\tilde{X}_1 = \mathrm{Ker}(\tilde{C}|\tilde{A}_1)$, $\tilde{X}_0 \oplus \mathrm{Ker}(\tilde{C}|\tilde{A}_1) = \mathrm{Im}(\tilde{A}_1|\tilde{B})$, $\tilde{X}_1 \oplus \tilde{X}_0 \oplus \tilde{X}_2 = \tilde{X}$. Here we make use of the fact that condition (i) is satisfied for $\Xi$ and $\tilde{\Xi}$. Relative to the decomposition $X = X_1 \oplus X_0 \oplus X_2$ we have

$$A_1 = \begin{pmatrix} * & * & * \\ 0 & (A_1)_0 & * \\ 0 & 0 & * \end{pmatrix}, \quad B = \begin{pmatrix} * \\ B_0 \\ 0 \end{pmatrix}, \quad C = \begin{pmatrix} 0 & C_0 & * \end{pmatrix}.$$

Relative to the decomposition $\tilde{X} = \tilde{X}_1 \oplus \tilde{X}_0 \oplus \tilde{X}_2$ we have

$$\tilde{A}_1 = \begin{pmatrix} * & * & * \\ 0 & (\tilde{A}_1)_0 & * \\ 0 & 0 & * \end{pmatrix}, \quad \tilde{B} = \begin{pmatrix} * \\ \tilde{B}_0 \\ 0 \end{pmatrix}, \quad \tilde{C} = \begin{pmatrix} 0 & \tilde{C}_0 & * \end{pmatrix}.$$

Then

$$C_0(A_1)_0^j B_0 = CA_1^j B = \tilde{C}\tilde{A}_1^j\tilde{B} = \tilde{C}_0(\tilde{A}_1)_0^j B_0, \qquad j \geq 0. \tag{5.21}$$

Note that our construction implies that

$$\mathrm{Ker}(C_0|(A_1)_0) = \{0\}, \qquad \mathrm{Im}((A_1)_0|B_0) = X_0,$$

$$\mathrm{Ker}(\tilde{C}_0|(\tilde{A}_1)_0) = \{0\}, \qquad \mathrm{Im}((\tilde{A}_1)_0|\tilde{B}_0) = \tilde{X}_0.$$

These relations and (5.21) imply that $\dim X_0 = \dim \tilde{X}_0$.

Next, let $\ell$ be a positive integer larger than $\dim X$ and $\dim \tilde{X}$. Introduce the operator

$$\Omega = \begin{pmatrix} \mathrm{col}(CA_1^j)_{j=0}^{\ell-1} \\ \mathrm{col}(CA_2A_1^j)_{j=0}^{\ell-1} \\ \mathrm{col}(CA_1A_2A_1^j)_{j=0}^{\ell-1} \\ \vdots \\ \mathrm{col}(CA_1^{\ell-1}A_2A_1^j)_{j=0}^{\ell-1} \end{pmatrix} \begin{pmatrix} B & A_1B & \cdots & A_1^{\ell-1}B \end{pmatrix},$$

and let $\tilde{\Omega}$ be the corresponding operator for $\tilde{\Xi}$. From (5.19) and (5.20) it follows that $\Omega = \tilde{\Omega}$. Since condition (ii) holds for $\Xi$ as well as for $\tilde{\Xi}$ we have

$$\mathrm{rank}\,\Omega = \mathrm{rank}\begin{pmatrix} B & A_1B & \cdots & A_1^{\ell-1}B \end{pmatrix} = \dim(X_0 \oplus X_1),$$

$$\mathrm{rank}\,\tilde{\Omega} = \mathrm{rank}\begin{pmatrix} \tilde{B} & \tilde{A}_1\tilde{B} & \cdots & \tilde{A}_1^{\ell-1}\tilde{B} \end{pmatrix} = \dim(\tilde{X}_0 \oplus \tilde{X}_1).$$

We already know that $\dim X_0 = \dim \tilde{X}_0$. So $\dim X_1 = \dim \tilde{X}_1$. Finally, consider

$$\Lambda = \begin{pmatrix} C \\ CA_1 \\ \cdot \\ \cdot \\ \cdot \\ CA_1^{\ell-1} \end{pmatrix} \Big( \mathrm{row}\,(A_1^jB)_{j=0}^{\ell-1} \;\; \mathrm{row}\,(A_1^jA_2B)_{j=0}^{\ell-1} \;\; \mathrm{row}\,(A_1^jA_2A_1B)_{j=0}^{\ell-1} \cdots \\ \cdots \; \mathrm{row}\,(A_1^jA_2A_1^{\ell-1}B)_{j=0}^{\ell-1} \Big),$$

and let $\tilde{\Lambda}$ be the corresponding operator for $\tilde{\Xi}$. Using (i) (which holds for $\Xi$ and $\tilde{\Xi}$) we see that

$$\dim(X_0 \oplus X_2) = \dim X - \dim X_1 = \operatorname{rank}\Lambda = \operatorname{rank}\tilde{\Lambda} = \dim\tilde{X} - \dim\tilde{X}_1 = \\ = \dim(\tilde{X}_0 \oplus \tilde{X}_2).$$

This implies that $\dim X_2 = \dim\tilde{X}_2$ and hence $\dim X = \dim\tilde{X}$. □

Let us consider a smaller realization domain, namely

$$\mathcal{D}_{ST} = \{(A_1A_2;X;B,C) \in N_2 \mid CA_1^i[A_1,A_2]A_1^jB = 0\}.$$

A node $\Xi$ in $\mathcal{D}_{ST}$ will be called *stationary* (cf. [19]). Observe that $\Xi = (A_1,A_2;X;B,C)$ is stationary if and only if

$$CA_1^iA_2A_1^jB = CA_1^jA_2A_1^iB, \qquad i,j \geq 0.$$

From Proposition 1.1 it follows that $(\Gamma',\mathcal{D}_{ST})$-minimality is the same as $(\Gamma',N_2)$-minimality. In other words conditions (i), (ii) and (iii) in Theorem 5.1 provide necessary and sufficient conditions for $\Gamma'$-minimality in the class of stationary nodes $\Xi$. Note that the defining property of the domain $\mathcal{D}_{ST}$ allows us to rewrite conditions (ii) and (iii) in the form

(ii)' $\quad \mathrm{Ker}_{ST}\,\Xi := \bigcap_{\nu=0}^{1}\bigcap_{i=0}^{n-1} \mathrm{Ker}\, CA_1^iA_2^\nu = \{0\},$

(iii)' $\quad \mathrm{Im}_{ST}\,\Xi := \bigvee_{\nu=0}^{1}\bigvee_{i=0}^{n-1} \mathrm{Im}\, A_2^\nu A_1^iB = X.$

Indeed, using the definition of $\mathcal{D}_{ST}$ one easily checks that

$$A_1(\mathrm{Ker}_{ST}\,\Xi \cap \mathrm{Im}\,(A_1|B)) \subset \mathrm{Ker}_{ST}\,\Xi,$$

$$A_1(\mathrm{Im}_{ST}\,\Xi + \mathrm{Ker}\,(C|A_1)) \subset \mathrm{Im}_{ST}\,\Xi,$$

which implies, in particular, that the spaces $\mathrm{Ker}_{ST}\,\Xi \cap \mathrm{Im}\,(A_1|B)$ and $\mathrm{Im}_{ST}\,\Xi + \mathrm{Ker}\,(C|A_1)$ are invariant under $A_1$. But then we may conclude that

(5.22) $\quad \mathrm{Ker}_{ST}\,\Xi \cap \mathrm{Im}\,(A_1|B) \subset \mathrm{Ker}\,\Xi \subset \mathrm{Ker}_{ST}\,\Xi,$

(5.23) $\quad \mathrm{Im}_{ST}\,\Xi + \mathrm{Ker}\,(C|A_1) \supset \mathrm{Im}\,\Xi \supset \mathrm{Im}_{ST}\,\Xi.$

Now assume that (i) holds. Then we see that $\mathrm{Ker}_{ST}\,\Xi = \mathrm{Ker}_{ST}\,\Xi \cap \mathrm{Im}(A_1|B)$ and $\mathrm{Im}_{ST}\,\Xi = \mathrm{Im}_{ST}\,\Xi + \mathrm{Ker}(C|A_1)$. By combining this with (5.22) and (5.23) we obtain that $\mathrm{Ker}_{ST}\,\Xi = \mathrm{Ker}\,\Xi$, $\mathrm{Im}_{ST}\,\Xi = \mathrm{Im}\,\Xi$.

Now we use the connection between the minimal systems $\theta = (A,B,C;N_1,N_2)$ and $(\Gamma',N_2)$-minimal nodes $\Xi_\theta = (A,P;X;B,C)$ as presented at the beginning of this section in order to reformulate Theorem 5.1 as a criterion for minimality of a boundary value system $\theta$. We shall use the following notations, where P will denote the canonical boundary value operator of $\theta$:

$$\mathrm{Ker}(C|A) = \bigcap_{j=0}^{n-1} \mathrm{Ker}\, CA^j; \qquad \mathrm{Im}(A|B) := \bigvee_{j=0}^{\infty} \mathrm{Im}\, A^jB,$$

$$\mathrm{Ker}\,\theta := \bigcap_{\nu=0}^{1} \bigcap_{i,j=0}^{n-1} \mathrm{Ker}\, CA^iP^\nu A^j; \quad \mathrm{Im}\,\theta := \bigvee_{\nu=0}^{1} \bigvee_{i,j=0}^{\infty} \mathrm{Im}\, A^iP^\nu A^jB.$$

Theorem 5.1 yields the following theorem.

THEOREM 5.5. *The system $\theta$ is minimal if and only if the following three conditions are satisfied:*

(i) $\mathrm{Ker}\,(C|A) \subset \mathrm{Im}\,(A|B)$

(ii) $\mathrm{Ker}\,\theta = \{0\}$

(iii) $\mathrm{Im}\,\theta = X$,

*where X denotes the state space of $\theta$.*

Note that Lemmas 5.2 - 5.4 provide a finite algorithm which can be used in order to compress the given system to a minimal one preserving the input/output map. A direct proof of Theorem 5.5 and other related results can be found in [12].

## III. MINIMALITY FOR N-D SYSTEMS

In this chapter we apply the theory developed in Chapters 1 - 2 to characterize minimality in some classes of N-D systems

### III.1. Preliminaries about 2-D systems

We shall deal with the Fornasini-Marchesini model for 2-D systems (see [6 - 7], also [2], [20]), i.e., with systems of the form

$$(1.1) \qquad \theta \begin{cases} x(k_1+1,k_2+1) = A_1x(k_1,k_2+1) + A_2x(k_1+1,k_2) + A_0x(k_1,k_2) + Bu(k_1,k_2), \\ y(k_1,k_2) = Cx(k_1,k_2), \\ x(k_1,0) = 0, \quad x(0,k_2) = 0, \quad k_1,k_2 = 0,1,\dots , \end{cases}$$

where $A_i : X \to X$ $(i = 0,1,2)$, $B : \mathbb{C}^p \to X$ and $C : X \to \mathbb{C}^m$ are linear operators acting between finite dimensional vector spaces. The space X is called the state space of the system (1.1).

To compute the transfer function of the system (1.1) one needs the 2-D z-transform Z, which is defined as follows. Let $\{x(k_1,k_2)\}_{k_1,k_2=0}^{\infty}$ be a $\mathbb{C}^r$-valued 2-D sequence. Then its z-transform $Z(\{x(k_1,k_2)\}_{k_1,k_2=0}^{\infty}) := \hat{x}(\lambda_1,\lambda_2)$ is given by

$$\hat{x}(\lambda_1,\lambda_2) = \sum_{k_1,k_2=0}^{\infty} \lambda_1^{-k_1}\lambda_2^{-k_2}x(k_1,k_2).$$

The following standard relations are useful:

$$Z(\{x(k_1+1,k_2)\}_{k_1,k_2=0}^{\infty}) = \lambda_1[\hat{x}(\lambda_1,\lambda_2) - \sum_{k_2=0}^{\infty} x(0,k_2)\lambda_2^{-k_2}]; \tag{1.2}$$

$$Z(\{x(k_1,k_2+1)\}_{k_1,k_2=0}^{\infty}) = \lambda_2[\hat{x}(\lambda_1,\lambda_2) - \sum_{k_1=0}^{\infty} x(k_1,0)\lambda_1^{-k_1}]; \tag{1.3}$$

$$\begin{aligned} Z(\{x(k_1+1,k_2+1)\}_{k_1,k_2=0}^{\infty}) = \lambda_1\lambda_2[\hat{x}(\lambda_1,\lambda_2) &- \sum_{k_2=1}^{\infty} x(0,k_2)\lambda_2^{-k_2} \\ &- \sum_{k_1=1}^{\infty} x(k_1,0)\lambda_1^{-k_1} - x(0,0)]. \end{aligned} \tag{1.4}$$

On taking the 2-D z-transform of the system θ given by (1.1) one obtains in view of (1.2) - (1.4) that

$$\hat{y}(\lambda_1,\lambda_2) = W_\theta(\lambda_1,\lambda_2)\hat{u}(\lambda_1,\lambda_2),$$

where the $m \times p$ matrix valued function

$$W_\theta(\lambda_1,\lambda_2) = C(\lambda_1\lambda_2 I_X - \lambda_2 A_1 - \lambda_1 A_2 - A_0)^{-1}B \tag{1.5}$$

is the *transfer function* of the system θ given by (1.1).

Now we introduce two basic operations on the system (1.1) which do not change its transfer function. Let $S : X \to \tilde{X}$ be an invertible operator. Substituting $\tilde{x}(k_1,k_2) = Sx(k_1,k_2)$ in (1.1) we obtain the system

$$\tilde{\theta} \begin{cases} \tilde{x}(k_1+1,k_2+1) = \tilde{A}_1\tilde{x}(k_1,k_2+1) + \tilde{A}_2\tilde{x}(k_1+1,k_2) + \tilde{A}_0 x(k_1,k_2) + \tilde{B}u(k_1,k_2), \\ y(k_1,k_2) = \tilde{C}\tilde{x}(k_1,k_2), \\ \tilde{x}(k_1,0) = 0, \quad \tilde{x}(0,k_2) = 0, \quad k_1,k_2 = 0,1,2,\dots , \end{cases} \tag{1.6}$$

where $\tilde{A}_i = SA_iS^{-1}$ $(i = 0,1,2)$, $\tilde{B} = SB$ and $\tilde{C} = CS^{-1}$. The systems θ and $\tilde{\theta}$, defined by (1.1) and (1.6), respectively, are called *similar*. It is obvious that the transfer function is not changed under the similarity transformation:

$W_{\tilde{\theta}}(\lambda_1,\lambda_2) = W_\theta(\lambda_1,\lambda_2)$.

Next, assume that the space X admits a direct sum decomposition $X = X_1 \oplus X_0 \oplus X_2$ relative to which the following partitionings hold true:

$$(1.7)\qquad A_i = \begin{pmatrix} * & * & * \\ 0 & A_i^{(0)} & * \\ 0 & 0 & * \end{pmatrix} \ (i=0,1,2); \quad B = \begin{pmatrix} * \\ B_0 \\ 0 \end{pmatrix}; \quad C = \begin{pmatrix} 0 & C_0 & * \end{pmatrix}.$$

The system

$$(1.8)\qquad \theta_0 \begin{cases} x(k_1+1,k_2) = A_1^{(0)}x(k_1,k_2+1) + A_2^{(0)}x(k_1+1,k_2) + A_0^{(0)}x(k_1,k_2) + B_0u(k_1,k_2), \\ y(k_1,k_2) = C_0x(k_1,k_2), \\ x(k_1,0) = 0, \quad x(0,k_2) = 0, \quad k_1,k_2 = 0,1,2,\dots , \end{cases}$$

is called a *reduction* of the system $\theta$ given by (1.1). In this case we also say that $\theta$ is a *dilation* of the system $\theta_0$, defined by (1.8). It is clear that $W_{\theta_0}(\lambda_1,\lambda_2) = W_\theta(\lambda_1,\lambda_2)$, i.e. the transfer function is invariant under the reduction (dilation) operation.

Next we consider *recognizable* systems (see, e.g., [2]), i.e. systems (1.1) of which the main operators satisfy the condition

$$(1.9)\qquad A_0 = -A_2A_1.$$

For such systems the transfer function (1.5) becomes simpler:

$$(1.10)\qquad W_\theta(\lambda_1,\lambda_2) = C(\lambda_1I_X - A_1)^{-1}(\lambda_2I_X - A_2)^{-1}B.$$

Remark that the class of recognizable systems is closed under reduction and similarity.

Now to each recognizable system $\theta$ defined by (1.1) and (1.9) we associate the node $\Xi_\theta = (A_1,A_2;X;B,C)$ in $N_2$. Conversely, any node $\Xi = (A_1,A_2;X;B,C)$ determines uniquely a recognizable system $\theta$ defined by (1.1) and (1.9) such that $\Xi = \Xi_\theta$. Let $\mathcal{D} \subset N_2$ be a realization domain in $N_2$. The class of all recognizable systems $\theta$ such that $\Xi_\theta \in \mathcal{D}$ will be denoted by $\{\mathcal{D}\}$. A recognizable system $\theta \in \{\mathcal{D}\}$ will be called *minimal* in the class $\{\mathcal{D}\}$ if $\dim X \le \dim \tilde{X}$ for any recognizable system $\tilde{\theta} \in \{\mathcal{D}\}$ such that $W_{\tilde{\theta}}(\lambda_1,\lambda_2) = W_\theta(\lambda_1,\lambda_2)$. Expanding the transfer function (1.10) in a neighbourhood of infinity one sees that $W_\theta(\lambda_1,\lambda_2)$ is uniquely determined by the moments $CA_1^iA_2^jB$, $i,j = 0,1,\dots$ . This yields the following proposition.

PROPOSITION 1.1. *Let $\mathcal{D} \subset N_2$ be a realization domain. A recognizable system $\theta \in \{\mathcal{D}\}$ is minimal in the class $\{\mathcal{D}\}$ if and only if the node $\Xi_\theta$ is $(\Gamma_2', \mathcal{D})$-minimal, where $\Gamma_2' = \{\gamma = (\underbrace{1,\ldots,1}_{q},\underbrace{2,\ldots,2}_{\ell-q}),\ q = 0,1,\ldots,\ell;$ $\ell = 1,2,\ldots\} \cup \{\emptyset\}$.*

III.2. Minimality in some classes of 2-D systems

In this section we present two classed of 2-D systems for which the minimality problem is reduced to restricted minimality of some dominating pairs.

Let $\alpha_1, \alpha_2$ be fixed complex numbers. Our first class of systems consists of all recognizable systems $\theta$, defined by (1.1) and (1.9), of which the main operators satisfy also the relation

$$(2.1)\qquad A_1A_2 - A_2A_1 = \alpha_1A_1 + \alpha_2A_2.$$

We call this class the *Lie class* of systems, and denote it by $\Delta_L^{\alpha_1,\alpha_2}$. Systems belonging to the particular class $\Delta_L^{0,0}$ (i.e. $\alpha_1 = \alpha_2 = 0$) are known in system theory as the Attasi model ([1], [20]). A minimality theory for this model can be found in [1].

Let us denote by $\mathcal{D}_L^{\alpha_1,\alpha_2}$ the Lie realization domain in $N_2$ defined by (II.2.1) with structural constants $\ell_{12}^1 = -\ell_{21}^1 = \alpha_1$, $\ell_{12}^2 = -\ell_{21}^2 = \alpha_2$. Then $\Delta_L^{\alpha_1,\alpha_2} = \{\mathcal{D}_L^{\alpha_1,\alpha_2}\}$ according to the notations of section III.1. We know from Proposition II.2.1 that the pair $(\Gamma_2', \mathcal{D}_L^{\alpha_1,\alpha_2})$ is dominating. Thus using Proposition 1.1 we can apply Theorem II.3.1, Theorem I.2.2 and Corollaries II.3.2 - II.3.3 to characterize the minimal systems in the class $\Delta_L^{\alpha_1,\alpha_2}$. If $\theta$ is a recognizable system defined by (1.1) and (1.9) we denote

$$N(\theta) := N(\Xi_\theta) = \bigcap_{|\gamma| \le n-1} \operatorname{Ker} C\omega_\gamma(A_1,A_2);$$

$$R(\theta) := R(\Xi_\theta) = \bigvee_{|\gamma| \le n-1} \operatorname{Im} \omega_\gamma(A_1,A_2)B.$$

THEOREM 2.1. *A system $\theta \in \Delta_L^{\alpha_1,\alpha_2}$ is minimal in the Lie class $\Delta_L^{\alpha_1,\alpha_2}$ if and only if $N(\theta) = (0)$ and $R(\theta) = X$, where $X$ stands for the state space of $\theta$.*

THEOREM 2.2. *Let $\theta \in \Delta_L^{\alpha_1,\alpha_2}$ and $\tilde{\theta} \in \Delta_L^{\alpha_1,\alpha_2}$ be minimal systems in the Lie class $\Delta_L^{\alpha_1,\alpha_2}$. Then the systems $\theta$ and $\tilde{\theta}$ are similar if and only if their transfer functions coincide: $W_\theta(\lambda_1,\lambda_2) = W_{\tilde{\theta}}(\lambda_1,\lambda_2)$.*

THEOREM 2.3. *Any system $\theta$ in the Lie class $\Delta_L^{\alpha_1,\alpha_2}$ defined by (1.1) and (1.9) is a dilation of a in $\Delta_L^{\alpha_1,\alpha_2}$ minimal system. More precisely, put $X_1 = N(\theta)$, let $X_0$ be a direct complement of $X_1 \cap R(\theta)$ in $R(\theta)$ and choose $X_2$ such that $X = X_1 \oplus X_0 \oplus X_2$. Then relative to this decomposition the* *partitionings* (1.7) *hold true and the system* $\theta_0$ *defined by* (1.8) *with* ($A_0^{(0)} = -A_2^{(0)}A_1^{(0)}$) *is minimal in the Lie class* $\Delta_L^{\alpha_1,\alpha_2}$.

The second class of systems we have in mind is the class of all recognizable systems $\theta$ defined by (1.1) and (1.9) of which the main operators satisfy additionally the relation

$$A_1A_2 - A_2A_1 = BC,$$

We call this class the *Pincus class* of systems (cf. [25], [4]) and denote it by $\Delta_P$. Recalling the definition (II.2.6.a) of a Pincus realization domain $\mathcal{D}_P$ we see that $\Delta_P = \{\mathcal{D}_P\}$. We have proved in Proposition II.2.2 that the pair $(\Gamma_2', \mathcal{D}_P)$ is dominating. So, using Proposition 1.1 and the theory of restricted minimality from Chapter II we obtain a characterization of the minimal systems in $\Delta_P$. To state the corresponding results one has to replace in Theorems 2.1 - 2.3 the name "Lie" by "Pincus" and the class $\Delta_L^{\alpha_1,\alpha_2}$ by the class $\Delta_P$.

In a similar way one can characterize minimal systems in the class $\Delta_P^{(a)} := \{\mathcal{D}_P^{(a)}\}$, where $\mathcal{D}_P^{(a)}$ is defined by (II.2.6.c) for an arbitrary complex number a. Note that the class $\Delta^{(0)} = \{\mathcal{D}^{(0)}\}$ coincides with the Attasi class of systems.

III.3. An example of an N-D system

Let N be a fixed integer and consider an N-D system $\theta$ defined as follows

$$(3.1)\qquad \theta\begin{cases} x(k_1+1,k_2+1,\dots,k_N+1) = \sum\limits_{s=1}^{N}\ \sum\limits_{j_1<j_2<\dots<j_s} R_{j_1,j_2,\dots,j_s}\cdot \\ x(k_1+1,\dots,k_{j_1-1}+1,k_{j_1},k_{j_1+1}+1,\dots,k_{j_2-1}+1,k_{j_2},k_{j_2+1}+1,\dots \\ \qquad\dots,k_{j_s-1}+1,k_{j_s},k_{j_s+1}+1,\dots,k_N+1) + Bu(k_1,k_2,\dots,k_N), \\ y(k_1,k_2,\dots,k_N) = Cx(k_1,\dots,k_N), \qquad k_1,\dots,k_N = 0,1,\dots\ , \\ x(k_1,\dots,k_N)\big|_{k_i=0} = 0,\quad i=1,\dots,N;\quad k_1,\dots,k_N = 0,1,\dots\ , \end{cases}$$

where $R_{j_1,j_2,\dots,j_s} : X \to X$, $B : \mathbb{C}^p \to X$ and $C : X \to \mathbb{C}^m$ are linear operators acting between finite dimensional spaces. Here X is called the state space of the system $\theta$. Similarity and reduction for such systems are defined by an obvious rephrasing of the appropriate definitions for 2-D systems.

Next, denoting the N-D z-transform by

$$\hat{x}(\lambda_1,\dots,\lambda_N) := \sum_{k_1,\dots,k_N}^{\infty} \lambda_1^{-k_1}\dots\lambda_N^{-k_N}x(k_1,\dots,k_N),$$

one writes (3.1) in the transform domain as follows

$$\begin{cases} \lambda_1\lambda_2\cdots\lambda_N\hat{x}(\lambda_1,\ldots,\lambda_N) = \\ \lambda_1\lambda_2\cdots\lambda_N \sum_{s=1}^{N} \sum_{j_1<j_2<\cdots<j_s} \lambda_{j_1}^{-1}\lambda_{j_2}^{-1}\cdots\lambda_{j_s}^{-1}R_{j_1,j_2,\ldots,j_s}\hat{x}(\lambda_1,\ldots,\lambda_N) \\ \qquad\qquad + B\hat{u}(\lambda_1,\ldots,\lambda_N), \\ \hat{y}(\lambda_1,\ldots,\lambda_N) = C\hat{x}(\lambda_1,\ldots,\lambda_N). \end{cases}$$

It follows that

$$\hat{y}(\lambda_1,\ldots,\lambda_N) = W_\theta(\lambda_1,\ldots,\lambda_N)\hat{u}(\lambda_1,\ldots,\lambda_N),$$

where

$$W_\theta(\lambda_1,\ldots,\lambda_N) := C\lambda_1^{-1}\lambda_2^{-1}\cdots\lambda_N^{-1}\Big[I_X - \sum_{s=1}^{N}\sum_{j_1<j_2<\cdots<j_s} \lambda_{j_1}^{-1}\lambda_{j_2}^{-1}\cdots\lambda_{j_s}^{-1}R_{j_1,j_2,\ldots,j_s}\Big]^{-1}B\hat{u}(\lambda_1,\ldots,\lambda_N). \tag{3.2}$$

It is clear that the transfer function (3.2) of a system $\theta$ is invariant under the similarity and reduction operations.

Now we consider a special class of systems $\theta$ consisting of systems (3.1) in which the main operators $R_{j_1,j_2,\ldots,j_s}$ are products of two operators $A_1$ and $A_2$ as follows

$$R_{j_1,j_2,\ldots,j_s} = (-1)^s A_{\sigma(j_s)}A_{\sigma(j_{s-1})}\cdots A_{\sigma(j_1)}, \tag{3.3}$$

where $\sigma(j) := \frac{1}{2}(3+(-1)^j)$. For such systems the transfer function (3.2) simplifies considerably. Namely, in this case

$$W_\theta(\lambda_1,\ldots,\lambda_N) = C(\lambda_1-A_1)^{-1}(\lambda_2-A_2)^{-1}\cdots(\lambda_N-A_{\sigma(N)})^{-1}B. \tag{3.4}$$

So the class of systems defined by (3.1) and (3.3) generalizes the class of recognizable systems defined in Section III.1 for $N = 2$. Thus we shall call systems $\theta$ defined by (3.1) and (3.3) *recognizable* also in the case $N > 2$. Note that this class is invariant under similarity and reduction.

Next we introduce the class $\Delta_N$ of all recognizable systems $\theta$ defined by (3.1) and (3.3) with $\dim X \le N/2$, where $X$ is the state space of $\theta$. A system $\theta \in \Delta_N$ is called *minimal* in the class $\Delta_N$ if $\dim X \le \dim\tilde{X}$ for any other system $\tilde{\theta} \in \Delta_N$ such that $W_{\tilde{\theta}}(\lambda_1,\ldots,\lambda_N) = W_\theta(\lambda_1,\ldots,\lambda_N)$. Here $\tilde{X}$ stands for the state space of $\tilde{\theta}$.

Now to each system $\theta$ defined by (3.1) and (3.3) we associate the node $\Xi_\theta = (A_1,A_2;X;B,C)$ in $N_2$. Conversely, each node $\Xi = (A_1,A_2;X;B,C)$ in $N_2$

determines uniquely a system $\theta$ defined by (3.1) and (3.3) such that $\Xi = \Xi_\theta$. It follows that a system $\theta \in \Delta_N$ is minimal in the class $\Delta_N$ if and only if the node $\Xi_\theta$ is $(\Gamma^{(N)},\mathcal{D}_N)$-minimal, where $\mathcal{D}_N$ is defined by (II.2.15). In view of Proposition II.2.3 the pair $(\Gamma^{(N)},\mathcal{D}_N)$ is dominating, and hence we can apply the theory of restricted minimality form Chapter II in order to characterize the minimal systems in the class $\Delta_N$. The statements of the results obtained in this way are similar to Theorems 2.1 - 2.3 in the preceding section and therefore they are omitted.

## IV. MINIMALITY FOR REALIZATIONS OF RATIONAL MATRIX FUNCTIONS IN SEVERAL VARIABLES.

In this chapter we study minimal realizations of rational matrix functions in several variables. This allows us to express the results developed in the previous chapters in terms of transfer functions and also to extend them. If the coefficients of the transfer function at infinity are moments, then the minimality theorems are the same as those for $(\Gamma,\mathcal{D})$-minimality for a certain $\Gamma$ and a certain $\mathcal{D}$ determined by the coefficients. In many natural cases (see Section IV.2 below) the coefficients at infinity are more complex and the earlier results can not be applied directly. The appropriate extension of the minimality theory is developed in this chapter.

### IV.1. Rational-matrix-valued maps and dominating pairs

Let $\mathcal{R}_s$ denote the set of all rational s-variate matrix functions, i.e. of all matrices of arbitrary sizes whose entries are rational functions in s complex variables. By a *rational-matrix-valued* map we mean a map $f : \mathcal{N}_k \to \mathcal{R}_s$ such that $f(\Xi)(\lambda_1,\dots,\lambda_s)$ is a sum of products of polynomials in the variables $\lambda_1,\dots,\lambda_s$ and the main operators $A_1,\dots,A_k$ of $\Xi$ and of inverses of such polynomials. Note that $f(\Xi)$ is independent of the input and output operators of $\Xi$. If $\Xi = (A_1,\dots,A_k;X;B,C) \in \mathcal{N}_k$ and $f : \mathcal{N}_k \to \mathcal{R}_s$, then the rational s-variate $m \times p$ matrix function

$$W_{\Xi,f}(\lambda_1,\dots,\lambda_s) := Cf(\Xi)(\lambda_1,\dots,\lambda_s)B$$

will be called the *f-transfer function of the node* $\Xi$. Conversely, let $W(\lambda_1,\dots,\lambda_s)$ be a rational s-variate $m \times p$ matrix function, let $f : \mathcal{N}_k \to \mathcal{R}_s$ be a rational-matrix-valued map and let $\mathcal{D} \subset \mathcal{N}_k$ be a realization domain. We say that a node $\Xi = (A_1,\dots,A_k;X;B,C)$ is a $(f,\mathcal{D})$-*realization* of W is $\Xi \in \mathcal{D}$ and

$$W(\lambda_1,\dots,\lambda_s) = W_{\Xi,f}(\lambda_1,\dots,\lambda_s) = Cf(\Xi)(\lambda_1,\dots,\lambda_s)B \tag{1.1}$$

for all points $(\lambda_1,\dots,\lambda_s) \in \mathbb{C}^s$ which are not singularities for both W and $f(\Xi)$. The right-hand side of (1.1) will also be called an $(f,\mathcal{D})$-realization of W.

Using the definitions of a rational-matrix-valued map and of a realization domain one easily checks the following two facts:

a) if $\Xi$ is an $(f,\mathcal{D})$-realization of W and $\tilde{\Xi} \in \mathcal{D}$ is similar to $\Xi$, then $\tilde{\Xi}$ is also an $(f,\mathcal{D})$-realization of W (in this case we say that the $(f,\mathcal{D})$-realizations $\Xi$ and $\tilde{\Xi}$ are *similar*);

b) if $\Xi$ is an $(f,\mathcal{D})$-realization of W and $\Xi_0$ is a reduction of $\Xi$, then $\Xi_0$ is also an $(f,\mathcal{D})$-realization of W (in this case we say that the $(f,\mathcal{D})$-realization $\Xi_0$ is a *reduction* of the $(f,\mathcal{D})$-realization $\Xi$ and $\Xi$ is said to be a *dilation* of $\Xi_0$).

Given a rational-matrix-valued map $f : N_k \to R_s$, we say that the f-transfer functions of two nodes $\Xi,\tilde{\Xi} \in \mathcal{D}$ coincide if

$$W_{\Xi,f}(\lambda_1,\dots,\lambda_s) = W_{\tilde{\Xi},f}(\lambda_1,\dots,\lambda_s),$$

for all points $(\lambda_1,\dots,\lambda_s) \in \mathbb{C}^s$ that are non-singular for both $W_{\Xi,f}$ and $W_{\tilde{\Xi},f}$. A node $\Xi \in \mathcal{D}$ is called $(f,\mathcal{D})$-*minimal* if among all nodes in $\mathcal{D}$ whose f-transfer function coincides with $W_{\Xi,f}$, the node $\Xi$ has the smallest state space dimension.

Next, we say that a rational-matrix-valued map $f : N_k \to R_s$ and a realization domain $\mathcal{D} \subset N_k$ form a *dominating pair* if for any two nodes $\Xi = (A_1,\dots,A_k;X;B,C) \in \mathcal{D}$ and $\tilde{\Xi} = (\tilde{A}_1,\dots,\tilde{A}_k;\tilde{X};\tilde{B},\tilde{C}) \in \mathcal{D}$ whose f-transfer functions coincide we have

$$C\omega_\gamma(A_1,\dots,A_k)B = \tilde{C}\omega_\gamma(\tilde{A}_1,\dots,\tilde{A}_k)\tilde{B}, \quad |\gamma| \le 2\max\{\dim X,\dim\tilde{X}\} - 1. \tag{1.2}$$

To be more explicit assume that f maps $N_k$ into the set of rational matrix functions that are analytic at infinity and write the power series expansion in the neighbourhood of infinity:

$$f(\Xi)(\lambda_1,\dots,\lambda_s) = \sum_{\alpha_1,\dots,\alpha_s=0}^{\infty} \lambda_1^{-\alpha_1}\cdots\lambda_s^{-\alpha_s}[f]_{\alpha_1,\dots,\alpha_s}(\Xi). \tag{1.3}$$

Then the assertion that $(f,\mathcal{D})$ is a dominating pair means that the equalities

$$C[f]_{\alpha_1,\dots,\alpha_s}(\Xi)B = \tilde{C}[f]_{\alpha_1,\dots,\alpha_s}(\tilde{\Xi})\tilde{B}, \qquad (\alpha_1,\dots,\alpha_s) \in \mathbb{N}_0 \tag{1.4}$$

imply (1.2). Note that in view of Theorem I.2.4 equalities (1.2) imply that all moments of $\Xi$ and $\Xi$ coincide: $M_\gamma(\Xi) = M_\gamma(\tilde{\Xi})$, $\gamma \in \Gamma_k$.

It is worth mentioning that if the coefficients $[f]_{\alpha_1,\dots,\alpha_s}(\Xi)$, $(\alpha_1,\dots,\alpha_s) \in \mathbb{N}_0^s$, happen to be just words $\omega_\gamma(A_1,\dots,A_k)$ for some subset $\Gamma \subset \Gamma_k$, then $(f,\mathcal{D})$-minimality of a node is the same as $(\Gamma,\mathcal{D})$-minimality and the notion of an $(f,\mathcal{D})$-dominating pair can be replaced by the notion of $(\Gamma,\mathcal{D})$-dominating pair. In general, the coefficients $[f]_{\alpha_1,\dots,\alpha_s}(\Xi)$ might be more complex expressions in $A_1,\dots,A_k$ than just words, as we shall see in the examples of the next section. However, the minimality theory for dominating pairs $(f,\mathcal{D})$ is much the same as the corresponding theory for dominating pairs $(\Gamma,\mathcal{D})$. We state now the results.

THEOREM 1.1. *Let $(f,\mathcal{D})$ be a dominating pair, and let $\Xi \in \mathcal{D}$. Then the following assertions are equivalent:*

a) *$\Xi$ is an $(f,\mathcal{D})$-minimal node;*

b) *$\Xi$ is a minimal node;*

c) *$N(\Xi) = 0$ and $R(\Xi) = X$, where $X$ is the state space of $\Xi$.*

THEOREM 1.2. *Let $(f,\mathcal{D})$ be a dominating pair. Two $(f,\mathcal{D})$-minimal nodes in $\mathcal{D}$ are similar if and only if their f-transfer functions coincide.*

THEOREM 1.3. *Let $(f,\mathcal{D})$ be a dominating pair. Two nodes in $\mathcal{D}$ are dilations of similar nodes if and only if their f-transfer functions coincide.*

The proof of these results goes along the same lines as the proof of Theorem II.3.1 and Corollaries II.3.2, II.3.3. One has only to take into consideration the following properties of rational-matrix-valued maps:

i) If $\Xi,\tilde{\Xi}$ are similar nodes with the similarity operator $S : X \to \tilde{X}$, then

$$f(\tilde{\Xi})(\lambda_1,\dots,\lambda_s) = Sf(\Xi)(\lambda_1,\dots,\lambda_s)S^{-1}.$$

ii) If $\Xi = (A_1,\dots,A_k;X;B,C) \in \mathcal{N}_k$ admits partitioning (I.2.1), then

$$f(\Xi)(\lambda_1,\dots,\lambda_s) = \begin{pmatrix} * & * & * \\ 0 & f(\Xi_0)(\lambda_1,\dots,\lambda_s) & * \\ 0 & 0 & * \end{pmatrix},$$

where $\Xi_0 = (A_1^{(0)},\dots,A_k^{(0)};X_0;B_0,C_0)$.

Note that in our considerations the rational-matrix-valued maps can be replaced by more general maps f mapping $\mathcal{N}_k$ into some sets of s-variate matrix functions provided those maps have the properties i) - ii) above.

If $k_1 < k_2$ are positive integers and $\Xi = (A_1,\dots,A_{k_2};X;B,C) \in \mathcal{N}_{k_2}$ we set $\Xi/\mathcal{N}_{k_1} := (A_1,\dots,A_{k_1};X;B,C)$. For later purposes we need the following two lemmas.

LEMMA 1.4. *Let $\mathcal{D}_1$ be a realization domain in $N_{k_1}$ and let the domain $\mathcal{D}_2 \subset N_{k_2}$ $(k_2 > k_1)$ be defined by*

$$\mathcal{D}_2 = \{\Xi = (A_1,\dots,A_{k_2};X;B,C) \mid \Xi/N_{k_1} \in \mathcal{D}_1, A_{k_1+j} = \tag{1.5}$$

$$= \sum_{\alpha\in A_j} C_\alpha^{(j)}\omega_\alpha(A_1,\dots,A_{k_1}), j=1,\dots,k_2-k_1\},$$

*where $A_j$ $(j=1,\dots,k_2-k_1)$ are some finite subsets of $\Gamma_{k_1}$ and $C_\alpha^{(j)}$ $(\alpha \in A_j, j=1,\dots,k_2-k_1)$ are some fixed complex numbers. Furthermore, let $f_1 : N_{k_1} \to R_s$ and $f_2 : N_{k_2} \to R_s$ be rational-matrix-valued maps which are analytic at infinity and assume that*

$$Cf_2(\Xi)(\lambda_1,\dots,\lambda_s)B = Cf_1(\Xi/N_{k_1})(\lambda_1,\dots,\lambda_s)B, \Xi \in \mathcal{D}_2. \tag{1.6}$$

*Then $(f_2,\mathcal{D}_2)$ is a dominating pair if and only if $(f_1,\mathcal{D}_1)$ is a dominating pair.*

PROOF. From the definition of $\mathcal{D}_2$ one easily sees that $\mathcal{D}_2$ is a realization domain. Let $\Xi = (A_1,\dots,A_{k_2};X;B,C) \in \mathcal{D}_2$ and $\tilde{\Xi} = (\tilde{A}_1,\dots,\tilde{A}_{k_1};\tilde{X};\tilde{B},\tilde{C}) \in \mathcal{D}_2$ be such that (1.4) holds with $f = f_2$. Then assumption (1.6) implies that

$$C[f_1]_{\alpha_1,\dots,\alpha_s}(\Xi/N_{k_1})B = \tilde{C}[f_1]_{\alpha_1,\dots,\alpha_s}(\tilde{\Xi}/N_{k_1})\tilde{B}, \quad (\alpha_1,\dots,\alpha_s) \in \mathbb{N}_0^s.$$

Thus, if $(f_1,\mathcal{D}_1)$ is a dominating pair, Theorem I.2.4 implies that

$$C\omega_\gamma(A_1,\dots,A_{k_1})B = \tilde{C}\omega_\gamma(\tilde{A}_1,\dots,\tilde{A}_{k_1})\tilde{B}, \quad \gamma \in \Gamma_{k_1}. \tag{1.7}$$

In view of the definition of $\mathcal{D}_2$ for any sequence $\beta \in \Gamma_{k_2}$ there is a finite set $\Delta_\beta \subset \Gamma_{k_1}$ and some fixed complex numbers $m_\delta^{(\beta)}$ $(\delta \in \Delta_\beta)$ such that

$$\omega_\beta(A_1,\dots,A_{k_2}) = \sum_{\delta\in\Delta_\beta} m_\delta^{(\beta)}\omega_\delta(A_1,\dots,A_{k_1}).$$

Using (1.7) we conclude therefore that

$$C\omega_\beta(A_1,\dots,A_{k_2})B = \tilde{C}\omega_\beta(\tilde{A}_1,\dots,\tilde{A}_{k_2})\tilde{B}, \quad \beta \in \Gamma_{k_2},$$

i.e. the pair $(f_2,\mathcal{D}_2)$ is dominating.

Conversely, assume that the nodes $\Xi = (A_1,\dots,A_{k_1};X;B,C) \in \mathcal{D}_1$ and $\tilde{\Xi} = (\tilde{A}_1,\dots,\tilde{A}_{k_1};\tilde{X};\tilde{B},\tilde{C}) \in \mathcal{D}_1$ are such that (1.4) holds with $f = f_1$. Set $\Xi_E :=$ $(A_1,\dots,A_{k_2};X;B,C)$ and $\tilde{\Xi}_E := (\tilde{A}_1,\dots,\tilde{A}_{k_2};\tilde{X};\tilde{B},\tilde{C})$, where

$$A_{k_1+j} = \sum_{\alpha\in A_j} C_\alpha^{(j)}\omega_\alpha(A_1,\dots,A_{k_1}), \quad \tilde{A}_{k_1+j} = \sum_{\alpha\in A_j} C_\alpha^{(j)}\omega_\alpha(\tilde{A}_1,\dots,\tilde{A}_{k_1}),$$
$$j=1,\dots,k_2-k_1.$$

Clearly, $\Xi_E,\tilde{\Xi}_E \in \mathcal{D}_2$ and $\Xi_E/N_1 = \Xi$, $\tilde{\Xi}_E/N_1 = \tilde{\Xi}$. It follows from the assumption (1.6) that

$$C[f_2]_{\alpha_1,\dots,\alpha_s}(\Xi_E)B = \tilde{C}[f_2]_{\alpha_1,\dots,\alpha_s}(\tilde{\Xi}_E)\tilde{B} \quad (\alpha_1,\dots,\alpha_s) \in \mathbb{N}_0^s.$$

If $(f_2,\mathcal{D}_2)$ is a dominating pair then, in view of Theorem I.2.4, the last equalities yield

$$(1.8) \qquad C\omega_\beta(A_1,\dots,A_{k_2})B = \tilde{C}\omega_\beta(\tilde{A}_1,\dots,\tilde{A}_{k_2})\tilde{B}, \quad \beta \in \Gamma_{k_2}.$$

Since $\Gamma_{k_1} \subset \Gamma_{k_2}$ the equalities

$$C\omega_\gamma(A_1,\dots,A_{k_1})B = \tilde{C}\omega_\gamma(\tilde{A}_1,\dots,\tilde{A}_{k_1})\tilde{B}, \quad \gamma \in \Gamma_{k_1},$$

are among the equalities in (1.8), i.e. the pair $(f_1,\mathcal{D}_1)$ is dominating. □

LEMMA 1.5. *Assume that two realization domains $\mathcal{D}_1 \subset N_{k_1}$ and $\mathcal{D}_2 \subset N_{k_2}$ $(k_1 < k_2)$ are related as in (1.5). Then for any node $\Xi = (A_1,\dots,A_{k_2};X;B,C) \in \mathcal{D}_2$ we have*

$$N(\Xi) = N(\Xi/N_{k_1}) = \bigcap_{|\gamma|\le n-1} \operatorname{Ker} C\omega_\gamma(A_1,\dots,A_{k_1}),$$

$$R(\Xi) = R(\Xi/N_{k_1}) = \bigvee_{|\gamma|\le n-1} \operatorname{Im} \omega_\gamma(A_1,\dots,A_{k_1})B,$$

*where* $n = \dim X$.

PROOF. In view of Proposition I.1.1, the space $N(\Xi/N_{k_1})$ is the greatest common invariant subspace for $A_1,\dots,A_{k_1}$ contained in Ker C. The definition (1.5) of $\mathcal{D}_2$ implies that $N(\Xi/N_1)$ is the greatest common invariant subspace for $A_1,\dots,A_{k_2}$ as well. Using again Proposition I.1.1 we infer that $N(\Xi/N_1) = N(\Xi)$. Similarly, on the base of Proposition I.1.2 one sees that $R(\Xi/N_1) = R(\Xi)$. □

## IV.2. Examples of dominating pairs $(f,\mathcal{D})$

In this section we present two examples of dominating pairs $(f,\mathcal{D})$ which we need for applications. In both examples the domain $\mathcal{D}$ is a Lie domain as defined by (II.2.1).

PROPOSITION 2.1. *Let $\mathcal{D} = \mathcal{D}_L$ be a Lie domain in $N_k$ and let the map $f = f^{(k)} : N_k \to R_k$ be given by*

$$(2.1) \qquad f^{(k)}(\Xi)(\lambda_1,\dots,\lambda_k) = (I - \sum_{j=1}^{k} \lambda_j^{-1}A_j)^{-1}.$$

*Then $(f^{(k)},\mathcal{D}_L)$ is a dominating pair.*

PROOF. If $\gamma = (\gamma_1,\dots,\gamma_r)$ is a sequence we shall use the notation $\{\gamma\}$ for the collection of all mutually distinct permutations of $\gamma$. With this notation we can write the power series coefficients of $f^{(k)}$ as follows:

$$[f^{(k)}]_{\alpha_1,\dots,\alpha_k}(\Xi) = \sum_{\gamma\in\{\alpha\}} \omega_\gamma(A_1,\dots,A_k).$$

where

$$\alpha = (\underbrace{1,\dots,1}_{\alpha_1},\underbrace{2,\dots,2}_{\alpha_2},\dots,\underbrace{k,\dots,k}_{\alpha_k}).$$

We shall show that if $\Xi = (A_1,\dots,A_k;X;B,C) \in \mathcal{D}_L$, $\tilde{\Xi} = (\tilde{A}_1,\dots,\tilde{A}_k;\tilde{X};\tilde{B},\tilde{C}) \in \mathcal{D}_L$ and if

$$\sum_{\gamma\in\{\alpha\}} C\omega_\gamma(A_1,\dots,A_k)B = \sum_{\gamma\in\{\alpha\}} \tilde{C}\omega_\gamma(\tilde{A}_1,\dots,\tilde{A}_k)\tilde{B} \tag{2.2}$$

for any $\alpha \in \Gamma_k$, then

$$M_\gamma(\Xi) = M_\gamma(\tilde{\Xi}) \tag{2.3}$$

for any $\gamma \in \Gamma_k$. To prove this assertion we use induction on the length of the words. For words of length one the relations (2.3) are just the same as (2.2). Assume for the induction hypothesis that (2.3) holds true for any $\gamma \in \Gamma_k$ with $|\gamma| \le \ell-1$ and take some $\alpha \in \Gamma_k$ with $|\alpha| = \ell$. Using the commutator relation (II.2.2) and the definition (II.2.1) of the Lie domain, we see that each word $\omega_\gamma(A_1,\dots,A_k)$ with $\gamma \in \{\alpha\}$ can be written as follows:

$$\omega_\gamma(A_1,\dots,A_k) = \omega_\alpha(A_1,\dots,A_k) + \sum_{\beta\in\mathcal{B}} m_\beta\omega_\beta(A_1,\dots,A_k), \tag{2.4}$$

where $m_\beta$ are some complex numbers and $\mathcal{B}$ is a subset of the set $\{\delta \in N_k \mid |\delta| = \ell-1\}$. Since the set $\mathcal{B}$ depends on $\gamma$ and $\alpha$ only, (2.4) clearly remains true if one substitutes $A_1,\dots,A_k$ by $\tilde{A}_1,\dots,\tilde{A}_k$, respectively. It follows that (2.2) can be rewritten in the form

$$M_\alpha(\Xi) + \sum_{\beta\in\hat{\mathcal{B}}} \hat{m}_\beta M_\beta(\Xi) = M_\beta(\tilde{\Xi}) + \sum_{\beta\in\hat{\mathcal{B}}} \hat{m}_\beta M_\beta(\tilde{\Xi}),$$

where $\hat{m}_\beta$ are some complex numbers and $\hat{\mathcal{B}}$ is again some subset of $\{\delta \in \Gamma_k \mid |\delta| = \ell-1\}$. In view of the induction hypothesis this implies immediately (2.3). □

PROPOSITION 2.2. *Let $\mathcal{D} = \mathcal{D}_L$ be a Lie domain in $N_2$ and let the map $f = f^{(a_1,a_2)} : N_2 \to R_2$ be given by*

$$f^{(a_1,a_2)}(\Xi)(\lambda_1,\lambda_2) = [\lambda_1\lambda_2 I - (\lambda_2 + a_1)A_1 - (\lambda_1 + a_2)A_2]^{-1}, \tag{2.5}$$

*where $a_1,a_2$ are fixed complex numbers. Then $(f^{(a_1,a_2)},\mathcal{D}_L)$ is a dominating pair.*

PROOF. If $\alpha_1,\alpha_2$ are positive integers we set

$$\alpha^{(k)} := (\underbrace{1,\dots,1}_{\alpha_1-k},\underbrace{2,\dots,2}_{\alpha_2-k},\underbrace{3,\dots,3}_{k}) \qquad (k = 0,1,\dots,\min\{\alpha_1,\alpha_2\}).$$

Introduce the operator $A_3 := a_1A_1 + a_2A_2$ and write

$$f^{(a_1,a_2)}(\Xi)(\lambda_1,\lambda_2) = \lambda_1^{-1}\lambda_2^{-1}(I - \lambda_1^{-1}A_1 - \lambda_2^{-1}A_2 - \lambda_1^{-1}\lambda_2^{-1}A_3)^{-1}.$$

With the above notations one can write the coefficients of the power series expansion of $f^{(a_1,a_2)}(\Xi)(\lambda_1,\lambda_2)$ in the neighbourhood of infinity as follows

$$[f^{(a_1,a_2)}]_{\alpha_1+1,\alpha_2+1}(\Xi) = \sum_{\gamma\in\{\alpha^{(0)}\}} \omega_\gamma(A_1,A_2) + R_{\alpha_1,\alpha_2}(A_1,A_2), \qquad (\alpha_1 \geq 0, \alpha_2 \geq 0),$$

where

$$R_{\alpha_1,\alpha_2}(A_1,A_2) := \sum_{k=1}^{\min\{\alpha_1,\alpha_2\}} \sum_{\gamma\in\{\alpha^{(k)}\}} \omega_\gamma(A_1,A_2,A_3). \tag{2.6}$$

Here the symbol $\{\beta\}$ denotes the set of all mutually distinct permutations of the sequence $\beta$. We have to show that $\Xi = (A_1,A_2;X;B,C) \in \mathcal{D}_L$, $\tilde{\Xi} = (\tilde{A}_1,\tilde{A}_2;\tilde{X};\tilde{B},\tilde{C}) \in \mathcal{D}_L$ and

$$\begin{aligned}&\sum_{\gamma\in\{\alpha^{(0)}\}} C\omega_\gamma(A_1,A_2)B + CR_{\alpha_1,\alpha_2}(A_1,A_2)B = \\ &= \sum_{\gamma\in\{\alpha^{(0)}\}} \tilde{C}\omega_\gamma(\tilde{A}_1,\tilde{A}_2)\tilde{B} + \tilde{C}R_{\alpha_1,\alpha_2}(\tilde{A}_1,\tilde{A}_2)\tilde{B} \qquad (\alpha_1 \geq 0, \alpha_2 \geq 0),\end{aligned} \tag{2.7}$$

implies

$$C\omega_\beta(A_1,A_2)B = \tilde{C}\omega_\beta(\tilde{A}_1,\tilde{A}_2)\tilde{B} \tag{2.8}$$

for any $\beta \in \Gamma_2$. To prove this we use induction on the length of words $\omega_\beta$. For a word $\omega_\beta$ of length one the equality (2.8) is among the equalities (2.7) (take $\alpha_1 = 0$ or $\alpha_2 = 0$). So, let (2.8) hold true for any word of length $\leq \ell-1$ and take a word $\omega_\beta(A_1,A_2)$ with $|\beta| = \ell$. Denote by $\beta^*$ the permutation of $\beta$ which is of the form

$$\beta^* = (\underbrace{1,\ldots,1}_{\beta_1},\underbrace{2,\ldots,2}_{\beta_2}).$$

From the definition of $R_{\alpha_1,\alpha_2}(A_1,A_2)$ in (2.6) one sees that

$$R_{\beta_1,\beta_2}(A_1,A_2) = \sum_{\gamma\in\Gamma} C_\gamma\omega_\gamma(A_1,A_2),$$

where $C_\gamma$ are some complex numbers and $\Gamma$ is a subset of the set $\{\delta \in \Gamma_2 \mid |\delta| \leq \ell-1\}$. Hence by the induction hypothesis,

$$CR_{\beta_1,\beta_2}(A_1,A_2)B = \tilde{C}R_{\beta_1,\beta_2}(\tilde{A}_1,\tilde{A}_2)\tilde{B},$$

and (2.7) implies

$$\sum_{\gamma\in\{\beta^*\}} M_\gamma(\Xi) = \sum_{\gamma\in\{\beta^*\}} M_\gamma(\tilde{\Xi}). \tag{2.9}$$

Using the commutator relations (II.2.2) and the definition (II.2.1) of the Lie domain one can write each word $\omega_\gamma(A_1,A_2)$ with $\gamma \in \{\beta^*\}$ as follows

$$(2.10)\qquad \omega_\gamma(A_1,A_2) = \omega_\beta(A_1,A_2) + \sum_{\delta\in\Delta} m_\delta\omega_\delta(A_1,A_2),$$

where $m_\delta$ are some complex numbers and $\Delta$ is a subset of the set $\{\delta \in \Gamma_2 \mid |\gamma| = \ell-1\}$. Substituting (2.10) into (2.9) and postmultiplying by $\beta_1!\beta_2!((\beta_1+\beta_2)!)^{-1}$ we obtain

$$(2.11)\qquad M_\beta(\Xi) + \sum_{\alpha\in A} r_\alpha M_\alpha(\Xi) = M_\beta(\tilde{\Xi}) + \sum_{\alpha\in A} r_\alpha M_\alpha(\tilde{\Xi}),$$

where $r_\alpha$ are some complex numbers and $A$ is a subset of the set $\{\delta \in \Gamma_2 \mid |\delta| = \ell-1\}$. In view of the induction hypothesis $M_\alpha(\Xi) = M_\alpha(\tilde{\Xi})$ for any $\alpha \in A$, and hence (2.11) reduces to the equality

$$M_\beta(\Xi) = M_\beta(\tilde{\Xi}).$$

This completes the proof of the proposition. □

IV.3. Applications to 2-D systems

In this section we consider again the Fornasini-Marchesini model of 2-D systems but we do not impose on the system the recognizability condition (III.1.9). Here to each system

$$(3.1)\qquad \theta \begin{cases} x(k_1+1,k_2+1) = A_1x(k_1,k_2+1) + A_2x(k_1+1,k_2) + A_0x(k_1,k_2) + Bu(k_1,k_2), \\ y(k_1,k_2) = Cx(k_1,k_2), \\ x(k_1,0) = 0, \quad x(0,k_2) = 0, \quad k_1,k_2 = 0,1,\dots , \end{cases}$$

with $A_i : X \to X$ $(i = 0,1,2)$, $B : \mathbb{C}^p \to X$, $C : X \to \mathbb{C}^m$, we associate the node $\Xi_\theta = (A_1,A_2,A_0;X;B,C)$ in $N_3$. Conversely, each node $\Xi = (A_1,A_2,A_0;X;B,C)$ in $N_3$ determines uniquely a system $\theta$ given by (3.1) such that $\Xi = \Xi_\theta$.

Next introduce the rational-matrix-valued map $g : N_3 \to R_2$ by

$$(3.3)\qquad g(\Xi)(\lambda_1,\lambda_2) = (\lambda_1\lambda_2I_X - \lambda_2A_1 - \lambda_1A_2 - A_0)^{-1}.$$

Then as is shown in Section III.1 the transfer function $W_\theta(\lambda_1,\lambda_2)$ of (3.1) is of the form

$$W_\theta(\lambda_1,\lambda_2) = Cg(\Xi_\theta)(\lambda_1,\lambda_2)B.$$

If $\mathcal{D} \subset N_3$ is a realization domain in $N_3$, the class of all systems $\theta$ defined by (3.1) such that $\Xi_\theta \in \mathcal{D}$ will be denoted by $\{\mathcal{D}\}$. A system $\theta \in \{\mathcal{D}\}$ with state space $X$ will be called *minimal in the class* $\{\mathcal{D}\}$ if $\dim X \le \dim \tilde{X}$ for any system $\tilde{\theta} \in \{\mathcal{D}\}$ with the same transfer function as $\theta$ : $W_\theta(\lambda_1,\lambda_2) = W_{\tilde{\theta}}(\lambda_1,\lambda_2)$. Here $\tilde{X}$ stands for the state space of $\tilde{\theta}$. Observe that a system $\theta \in \{\mathcal{D}\}$ is minimal in the class $\{\mathcal{D}\}$ if and only if the node $\Xi_\theta \in \mathcal{D}$ is $(g,\mathcal{D})$-minimal, where the rational-matrix-valued map $g : N_3 \to \mathcal{D}_2$ is defined by (3.3). Thus, if the pair $(g,\mathcal{D})$ is dominating, the results of Section IV.1 can be applied in order to characterize minimal systems in $\{\mathcal{D}\}$. The fact that $(g,\mathcal{D})$ is a dominating pair means that $\mathcal{D}$ is a realization domain with the following extra property: if $\Xi,\tilde{\Xi} \in \mathcal{D}$ and $\theta,\tilde{\theta}$ are systems defined by (3.1) such that $\Xi = \Xi_\theta$, $\tilde{\Xi} = \Xi_{\tilde{\theta}}$ and $W_\theta(\lambda_1,\lambda_2) = W_{\tilde{\theta}}(\lambda_1,\lambda_2)$, then

$$M_\gamma(\Xi_\theta) = M_\gamma(\Xi_{\tilde{\theta}}), \qquad \gamma \in \Gamma_3 \tag{3.4}$$

(of course, in (3.4) one can take $|\gamma| \le 2\max\{\dim X, \dim \tilde{X}\} - 1$ where $X$ and $\tilde{X}$ are the state spaces of $\theta$ and $\tilde{\theta}$, respectively.) Realization domains with the above property we call FM-domains (the letters FM stand for Fornasini and Marchesini). The examples of section III.2 can be interpreted in these terms. In fact, we have seen there that the domains

$$\tilde{\mathcal{D}}_L = \{\Xi = (A_1,A_2,A_0;X;B,C) \in N_3 \mid A_0 = -A_2A_1, (A_1,A_2;X;B,C) \in \mathcal{D}_L^{\alpha_1,\alpha_2}\}$$

and

$$\tilde{\mathcal{D}}_P^{(a)} = \{\Xi = (A_1,A_2,A_0;X;B,C) \in N_3 \mid A_0 = -A_2A_1, (A_1,A_2;X;B,C) \in \mathcal{D}_P^{(a)}\}$$

are FM-domains. In this section we shall present an additional example of an FM-domain. But first we shall state some general theorems on minimality of systems in FM-domains.

For a system $\theta$ defined by (3.1) we shall use the notations

$$N(\theta) := N(\Xi_\theta) = \bigcap_{|\gamma|\le n-1} \operatorname{Ker} C\omega_\gamma(A_1,A_2,A_0),$$

$$R(\theta) := R(\Xi_\theta) = \bigvee_{|\gamma|\le n-1} \omega_\gamma(A_1,A_2,A_0)B,$$

where $n$ is the dimension of the state space $X$ of $\theta$.

THEOREM 3.1. *Let $\mathcal{D}$ be an FM-domain. A system $\theta \in \{\mathcal{D}\}$ is minimal in the class $\{\mathcal{D}\}$ if and only if $N(\theta) = 0$ and $R(\theta) = X$, where $X$ stands for the state space of the system $\theta$.*

This result follows immediately from Theorem 1.1.

THEOREM 3.2. *Let $\mathcal{D}$ be an FM-domain, and let $\theta \in \{\mathcal{D}\}$ and $\tilde{\theta} \in \{\mathcal{D}\}$ be minimal systems in the class $\{\mathcal{D}\}$. Then the systems $\theta$ and $\tilde{\theta}$ are similar if and only if $W_\theta(\lambda_1,\lambda_2) = W_{\tilde{\theta}}(\lambda_1,\lambda_2)$.*

This theorem follows from Theorem 1.2.

THEOREM 3.3. *Let $\mathcal{D}$ be an FM-domain. Then any system $\theta \in \{\mathcal{D}\}$ defined by (3.1) is a dilation of a system which is minimal in the class $\{\mathcal{D}\}$. More precisely, put $X_1 = N(\theta)$, let $X_0$ be a direct complement of $X_1 \cap R(\theta)$ in $R(\theta)$ and choose $X_2$ such that $X = X_1 \oplus X_0 \oplus X_2$. Then relative to this decomposition the partitionings (III.1.7) hold true and the system $\theta_0$ defined by (1.8) is minimal in the class $\{\mathcal{D}\}$.*

This result is a direct consequence of Theorems 1.1, 1.3 and Theorem II.2.2.

Note as in [20] that introducing the variable $\xi(k_1,k_2) = x(k_1,k_1+1) - A_2x(k_1,k_2)$ one can write the system (3.1) in Roesser's form (see e.g. [27], [9-10], [20]):

$$(3.5)\qquad \begin{cases} \begin{pmatrix} \xi(k_1+1,k_2) \\ x(k_1,k_2+1) \end{pmatrix} = \begin{pmatrix} A_1 & A_0 + A_1A_2 \\ I & A_2 \end{pmatrix} \begin{pmatrix} \xi(k_1,k_2) \\ x(k_1,k_2) \end{pmatrix} + \begin{pmatrix} B \\ 0 \end{pmatrix} u(k_1,k_2), \\ \\ y(k_1,k_2) = \begin{pmatrix} 0 & C \end{pmatrix} \begin{pmatrix} \xi(k_1,k_2) \\ x(k_1,k_2) \end{pmatrix}, \quad k_1,k_2 = 0,1,\dots . \end{cases}$$

Introducing similarity, reduction and minimality for systems of the form (3.5), as suggested by the corresponding notions for systems of the form (3.1), one can rephrase Theorems 3.1 - 3.3 as theorems about minimality in classes of systems of the type (3.5). However, we prefer to state the results in the framework of systems written in form (3.1), because the notions of similarity and reduction as introduced in this section seem to be more natural in the Fornasini-Marchesini framework.

Now we present an example of an FM-domain. Let $\alpha_1,\alpha_2$ and $a_1,a_2$ be fixed complex numbers. Consider the class $\Delta_L(\alpha_1,\alpha_2;a_1,a_2)$ of all systems (3.1) of which the main operators satisfy

$$(3.6)\qquad A_1A_2 - A_2A_1 = \alpha_1A_1 + \alpha_2A_2,$$

$$(3.7)\qquad A_0 = a_1A_1 + a_2A_2,$$

The realization domain in $N_3$ defined by (3.6) - (3.7) will be denoted by $\mathcal{D}_L(\alpha_1,\alpha_2;a_1,a_2)$. Let us denote by $\mathcal{D}_L$ the Lie realization domain in $N_2$ defined by (II.2.1) with structural constants $\ell_{12}^1 = -\ell_{21}^1 = \alpha_1$, $\ell_{12}^2 = -\ell_{21}^2 = \alpha_2$. Then, clearly,

$$\mathcal{D}_L(\alpha_1,\alpha_2;a_1,a_2) = \{\Xi = (A_1,A_2,A_0;X;B,C) \mid \Xi/N_2 \in \mathcal{D}_L,\ A_0 = a_1A_1 + a_2A_2\}$$

In view of (3.7) the map g defined by (3.3) can be written in the form

$$g(\Xi)(\lambda_1,\lambda_2) = [\lambda_1\lambda_2 I - (\lambda_2+a_1)A_1 - (\lambda_1+a_2)A_2]^{-1}, \Xi \in \mathcal{D}_L(\alpha_1,\alpha_2;a_1,a_2),$$

and hence for any node $\Xi \in \mathcal{D}_L(\alpha_1,\alpha_2;a_1,a_2)$ we have

$$Cg(\Xi)(\lambda_1,\lambda_2)B = Cf^{(a_1,a_2)}(\Xi/N_2)(\lambda_1,\lambda_2)B,$$

where the map $f^{(a_1,a_2)}$ is defined by (2.5). Now use Proposition 2.2 and Lemma 1.4 to conclude that $\mathcal{D}_L(\alpha_1,\alpha_2;a_1,a_2)$ is an FM-domain. Thus, minimal systems in the class $\Delta_L(\alpha_1,\alpha_2;a_1,a_2)$ can be characterized by means of Theorems 3.1 - 3.3. Lemma 1.5 implies that the subspaces $N(\theta)$ and $R(\theta)$ in the statement of Theorems 3.1 and 3.3 can be found as follows:

$$N(\theta) = \bigcap_{|\gamma|\le n-1} \operatorname{Ker} C\omega_\gamma(A_1,A_2), \quad R(\theta) = \bigvee_{|\gamma|\le n-1} \operatorname{Im} \omega_\gamma(A_1,A_2)B.$$

## IV.4. A class of systems governed by partial differential equations

Consider linear systems of the following form

$$(4.1) \qquad \theta \begin{cases} \left(\frac{\partial}{\partial t_0} - \sum_{i=1}^{k} A_i \frac{\partial}{\partial t_i}\right) x(t_0,\dots,t_k) = A_0x(t_0,\dots,t_k) + Bu(t_0,\dots,t_k), \\ y(t_0,\dots,t_k) = Cx(t_0,\dots,t_k), \\ x(t_1,\dots,t_{i-1},0,t_{i+1},\dots,t_k) = 0 \quad (i = 0,1,\dots,k),\ t_j \ge 0, \\ \qquad\qquad j = 0,1,\dots,k, \end{cases}$$

where $A_i : X \to X$ $(i = 0,\dots,k)$, $B : \mathbb{C}^p \to X$ and $C : X \to \mathbb{C}^m$ are linear operators acting between finite dimensional spaces. In this section we identify the system (4.1) with the node $\theta = (A_0,A_1,\dots,A_k;X;B,C) \in N_{k+1}$. For an X-valued function $x(t_0,\dots,t_k)$ we shall use the symbol $\hat{x}(\lambda_0,\dots,\lambda_k)$ to denote its Laplace transform, provided the latter exists (see e.g. [28]):

$$\hat{x}(\lambda_0,\dots,\lambda_k) = \int_0^\infty \dots \int_0^\infty e^{-\sum_{i=0}^k \lambda_i t_i} x(t_0,\dots,t_k)dt_0 \dots dt_k.$$

On taking the Laplace transform of (4.1), one obtains

$$\hat{y}(\lambda_0,\dots,\lambda_k) = W_\theta(\lambda_0,\dots,\lambda_k)\hat{x}(\lambda_0,\dots,\lambda_k),$$

where the *transfer function* W of the system (4.1) is given by

$$(4.2) \qquad W_\theta(\lambda_0,\dots,\lambda_k) = C(\lambda_0 I - A_0 - \sum_{i=1}^{k} \lambda_i A_1)^{-1}B.$$

Two systems $\theta = (A_0,\dots,A_k;X;B,C)$ and $\tilde{\theta} = (A_0,\dots,A_k;X;B,C)$ are called *similar* if the nodes $\theta \in N_{k+1}$ and $\tilde{\theta} \in N_{k+1}$ are similar. Also, a system $\theta_0 = (A_0^{(0)},\dots,A_k^{(0)};X_0;B_0,C_0)$ is called a *reduction* of the system $\theta = (A_0,\dots,A_k;X;B,C)$ if the node $\theta_0$ is a reduction of the node $\theta$, and in this case $\theta$ is referred to as a *dilation* of $\theta_0$. Note that similarity and reduction operations do not change the transfer function of the system.

By $\Delta_L$ we denote the class of all systems (4.1) of which the main operators satisfy the relations

$$(4.3)\qquad A_iA_j - A_jA_i = \sum_{\nu=0}^{k} \ell_{ij}^{\nu}A_\nu \quad (i,j = 0,\dots,k),$$

where $\ell_{ij}^{\nu}$ $(i,j,\nu = 0,\dots,k)$ are fixed complex numbers. The Lie realization domain in $N_{k+1}$ defined by (4.3) will be denoted by $\mathcal{D}_L$. A system $\theta = (A_0,\dots,A_k;X;B,C) \in \Delta_L$ will be called *minimal in the class* $\Delta_L$ if $\dim X \le \dim \tilde{X}$ for any other system $\tilde{\theta} = (\tilde{A}_0,\dots,\tilde{A}_k;\tilde{X};\tilde{B},\tilde{C}) \in \Delta_L$ such that $W_{\tilde{\theta}}(\lambda_0,\dots,\lambda_k) = W_\theta(\lambda_0,\dots,\lambda_k)$.

Writing

$$(\lambda_0 I - A_0 - \sum_{i=1}^{k} \lambda_i A_i)^{-1} = \mu_0^{-1}(I - \sum_{i=0}^{k} \mu_i^{-1}A_i)^{-1} =$$
$$= \mu_0^{-1} f^{(k+1)}(\theta)(\mu_0,\dots,\mu_k)$$

with $\mu_0 := \lambda_0$, $\mu_i := \lambda_0\lambda_i^{-1}$ $(i = 1,\dots,k)$, one concludes that a system $\theta = (A_0,\dots,A_k;X;B,C) \in \Delta_L$ is minimal in the class $\Delta_L$ if and only if the node $\theta$ is $(f^{(k+1)},\mathcal{D}_L)$-minimal. As the pair $(f^{(k+1)},\mathcal{D}_L)$ is dominating (see Proposition IV.2.1) we can apply Theorems 1.1 - 1.3 to obtain the following characterization of minimal systems in the class $\Delta_L$.

THEOREM 4.1. *A system $\theta \in \Delta_L$ is minimal in the class $\Delta_L$ if and only if $N(\theta) = \{0\}$ and $R(\theta) = X$.*

Here X denotes the state space of the node $\theta$ and

$$N(\theta) := \bigcap_{|\gamma|\le n-1} \operatorname{Ker} C\omega_\gamma(A_0,A_1,\dots,A_k),$$

$$R(\theta) := \bigvee_{|\gamma|\le n-1} \operatorname{Im} \omega_\gamma(A_0,A_1,\dots,A_k)B,$$

where $n = \dim X$.

THEOREM 4.2. *Let $\theta$ and $\tilde{\theta}$ be minimal systems in the class $\Delta_L$. Then the systems $\theta$ and $\tilde{\theta}$ are similar if and only if $W_\theta(\lambda_0,\dots,\lambda_N) = W_{\tilde{\theta}}(\lambda_0,\dots,\lambda_N)$.*

THEOREM 4.3. *Any system $\theta \in \Delta_L$ is a dilation of a system which is minimal in the class $\Delta_L$. More precisely, put $X_1 = N(\theta)$, let $X_0$ be a direct complement of $X_1 \cap R(\theta)$ in $R(\theta)$ and choose $X_2$ such that $X = X_1 \oplus X_0 \oplus X_2$. Then* *relative to this decomposition the following partitionings hold true*

$$A_i = \begin{pmatrix} * & * & * \\ 0 & A_i^{(0)} & * \\ 0 & 0 & * \end{pmatrix}, \quad (i = 0,1,\dots,k), \quad B = \begin{pmatrix} * \\ B_0 \\ 0 \end{pmatrix}, \quad C = \begin{pmatrix} 0 & C_0 & * \end{pmatrix},$$

*and the system* $\theta_0 = (A_0^{(0)}, A_1^{(0)}, \dots, A_k^{(0)}; X_0; B_0, C_0)$ *is minimal in the class* $\Delta_L$.

Note that systems of type (4.1) (in a somewhat more general form) have been studied in [21] (see also [8], [29]), where the following two results have been established: 1) if $\theta = (A_0,\dots,A_k;X;B,C)$ and $\tilde{\theta} = (\tilde{A}_0,\dots,\tilde{A}_k;\tilde{X};\tilde{B},\tilde{C})$ are systems of the form (4.1) with $\operatorname{Ker}\theta = \operatorname{Ker}\tilde{\theta} = (0)$, $\operatorname{Im}\theta = X$, $\operatorname{Im}\tilde{\theta} = \tilde{X}$ and $W_\theta(\lambda_0,\dots,\lambda_k) = W_{\tilde{\theta}}(\lambda_0,\dots,\lambda_k)$, then $\theta$ and $\tilde{\theta}$ are similar; 2) for any system of type (4.1) there is a system $\theta_0 = (A_0^{(0)},\dots,A_k^{(0)};X_0;B_0,C_0)$ such that $\operatorname{Ker}\theta_0 = (0)$, $\operatorname{Im}\theta_0 = X_0$ and $W_{\theta_0}(\lambda_0,\dots,\lambda_k) = W_\theta(\lambda_0,\dots,\lambda_k)$. The theory developed in the present paper adds to this the fact that conditions $\operatorname{Ker}\theta = (0)$ and $\operatorname{Im}\theta = X$ are necessary and sufficient for a system $\theta = (A_0,A_1,\dots,A_k;X;B,C)$ to have minimal state space dimension among all systems with the same transfer function as $\theta$.

Finally, note that the transfer function (4.2) is not proper (see [2], pg. 264), and it can not be realized in the Roesser form.

REFERENCES


1. Attasi, S.: Modelling and recursive estimation for double indexed sequences, in System Identification: Advances and Case Studies, ed. R.K. Mehra and D.G. Lainiotis, Mathematics in Science and Engineering, Vol. 126, 1976, pp. 289-348.

2. Bose, N.K.: Applied multidimensional systems theory, Van Nostrand Reinhold, 1982.

3. Brodsky, M.S.: Triangular and Jordan representations of linear operators. Transl. Math. Monographs, Vol. 32, Amer. Math. Soc. Providence R.I., 1970.

4. Carey, R.W., Pincus, J.D.: Almost commuting pairs of unitary operators and flat currents, Integral Equations and Operator Theory 4 (1981), 45-122.

5. Donaldson, S.K.: Instantons and Geometric Invariant Theory, Commun. Math. Phys. 93 (1984), 453-460.

6. Fornasini, E., Marchesini, G.: Algebraic realization theory of two-dimensional filters, in Variable Structure Systems, A. Ruberti and R. Mohler, Eds. New York: Springer Verlag (Springer Lecture Notes in Economics and Mathematical Systems), 1975.

7. Fornasini, E., Marchesini, G.: State-space realization theory of two-dimensional filters, IEEE Trans. Auto. Control, 21 (1976), 484-491.

8. Gauchman, H.: On non-self-adjoint representation of Lie algebras, Integral Equations and Operator Theory 6 (1983), 672-705.

9. Givone, D.D., Roesser, R.P.: Multidimensional linear iterative circuits-general properties, IEEE Trans. Computers, 21 (1972), 1067-1073.

10. Givone, D.D., Roesser, R.P.: "Minimization of multidimensional linear iterative circuits", IEEE Trans. Comput., vol. C-22, (1973), 673-678.

11. Gohberg, I., Kaashoek, M.A.: Time varying linear systems with boundary conditions and integral operators, I. The transfer operator and its properties, Integral Equations and Operator Theory, 7 (1984), 325-391.

12. Gohberg, I., Kaashoek, M.A., Lerer, L.: Minimality and irreducibility of time-invariant linear boundary value systems, Int. J. Control, 44 (1986), 363-379.

13. Gohberg, I., Kaashoek, M.A., Lerer, L.: On minimality in the partial realization problem, Systems and Control Letters 9 (1987), 97-104.

14. Helmke, U.: Linear dynamical systems and instantons in Yang-Mills theory, IMA Journal of Mathematical Control & Information 3 (1986), 151-166.

15. Kailath, T.: Linear Systems, Prentice-Hall, Englewood Cliffs, NJ, 1980.

16. Kalman, R.E.: Mathematical description of linear dynamical systems, SIAM J. Control and Optimization, 1 (1963), 152-192.

17. Kalman, R.E.: On minimal partial realizations of a linear input/output map, in: Aspects of Networks and System Theory (Eds. R.E. Kalman and N. De Claris), Holt, Rinehart and Winston, New York, 1971, pp. 385-407.

18. Kalman, R.E., Falb, P.L., Arbib, M.A.: Topics in Mathematical Systems Theory, McGraw-Hill, New York, NY, 1969.

19. Krener, A.J.: Acausal realization theory. Part I. Linear deterministic systems. Submitted for publication, 1986.

20. Kung, S.Y., Levy, B.C., Morf, M., Kailath, T.: New results in 2-D systems theory, Part II: 2-D state-space models-realization and the notions of controllability, observability, and minimality, Proc, IEEE, 65 (1977), 945-961.

21. Levin, S.: Linear dynamical systems with partial derivatives, Integral Equations and Operator Theory, 7 (1984), 118-137.

22. Livšic, M.: On the spectral decomposition of linear non-selfadjoint operators, Mat. Sb. 34 (76) (1954), 149-199. English transl., Amer. Math. Soc. Transl. (2) 5 (1957), 67-114.

23. Livšic, M.: On commuting non-selfadjoint operators, Integral Equations and Operator Theory, 9 (1986), 121-133.

24. Livšic, M., Jantsevich, A.: Operator colligations in Hilbert spaces (1971), Kharkov Univ. U.S.S.R., English transl., J. Wiley, New York, 1979.

25. Pincus, J.D.: Commutators and systems of singular integral equations. I., Acta Mathematica 121 (1968), 219-249.

26. Rosenbrock. H.H.: State Space and Multivariable Theory, Nelson, London, 1970.

27. Roesser, R.P.: A discrete state-space model for linear image processing, IEEE Trans. Auto. Control, 20 (1975), 1-10.

28 Voelker, D., Doetsch, G.: Die zweidimensionale Laplace tranformation (in German), Birkhäuser, Basel, 1950.

29. Waxman, L.: On characteristic operator-functions of Lie-algebras, Kharkovskogo Univ., USSR Kharkov, 83 (1972), pp. 42-45; Integral Equations and Operator Theory, 6 (1983), 312-218.

30. Youla, D.C.: The synthesis of linear dynamical systems from prescribed weighting patterns, SIAM J. Appl. Math., 14 (1966), 527-549.

I. Gohberg
Dept. of Mathematical Sciences
The Raymond and Beverly Sackler
Faculty of Exact Sciences
Tel-Aviv University
Ramat-Aviv
Israel

M.A. Kaashoek
Dept. of Mathematics and Computer Science
Vrije Universiteit
Postbus 7161
1007 MC Amsterdam
The Netherlands

L. Lerer
Dept. of Mathematics
Technion-Israel Institute of Technology
Haifa 32000
Israel

Operator Theory:
Advances and Applications, Vol. 29



# ON THE MULTIPLICITY OF THE COMMUTANT OF OPERATORS

László Kérchy

Dedicated to Professor M. S. Livsic on the occasion of his 70th birthday

The following problem was posed by D. A. Herrero in [7]: "Is the multiplicity of the commutant of operators a quasisimilarity invariant?". Studying this question it is shown that this multiplicity is constant, actually, it is 1, in the quasisimilarity orbits of normal operators, $C_0$-contractions, weak contractions and of isometries whose completely non-unitary parts are of finite multiplicity. Finally, an operator T is constructed, with commutant of infinite multiplicity, so that T is "close" to the quasisimilarity orbit of the unilateral shift of infinite multiplicity.

## 1. INTRODUCTION

Let H be a separable, complex Hilbert space, and let B(H) denote the set of bounded, linear operators acting on H. The multiplicity of a non-empty subset G of B(H) is the minimum of the cardinalities of those sets $F \subset H$ of vectors, which are generating for G, that is for which the span $\vee G F = \vee \{Ax : A \in G, x \in F\}$ coincides with the whole space H. The multiplicity $\mu_T$ of a single operator $T \in B(H)$ is by definition the multiplicity of the set of iterates $\{T^n\}_{n \geq 0}$. The commutant $\{T\}'$ of T consists of the operators $A \in B(H)$ which commute with T : AT = TA. In the sequel $\mu'_T$ will stand for the multiplicity of the commutant $\{T\}'$ of T.

In [4] a bilateral weighted shift W was given with multiplicity $\mu'_W = 2$. While in [12], answering for a conjecture of D. A. Herrero, W. R. Wogen proved that, for every cardinality $1 \leq n \leq \infty$, there exists an operator $T \in B(H)$ with commutant of multiplicity n.

For any two operators $T_1 \in B(H_1)$ and $T_2 \in B(H_2)$, $I(T_1, T_2)$ will denote the set of intertwining operators $A \in B(H_1, H_2)$: $AT_1 = T_2A$. $T_1$ is called the quasiaffine transform of $T_2$, in notation $T_1 \prec T_2$, if $I(T_1, T_2)$ contains a quasi-affinity, that is if it contains an operator with trivial kernel and dense range. $T_1$ can be injected into $T_2$ : $T_1 \overset{i}{\prec} T_2$ , if $I(T_1,T_2)$ contains an injective operator. $T_1$ can be completely injected into $T_2$ : $T_1 \overset{ci}{\prec} T_2$ , if there exists a family of injections in $I(T_1,T_2)$ the span of whose ranges is the space $H_2$ . Finally, the operator $T_1$ can be densely mapped into $T_2$ : $T_1 \overset{d}{\prec} T_2$ , if $I(T_1,T_2)$ contains an operator with dense range.

We say that $T_1$ and $T_2$ are quasisimilar: $T_1 \sim T_2$ , if both $T_1 \prec T_2$ and $T_2 \prec T_1$ hold. Injection-similarity $T_1 \overset{i}{\sim} T_2$ , complete injection-similarity $T_1 \overset{ci}{\sim} T_2$ , and dense similarity $T_1 \overset{d}{\sim} T_2$ are defined in an analogous way. Similarity and unitary equivalence of $T_1$ and $T_2$ will be denoted by $T_1 \approx T_2$ and $T_1 \cong T_2$ , respectively.

The notions of the relations above were introduced by B. Sz.-Nagy and C. Foiaş /cf. [10]/ and have been studied by many authors. It is easy to see that if $T_1 \overset{d}{\prec} T_2$ , then $\mu_{T_2} \leq \mu_{T_1}$ . Hence dense similarity, and so in particular quasisimilarity, preserves the multiplicity of operators. In [7] D. A. Herrero raised the problem whether the multiplicity of the commutant is also a quasisimilarity invariant. It is worth mentioning here that quasisimilarity preserves the existence of non-trivial hyperinvariant subspaces /see e. g. [6]/.

The purpose of the present note is to show that the multiplicity of the commutant is indeed constant in the quasisimilarity orbits of normal operators, $C_0$-contractions, weak contractions and of isometries with completely non-unitary parts of finite multiplicity. The quasisimilarity orbit of the unilateral shift of infinite multiplicity is also investigated.

## 2. NORMAL OPERATORS

Let us recall that a set $F \subset H$ of vectors is called to be separating for a family $A \subset B(H)$ of operators if $C = 0$ whenever $C \in A$ and $Cx = 0$, for every $x \in F$. We start with the following general lemma.

LEMMA 2.1. Let us assume that the operators $T_1 \in B(H_1)$ and $T_2 \in B(H_2)$ satisfy the conditions:

/1/ $T_2 \prec T_1$ ,

/2/ $T_1 \overset{i}{\prec} T_2$

and

/3/ $F \subset H_2$ is cyclic for $\{T_2\}'$ whenever it is separating for $\{T_2\}''$ .

Then we have $\mu'_{T_1} \leq \mu'_{T_2}$ .

PROOF. By /1/ and /2/ there exist operators $X \in I(T_1,T_2)$ and

$Y \in I(T_2, T_1)$ such that $X$ is injective and $Y$ is a quasiaffinity. Let $F \subset H_2$ be a set cyclic for $T_2$ and with card $F = \mu'_{T_2}$. Then card $G$ = card $F$ holds for the set $G = YF \subset H_1$. Since, for every $C \in \{T_2\}'$, the operator $YCX$ belongs to $\{T_1\}'$, it follows that

/4/ $$H_1 \supset \vee \{AG : A \in \{T_1\}'\} \supset \vee \{YCXG : C \in \{T_2\}'\} = (Y \vee \{C(XYF) : C \in \{T_2\}'\})^{-}.$$

The set $F$, being cyclic for $\{T_2\}'$, is separating for $\{T_2\}''$. Hence $XYF$ also separates $\{T_2\}''$, because the operator $XY \in \{T_2\}'$ is injective. By /3/ we obtain that $XYF$ is cyclic for $\{T_2\}'$. Therefore, taking into account that $Y$ has dense range, we infer by /4/ that $H_1 = \vee \{AG : A \in \{T_1\}'\}$. But this yields the inequality $\mu'_{T_1} \leq$ card $G = \mu'_{T_2}$. //

The next proposition shows that this lemma is applicable for normal operators.

PROPOSITION 2.2. If $N \in B(H)$ is a normal operator then $\mu'_N = 1$, and a vector $x \in H$ is cyclic for $\{N\}'$ if and only if $x$ is separating for $\{N\}''$.

PROOF. By the Fuglede - Putnam theorem and the Double commutant theorem we know that $\{N\}''$ coincides with the von Neumann algebra generated by $N$. Since $\{N\}''$ is commutative, it has a separating vector $x \in H$ /cf. [3, Corollary IX.7.9]/. The scalar-valued measure $\mu_x(\cdot) = (E(\cdot)x, x)$ will be equivalent to the spectral measure $E(\cdot)$ of $N$ /see [3, Theorem IX.8.9]/. Hence a look at the functional model of $N$ shows that the vector $x$ is cyclic for $\{N\}'$ /see [3, Theorems IX.10.1,16,20]/. //

Combining the preceding two results we get the following

THEOREM 2.3. Let $N \in B(H_2)$ be a normal operator and $T \in B(H_1)$. If $T \overset{i}{\prec} N \prec T$, then $\mu'_T = 1$.

COROLLARY 2.4. Let $T \in B(H)$ be a power-bounded operator of class $C_{11}$, which means that $\sup_n \|T^n\|$ is finite and the sequences $\{T^n x\}_n$ and $\{T^{*n} x\}_n$ do not converge to zero, for every non-zero $x \in H$. Then $\mu'_T = 1$.

PROOF. In virtue of [10, Proposition II.5.3] $T$ is quasisimilar to a unitary operator. //

In [9] an operator $T \in B(H)$ was called to be a quasi-$C_{11}$-contraction if $\|T\| \leq 1$, $\lim_n \|T^{*n} x\| \neq 0$ for every $0 \neq x \in H$, and if the values $\Theta_T(z)$ of the characteristic function of $T$ /cf. [10]/ are quasiaffinities for a. e. $z$ on the unit circle. We note that the class of quasi-$C_{11}$-contractions properly includes the class of $C_{11}$-contractions /cf. [9]/.

COROLLARY 2.5. For every quasi-$C_{11}$-contraction $T \in B(H)$ we have $\mu'_T = 1$.

PROOF. By [9, Sections 3 and 6] there exists a unitary operator $U \in B(K)$ and there are operators $X \in I(H,K)$ and $Y \in I(K,H)$ such that $Y$ is a quasiaffinity and $XY$ is injective. Looking at the proof it can be seen that Lemma 2.1 holds validity if the injectivity of the intertwining operator $X \in I(H,K)$ is replaced by the injectivity of the operator $XY$. This stronger version of Lemma 2.1 and Proposition 2.2 imply the statement. //

## 3. $C_0$-CONTRACTIONS

Let $S$ denote the unilateral shift on the Hardy space $H^2$, that is $Su = \chi u$, for every $u \in H^2$, where $\chi(z) \equiv z$. To every inner function $m \in H^\infty$ there corresponds an operator $S(m)$ which is the compression of the shift $S$ to the subspace $H(m) = H^2 \ominus mH^2$ : $S(m) = P_{H(m)} S|H(m)$. /Here $P_{H(m)} \in B(H^2)$ stands for the orthogonal projection onto $H(m)$./ Let $M = \{m_n\}_{n=1}^\infty$ be a sequence of inner functions such that $m_{n+1}$ divides $m_n$, for every $n$. The model-operator $S(M)$ attached to $M$ is defined as the orthogonal sum $S(M) = \bigoplus_n S(m_n)$, acting on the Hilbert space $H = \bigoplus_n H_n$, where $H_n = H(m_n)$. Note that $H_n = \{0\}$ if $m_n \equiv 1$. /In connection with Hardy spaces the reader is referred to [10, Chapter III] and to [8]./

We want to determine the cyclic sets for the commutant of the model-operator $S(M)$. First we provide some basic operators in $\{S(M)\}'$. For every $n$, let $P_n \in B(H)$ denote the projection onto $H_n$, and for any $k < l$ let $P_{l,k}$ and $Q_{k,l} \in B(H)$ be the operators: $P_{l,k}(\bigoplus_n x_n) = \bigoplus_n y_n$, where $y_n = P_{H(m_l)} x_k$ if $n = l$ and $y_n = 0$ otherwise, $Q_{k,l}(\bigoplus_n x_n) = \bigoplus_n z_n$, where $z_n = (m_k/m_l) y_l$ if $n = k$ and $z_n = 0$ otherwise. It is clear that these operators belong to $\{S(M)\}'$. Taking into account that the commutant $\{S(m_n)\}'$ is of the form $\{u(S(m_n)) : u \in H^\infty\}$, and using the previous operators it can be easily shown that the bicommutant of $S(M)$ consists of the functions of $S(M)$: $\{S(M)\}'' = \{u(S(M)) : u \in H^\infty\}$. /Here the Sz.-Nagy, Foias functional calculus is applied for $S(M)$; see [10, Chapter III]./

PROPOSITION 3.1. The multiplicity $\mu'_{S(M)} = 1$ for the model-operator $S(M)$. Furthermore, a vector $h = \bigoplus_n h_n \in H$ is cyclic for $\{S(M)\}'$ if and only if $h$ separates the bicommutant $\{S(M)\}''$.

PROOF. Let $u$ be an arbitrary function in $H^\infty$. Then $u(S(M))h = 0$ if and only if $P_{H(m_n)}(uh_n) = u(S(m_n))h_n = 0$, for every $n$. This latter means that $m_n$ divides $uh_n$ , that is $m_n/(m_n \wedge h_n)$ divides u, for every n. Hence $u(S(M))h = 0$ holds exactly when the least common multiple $\bigvee_n m_n/(m_n \wedge h_n)$ of the inner functions $m_n/(m_n \wedge h_n)$ divides u.

On the other hand, the minimal function of S(M) is $m_1$ , so $u(S(M)) = 0$ if and only if $m_1$ divides u. Summerizing these facts we conclude that the vector $h = \oplus_n h_n \in H$ is separating for the bicommutant $\{S(M)\}''$ exactly when $\bigvee_n m_n/(m_n \wedge h_n) = m_1$ . In particular, if $h_1 = P_{H(m_1)} 1$ and $h_n = 0$ for $n \geq 2$, then $h = \oplus_n h_n$ will be separating for $\{S(M)\}''$.

Let us assume now that $h = \oplus_n h_n$ is an arbitrary separating vector of $\{S(M)\}''$. The proof will be completed if we show that h is cyclic for $\{S(M)\}'$.

Let $H'$ denote the hyperinvariant subspace induced by h : $H' = \vee \{Ah : A \in \{S(M)\}'\}$. Then, for any n, the subspace $H'_n = \bigvee_{j \geq 0} S(M)^j P_n h = \bigvee_{j \geq 0} S(m_n)^j h_n$ is invariant for $S(m_n)$ and is contained in $H'$. By Beurling's theorem there exists a unique inner function $\psi_n$ in $H^\infty$ such that $\psi_n$ divides $m_n$ and $H'_n = \psi_n H^2 \ominus m_n H^2$. A short computation shows that $\psi_n$ coincides with the greatest common divisor of $h_n$ and $m_n$ : $\psi_n = h_n \wedge m_n$.

For every $n > 1$, the subspace $Q_{1,n} H'_n$ is contained in $H' \cap H_1$, is invariant for $S(m_1)$ and $S(m_1) | Q_{1,n} H'_n \cong S(m_n) | H'_n \cong S(m_n/(h_n \wedge m_n))$ . Hence the minimal function of the restriction of $S(m_1)$ to $Q_{1,n} H'_n$ is $m_n/(h_n \wedge m_n)$. Similarly, the minimal function of $S(m_1) | H'_1$ is $m_1/(h_1 \wedge m_1)$ . Since the vector $h = \oplus_n h_n$ is separating for $\{S(M)\}''$ , the least common multiple of the inner functions $m_n/(h_n \wedge m_n)$ $/n \geq 1/$ is $m_1$. Therefore, the subspaces $H'_1$, $Q_{1,2}H'_2$, $Q_{1,3}H'_3, \ldots$ span $H_1$, hence $H_1$ is included in $H'$. Then $H_n = P_{n,1} H_1$ is contained in $H'$ too, for every $n > 1$, and so $H' = H$.

Consequently, the vector h is cyclic for $\{S(M)\}'$. //

Let $T \in B(H)$ be a completely non-unitary contraction, that is $\|T\| \leq 1$ and for no non-zero reducing subspace $H'$ for T is $T|H'$ a unitary operator. T is called to be of class $C_o$ if there exists a non-zero function u in $H^\infty$ such that $u(T) = 0$.

THEOREM 3.2. If the operator $T \in B(K)$ is quasisimilar to a $C_o$-contraction, then $\mu'_T = 1$ .

PROOF. Let $T' \in B(K')$ be a $C_o$-contraction quasisimilar to T. By the basic result of [2] we know that $T'$ is quasisimilar to a unique model-operator S(M). Hence Proposition 3.1 and Lemma 2.1 yield that $\mu'_T = 1$ . //

Note that if $T_1$ and $T_2$ are completely non-unitary contractions and

$T_1 \prec T_2$, then $T_1$ is of class $C_0$ if and only if so is $T_2$. Moreover, if $T_1$ and $T_2$ are $C_0$-contractions, then $T_1 \prec T_2$ implies the quasisimilarity $T_1 \sim T_2$.

Finally, we remark that if T acts on a finite dimensional Hilbert space, then cT is a $C_0$-contraction for an appropriate scalar $c > 0$, and so $\mu'_T = \mu'_{cT} = 1$.

4. WEAK CONTRACTIONS

Let $T \in B(H)$ be a weak contraction, which means that $\|T\| \leq 1$, the defect operator $I - T^*T$ has finite trace, and the spectrum of T does not cover the whole unit disc. It is known /cf. [13]/ that T is quasisimilar to the orthogonal sum $T_0 \oplus T_1$ of a $C_0$-contraction $T_0 \in B(H_0)$ and a $C_{11}$-contraction $T_1 \in B(H_1)$. Consequently, T is quasisimilar to an operator of the form $S(M) \oplus U$, where $S(M)$ is the model-operator corresponding to a sequence $M = \{m_n\}_n$ of inner functions /$m_{n+1}$ divides $m_n$/ and U is unitary. Since the commutant of $S(M) \oplus U$ splits into the direct sum: $\{S(M) \oplus U\}' = \{S(M)\}' \oplus \{U\}'$, by Propositions 3.1, 2.2 and Lemma 2.1 we get the following

THEOREM 4. If the operator $T \in B(H)$ is quasisimilar to a weak contraction, then $\mu'_T = 1$.

5. ISOMETRIES

For an isometry V it is not true in general that every separating vector of $\{V\}''$ is necessarily cyclic for $\{V\}'$. Indeed, let us consider the unilateral shift $S \in B(H^2)$, $Sh = \chi h$ /$h \in H^2$, $\chi(z) \equiv z$/. Since $\{S\}' = \{S\}'' = \{u(S) : u \in H^\infty\}$, and since any non-zero function f in $H^2$ does not vanish a. e. on the unit circle, it follows that every non-zero $f \in H^2$ is separating for $\{S\}''$. On the other hand, $f \in H^2$ is cyclic for $\{S\}'$ if and only if f is an outer function.

In the next lemma we consider the unilateral shift $S_n$ of arbitrary finite multiplicity n. Up to unitary equivalence $S_n$ can be given as the multiplication by $\chi$ on the vector-valued Hardy space $H^2(\mathbb{C}^n)$.

LEMMA 5.1. For every $1 \leq n < \infty$, the multiplicity of the commutant of the unilateral shift $S_n$ is $\mu'_{S_n} = 1$. Furthermore, if the operator $Z \in \{S_n\}'$ has dense range and $x \in \mathbb{C}^n$ is cyclic for $\{S_n\}'$, then Zx will be cyclic for $\{S_n\}'$ too.

PROOF. The Hilbert space $H^2(\mathbb{C}^n)$ is isomorphic to the orthogonal sum of n copies of the scalar Hardy space $H^2$. Hence every vector $x \in H^2(\mathbb{C}^n)$ can be written in the form $x = \bigoplus_{j=1}^{n} x_j$, where $x_j \in H^2$. An immediate consequence of

Beurling's theorem is that x is cyclic for $\{S_n\}'$ if and only if $\bigwedge_{j=1}^{n} x_j = 1$ . So $\{S_n\}'$ does have cyclic vectors.

The operator $Z \in \{S_n\}'$ is a multiplication $Z = M_\Theta$ by a bounded, analytic operator-valued function $\{\Theta(z), \mathbb{C}^n, \mathbb{C}^n\}$ defined on the unit disc $\mathbb{D}$. /Cf. [10, Lemma V.3.2]./ If Z has dense range, then $\det \Theta \in H^\infty$ is an outer function /see [10, Proposition V.6.1]/. Let $\Omega(z)$ be the algebraic adjoint of $\Theta(z)$ /$z \in \mathbb{D}$/; $\{\Omega(z), \mathbb{C}^n, \mathbb{C}^n\}$ is also a bounded, analytic function, and $\Omega(z)\ \Theta(z) = \det \Theta(z) I$ for every $z \in \mathbb{D}$.

Let $x = \bigoplus_{j=1}^{n} x_j$ be a vector cyclic for $\{S_n\}'$ , and let us consider the hyperinvariant subspace $H' = \vee \{Ay : A \in \{S_n\}'\}$ induced by the vector $y = Zx$. Let us assume that $H' \neq H^2(\mathbb{C}^n)$. Since $M_\Omega \in \{S_n\}'$ , it follows that $M_{\det\Theta} x = M_\Omega M_\Theta x = M_\Omega y \in H'$. Hence $M_{\det\Theta} x$ is not cyclic for $\{S_n\}'$ , so $\bigwedge_{j=1}^{n} (\det\Theta) x_j \neq 1$. But the function $\det\Theta$ being outer, we infer that $\bigwedge_{j=1}^{n} (\det\Theta) x_j = \bigwedge_{j=1}^{n} x_j = 1$, which is a contradiction. Therefore, the vector $y = Zx$ is cyclic for $\{S_n\}'$. //

Let us consider now an arbitrary isometry $V \in B(H)$. It is well-known that H can be uniquely decomposed into the orthogonal sum $H = H_s \oplus H_a \oplus H_c$ , reducing for V, such that $U_s = V|H_s$ is a singular unitary operator /its spectral measure is singular with respect to the Lebesgue measure on the circle/, $U_a = V|H_a$ is an absolutely continuous unitary operator, and $V_c = V|H_c$ is a completely non-unitary isometry, so $V_c \cong S_n$ for some $0 \leq n \leq \infty$ . We shall prove the following

THEOREM 5.2. If the operator $T \in B(K)$ is densely similar to an isometry $V : T \overset{d}{\sim} V$, whose completely non-unitary part $V_c$ is of multiplicity $0 < n < \infty$, then $\mu_T' = 1$ .

PROOF. By the assumption there exist operators $X \in I(T,V)$ and $Y \in I(V,T)$ with dense ranges. The product $Z = XY \in \{V\}'$ will be also quasi-surjective. Since the commutant of V splits into the direct sum $\{V\}' = \{U_s\}' \oplus \{U_a \oplus S_n\}'$ /cf. [5]/, it follows that Z is of the form $Z = Z_s \oplus Z'$, where $Z_s \in \{U_s\}'$ and $Z' \in \{U_a \oplus S_n\}'$ . Again by [5, Lemma 4.1] we know that $(\ker Z_s)^\perp$ reduces $U_s$ and $U_s|(\ker Z_s)^\perp \cong U_s$ . Taking into account Proposition 2.2 we can see that there exists a vector $x_s \in H_s$ such that $z_s = Z_s x_s$ is cyclic for $\{U_s\}'$.

Since $I(U_a, S_n)$ consists only of the zero operator, we infer that the entry $Z_{21} = 0$ in the matrix $[Z_{ij}]_{1\leq i,j\leq 2}$ of the operator $Z' \in B(H_a \oplus H_c)$ . It follows that $Z_{22} \in \{S_n\}'$ has dense range, and so Lemma 5.1 provides us a vector $x_c \in H_c$ such that $Z_{22}x_c$ is cyclic for $\{S_n\}'$. Considering the functional model of $U_a$ we conclude that $Z'(0 \oplus x_c) = Z_{12}x_c \oplus Z_{22}x_c$ is cyclic for $\{U_a \oplus S_n\}'$. Consequently, the vector $z = Zx$ will be cyclic for $\{V\}'$, if $x = x_s \oplus 0 \oplus x_c$.

Let us consider the vector $y = Yx \in K$. The chain of relations $K \supset \vee\{Ay : A \in \{T\}'\} \supset \vee\{YBXYx : B \in \{V\}'\} = (Y \vee\{Bz : B \in \{V\}'\})^{-} = (YH)^{-} = K$ shows that $y$ is cyclic for $\{T\}'$. //

We remark that in [14] P. Y. Wu characterized the contractions $T$ which are quasisimilar to an isometry $V = U_s \oplus U_a \oplus S_n$, where $n < \infty$. It was also proved there that under some additional assumptions, for example if $T$ is hyponormal, the dense similarity $T \overset{d}{\sim} V$ implies the quasisimilarity $T \sim V$.

6. THE SHIFT OF INFINITE MULTIPLICITY

The proof of Lemma 5.1 works only for shifts of finite multiplicity. This raises the question whether there exists an operator $T$ with multiplicity $\mu'_T > 1$ such that $T$ is quasisimilar to the unilateral shift $S_\infty$ of infinite multiplicity. Since $\mu'_{S_\infty} = 1$, a positive answer would settle Herrero's problem in the negative. Though we are not able to prove the existence of such an operator, the next theorem provides us operators $T$ with $\mu'_T = \infty$, which are "almost" quasisimilar to $S_\infty$.

THEOREM 6. For every $\varepsilon > 0$, there exists an operator $T \in B(H)$ with the following properties:

/5/ $\mu'_T = \infty$,

/6/ $S_\infty \overset{i}{<} T < S_\infty$ and $(1+\varepsilon)S_\infty < T$,

/7/ there exists an operator $\tilde{T} \in B(H)$ such that $T - \tilde{T}$ is compact, $\|T - \tilde{T}\| < \varepsilon$ and $\tilde{T}$ is quasisimilar to $S_\infty$.

PROOF. Our construction is based on Wogen's paper [12].

Let $H_0, H'_1, H'_2, \dots$ be infinite dimensional separable Hilbert spaces, and let $H' = H_0 \oplus (\oplus_n H'_n)$. Let us consider unitary operators $U_0 : H_0 \to H'_1$, $U_n : H'_n \to H'_{n+1}$ /$n \in \mathbb{N}$/, and define $U \in B(H')$ as $U|H_0 = U_0$, $U|H'_n = U_n$ /$n \in \mathbb{N}$/.

Let us given the decomposition $H'' = \bigoplus_{m,n \in \mathbb{N}} H_{m,n}$ of the separable Hilbert space $H''$ into the orthogonal sum of infinite dimensional subspaces $H_{m,n}$, and let $U_{m,n} : H_{m,n} \to H_{m+1,n}$ be unitary operators /$m,n \in \mathbb{N}$/. Let us consider sequences $\{r_n\}_n$ and $\{s_n\}_n$ of positive integers such that $r_n < s_n < r_{n+1}$ and $s_n - r_n$ is even, for every $n \in \mathbb{N}$. Set $p_n = 2^{-1}(r_n + s_n)$ and $d_n = s_n - r_n$. Moreover, let $\{q_n\}_n$ be a sequence of real numbers, where $1 < q_n < 1 + (\varepsilon/2)$, for every $n \in \mathbb{N}$. We define the operator $V \in B(H'')$ in the following way: $V|H_{m,n} = q_n U_{m,n}$ if $r_n \leq m < p_n$, $V|H_{m,n} = q_n^{-1} U_{m,n}$ if $p_n \leq m < s_n$, and $V|H_{m,n} = U_{m,n}$ otherwise.

Let $\{e_n\}_n$ be a sequence of unit vectors dense in the unit sphere of $H_o$, and set $A_n = I_{H_o} - (1-n^{-1}) e_n \otimes e_n$. Choose unitary operators $V_n : H_o \to H_{1,n}$, and form the products $Q_n = V_n A_n$ $/n \in \mathbb{N}/$. Then the operator $Q \in B(H', H'')$ is defined by $Q(\bigoplus_{j \geq o} x_j) = \bigoplus_{n \geq 1} \varrho_n Q_n x_o$, where $\{\varrho_n\}_n$ is a sequence of positive numbers with $\sum_n \varrho_n^2 < \varepsilon^2$. It is clear that $Q$ is compact and $\|Q\| < \varepsilon$.

Our operator $T$ will act on the orthogonal sum $H = H' \oplus H''$ and is defined by the matrix

$$T = \begin{bmatrix} U & O \\ Q & V \end{bmatrix}.$$

The Hilbert space $H$ can be decomposed into the orthogonal sum $H = \bigoplus_{n \geq o} H_n$, where $H_n = H'_n \oplus (\bigoplus_l H_{n,l})$, for $n \geq 1$. Since $TH_n \subset H_{n+1}$ for every $n \geq o$, $T$ is a weighted shift with operator weights $T_n = T|H_n \in B(H_n, H_{n+1})$ $/n \geq o/$. It follows that the matrix $[S_{m,n}]$ /with respect to the decomposition $H = \bigoplus_{n \geq o} H_n$/ of any operator $S \in \{T\}'$ is lower triangular, and for its diagonal entry $S_n = S_{n,n}$ the equation $S_{n+1} T_n = T_n S_n$ holds $/n \geq o/$. Consequently, the operator $R_n = T_{n-1} T_{n-2} \ldots T_o \in B(H_o, H_n)$ fulfills the commuting relation $S_n R_n = R_n S_o$, and so we get the inequality

$$/8/ \qquad \|S\| \geq \sup_n \sup_{o \neq x \in H_o} \|S_n R_n x\| \, \|R_n x\|^{-1} = \sup_n \sup_{o \neq x \in H_o} \|R_n S_o x\| \, \|R_n x\|^{-1}.$$

Let us assume that $x$ and $y$ are linearly independent vectors of $H_o$. Then there exists a strictly increasing function $k : \mathbb{N} \to \mathbb{N}$ such that $\|Q_{k(n)} x\| < n^{-1} \|x\|$, for every $n$, and $\inf_n \|Q_{k(n)} y\| = c > 0$. Since, for any vector $z \in H_o$, we have

$$\|R_{p_{k(n)}} z\|^2 = \|z\|^2 + \varrho_{k(n)}^2 \|Q_{k(n)} z\|^2 q_{k(n)}^{d_{k(n)}} + \sum_{i \neq k(n)} \varrho_i^2 \|Q_i z\|^2,$$

it follows that

$$/9/ \qquad \|R_{p_{k(n)}} y\|^2 \cdot \|R_{p_{k(n)}} x\|^{-2} \geq c^2 a_{k(n)} \left((1 + \varepsilon^2) \|x\|^2 + n^{-2} \|x\|^2 a_{k(n)}\right)^{-1},$$

where $a_n = \varrho_n^2 q_n^{d_n}$. Hence we infer that if

$$/10/ \qquad \lim_n \varrho_n^2 q_n^{d_n} = \infty,$$

then, in view of /9/, the sequence $\{\|R_n y\| \cdot \|R_n x\|^{-1}\}_n$ will not be bounded. Therefore, taking into account /8/ we get that the operator $S_o$ must be of the form $S_0 = dI_{H_0}$, where $d \in \mathbb{C}$ is a scalar. This implies that the multiplicity $\mu'_T = \dim H_0 = \infty$, so /5/ is fulfilled.

The operator $V' \in B(H'')$ defined by $V'|H_{m,n} = U_{m,n}$ /m,n $\in \mathbb{N}$/ is unitarily equivalent to the shift $S_\infty$. Since V is evidently quasisimilar to V', it follows that $S_\infty \overset{i}{\prec} T$. Moreover, it is easy to verify that the quasiaffinity $X \in I(V,V')$ can be chosen in such a manner that $Xh = h$ holds, for every $h \in \oplus_n H_{1,n}$. Then the quasiaffinity $X' = I \oplus X \in B(H' \oplus H'')$ will intertwine T with the operator $T' = \begin{bmatrix} U & 0 \\ Q & V' \end{bmatrix}$, $X' \in I(T,T')$. Considering a new norm $[\![h]\!] = \lim_n \|T'^n h\|$ on H it can be shown that $T'$ is similar to $S_\infty$. Hence we obtain that $T \prec S_\infty$. On the other hand, because $\|T\| \leq \max(1+(\varepsilon/2),(1+\varepsilon^2)^{1/2}) < 1 + \varepsilon$, applying [1, Theorem 3.12] we can write that $(1+\varepsilon)S_\infty \prec T$, and so /6/ is also valid.

Finally, it is easy to check that the operator $\tilde{T} = U \oplus V \in B(H' \oplus H'')$ satisfies the conditions of /7/. //

We remark that if in our example $P_0 h \neq 0$ for a vector $h \in H$, where $P_0$ denotes the projection onto $H_0$ in H, then the sequence $\{\|T^n h\|\}_n$ is not bounded. This results in that the range of any operator $Y \in I(S_\infty, T)$ is orthogonal to $H_0$, hence the relation $S_\infty \overset{c.i}{\prec} T$ does not hold. Consequently, $T \prec S_\infty$ does not imply in general that $S_\infty \overset{c.i}{\prec} T$. In [11] it was proved that such an implication does hold if T is a completely non-unitary contraction.

REFERENCES

1. C. Apostol, H. Bercovici, C. Foiaş and C. Pearcy, Quasiaffine transform of operators, Michigan Math. J., 29 /1982/, 243-255.

2. H. Bercovici, C. Foiaş et B. Sz.-Nagy, Compléments à l'étude des opérateurs de classe $C_0$. III, Acta Sci. Math. /Szeged/, 37 /1975/, 313-322.

3. J. B. Conway, A course in functional analysis, Springer-Verlag /New York - Berlin - Heidelberg - Tokyo, 1985/.

4. J. A. Deddens, R. Gellar and D. A. Herrero, Commutants and cyclic vectors, Proc. Amer. Math. Soc., 43 /1974/, 169-170.

5. R. G. Douglas, On the operator equation $S^*XT = X$ and related topics, Acta Sci. Math. /Szeged/, 30 /1960/, 19-32.

6. L. Fialkow, A note on quasisimilarity. II, Pacific J. Math., 70 /1977/, 151-161.

7. D. A. Herrero, On multicyclic operators, Integral Equations and Operator Theory, 1 /1978/, 57-102.

8. K. Hoffman, Banach spaces of analytic functions, Prentice-Hall /Englewood Cliffs, N. J., 1962/.

9. L. Kérchy, On the residual parts of completely non-unitary contractions, to appear in Acta Math. Acad. Sci. Hungar.

10. B. Sz.-Nagy and C. Foias, Harmonic analysis of operators on Hilbert space, North Holland - Akadémiai Kiadó /Amsterdam - Budapest, 1970/.

11. K. Takahashi, Quasiaffine transform of unilateral shifts, preprint.

12. W. R. Wogen, On cyclicity of commutants, Integral Equations and Operator Theory, 5 /1982/, 141-143.

13. P. Y. Wu, Quasisimilarity of weak contractions, Proc. Amer. Math. Soc., 69 /1978/, 277-282.

14. P. Y. Wu, Contractions quasisimilar to an isometry, to appear in Acta Sci. Math. /Szeged/.

Bolyai Institute
University Szeged
Aradi vértanuk tere 1
6720 Szeged, Hungary

Submitted: March 6, 1987